NATURAL ENEMIES

By Alexander Klein

NATURAL ENEMIES⁇

ENEMIES

YOUTH AND THE CLASH OF GENERATIONS ■ ■ ■

collected and edited by
ALEXANDER KLEIN

J. B. LIPPINCOTT COMPANY | PHILADELPHIA & NEW YORK

ACKNOWLEDGMENTS

Grateful acknowledgment is made to all authors, publishers, magazines, and agents for permission to include copyrighted material:

"Why Youth Seeks New Values" (Why Young People Are Seeking New Values) by Richard Schickel: copyright © 1966 by McCall Corporation; reprinted by permission of the author and through the courtesy of *Redbook Magazine.* "Youth—the Oppressed Majority" by Nat Hentoff: copyright © 1967 by HMH Publishing Co., Inc.; originally appeared in *Playboy* Magazine; reprinted by permission of the author. "We Can't Appease Them" (We Can't Appease the Younger Generation) by Spencer Brown: copyright © 1966 by The New York Times Company; also published in an edited version in *The Reader's Digest;* reprinted by permission. "You Force Us to Rebel" (You Force Kids to Rebel) by Steven Kelman: copyright © 1966 by The Curtis Publishing Company; reprinted from *The Saturday Evening Post* by permission of the author. "Nirvana Now" by Daniel P. Moynihan: copyright © 1967 by the United Chapters of Phi Beta Kappa; reprinted from *The American Scholar,* Vol. 36, No. 4, Autumn, 1967, by permission of the publisher and the author. "Growing Up in America" by Margaret Mead, from "The Young Adult" in *Values and Ideals of American Youth* (Columbia University Press): copyright © 1961 by National Committee for Children and Youth; reprinted by permission of the author and the publisher. "Let It Be Vivid, Let It Be Now!": copyright Time Inc., 1967; reprinted by permission from *Time,* The Weekly Newsmagazine. "An Under-Twenty-Five Reply to *Time*" (Beyond the Man of the Year) by Marilyn Swartz: copyright © 1967 by the United Chapters of Phi Beta Kappa; reprinted from *The American Scholar,* Vol. 36, No. 4, Autumn, 1967, by permission of the publisher and the author. "Perspectives on the Campus Arena" (The War Between the Generations) by Christopher Jencks and David Riesman: copyright © 1967 by *Teachers College Record*, Columbia University Teachers College; by permission of the authors and the publisher. "Students and the Velocity of History" (Joe College: R.I.P.) by Arthur M. Schlesinger, Jr.: copyright © 1968, 1969 by Arthur M. Schlesinger, Jr.; first published in *The Saturday Evening Post*; by permission of the author. "Students in Rebellion" by Henry Steele Commager: copyright © 1968 by *The New York Post*; reprinted by permission of the author and publisher. "What's Bugging Them?" (What's Bugging the Students) by Irving Kristol: copyright © 1965 by the Atlantic Monthly Company, Boston, Mass. 02116; reprinted by permission of the author and publisher. "Two, Three, Many Columbias" by Tom Hayden: copyright © 1968 by Ramparts Magazine, Inc.; reprinted by permission of the publisher and the author. "Beginning in Doubt" by Russell Kirk: copyright © 1968 by National Review, Inc.; reprinted by permission of the author and publisher. "Riots, Wars, and American Education" by Harold Taylor: copyright © 1968, 1969 by Harold Taylor; by permission of the author. "The Responsibilities of the Student" by William F. Buckley, Jr.: copyright © 1968, 1969 by William F. Buckley, Jr.; by permission of the author. "What We Want—and Why" (What Students Want) by Edward Schwartz: copyright © 1968 by The Progressive, Inc.; reprinted by permission of the author and publisher. "Faculty Power" by McGeorge Bundy: copyright © 1968 by McGeorge Bundy; reprinted from *The Atlantic Monthly* by permission of the author. "The War Against the Young" by Richard Poirier: copyright © 1968 by The Atlantic Monthly Company, Boston, Mass. 02116; reprinted by permission of the author and publisher. "What Are They Telling Us?" (What Are Young People Telling Us?) by Norman Cousins: copyright © 1968 by Saturday Review, Inc.; reprinted by permission of the author. "Columbia: Symbol and Substance" from Stephen Donadio's interview with Lionel Trilling: copyright © 1968 by Partisan Review; reprinted by permission of the authors and the publisher. "How We Got That Way" by Sherman B. Chickering: copyright © 1967 by Sherman B. Chickering; reprinted from *The American Scholar*, Vol. 36, No. 4, Autumn, 1967, by permission of the author. "The New Mutants" by Leslie A. Fiedler: copyright © 1965 by Partisan Review; reprinted by permission of the author and the publisher. "As Much an Experience as an Idea" from "What's Happening to America" by Susan Sontag: copyright © 1967 by Susan Sontag; reprinted with the permission of Farrar, Straus & Giroux, Inc., and the author; published in *Partisan Review*. "Buchwald's Guide to Campus Capers" (Capers on the Campus) by Art Buchwald: copyright © 1968 by New York Post; reprinted by permission of the author. "Yes and No" by Norman Podhoretz (interviewed by Alexander Klein): copyright © 1969 by Norman Podhoretz and Alexander Klein. "The Party of Hope" by Alfred Kazin: copyright © 1968 by The Condé Nast Publications Inc.; reprinted from *Vogue* by permission of the author and the publisher. "In the Name of Life" by Erich Fromm: copyright © 1968, 1969 by Erich Fromm; by permission of the author. "The New Aristocrats" by Paul Goodman: copyright © 1967 by Paul Goodman; originally appeared in *Playboy* Magazine; reprinted by permission of the author. "The Alienated" from *Young Radicals* by Kenneth Keniston: copyright © 1968 by Kenneth Keniston; reprinted by permission of Harcourt, Brace & World, Inc. "Black Youth Search for Identity" (Contemporary Negro Youth—Some Problems of Identity) by Kenneth Clark: copyright © 1967 by Johnson Publishing Co., Inc.; reprinted from *Ebony Magazine* by permission of the author and the publisher. "From Dreams of Love to Dreams of Terror" by James Baldwin: copyright © 1968 by James Baldwin; reprinted from *Los Angeles Free Press* by permission of the author, his agent, Robert Lantz, and the publisher. "Jewish Campus Youth" by Theodore Bikel: copyright © 1968, 1969 by American Jewish Congress and Theodore Bikel; reprinted by permission of the author and the American Jewish Congress. "Catholic Teen-agers Debate Adult Critics" (Today's Rebellious Generation): copyright © 1966 American Press, Inc.; reprinted with permission from *America, The National Catholic Weekly Review*. "Knights in Chino Pants: The Vanishing Adolescent" from *The Vanishing Adolescent* by Edgar Z. Friedenberg: copyright © 1959, 1964 by Edgar Z. Friedenberg; reprinted by permission of the Beacon Press. "Rebellion in Adolescence" by Benjamin Spock: copyright © 1966 by McCall Corporation; reprinted by permission of the author and through the courtesy of *Redbook Magazine*. "The Affluent Drop-Out" by Haim Ginott: copyright © 1969 by Haim Ginott; by permission of the author. "Sex, My Daughters, and Me" by Midge Decter: copyright © 1967 by *Harper's* Magazine, Inc.; reprinted from the August, 1967, issue of *Harper's Magazine* by permission of the author. "What We Offer" by Walter Lippmann and "To Mr. Lippmann" by Rita Dershowitz: copyright © 1967 by Harper's Magazine, Inc.; reprinted from the October, 1967, issue of *Harper's Magazine* by permission of the authors. "The Real Iron Curtain" by Harry Golden: copyright © 1969 by Harry Golden; by permission of the author. "Let's Establish Diplomatic Relations" (Letter to the Young) by Marya Mannes: copyright © 1966 by McCall Corporation; reprinted by permission of the author and through the cour-

1966 by Katherine Anne Porter, published in *Mademoiselle;* reprinted by permission of Katherine Anne Porter, Roy Newquist, Cyrilly Abels, Theron Raines, and the publishers. "Sex and Students" by Robert Coles: copyright © 1966, Harrison-Blaine of New Jersey, Inc.; reprinted by permission of *The New Republic* and the author. "The Sexual Revolution—in Living Color" by Harriet Van Horne: copyright © by McCall Corporation; reprinted by permission of *McCall's Magazine* and the author. "Happeners" from *It's Happening* by J. L. Simmons and Barry Winograd: copyright © 1966 by J. L. Simmons and Barry Winograd; reprinted by permission of the authors and Marc-Laird Publications, Santa Barbara, California. "Some *Playboy* Views" from "The Playboy Philosophy" by Hugh M. Hefner: copyright © 1962, 1963, 1964, 1965, 1966 by HMH Publishing Co., Inc.; originally appeared in *Playboy* Magazine; reprinted by permission of the author and publisher. "An Open Letter to Allen Ginsberg" by Harvey Cox: copyright © 1967 by Commonweal Publishing Co., Inc.; reprinted by permission of the author and *Commonweal.* "Public Solitude" by Allen Ginsberg: copyright © 1967 by Allen Ginsberg; reprinted from *Respond,* published by the Laymen's League of the Unitarian Universalist Association, by permission of the publisher and the author. "Allen and I" by Louis Ginsberg: copyright © 1969 by Louis Ginsberg; by permission of the author. "Drugs and Dissent" by Robert Coles: copyright © 1967 by Partisan Review; reprinted by permission of the publisher and author. "The Hippies" from an interview with John Kenneth Galbraith: copyright © 1968 by HMH Publishing Co. Inc.; originally appeared in *Playboy* Magazine; reprinted by permission of the pubisher. "What Can the Young Believe?" by Robert F. Kennedy: copyright © 1967, Harrison-Blaine of New Jersey, Inc.; reprinted by permission of *The New Republic* and the author. "Thoughts for Young Americans" by Dwight D. Eisenhower (The *Reader's Digest,* April, 1966): copyright © 1966 by Dwight D. Eisenhower; reprinted by permission of Doubleday & Company, Inc. "The Youth Revolution: A Positive Response" by John D. Rockefeller III: copyright © 1968, 1969 by John D. Rockefeller III; published in another version in *Saturday Review;* copyright © 1968 by Satuday Review, Inc.; by permission of the author. "How to Change the World" from "On the City" by John V. Lindsay: copyright © 1968 by Hearst Corporation; reprinted by permission of the author and the publisher from *Eye* Magazine, Vol. 1, No. 2 (April, 1968). "They Are Protesting *For*" (The Concerned Generation) by Eugene J. McCarthy: copyright © 1968 by The Condé Nast Publications Inc.; reprinted from *Mademoiselle* by permission of the author. "Joan Baez: Actually I'm a Square" (Joan

To S. R. Slavson
to whose wisdom, insight and
sinew many future generations
will be so deeply indebted
(if man has a future)

CONTENTS

Contents

INTRODUCTION

Plymouth Rock: as the Mayflower anchors, a boy picks up his father's musket and fires a bullet that barely misses some powder kegs, almost blowing up the ship. Upon landing, another youngster runs off into the woods; he is discovered days later some twenty-odd miles away encamped with a group of Indians.

1969: a student leader (who has been a page at the 1968 Republican National Convention) tells parents and professors: "Today, as we leave Yale, a sense of frustration and despair overwhelms us."

A black teenager contemplates his future: "You turn 18 and they send you away to kill people you never met. I'd rather kill a person here I hated." And the valedictorian at a leading women's college (quietly) sums up: "That rosy future . . . it is a hoax. Our days as a species on this planet are numbered . . . I'm terribly saddened that the most humane thing for me to do is to have no children at all." While another student calls prayerfully for a miracle: "Let there be born in us a strange joy!"

In all dynamic societies the clash of generations is an unavoidable bane and essential catalyst. It is a natural function of the young to assert their independence, to challenge their elders' traditions and preconceptions, logically and validly, as well as "imprudently" and "outrageously"—even going so far as to insist that avowed principles actually be practiced. In turn, it is the natural propensity of the parent generations to resist the challenge, moderately and immoderately, rationally and irrationally, to be overcautious and to "just stand there," while pressing problems fail to yield to "outmoded methods" based on "outdated conceptions and vision."

In the family, parents and children, readiest targets of one another's varied ambivalent emotions, both love and hate each other—are natural allies and natural enemies, mutual sources of satisfaction and frustration, pride and guilt.

Socially, only a minority of the young rebel overtly. But they are often the bellwether minority, including many who are more aware, more sensitive, with more integrated, stronger personalities, enabling them to express and act on their views and feelings—feelings shared, consciously and unconsciously, by a large number of their outwardly conformist peers. Bob Dylan's call on the elders to "Get out of the way of what you don't understand, Mr. Jones!" ricochets down the dark tunnel-corridors of history.

Perennial, too, from ancient clay tablets, through Plato, to the latest television panel discussion are the elders' complaints about youth—together with the sage advice that all would be well if only the young would follow the old ways; that is, the very ways which led to the problems the elders are lamenting.

Unfortunately, even the best of the new generation usually have only a hazy, often contradictory conception of what needs to be done and how, and almost no viable strategy for moving society along the lines they favor. Moreover, the generational clash itself, with its multi-rooted, high-octane passions, displaces much energy and concern from central to peripheral, symbolic targets and distorts both methods and goals, in what can become a vicious recriminatory spiral.

In our era this could be fatal. Today, unless youth and their elders join to act in concert, and act far more wisely and effectively than ever before, mankind is unlikely to muddle through.

Collected in this volume is some of the best available thought on today's fateful generational encounter by both specialists and generalists, by over- and under-30's, as well as representative views of public figures and of various segments of opinion. Some were specially commissioned. Many were edited from longer essays or from books; for this excerpting I assume full responsibility, as well as for juxtaposing contrasting views, at times forming a sort of chain-debate. By providing some counterpoint throughout (my own biases remain obvious) clues to truer insight may be more likely to emerge, as well as more balanced guides to action.

Lack of, or tragically inadequate, action on soul-destroying injustices and deadly problems which threaten us all is almost universally acknowledged to be a central factor in the extent and sharpness of America's "youth revolt" and "student unrest." Buckminster Fuller estimates that we have perhaps fifteen years left to "choose between Utopia and oblivion" for our species. George Wald declares that the "younger generation is no longer sure it has a future," mentioning nuclear holocaust and population explosion. But the future can be irretrievably damaged and even destroyed in many other ways, including continuing technological and ecological anarchy and mismanagement, and the industrious application of the quantum-leaps in genetics and surveillance to create a super-1984.

Meantime, the young see all our institutions (schools, hospitals, courts, Congress, etc.) deeply inadequate, our cities dying, our highest officials' public lying taken for granted. They see money earned by work taxed far more heavily than money acquired by manipulation; and pittance aid to the poor frowned on while lavish government subsidies and family inheritance for the rich are socially approved. They see an "affluent" society in which public services and the quality of life decline precipitously, and 50 percent of white families' income—85 percent of blacks'—is at a level you and I would consider abject poverty ($1500 to $6500 after taxes for a family of four).

Contrary to patronizing adult strictures, most of the young know full well that *all* societies are "hypocritical," with a considerable gap between values professed and values lived. But youth is "historical" enough to know that if all hell isn't raised, very little narrowing of the gap will occur. Convinced that we have the productive ability to fill all our people's material needs at a decent level—and still have ample luxuries for the "elite" —youth finds our not doing so inexcusable. They are further shocked when they discover that our society—relative to its capacities—is not even trying to solve its people's pressing problems, *really* trying, with a fraction of the commitment with which it tries to "win" wars. At most, nibbling, Band-Aid measures are taken. Indeed, housing "programs" decrease housing for the poor and lower middle-class, while funding luxury dwellings. Income is as unfairly distributed as thirty years ago. More black children go to segregated schools than in 1954; black unemployment is hardly dented; and the average black college graduate is paid $1,000 a year less than the average white high-school dropout.

Eighteen months after seeing starving American children on television the young read that most states still criminally keep food stamps from reaching the hungry. And the federal government won't let those hungry grow corn for their children on nearby unused land, because the well-to-do owners are being handsomely paid to keep it fallow!

So the crises of morality, credibility and confidence deepen, the likelihood of major civil strife, concentration camps and the police state increases. And all but a few of those from whom youth might have expected the best—their professors and liberals in general (myself included)—appear either oblivious or helpless.

Consistently the young experience a basic contempt by "the elite" for people, a low estimate of what people can be educated and inspired to do. Indeed the human being—the unique individual we claim to value—is more and more being treated by our society as a nuisance, a glut on the market. If only there were fewer commuters, no blacks, poor, aged, mentally ill, no annoying dissidents, no unprogrammed people (except us happy elite), no underdeveloped masses.

One can anticipate a secret "Iron Mountain" government report recommending simultaneous scientific, computer-selected mass euthanasia (by painless, even joyous, drugged method) of, say, 87.92431 percent of the world's population, to relieve their suffering and to bring about more well-being for the remaining Americans and the human race generally. (Hysterical? President Nixon's science advisor publicly agreed with other experts that in a few years hundreds of millions will be starving to death; but (while we Americans consume 60 percent of the world's output of irreplaceable natural resources) we are *not* taking feasible steps to avert that famine. If you and I should be consulted, too late to save them, would we let them die painfully or vote for mass mercy killing?)

Telling the young, in this context, that "the United States has the highest standard of living in the world" and the most individual freedom of any mass-society is no consolation. It only deepens their despair, reminds them there's no decent, truly just society they can look to anywhere, suggests that humanness may simply not be adequate to save us. And youth has neither otherworldly nor secular faith to turn to; for them progress and science have become synonyms for Satan.

Whereupon, deep in their unconscious profound anger, revulsion and anxiety take root—with premonitions of *self*-loathing, of a conception of self, of man, and man's history that is loathsome and unacceptable, that they must deny or anaesthesize if they are to survive.

The truisms of our age, over which we all slide, contain terrible, pervasive truth which plunges deep into the young and secretly lives and works there: Auschwitz and Hiroshima, and crouching under school desks while Kennedy and Khrushchev, eyeball to eyeball, risk nuclear incineration for us all/ bombing of civilians in London, Dresden, Vietnam/ American, Saigon, Vietcong tortures and murders/ the Allies failing to take steps which could have saved millions from Nazi death camps/ Soviet admission of mass-oppression and slaughter of their own people/ and the stabbing realization that a less virulent, less overtly evil, but far more long-lasting form of "Nazism" has been and still is being practiced here at home, searing the minds and spirits of millions of non-white people with the hot irons of prejudice and discrimination, and by slow, silent, steady, crushing "violence"—poverty, bad education, forced overcrowding, inferior medical care—making them (and the white poor, too) fall ill more often and die years earlier. (Black life expectancy is 7 years less than white; death rate of black children under 5 is twice that of whites.)

They may not know the specifics, but the sense of all this unacceptable history, and more, has long ago seeped through the cocoon of "affluence" we wrapped around our lucky young and through the rat-rich walls of the ghetto, too; created a profound feeling deep inside that violence and evil are pervasive, potential in all men—themselves included—and that normal "rational," "good" men are permitting and committing normal, regular horrors, on small and vast scales daily, now, at this moment. And the young sense that they are being groomed to continue not only their nation's and mankind's constructive work but also, inevitably, its mass-evil, mass-violence, mass-manipulation, mass-murder. Original sin of unprecedented magnitude has been traumatically rediscovered by the unconscious, and there is no salvation anywhere.

Instead, punishment of equally unprecedented magnitude has been provided: species-suicide, for our very best successes—in medicine, communications, power and other technologies—have brought us to the brink of both dreams and disasters, of utopian beneficence, and also of ever-spiraling physical and psychic dangers, some perhaps still as unknown to us today as was the unwitting grinding of sandstone dust daily into their corn meal by the Basketweavers' implements 1500 years ago, dust which wrecked their constitutions and destroyed their society from within even as they were growing more and more abundant harvests and were successfully defending their cliff dwellings against outside enemies. (P.S. We've only just learned that mother's milk, U.S.A., 1969, can no longer pass federal health inspection; too much DDT in it to qualify for interstate sale!)

Power accrues to our technological society like riches to Midas, and upon this ever-rising summit of power we are impaled and imprisoned, *feeling* more powerless perhaps than man ever has before.

Which brings us back to that unconscious sense of loathing for man, as violent, evil, and mass suicidal. This man—Western man—the young must deny in themselves, if possible extirpate entirely; in innumerable ways, their twin paths of revolt—the Life-Style Revolution or Counter Culture, and new-style Political Activism (which merge in many of the young)—tell their elders: "We are not like you, we are different, we are a new kind of man, a *different species*, with deeper insight, truer love, fuller joy, finer conscience, abiding peacefulness. We *can* achieve salvation."

Hence the thoroughgoing, determined effort to be different— in dress, hair, manners, bearing, ways of moving and modes of thought, aesthetic and other standards, speech and types of political action. The turning away from conventional competitiveness, acquisitiveness, achievement—from all adult "adjustment" which for them spells death-of-the-spirit. The rejection of "failed" authority and institutions. The romantic revolt against reason (so long and so badly abused by the elders that it is mistakenly shunned as essentially inimical). With the elders so discredited, youth's anxiety is intensified. Some call the young bored. In truth many are understandably panicked and retreat into protective apathy. Hence, in part, the importance of sex, rock, drugs—to still anxiety against the old world's terrors not yet fully exorcised and to come alive again, to give birth to a new consciousness, de-emphasizing duration, the horror of cumulative events, and stressing spontaneity, pagan hedonism and immediate sensation, love intimacy, the personal and private. (Lapses are common, of course. Thus, abhorring violence, many stress a cult of gentleness, but then proselytize for "nonviolence" and "love" with a fanatic salvationism which projects aggressive hateful "vibrations." Politically a few have consciously embraced "violence-for-good," thereby echoing official doctrine.)

When Gandhi was once asked his opinion of Western civilization, he replied: "It would be a good idea." That is what our domestic "youth revolt" is all about: questing, protesting, trying to create a more fulfilling, harmonious, viable, just social order and personal life. That includes values the young can act on sufficient for good-conscience and a community they can feel deeply committed to, a dedication transcending self and mortality. Contrary to most parents' view, things are not "easier" for their children, particularly if they are aware, sensitive, intelligent. Today the hard but clear tasks that preempted the efforts of many parents (going to college, scrambling for economic security, defeating the Nazis) have been replaced by a host of "impossible" tasks (righting national wrongs; stopping wars; living a good, significant life in a society whose wide "opportunities" many young feel are predicated on unacceptable anti-life styles, values, roles. (Girls are caught in a complex, ambivalent struggle between the old male-dominated family-bound roles and the new developing modes of woman-as-full-and-equal-person, in a society still heavily discriminating against women.)

There are, of course, youths who work for reform within the system, like advocacy lawyers who make their firms give them time off to handle civil rights and poverty cases for free. The more dramatic Life-Style and Political Activism revolts, however, aim to provide a different, better self, ethic faith, society *now*—"Paradise Now," precisely.

Central to the rebel ethos is diminution of repression, social and personal, resistance to being "programmed," insistence on free, individual choices and open feeling. In proper balance all this is life-affirming. But the young become life-denying if they insist on repressing, in themselves and others, the pleasures and benefits of human reasoning, planning, cumulative experience, discipline, organization. And reason and organization *can* coexist with spontaneity and "grooving."

But a better-balanced, more productive and fulfilling approach will certainly not be fostered by elders' rhapsodically hailing the rebels as saviors of Western Technological Man, nor by the even more prevalent curt or vitriolic putdown and syllogistic demonstration of youth's error in abandoning reason. Only adult appreciation of the positive, humanistic values of the "feeling" culture, combined with reason-based, effective, *action* by those elders on the crucial "impossible" tasks of our age will cut any ice with the young, will inspire them to rediscover the virtues, exhilarations and achievements of right reason in action.

Some enthusiasts predict that the counter culture will attract more and more youth and increasingly undercut and transform the ethos of "the system," bringing "revolutionary" changes to our whole society. This is most unlikely. The prevailing culture will continue selectively to cannibalize chunks from the rebel culture, and to blunt the rest without too much difficulty. Besides, even at today's accelerated pace it would take quite a while for cultural change to be translated into governmental and economic change. And the science revolution will be moving much faster, with profounder social effects, including genetic and chemical means for curbing the rebel culture.

Meantime, by withdrawing in panic from the insane outside world, most of the young would-be pagans are "copping out," leaving politics and the social order to the fumbling "nibblers" and crackpot "realists" in charge. While time runs out. . . .

But the Political Activists, by their impatient confrontation-ultimatums, are also taking a dangerous, *slow* road to the type of fundamental social change they seek. Sparked by young Negroes sitting-in down south, confrontation politics became a national call to conscience. It achieved some civil rights gains, served as one of the midwives of deeper black pride.

Protests, marches and the romantic, mock-power building seizures, magnified in "radicalizing" effect by needless police brutality, have highlighted the urgency of our problems and exerted a limited educational effect on sleeping liberals (like myself) and on many youths who otherwise would have been apolitical. Students have forced professors to begin to realize some of the profound shortcomings of the university and even start superficial reforms. And anti-war civil disobedience and militancy did keep the Vietnam issue and the resistance in dramatic focus before the nation. Whether the *continuing* unorthodox nature of much anti-war activity has scared people off and delayed widespread, legal, moratorium-type opposition is a moot point.

In any event confrontation-politics, apart from the war, being sporadic and only semi-organized, shunning electoral methods, often using tactics which (questions of morality aside) soon alienated sympathizers, could hardly build a mass base. It has already become a contributing cause to serious "backlash."

In truth, most young radical leaders have no illusions about winning. One prominent New Leftist recently told me he "expects the police state, in any event, in four or five years, so we had better radicalize all we can. Then maybe in twenty years we can crack it." Grim scenario, especially since major modern police states are rarely deposed unless defeated in war by another country. And a New Left writer, Michael Rossman, has written, poignantly: "We do not act from hope . . . there is much to love, no reason to hope, be free."

Actually young radicals have often first worked within "the system," with one of the parties, and in unsuccessful attempts at "dialogue" with university officials. It was the liberal elders' minimal sense of urgency, the discovery of the universities' subversion-by-research, and liberal complicity in the Vietnam war that spurred the young into protest-politics and anti-liberalism. And, the moment conventional politics offered them a faint, brief glimmer of hope—the McCarthy and Kennedy anti-war candidacies—the young streamed back into the democratic process.

When some of the young do "give up on liberalism and the democratic process" they are actually doing their elders too much honor. The implication is that those elders have really tried to effect basic reform by democratic means, and by their failure have proven it is unfeasible. Not so.

Only a tiny handful of liberal academics and intellectuals— of *all* the millions of liberals—have been *regularly* active in conventional politics, in the party system. Conforming to our culture's overemphasis on specialization and status, most of us have narrowed our areas of function to career and home, so that no tradition of citizen politics has developed. Even involved liberal intellectual leaders have limited their action to elitist modes and maneuverings: writing, making speeches, advising candidates and officials and forming relatively small groups, such as Americans for Democratic Action, to influence issues and poli-

ticians. But liberal leaders, both practical and intellectual, have never rolled up their sleeves and *pervasively, massively* organized fellow citizens to flock into the Democratic Party, take it over from the Bosses and make it *democratic.*

Just as our government left serious planning to the corporations, so we liberals have left organized, sustained politics largely to the professional politicians and to those other organized citizens who do work hard at the democratic process (and are handsomely rewarded for their efforts): the oil, automobile, steel, gun, Mafia, AMA, drug, Pentagon and other special-interest lobbies, and some labor leaders. Since our party and governmental systems are geared anti-democratically (via states' rights; committee tyranny; the funding of political campaigns by the monied, etc.), to resist broadly beneficial reform, the absence of major liberal citizen-politics has guaranteed that *significant* social change would usually come very slowly, even under so-called "liberal" administrations. Liberals, however, wrote and spoke so copiously, cogently and attractively that they created the illusion—for themselves, their opponents and many millions—not only that liberalism was official doctrine but that a full liberal program was in being. Liberal intellectuals' status, as culture heroes and counselor-mentors to officials, inevitably heightened this illusion and fostered complacency and oligarchic "cult-of-personality" politics.

Moreover, we are the victims of media-overkill. The daily oceans of ink, the billion Milky-Ways of electronic images, the Babel of Voices to-the-nth-power cacophonized, the continuous media-orchestration of crises, force us into protective numbness. ("ears have walls" said one of the Paris student revolt graffiti). Worse, the media (including, very likely, the words you are reading now) more and more become not guides and spurs to action, but *substitutes* for action. Receiving information, sharing a favorite newscaster's, columnist's or Senator's indignation, and venting it to friends, is for most of us vicarious action, our only sustained "action" on public matters. Thus, most of us are *consumers* of politics. And commentators and editorial writers

are simply *processors* and *purveyors* of political drama, creators
of shared pseudo-action, turning off real action. The Republic
is bleeding to death and we stand by watching as though it were
a spectator sport!

Yet the present is also a moment of unprecedented opportunity. For the very disillusion and frustration abroad in the land,
combined with the national and global threats to our common
survival and to the quality of all our lives, could all be focused
for the country as a far deeper crisis than either the Great Depression or World War Two. The majority might then be led to
rise to the challenge, to join in a new democratic Citizen Politics
of Common Purpose, that would offer a chance—perhaps the
only chance—of averting disaster. And this time, instead of a
limited "New Deal" we might (with our increased educational
level and heightened political and moral consciousness) be
able to create a democratic, evolutionary "revolution"—socioeconomic, ethical, cultural, transforming institutions and attitudes and values through gradations of communal social and
political action, locally and nationally.

To expect this to evolve via present structures in time to save
us is fatal naïveté. Yet liberals have not been suggesting, much
less taking, *major* new directions, even as they write fearfully
of the political process breaking down, and of polarized left-
right, black-white "chiliastic direct-action" undermining the social order and moving us toward the total state. A noted perceptive Establishment liberal recently reiterated in an elegant
essay that today's crisis is religious, not political, that the young
are seeking new faith, and warned that ideological (undemocratic) "politicization of all things" is going to spread more and
more among youth. But he, too, offered no promising, new, *democratic* political alternatives for the young, and no basis for faith,
just a vague futile plea for better "moral philosophy." But
clearly faith will not be created in these young by any mount of
"moral philosophizing," but precisely through democratic communal citizen politics—and social action.

Through participation in such a movement—and the changes

in people, government and society it would bring—outlets for moral energy would be supplied and the energies now flowing towards "extremist totalism" would be converted to constructive tasks of humanistic, democratic transformation; values would be renewed; meaning recovered in action; at least some of the legitimacy of authority re-earned; and faith lived and found in good works. (The lesson to be learned from the failures of past student and youth movements is that positive adult action and guidance, dedicated major reform movement that can lead to intergenerational partnership is essential if mounting polarization and destructiveness are to be avoided, and productive results achieved.)

The young are right: conventional, party politics cannot begin to be sufficient for this crisis epoch (though it *is*, of course, necessary), wide participation is essential, and "parallel institutions" will have to be set up. To achieve racial justice more swiftly/ to guarantee jobs at decent pay for all/ to make massive socially productive public investments, under citizen—not bureaucratic—control/ to revitalize and democratize the labor unions as *enhancers* of citizen power/ to make our schools truly serve the citizenry (not the old oligarchies nor the new demagogues) rather than largely perpetuating class division/ to provide, for the first time in our history, adequate representation for the interests and pressing needs of the *majority:* of Middle Americans and of the young, the poor, the non-white, all the excluded segments of the population (some of whom are withdrawing their consent to be governed)/ to counter the pervasive sense of impotence/ to develop a sense of community—towards all this, and more, we obviously cannot simply amend and extend the major political parties. We must also, rapidly, create *new* channels and institutions for political and social action—unified, for the first time in our history, in a *non*-party, citizen-participation, issue-oriented organization, democratic, but on a scale and in forms we have never had before.

Unions and business work within the parties, but they also organize separately; so must liberals, but on a mass-basis. (A third party would not only widen liberal-radical splits, but be condemned to long-time minority status.) Aimed at *basic* reform, carrying out its own social action program (as indicated later), and utilizing both electoral and non-violent "movement" tactics, the new *non*-party organization could attract many of the disillusioned young and black who shun party politics. It would also provide a *permanent* channel for Republican and Democratic liberals to work together, locally and nationally, on issues. It would be both a mass-membership organization *and* a coalition; and many members would also belong to other groups as well as to a major political party, thereby speeding the reform of the parties by acting en masse within them as well as by posing a *potential* third-party threat. In time, citizen influence on the Democratic Party should be decisive, with liberal tendencies also increased in the Republican Party.

Launched by a broad spectrum of leadership, such a citizen movement would set up varied forms of membership and affiliation: state, city, neighborhood chapters, as well as church, union, ethnic, faculty, student, business, professional, scientific and other types of chapters, including major newspaper, magazine, network and corporation employee chapters. Thus it would be strategically suited for varieties of democratic action far beyond the scope of a party.

National *group* leadership would exist, but local initiatives would be stressed. Members would apply a creative synthesis of the methods of electoral politics, lobbies, labor unions, the civil rights movement, and the peaceful demonstrations of the students and activists. Because such a mass organization could make citizen power at long last effective in the electoral process and push through structural government reforms, it would tend to make it less frequently necessary to use non-violent "demonstration" methods. And all tactics would tend to be more restrained, because the members would not feel themselves isolated rebels, or need to shout very loud to get attention. New tactics could also be developed, including dramatic, media and personal means of mass political education. Also methods of educating elite groups to a better understanding of how their true self-interest today often merges with that of other population segments and with the common good.

As indicated, both as a national organization and as an association of local citizens' groups, we would base ourselves squarely on a *Politics of Common Purpose*. That means a program which can win the support of considerable portions of masses as diverse as suburbanites, farmers, blacks, poor, liberals (regular and left), labor, moderate radicals, students, professors, the "enlightened" new classes of professionals, and white Middle Americans (incomes $5,000 to $15,000) many of whom are part of "the backlash."

This is by no means an impossible dream. A relatively small shift can swing elections. And the large mass of "forgotten Americans" has not been offered a significant program by anybody nor accorded true respect; and they know it—with Nixon in the White House, the huge majority, according to a recent national poll, still expect things to "change for the worse." Moreover in that same poll, these troubled whites placed highest on their list of "problems the government should be spending more money on" (in this order) job-training of unemployed/ ending pollution/ medical care for needy and old/ fighting crime/ improving schools/ providing better housing, especially for Negroes. And they want less spent on space and the military. That's not a bad start toward a liberal re-ordering of national priorities. *Real* tax reform and more local control could also appeal to them, as well as better schools and colleges and other career pathways for their children. And if genuine concern for their problems is shown, dangers highlighted, but a way and a vision projected in which they can count and participate, many of these white "squares" would respond positively.

There are also reservoirs of untapped generosity and idealism in their self-image waiting to be spoken to. And who is to say— without first trying—that they could not be educated to realize that—for example—righting racial wrongs *committedly* would reduce crime and welfare rolls, benefit the whole economy, raising whites' real incomes, too, and saving whites' children from facing thorny racial problems? To realize that their self-interest would be served better by a true pro-development, living-standard-raising foreign policy than by our present and costly, unjust guardianship of the status quo abroad? That any swing to reaction" is very much to their own *dis*advantage? A coordinated mass politics, not dependent on a few charismatic leaders, but involving many thousands of community-level democratic political "educators" might well accomplish what now appears "impossible."

Most important, too, the new institution would constitute— for the first time in the history of our democracy—a truly powerful citizens'-lobby, for the interests of the majority and the needs of hitherto almost totally excluded minorities. It would represent many millions of active, issue-oriented voters more than all the other vested interest lobbies combined. And it could have funds to match, if not surpass, them. Big-Steel, Big-Oil and all the other Big-Bigs might find themselves outclassed by Big-and-Little-Citizen.

Such a vigorous, solid, national citizen politics would also help make "local control" truly feasible, not permitting "citizen participation" to become extensions of federal bureaucracy as so disastrously has occurred in recent years. Also by providing channels for people to exert significant control over national and state government, it would moderate the emotional overemphasis on "localism" that present impotence fosters. Thus, while matters best handled locally would be rendered unto the localities, key national programs and planning would also be stepped up, as clearly they must.

With its numerous, varied chapters in the sciences and corporations, the citizen movement could also maintain a thoroughgoing "technology check" which, backed by its mobilized political muscle, could prevent grave ecological errors in time. It could be immensely beneficial, too, in counteracting the tendency toward monopolization of knowledge-power, of scientific research and development by government and the corporations.

At the same time it could encourage scholars and scientists hitherto perhaps too rigid about pursuing only so-called "disinterested" research, to be less fearful of cooption and to act on the principle that scholarship in the service of man need not be either meretricious or corrupting. . . .

Despite the existence of various volunteer groups, we do not have a real tradition of citizen-social-action, either. In that sense we are a very poor, underdeveloped people. The vast majority of citizens are locked into their work and private worlds. They are thus completely cut off from the responsibilities and satisfactions of varieties of public and social service in their communities, which could give them a sense of wider purpose and responsibility and power, direct contact with persons of other segments of the population, and the pleasure and fulfillment of seeing vivid, social, human results from their freely given efforts. (Among college students only one out of thirty is participating in any social action.) This also has been one factor in keeping low the horizons of "the possible" in many vital areas in which citizen effort could make a tremendous continuing contribution.

The new citizen movement would foster and coordinate (with unions, universities, the private sector) a comprehensive social-action program, ranging from local information services to mass job-training, tutoring and teachers'-aide corps thousands of times larger than now in being. A pervasive, imaginative anti-prejudice campaign, far eclipsing present efforts, could be mounted, aimed at making stomping on a human being as anathema as stomping on the flag. For the first time major white commitment could be demonstrated to eliminating at least overt expression of racism which daily sears not just poor but also "successful" non-whites. Models of coherent community could be created, with students and faculty joining the general citizenry in constructive "direct experience" beneficial both to the learning process and the community.

The young from high-school age on would flock to join their elders in making such memorable "history" in concert, and

youth would be provided with significant, productive useful
roles and work during their protracted schooling. And for all
of us, the combination of mass-participation politics and social
action might in time create a new ethos, a new communal tradition, an involvement with our fellow-citizens that would deeply
engage us, so that social action would become the norm rather
than the exception. Let me add that such participation can be
readily integrated into business or professional careers and family schedules, and for most persons would be life-enhancing, a
badly needed supplement to the narrow, limited, non-communal,
diminished humanity into which most of us have been molded.

Paradoxically, our so-called "post-industrial" society is in
some ways faced with the sort of perils that beset pioneer settlements in a strange new world. Our physical and spiritual survival is profoundly threatened and we too are primitively un-
organized to deal with our common dangers and problems, and
desperately need participatory, pioneering spirit and channels
for action. This, also, is one of the emphases of the young, that
we all become our brothers' keepers. Both in the act and by the
result we might recover our lost confidence and humanity and
transform our society, without apocalypse, rendering our democracy viable and responsive enough not to keep coming apart
(until the total state takes over) and more fit to cope with the
urgent, complex "Utopia or oblivion" decisions upon which all
our fates depend.

If we do not heed the message of the young and fail to pioneer
new forms for organized, intelligent sociopolitical action on a
vast scale; if the vacuum of leadership continues as some of our
best minds persist in their non-participatory, ostrich overspe-
cialization, then all the deep anxieties and fears of the young—
and the warnings of Buckminster Fuller, still the youngest of
the young—will come to pass.

History—that nightmare to which so many of our young
are understandably allergic—does not provide much basis for
optimism. And it has been a long time now that the young, and
black, have been crying and biting, kicking and drawing blood,

yet the elders have responded chiefly by drawing the wagons in a circle, tossing some crumbs, confetti and ritual phrases at the troublemakers, and cocking their rifles. The Maginot Line of the psyche, collectivized in "the system"—all the systems—is our foremost wonder and horror, relentlessly collaborating with its own technical genius to create the ultimate, all-encompassing "work of art" that may soon succeed in negating, replacing life.

Some years ago Albert Einstein (who had been actively pressing for world disarmament initiatives and had previously commented optimistically on an essay of mine on foreign policy) wrote me a letter in which he expressed his deep disillusionment: reluctantly he had concluded that mankind was on the wrong track and could not—perhaps did not want to—be saved. I now throw into the breech a story I recently heard which, had I known it then, I would have included in my attempt at a consolatory reply:

Bushman tribal society and intertribal relations were cooperative, with minimal conflict and no murder. Until one day a young man rebuffed by a girl from another tribe was so smitten that, with the aid of friends, he kidnapped her and took her home as his forced-bride. Violence then broke out between the two tribes, but ceased abruptly when one man was killed. The leaders conferred and decided that to avoid future murder the two tribes would shun further contact with each other. A territorial dividing line was agreed on. It has never been violated. And each year both tribes separately re-enact the war-and-murder as ritual reminder never to permit its recurrence in real life.

Perhaps, then, we, too, facing unprecedented peril, can come to wisdom and to action, in time. If not, perhaps nature *will* heed the young and—next time a different, better species.

RICHARD SCHICKEL

why youth seeks
new values

**Our society—any society—gets
the kind of children it deserves.**

Erik H. Erikson [the distinguished Harvard psychologist] points out that the adolescent's energetic exuberance, his eager quest after new ideals and excitement for its own sake, are quite normal; they appear in all Western societies. Even when these energies sometimes spill over into criminal activity, it is not necessarily a sign that the whole younger generation is going to hell in a handcart. Nor is it a symptom of some frightening and mysterious sickness peculiar to our age. On the contrary, it is often a young person's direct statement of disgust over the current ways of the world, over being made, as Margaret Mead puts it, "scapegoats for adult apathy, indifference, lack of responsibility and lack of imagination."

To state it bluntly, Erikson believes that our society—any society—gets the kind of children it deserves, even secretly wants. If our children disappoint us, he suggests, it is because the world we create for them—and which, of course, influences their values and aspirations—disappoints us even more. Preadult young men and women are often confused. In any era they want to know what they should believe in, what they should try to become. What frightens some adults is the fact that many adolescents work at these questions with furious intensity. And adolescent frustration when the answers refuse to come easily is often terrible to behold.

In his remarkable book *Childhood and Society*, Erikson sug-

gests one possible answer to their questions. He reminds readers
that when Freud was asked what he thought a normal person
should be able to do well, he replied simply, "To love and to
work."

It is a simple formula, but not, in Erikson's view, an oversim-
plified one. To love successfully and to work successfully and
to keep the demands of each in reasonable balance are, for him,
universal goals to which everyone, regardless of class or natural
gifts, may reasonably aspire. But Erikson does not claim that
the ability to love and to work is easily attained. On the contrary, he is greatly concerned over the ways society conspires to
rob us all of this ability.

A child is, naturally, dependent upon the adults around him
for his image of the world, and the chances are that they will
show him a distorted image. This can be critical, for as Erikson
sees it, each of the child's stages of growth hinges on a major
choice as to how he sees himself in relation to the world. If a
wrong choice is forced upon him at one stage or another by the
image he sees, his succeeding choices will be more difficult. The
process may be likened to a minor navigational error that may
put a plane a mile or so off course when it is made but that, if
not corrected, can cause the plane to be hundreds of miles off
when it should be reaching its destination.

By the time a child arrives at adolescence he will have made,
according to Erikson, four momentous choices. As a tiny baby
he will have learned either trust or mistrust at his mother's
breast; in the course of toilet training he will have gained either
a sense of autonomy or a feeling of shame and doubt; learning
to walk during the period when the numerous terrors of infantile
sexuality are first encountered, he will experience either a
healthy sense of initiative or, if things go badly, a sense of guilt
over goals and acts attempted or even contemplated. Finally, in
school and on the playground he will meet for the first time the
"inorganic laws of the tool world," and out of that encounter
will come either a taste for the pleasure of productivity or pos-

sibly a lingering sense of inferiority if he is unable to master this stage.

In the worst of circumstances, then, a youngster may approach adolescence full of distrust, shame, doubt, guilt and inferiority—in short, in a terrible mess before life has even fairly begun. In point of fact, most people reach adolescence in a rather mixed-up state, with odd strengths and hidden weaknesses already part of their personalities. The great task of adolescence, according to Erikson, is the formation of a mature identity out of these bits and pieces; the problem is to decide who you are and what you want to be.

Obsessed with the question of "what they appear to be in the eyes of others as compared with what they feel they are," adolescents keep themselves together, Erikson says, by temporarily overidentifying with the heroes of cliques and crowds. This helps to explain the phenomenal appeal of characters like the Beatles or the uncanny influence that one particularly admired youth—whose virtues are usually quite unapparent to adults—can exert on a group of teen-agers. This overidentification also provides the basis for some social criticism. If the ideals of the day are entertainers, athletes, hucksters and hustlers, it is no wonder adolescents are confused; no wonder they are embarrassingly curious about the gap between the figures we ritualistically hold up for their admiration (ministers, teachers, professional men) and those in whom, as our popular culture makes abundantly clear, we are really most interested.

But the search for identity is not the only thing that preoccupies adolescents. There is also, in the late teens, the beginning of the search for love—or, as Erikson puts it, the struggle to master the problems of intimacy. This is a necessary prelude to love—but it seems to him that our social system in general and our educational system in particular are designed to limit the opportunities for the kinds of close friendships and inspirational teaching that help a youngster develop a capacity for love. When education is geared mainly to preparation for economic success and when success is defined mainly as learning to get along in order to get ahead, human intimacy is bound to be regarded as a dangerous distraction from the one true path.

Paul Goodman's *Growing Up Absurd* is the great text on this point. He describes our society as "an apparently closed room in which there is a large rat race as the dominant center of attention." In this closed room there is no alternate to the rat race —that is, to material values. So even if one despises the race, he cynically continues to run it. It is very hard to grow up under this condition, Goodman says, for we share no true sense of community that might sustain, inspire and nurture young people until they can act on their own with fully developed powers.

Living in a closed room may not weigh too heavily on adults, says Goodman. They may not be very happy, but they can "fight and work anyway." But youngsters cannot do that. For them, "it is indispensable to have a coherent, fairly simple and viable society to grow up into; otherwise they are confused and some are squeezed out." In today's world, traditions are being broken constantly, and there are not yet enough new standards to affirm. Goodman is vague about where to place the blame for this situation; apparently it belongs to all of us, and our fathers and grandfathers as well; therefore it belongs to none of us. Which makes that amorphous thing, history, the villain of the piece.

That is exactly what Bruno Bettelheim argues. . . . Bettelheim says our world has changed from an individualistic, agrarian society to a mass, urban one, but our notion of what constitutes the good life remains fixed in the past. Unable to find the old satisfactions in our new world, achingly aware of the gap between ideals and reality, many frustrated parents apply "overt and covert pressures on youth to provide . . . what was lacking in their own lives."

[Sociologist Edgar Z.] Friedenberg declares that the problem is not that so many youths rebel against such pressures, but that so few do. The typical teen-ager, he says, "is enraged not at the tyranny of adults but at their blandness, their weakness, their emptiness. . . . Rebellion would be a lot cozier than his feeling that one has been gutted, that one is trapped, because there are no possibilities in humanity itself."

Thus both children and adults are victimized by society. But the burden falls more heavily on young people simply because adults have power over them. The natural parental abhorrence over the fact that they can't fully control adolescents is intensified, Friedenberg thinks, by what amounts to a deep envy of youth and their "life not yet squandered." But since much of this antagonism to the young is not conscious, it festers dangerously in the dark—only to break out in the schools, to which parents have delegated the job of keeping young people in line.

Our schools, Friedenberg says, have two great responsibilities: to help the student find a meaning in life that makes sense in *his* terms, and to help him find a sense of self-esteem. The achievement of these goals is blocked, he says, by the history of public education in this country. The traditional function of our schools has been to train the children of immigrants to work docilely in factories and offices and to give them the guidelines by which they can pull themselves up into the middle class and beyond. This has led to an emphasis on smoothing off rough edges, learning to get along with the group to which one aspires and curbing one's individuality. The school has been the melting pot in a society that prides itself on its ability to assimilate all kinds of people. Thus schools and teachers are unlikely to respond happily to signs of originality, nonconformity or eccentricity on the part of students. The result is an education that narrows the world instead of opening it up.

In his book *Coming of Age in America* Friedenberg is devastatingly specific in his charges against our schools. Their spirit may be recaptured by any reader who remembers his school days' myriad rules of conduct and deportment, the ostensible function of which was to make you "a nice person" but which had as its real purpose the "infantilization" of adolescence and the ensnarement of youngsters "in the trailing remnants of childhood emotions which always remain to trap them."

To add to the problem, Friedenberg says, we have turned over to the schools functions that used to take place elsewhere, placing the schools in a position to alter the way a child grows, his values, his sense of his own worth, even his patterns of anxiety. And these, Friedenberg insists, are matters too important to be left to those whose major concern is formal education. In exercising this vast authority, the schools are quite democratic. We are familiar with the extent of the dropout problem in the slums, which many authorities believe is heightened by the ludicrous conflict between the middle-class values the school tries to enforce and the values that the students encounter every day in the school of hard knocks. To Friedenberg the wonder is that more slum kids don't drop out; for if middle-class youngsters are no longer stimulated by the prospect of carrying on a meaningless tradition, why should we expect to gain recruits for it in the slums?

But the prejudice against "different" children extends to more than just the poor. The school, Friedenberg charges, tries to break or drive out everyone who deviates from the norm—the rich, the excessively bright or imaginative or specialized—because in a mass society "the most serious threat to self-esteem is the possibility of meeting someone who really *is* qualified and does know how to do something special, thus opening . . . limitless vistas of inferiority."

The high school, then, does not help the student test various roles and identities; it does not help him to "connect" his unique gift with some suitable adult role. Instead, it attempts to force everyone into the current statistical model of normality. Any tentative step toward trying another role is frowned on or laughed at or ignored. Most likely the odd youth will simply be left behind, standing on the corner with the other dropouts, watching the swelling parade to college.

And college, according to Paul Goodman, is now organized like a model of the great rat race that students are going to enter upon graduation. Instead of a leisurely, civilized pursuit of knowledge for its own sake, the college student finds he must pursue good grades that will ensure the good job in the good, materially rich life to come. College is no longer the refreshing contrast it once was to high school; too often it is nothing but a sophisticated extension of that dreary, regulation-bound place. No wonder the colleges are hurrying to re-create some of the old atmosphere of higher learning; no wonder the student body is restless with revolt.

It can be argued, of course, that the critics, in order to make their point, overstate their case. We all know sensitive, humane and intelligent teachers who believe that the proper function of education is the cultivation of diversity and of the singular student's singular gifts—and sometimes, somehow, such teachers manage to break through the paper curtain of forms, reports and administrative edicts to touch the hearts and minds of their students. And we all know students who resist the effects of the great educational blender and emerge from it intact and, oddly enough, even enhanced by the experience.

But if even part of the critics' charges are true, it is clear that our approach to the problems of educating adolescents and young adults is wrong, that all the wondrous and expensive new educational technology, all our surveys, studies and seminars, will not accomplish what we so fervently wish of them. It is clear that our troubles lie not in the technology of education but in its very atmosphere.

According to Friedenberg, the essential first step in true reform is to end the connection in our minds between schooling and economic opportunity. We will not, he assures us, solve the dropout problem by repeating the formula that those with a high-school diploma do better economically than those without one. The kids understand perfectly well that the truly significant difference in income hinges on a college degree—and that college is not a choice available to everyone.

If that is true, it follows that the American high school itself, largely oriented toward college preparation, does not make sense for everyone. What is needed, says Friedenberg, is a wider range of alternatives than the present choice between a high-school diploma and dropping out. He contends that the public

school now adequately serves "ambitious, conventional youth
who accept with equanimity the commonplace folkways of their
community" and who can comfortably express their talents in
conventional ways. What we need is something equally comfortable for the others. He suggests two possibilities.

The first is a series of residential schools, open to all but
mainly for the benefit of poor children. The idea is to lift them
bodily out of the atmosphere of despair that surrounds them on
their home turf. He is not urging, as some have, revivals of the
semimilitary CCC camps. On the contrary, he believes that "generally speaking, slum children may be assumed to have received
whatever virtues austerity might confer." So he proposes that
these schools have a minimum of rules, provide students with
pocket money and be lavish with food, care and facilities. "The
youngsters . . . should be treated in a way that means respect
to them, and for the deprived this must include a large measure
of material and sensual indulgence." In addition to these schools
he suggests a sort of G.I. bill of rights for youngsters, under
which the government would pay the fees of students in need of
experimenting with other alternatives, ranging from the upper-
class Eastern prep schools to first-rate private vocational schools.

If we encouraged a new diversity in education, Friedenberg
believes, we would also improve the conventional high school,
relieving it of the pressure created by its attempt to accommodate those students who least like it and whom it least likes.

It is a visionary proposal. But Paul Goodman goes even further. For instance, he suggests experimenting in the primary
grades with no school at all for some children, to see if they
might not pick up on their own the elementary essentials of education. A great many children do learn to read without formal
instruction, while many are actually blocked by their encounter
with a system of rewards and punishments. Goodman would also
experiment with learning outside the classroom, with smaller
schools, with classes of mixed age groups, with an end to compulsory attendance. He proposes at the college level immediate
abandonment of the grading system by some of our more pres-

tigious colleges to eliminate the pressures grading imposes on the student. He also thinks some colleges might insist on two years of work or travel or public service as a condition for entrance "to get students with enough life experience to be educable . . . to break the lock step of 12 years of doing assigned lessons for grades." Out in the world, young people might acquire some motivation other than future money rewards for continuing their education. He believes that "educational policy must allow for periodic quitting and easy return to the scholastic ladder so that the young have time to find themselves and to study when they are themselves ready." In short, Goodman is willing to try anything that will make education more flexible, anything that will acknowledge and emphasize individual differences in aptitudes and interests, in psychological and intellectual growth rates, in styles of life and thought.

But having said this, the argument begins to circle back on itself. There would be no need for a radical revision of education if society itself were not caught in a lock step that the schools must join. As Goodman puts it, "Fundamentally, there is no right education except growing up in a worthwhile world. Indeed, our excessive concern with poblems of education at present simply means that the grownups do not have such a world."

Whether Goodman and Friedenberg are practical or impractical, it can do no harm, in the midst of the current ferment over the problems of youth, to be reminded that the young have a right to expect more from their schools than mere vocational training or the promise of good jobs at good pay. Education, rightly conceived, must help parents offer their youngsters a sense that the community they are being prepared to join is a worthwhile place.

This is not merely an abstract question of social justice; it is a matter of vital self-interest to everyone. As Erik Erikson says, "It is the young who, by their responses and actions, tell the old whether life as represented by the old and presented to the young has meaning." Young people at the moment are withholding any such assurance. That some among us are willing to ponder these deeply disturbing questions is a good omen. But if we are to take critics like Friedenberg and Goodman seriously, we must look beyond piecemeal reform, beyond nuts-and-bolts adjustments. We must do nothing less than take up the ultimate question of what constitutes a good life in a good society for all of us.

NAT HENTOFF

youth—the oppressed majority

It's the color of your mind they want to control.—an Indian girl

Teachers and schools tend to mistake good behavior for good character.—John Holt

We are warned not to waste our time, but we are brought up to waste our lives. —Eric Hoffer

To most adults who read about it, the analogy must have seemed preposterous. Here was John Lindsay, the mayor of New York, actually telling a group of Princeton undergraduates last November that they were like black youngsters in a ghetto. "The distance between these groups—educationally, economically, socially—has certain psychological bridges," he said. "The frustration of the sophomore alienated from his university by its size and impersonality is not very much different from the resentment of the ghetto youth who is alienated from his city because its opportunities and rewards are foreclosed to him. Both suffer the malady of powerlessness—powerlessness in the face of huge, authoritarian institutions that routinely cause fundamental dislocations in the lives of the people they affect each day."

The young powerless? According to Al Capp, J. Edgar Hoover, editorial writers for *The New York Times* and practically any parent, the trouble with the young—the poor dutifully excepted—is that they have too *much* power. They are self-indulgent, willful and more disrespectful of their elders than any previous generation of adolescents. Accordingly, they must be curbed and prepared for "responsibility," for unfortunately, they *will* inherit the earth. The more the young rebel, the more firmly they must be suppressed; for is it not the obligation of their elders to make certain that the young grown up into replicas of themselves? If the young do not, what meaning has there been in the lives of their parents? "We must die," say the old, not really believing it, "but at least the values we lived by will remain."

And it is there that the dissident among the young make their attack: the values of those responsible for society as it is. In December 1966 Ray Mungo, then editor of the student-run *Boston University News*, wrote, under the head "BLACK CHRISTMAS": "We are nothing if not an educational institution, and yet our graduates tend to fall, unquestioningly, into the same narrow sphere of exclusive self-interest in which most men move. And even this self-interest does not pervade the self; we know ourselves as little as we know others. . . . So we do not examine our own sexuality, we won't study the history of China and we're unspeakably cold to murder by the thousands in Vietnam. We have ceased functioning as human beings capable of some sympathies beyond our own offices . . . our Beauty is an idealized Beauty rather than the one we'd joyously climb on and inseminate."

That's one skirmish in the generational war. Others of the young do not attack at all but try to remain private. "It goes beyond your class or the color of your skin," a wiry Indian girl from Maine declares. "It's the color of your mind they want to control. They want you preprocessed before you can have what they call autonomy. But they won't get *me*." Lines are continually being drawn by the young to preserve what they can of their youth—ways of dress, of wearing hair, of music, of speech. But most learn that in terms of making the most basic decisions about their lives, they are indeed without power. "Adolescents," writes sociologist Edgar Z. Friedenberg, "are among the last social groups in the world to be given the full 19th Century Colonial treatment."

One way to measure this society's attitude toward the young is their status in the courts. In many states, juveniles accused of breaking the law are deprived of such essential elements of due process as the right to appeal, access to records, the right to trial by jury and even the right to make bail. The rationale is that the proceedings are not "criminal" in nature, since they take place in a civil court and besides are intended to "protect" the young. However, juvenile courts do have the power to confine the adolescent or administer other punishment. And as many as one fourth of the young who are confined are placed in adult jails.

Some progress toward applying constitutional guarantees to juveniles was made in a [recent] landmark decision by the Supreme Court, which ruled that the young must at least be given notification of the right to counsel, who, if necessary, will be appointed by the court; the right to confront and cross-examine witnesses, including complainants; warning of the privilege against self-incrimination and the right to remain silent; and timely notice of the charges against them. The case before the Court involved a 15-year-old accused of making obscene phone calls. The juvenile-court judge, without informing the adolescent of his constitutional rights and without giving him a chance to confront his accuser, sent him away for six years to a state training school. The sentence was upheld by Arizona's highest court, then was reversed by the U. S. Supreme Court.

Although Justice Abe Fortas, speaking for the majority, noted that "it would, indeed, be surprising if the privilege against self-incrimination were available to hardened criminals but not to children," the courtroom reforms introduced by the Justice still omit a number of other basic constitutional guarantees—from the right to bail to the right of appeal. Furthermore, as Fred P. Graham noted in *The New York Times*, "Experience has demonstrated . . . that merely informing a child's parents that counsel will be provided upon request . . . will not bring many lawyers into juvenile courts. In the District of Columbia, where free counsel has been offered, between 85 and 90 percent of the parents have waived their children's rights to legal assistance. By comparison, when adults are defendants in felony cases, approximately the same percentage—85 to 90 percent— accept assigned counsel for themselves."

Nor does the new Supreme Court decision affect how adolescents are treated by police—before they come to court. Juveniles are still not protected, for example, from self-incrimination in police interrogation. And in other respects as well, their position as colonials in the way they are treated by the police in most communities will undoubtedly remain the same for the foreseeable future. Since police attitudes are consonant with how most adults feel about the young, cops regularly roust not only teenagers in black ghettos but also white middle-class youngsters who dress, talk and otherwise disport themselves in a manner considered "oddball," "rebellious" or "disrespectful."

For more than a year, Los Angeles police have not only established a ten-P.M. curfew for those under 18 on Hollywood's Sunset Strip but they frequently arrest any adolescent who "appears" rowdy or who "jaywalks." On November 28, 1966, *The New York Times* reported: "Baton-swinging armed officers marched shoulder to shoulder down Sunset Boulevard, the main artery, shoving the protesters into side streets or clubbing them to the pavement. Those arrested were often prodded with night sticks or repeatedly shoved to the ground before being loaded into police buses.". . .

In Chicago, during the first six months of 1965, Peter Meyerson writes in *The Young Americans*, "a total of 10,660 teenagers were arrested for violations of a curfew that, one youth lamented, would be 'martial law' if applied to adults." In Philadelphia's Rittenhouse Square, interracial groups of the young with long hair, sandals and occasional beards—though otherwise innocent of breaches of the peace—are not allowed to gather in groups of more than six, are told where they can and cannot sit and have been swept up indiscriminately in "narcotics" raids. And in Jackson Square, in New Orleans' French Quarter, a group of youngsters was sitting and singing on a Sunday last November. Suddenly, 17 of them were hustled into a police wagon. The charges: "littering and creating a scene.". . .

It is in the schools that adult compression of the young is most insistent, most pervasive and—in terms of the final product— most terrifying. In his book *How Children Fail,* which is about upper-middle-class, not slum, schools, John Holt documents his contention that, except for a handful, almost all children who are processed through American schools "fail to develop more than a tiny part of the tremendous capacity for learning, understanding and creating with which they were born and of which they made full use during the first two or three years of their lives."

To begin with, they are often treated as if spontaneity were subversive to the processes of education. Too many classrooms and too many halls in the schools are deadly quiet. Trust, moreover, is not for the young. It is not uncommon for adult spies to be placed in the bathrooms of high schools. There are classrooms with two-way P.A. systems, so that functionaries can listen in to what's going on.

Principals, running their schools like authoritarian dukedoms, issue edicts of stunning and usually irreversible absurdity. The principal of University High School in Los Angeles, for instance, ordered an 18-year-old from Uruguay, who has always worn his hair long, to cut it forthwith. When he refused, the principal had him arrested. In jail, the irrepressible criminal began to sing. This failure to be penitent, this resiliency before adult power, compelled the police to choke him, punch him and handcuff him.

Other punitive measures are increasingly taken against those who choose to wear their hair long—a form of rejection of "proper" (that is, mass) behavior that particularly enrages adults. In Oyster Bay, Long Island, some months ago, five high school students were quarantined on a separate floor—called "the zoo" by their fellow inmates—and denied water as long as they refused haircuts.

In reaction to this and to similar stern pronunciamentos by principals who equate conformity with responsibility, Marya Mannes observed in *The New York Times* that so oversized an emotional reaction by adults "may be more a sign of our own rigidity than of [the students'] folly; one more example of a society grown set in its ways; resistant to change, hostile to difference." To which *The New Yorker* added: "It may be that smooth chins, cheeks and skulls represent to us something preciously modern—smoothness as an ideal, man as interchangeable, frictionless—and that all this bristling and flowing going on around us threatens to gum up the machine. Well, is the machine really that fragile? And was it designed to be eternal? We were furry primates before we were robots."

There is pathos as well as obtuseness in the nearly hysterical antipathy of many adults, in and out of schools, to long hair on young men. They are disturbed by the nerve, the sheer nerve, of those who defy smoothness as an ideal. Their own smoothness of morals, of sexual response, of attenuated life goals are also called into question by this luxuriance of hair and the other sensual "excesses" it connotes. One such long-haired, bearded youngster, drummer Bobby Moses of the Free Spirits, a rock group, was ambling along a street on New York's Lower East Side when a middle-aged stranger, in a suit and tie, stopped, stared and, his face contorted, rasped: "In two months you're going to be in Vietnam and you're going to be killed." Moses looked at him coolly and said, "Listen, mister, the only reason you're complaining is because you're old and you're going to die before I do."

In other ways besides preordained hair styles, the young in school are prepared for "responsibility" by being allowed hardly any. High-school and many college newspapers are rigorously—often bizarrely—censored. Controversial speakers are not invited. Student protests are squashed. At Cass Technical High School in Detroit, a 17-year-old semifinalist in the National Merit Scholarship competition had been forced to cut his hair on pain of permanent suspension from school. Later, when he and three other students wore black arm bands to protest the school's observance of "Military Day," all four were "temporarily excluded." Said the young man: "I got my hair cut, but now they're regulating ideas and I can't get my ideas cut. I'm keeping *them*."

In many other schools, antiwar demonstrators have been stripped of their arm bands; and at a high school in Great Neck, New York, when the student government voted to forgo one lunch in sympathy with the famine-threatened people of India, its plan was vetoed by the administration.

In classes throughout the country, teachers ritualistically underline the importance of political commitment for citizens in a democracy. But the young are trained for this role in situations devoid of political activity. When a senior in a large suburban high school in New Jersey asked that the school's World Affairs Club be permitted to cosponsor a lecture with an outside political organization, the director of student activities peremptorily informed him that no student political advocacy of any kind was permitted in the school.

The same student, Daniel Gladstone, wrote a review of a history textbook for the school newspaper. In it, Gladstone reported in a *Saturday Review* article, "High School Students Have No Voice," "I established criteria for textbooks and showed how the book failed to meet them. Because the sponsor of the newspaper was not in school the day the articles were sent to the printer, he did not see the review until it was published. Then he, the vice-principal and the chairman of the history department all told me that I had acted 'out of line' in writing the review and that I had no right to criticize an action of a faculty member or group."

No high school is more respected for the academic achievements of its student body than is the Bronx High School of Science. Yet a few years ago, its students were instructed that during a civil-defense drill simulating an atomic attack, they must kneel and hold a book over their heads. "An interesting medievalism for a school of science," commented social critic Paul Goodman, father of one of several young empiricists who disobeyed the command. They were suspended, of course, and the parents of the disobedient youngsters were informed that "behavior of this type can do immeasurable harm to [the students'] future possibilities for recommendations and college entrance." Paul Goodman pointed out to the New York City Board of Education . . . that "this attitude of the organized system is not calculated to make creative scientists." But it can help produce scientists trained to function in teams and easily able to involve themselves in all manner of assignments—biological warfare, for instance—on orders from the organized system.

If the young are prohibited from learning how to govern themselves and from following their best instincts, including common sense, in high school, they do not receive appreciably more growing room in most colleges. There they continue to be prepared for the basic feeling of powerlessness of American life—the powerlessness of the individual, young or adult, to affect what Mayor Lindsay terms the "huge, authoritarian institutions that routinely cause fundamental dislocations in the lives of the people they affect each day." S. E. Luria, professor of biology at Massachusetts Institute of Technology, points out that "a most distressing aspect of university life is the mock parliamentarianism of formal campus democracy. Students engage in meaningless campaigns and elections for student governments that are concerned mainly with trivia such as curfew hours. . . . The empty, formal democracy of the campus is not only a frustrating experience; it becomes also a training ground for the acceptance of patterns of pseudodemocratic government, in which political machines determine the choices presented to the voters, and a willful executive can frustrate the spirit of the Constitution by turning a legislative assembly into a rubber-stamp body."

Here, again, there is pathos in the repression of the young by adults. Those who are without power in the "real world"—without power in relation to the corporations that employ them, to the governments that make war and raise taxes in their name, to the social forces that make their cities unsafe and their air polluted—resent assumptions by the young that they can run *their* lives, that they can somehow avoid fundamental impotence. Father knows best, damn it. There is no hope. Settle down and hold onto a comfortable niche in the system. The son who defies authority shows up the weakness of his father and must be taught a lesson, the lesson being that passivity is wisdom, that survival is all.

The young, meanwhile, are prepared for "real life" not only by their subject status and by the meaningless regulations keeping them in place in the educational zoo. Also, *what* they are taught, as well as how they are taught, prepares them to fit smoothly into the system. One of the most basic of all needs—especially during adolescence—is to shape an identity, to find out what in the world is most relevant to you. But the American educational system operates all too often directly counter to that goal. The schools consider their function to be the adaptation of their pupils to the requirements of society as it is now and as they think it must develop. And increasingly, this is a society of specialization. Certain basic skills must be instilled to lay a foundation for the specialized skills to come. Recently, during the course of a series om lectures he delivered on the BBC, John Kenneth Galbraith asked: "Can we be altogether happy about education that is so motivated? There is the danger that it will be excessively vocational. We shall have a race of men who are strong on telemetry and space communications but who cannot read anything but a blueprint or write anything but a computer program."

But the schools, with few exceptions, have no time to worry about that question. Nor do they allow their pupils time to worry about who they are. Too much information has to be funneled into them so that they can go on to the "better" colleges and then to the "better" specialized jobs. The independent youngster with strong interests in particular areas that are not currently regarded as having a high degree of social usefulness gets in the way—particularly if he has questions for which answers are not to be found in the textbooks or the teachers at hand. He takes too much time and must either be cut to fit or leave school. He also gets in the way if his learning style is not geared to speedy achievement on predetermined tracks. . . .

The concept of education as a way to *individual* growth, as a way to retain and build on the spontaneity of real interests and organic motivations, is alien to the schools. The "achievers" learn that success in school means playing back to the teachers what the teachers want to hear. In this circular game of manipulation, the free play of intelligence and individual initiative becomes dangerous, for it can lead to bad grades. A youngster who continually questions the worth of what he is being taught and the values of the society for which he is being shaped becomes a "problem." As John Holt says, "Teachers and schools tend to mistake good behavior for good character."

Recently, through the International Teacher Development Program, over 600 teachers from a number of countries visited classrooms throughout the United States. Most were saddened by what they saw. "You will find," observed a teacher from Chile, "that the examination questions that determine success or failure in American schools are chiefly those for which answers can be memorized. Hence, they test training, not thinking. The trained person depends upon others for his instruction. The great goal of the school should be to produce the independent learner." And an appalled teacher from Japan observed: "Students raised their hands and asked questions industriously. But somehow they seemed to be driven from lesson to lesson, having only minutes between periods. Why this hurriedness?". . .

The pressures begin in grade school. . . . Get with it or you'll be sidetracked. And so the young are continually tested, grouped, evaluated—not according to their individual bents and strengths but through standardized measurements. Look, say the parents and guidance counselors: In 1965 alone, more than 100,000 *qualified* students couldn't find any openings in any but the most arcane colleges. You have to be better and better and *better!* . . .

But what if you have different criteria for a successful life from the kind to which all that accumulation of credits will lead? An American mother writes to A. S. Neill, headmaster of the Summerhill School in England, that her 11-year-old daughter won't do her homework and is failing in school. "Shall I push her to study," the woman asks, "or shall I let her fail?" "Woman, you *cannot* push her," Neill begins in his new book, *Freedom—Not License!* "She already knows the consequences and has made her choice. Your child is alive and shows a healthy criticism of the system by refusing to take part in it. How can you as an individual remedy a situation in which your daughter is the victim of a barbarous system? What good did homework ever do anyone? Home study—forced on a child—is *dead* study. Such forced study wrenches the child away from her play hours. Homework is resented because it has no true place in your daughter's sense of living. It occurs to me: Maybe your daughter is not much of a scholar. Maybe her natural interests do not gravitate toward study. Must you force your values and ambitions on her? Far better for her to be a happy human being without a college degree than an unhappy, neurotic girl fighting her inner drives and armed with a college diploma."

The advice is far too subversive of prevalent values for all but a few parents to accept. And, more tragically, most of the young have already been so deadened by the educational system that they see failure as the only alternative to "making it" in the established middle-class way. A high school senior in Lexington, Massachusetts, is stiff with fear the night before she is to take the crucial college boards: "Everything is on the line tomorrow. You determine your next four years. And perhaps your whole future.". . .

As if one can learn only in school. As if there are no meaningful experiences for the young except in school. As if all vocations but those requiring academic training have by fiat been made of lesser value. As if one could not go back to a school when one *wanted* to. Having been trained not to think but to respond in predetermined ways, too many of the young are unable to recognize alternatives to breaking out of the lock step that is American education. And so, youth, which should be a time of wide-ranging curiosity, joy in discovery and a reaching out to experience, becomes a time of fear. "Even in the kindest and gentlest of schools," John Holt writes, "children are afraid, many of them a great deal of the time, some of them almost all the time . . . afraid of failing, afraid of being kept back, afraid of being called stupid, afraid of feeling themselves stupid." If you think Holt exaggerates, consider how many adults return in their nightmares to fantasies of failure in school. . . .

[In college] the testing and the evaluating is even more onerous and incessant, for there aren't enough places in the "better" graduate schools and everyone now knows that a mere B.A. or B.S. is not enough for the "best" careers. Last year, the Yale graduate department of English had 529 applications but places for only 45 students. In economics, there were more than ten applicants for every opening. In the course of a year, as many as 30 people with Woodrow Wilson fellowships are turned down. The same compression exists in practically all of the more renowned graduate schools.

The undergraduate, therefore, pressing to be as close as he can to the top of his class, still has no time for what interest *him*. As Nevitt Sanford and Dr. Joseph Katz of Stanford's Institute for the Study of Human Problems point out: "The indications are that increased work demands, competitiveness and a resultant pervasive guilt when one is not occupied with studying have also considerably diminished the opportunities for forming friendships with other students, at least the kind of deep and meaningful friendships that require time and freedom from psychological encumbrance in order to grow."

Later, in the graduate schools, says John Perry Miller, dean of Yale University's graduate school, "the pressure is already worse than in the undergraduate colleges.". . .

The majority, having wasted their chance to find out who

they are in adolescence, are now sufficiently numbed to function as docile members of the society. Paul Goodman has described this educational "treatment" succinctly: "The scholastically bright are not following their aspirations but are being pressured and bribed; the majority—those who are not especially bright but have other kinds of vitality—are being subdued. . . . Few look toward vocations that will peculiarly fulfill them. Few really believe that they will have a say in their jobs or in how their city is run, any more than they have had in how they grow up."

There are those who resist the treatment. Not all high-school dropouts, for example, have necessarily made the wrong choice —for *themselves*. Dr. Joseph L. French of Pennsylvania State University has studied a sample of the 7.8 percent of all school dropouts in Pennsylvania with I.Q.s of 110 or better. The results, as reported in the *Roosevelt Torch* of Roosevelt University in Chicago, indicated that "compared with those who remain in school, the intellectual dropouts were by nature less inhibited and more happy-go-lucky. They were also more independent, unconventional and rebellious. Their homes had been more permissive and less protected." The vocational interests of the dropouts, French found, tended toward "mechanical activities— machine operation and design, or home repair of machinery and electronic gadgets." In view of those interests, only 22 percent of the male dropouts "anticipated a professional career as opposed to a trade, while the figure for [those who stayed in school] stood at 60 percent." Interestingly, however, 90 percent of the dropouts said they were interested in eventually furthering their education. They had refused to be conned into believing that moving out of the lock step meant that education had to be at an end for them. Therefore, those who do return to school are likely to go back when they *want* to and to study what really interests them.

And the number of college dropouts is increasing. The consensus of many of the contributors to the new book *The College Dropout and the Utilization of Talent* is that it is not at all essential and often not advisable that a student spend four consecutive years in college. Today's student life, the book points out, is characterized by "increased unrest and subsequent mobility among academically sound undergraduate students. Some go to Europe for a year of study and/or travel, others into the Peace Corps and still others to an entirely different type of college to gain varied experience." And more and more of these college dropouts report that this break in the pattern has been of great value in allowing them to discover themselves. Some also discover that there is no *personal* need for them to return to college. But to drop out positively, not in self-judgment as a failure, requires students who have not been entirely subdued by the system, and they are not by any means in the majority.

New recruits to the intensely private life are coming from those of the young who were once involved in civil rights activity and in other hopes for changing society. The rise of the Black Power ethos in groups such as SNCC and CORE makes a growing number of white former activists feel there is no longer any place for them in the front lines of the Movement. Others are convinced that, in any case, nothing can really be changed. . . .

And so the increase in the use of consciousness-expanding drugs among the young continues. Dr. James Fox of the U.S. Food and Drug Administration's Bureau of Drug Abuse Control estimates that by now about one in every hundred college students has used LSD at one time or another. Marijuana is easily obtained at most major universities. At the University of California at Berkeley, more than half the student body has tried marijuana at least once, and perhaps a third has gone back for more. Nor are high-school and junior-high-school students unfamiliar with hallucinogens. The incidence of their use among those that young is growing.

Parents and other adults are disturbed, appalled and grimly censorious of the young who have gotten off the world. They agitate and vote for restrictive laws and demand investigations of the schools, ignoring their own role in convincing these young to "turn on, tune in and drop out." Harvard psychiatrist Norman Zinberg says of the young drugtakers: "They don't trust life as it is. They look for something more beautiful, more real." More beautiful and real than the lives of the adults they know. Than the lives of those in their 40s, let's say, whom New York reporter Jimmy Breslin has called "the young old men. . . . Every day, they are losing the world of the young girls and they try to hold onto it with their eyes and their one-line jokes and every day they are losing. Every day that they go home and eat and fall asleep in front of the television and then get up in the morning and go to work on jobs they don't like. Every day that they spend going to a golf course as if it were a church, and polishing a car, and then going to a house party and talking about the same things that they talked of last week. . . . And the women, their bodies coming apart from having too many children, talking with the first old-lady stories of operations coming into the conversation."

These are the fading adults who illustrate Eric Hoffer's threnody: "In this country we are warned not to waste our time, but we are brought up to waste our lives." And these are the adults who look at the young with envy and barely suppressed sighs of self-pity at the waste of their own years. But they cannot fundamentally concede that waste and therefore must condemn "deviant" behavior and try to "straighten out" those of their children who won't take the prescribed routes to death on the installment plan. They send them to psychiatrists, they cut off their allowances, but they cannot talk to them—for what have they to say?

It is the increasingly free-and-easy sexuality among some of the young that especially torments adults. For American adults have been brought up on the Puritan ethic. Pleasure is suspect. Pleasure has to be earned. Pleasure has to be postponed. And so pleasure—in its most intense, releasing forms—is often postponed until death. Imagine the stab of loss at breakfast tables and on commuter trains the morning last December on which the wire services carried—and newspapers prominently displayed—the view of a 19-year-old University of Minnesota coed that "Sexual intercourse is a form of communication be-

tween two people, which, because of available contraceptive
pills, should be no more regulated than any other form of communication, such as conversing, dancing and holding hands."
What is the world coming to? But they'll learn, they'll learn.
They'll get married and they'll learn. And probably many of the
now sexually liberated young *will* slide into habit in sex as in
all else. But it may be that today's adolescents' one permanent
legacy to their own young is the shattering of unnatural and
anachronistic barriers to sex, at least before marriage. For the
premium on virginity is becoming obsolete; and on many campuses, living together is simply part of the scene.

There is persistent ferment among a minority of the young to
change the ways in which they are being educated—from within
the system and by setting up parallel institutions out of the system's control. With regard to the latter, students, sometimes
with faculty help, have set up their own "free universities" and
"experimental colleges.". . . There the students themselves decide the courses to be given, which are then taught by student
specialists or by professors drawn to the heady prospect of a
totally *voluntary* learning situation. . . .

The faculty members who participate in these parallel schools
are those rare adults who understand that education should not
be a passive process, that people should not *be* educated but
ought to educate themselves, with the teacher as a catalyst. John
Clayton, for example, an assistant professor of humanities at
Boston University, who delivered lectures on Saul Bellow in the
Experimental Seminar Program, writes in the *Boston University
News:* "Ideas are not abstractions but experiences; they must
be carried alive into the heart; they should be richly loaded
with values; they should lead to action—either social or personal. I remember a couple of years ago teaching Thoreau's
Walden. . . . I quoted the passage criticizing university education, laughing at the irony that even this idea students had to
write in their notebooks. I said, if you believe what Thoreau
says, what are you doing here? So one student—John Kaplan—

got up and walked out! Joy! Like the Baal-Shem-Tov, he was in
the truth, not just in possession of the truth.

"The teacher's main job," Clayton continues, "is to draw
the student into living communication and thought. The job is
to shatter the existing knowledge structures in the student so he
can form new structures that will let new data in. The job is to
open him up. It's to let him relate new ideas to his old values.
The job is to blow his mind. Freshmen need to study alienation
in America or to study problems of identity in Boston. If sociological tools are needed, if economic concepts are needed, in-
troduce them. But don't make a student go through years of di-
gested, analytical, disciplinary structure before he finds out
why. We need courses that involve the student's life at home, in
the dormitory, at work. We live in Boston."

It may be that the existence of such experiments as Boston
University's experimental courses may draw more such men as
Clayton into teaching. And some of the professors of the future
may come from the young in this academic underground. Already, pressures from the young have begun to elasticize, to a
small extent, the courses and the way they're conducted in some
schools. *Moderator* reports as illustrations: "A psychology
course at the University of Michigan gives course credit for one
third of the time students spend working in a community tutorial
program, mental hospital or social-service project. . . . Next year
at Western Michigan University, students will be able to receive
academic credit for work overseas in the Peace Corps."

And while there are still only a very few colleges that have
liberated their students and teachers from grades, a growing
number of colleges and universities are permitting students to
take courses in which the only grade they will be given is "pass"
or "fail." Thereby, time and spirit will not be wasted on regurgi-
tation under the name of examinations and on worry as to
whether taking a course outside your field may lower your aver-
ages. Deep down in the system, at the beginning of the compression process—the elementary school—there are beginnings of
nongraded classes and of discovering what the *child* wants to

know. But from elementary school to college, these are only beginnings. The system is too deeply rooted in its rigidity and in the undeviating length of its tracks to be radically changed soon.

But at the colleges and universities, some of the young still try to have a voice in how they are educated. . . . A remarkable example of the questioning of "official" adult values that can be set in turbulent motion by a candid, committed and unafraid group of students is the rebellion at Boston University led by Ray Mungo, his staff and such colleagues as Julian Houston, president of the Student Congress. A relentless campaign by the *Boston University News* to abolish the R. O. T. C. on campus, for instance, has helped spur similar movements at Ohio Wesleyan, Cornell, Duke, Harvard and other schools. Its raising of the issue also provoked a controversy as to whether the R. O. T. C. has the right to continue to receive academic standing and official curricular recognition. The *News* has also called for noncooperation with the draft, for the end of grades and for sexual freedom. ("Because the matter is entirely personal, we believe the student should be free to practice his own approach to sexual discovery and wonder without the prurient shadow that the administration throws over him, in the form of unyielding parietal rules. But, far more important, we believe the university has rejected its responsibility to provide information and advice regarding birth control to students who often do themselves tragic harm for lack of sound, available consultation.")

Mungo and his associates have created a ferment of ideas and self-questioning in what used to be a placid, conformist school with a largely moribund faculty. Mungo has, of course, been attacked by the adult community—in Boston's newspapers, from pulpits in the city's largest churches, by former United States Senator Leverett Saltonstall and by the university's Board of Trustees. But he thrives on his attempt to make BU a place where "real persons" can learn and teach, because he is experiencing that rare joy of, as the Quakers say, speaking truth to power. And he is trying to spread that joy by advocating a national union for students—"a union providing an autonomous power group on and off campus, capable of collective power and, ideally, force." The concept of a union, he continues, "is particularly applicable because students are at last demanding their rights here and elsewhere; because they have learned that Federal aid to education is meager compared with war budgets; because they pay immense sums for their education, and thus they remain physically tied to parents (when they deserve, as most European nations have long ago recognized to be educated at national expense); and because their training in submission to university authorities is specifically intended to prepare them for lives of submission—to employers, to governments, to fear."

There are other signs, it is claimed, that the values of the young may be changing. Michael Harrington writes: "In 1964, *The Wall Street Journal* reported that 14 percent of Harvard's senior class entered business, as contrasted with 39 percent in 1960. In 1966, the Harris Poll surveyed college seniors for *Newsweek* and found that this trend was deepening. Only 12 percent of the sample were looking forward to business careers." Where do they go? Into research, the professions, academic life. Education, for instance, is now a 60-billion-dollar business in the United States. Is there sufficient reason, however, to believe that a rejection of business as a vocation also involves a rejection of present societal values? Will those in research refuse to work on projects of destruction? Will those in the professions be any less addicted to self-interest, any more critical of political and economic power blocs, than their elders are?

And will those who go into education be significantly different from the present educational establishment? Will their effect on the young to come be significantly different from that described by Carl Davidson, vice-president of Students for a Democratic Society? "We have named the system in this country," he wrote in SDS' *New Left Notes,* "corporate liberalism, and if we bother to look, its penetration into the campus community is awesome. Its elite is trained in our colleges of business administration. Its defenders are trained in our law schools. Its apologists can be found in the political-science departments. The colleges of social sciences produce its manipulators. For propagandists, it relies on the schools of journalism. It insures its own future growth in the colleges of education. If some of us don't quite fit in, we are brainwashed in the divisions of counseling.". . .

Historian Arthur Schlesinger, Jr., predicts that by the end of the Sixties, alongside the fact that those in their 20s will constitute the biggest voting bloc in America, there will be 7,000,000 students in college. We will be a country of the young; and within that young, there will be a special-interest group, says Schlesinger, which "will formulate its demands and fight for them." But if most of those young, in and out of college, are already young-old men, how far-reaching will their demands be? Placing American youth in a ghetto has, in the majority of cases, worked as intended. When they are ready to be released into the world, the values of the majority of them will be of the world as it is now.

And yet the dissenters persist. Some, such as Ray Mungo, persist in working and organizing for change. Others travel into their own minds. Both the outer-directed and the inner-directed dissenters believe they can hold out. Such as a 17-year-old girl from Boston who insists: "I could never join the mainstream of society now. If you've been made aware, then you can't suddenly bury yourself. So society is just going to have to accept us. Either that or this darned society is just going to collapse. You can't have a society full of unaware people."

She ignores the much more likely third choice—that society will neither collapse nor become en masse that much more "aware." However, even as efficiently dehumanizing a society as ours will be unable to force all in the vivid minority of today's young to adjust to what most adults call reality. If the best of the young do not prevail—and the odds are heavily against them—many will remain a conspicuous community of refusal to accept shallow or counterfeit lives. What will society do with them? It will try to ignore them while they, in turn, keep trying to discover and fulfill their potentiality in enclaves in the larger cities and in university towns.

A New Yorker in his early 20s who dropped out of college to work with CORE and then to engage in community organizing in Syracuse is now at the London School of Economics. On his Christmas card last year, he wrote a line from Henry Miller: "I believe because not to believe is to become as lead, to be prone and rigid, forever inert, and to waste away." He intends to come back to engage in further action for social change. He will probably be able to save himself from becoming as lead, as will Ray Mungo. They have avoided being pressed flat in the ghetto of American youth. But not many do. Not yet enough, anyway, to do much more than keep themselves alive and growing. This is a country of waste—from natural resources to armaments. But especially it is a country that wastes its young.

If that wastage is to be significantly reduced, it can be done only by the young themselves. Accordingly, today's young are sharply divided, as never before, between those who have already been processed and those who are resisting their ghetto status and corollary powerlessness. The latter recognize that they are in a fight for their lives—figuratively and, in view of the lessons of Vietnam, quite often literally.

SPENCER BROWN

---

we can't
appease them

**We have been had. . . . I ask that we examine our
vocabulary, our thinking and our moral nerve.**

It is high time for someone not committed to a rigid
curriculum, for an admirer of Freud and Dewey, for one who
has voted against conservative candidates in every election since
1932 . . . for such a one to argue against victory by the young
in their warfare with the old. . . . I wish to examine the common
claim that today's younger generation—the young people in the
last years of high school and in college—are uniquely miserable, uniquely persecuted, uniquely virtuous. And in determining what we adults should answer to that claim, I ask that we
examine our vocabulary, our thinking and our moral nerve. . . .
When we speak of the young, we often fall into gobbledygook
sociologese-psychologese. We say that our young people are un-
dergoing an "identity crisis," and we think of them as "alienated" and suffering from "anonymity." We remark that they
are "acting out" their problems. We sympathize with their "rebellion" and admire their courage when they "speak out"
against their "exploitation."

Phrases like these . . . corrupt our thinking. They suggest that
these troubles are new, whereas they are as old as the human
race. They merely change their form with each generation, sometimes oftener. But our cant phrases, suggesting unprecedented
gravity, deprive us of perspective. "Growing pains" is an older
phrase—half-mocking, half-tolerant—quite as useful as "identity crisis," since it suggests the recurring nature of the phenom-

enon. And what has "alienation" got that differentiates it from old-fashioned loneliness? Youth has *always* been lonely. And youth generally "acts out" its problems by raising hell—hardly a modern monopoly.

That youth has very real grievances no sane man can doubt. Yet, just as surely, no sane man should subscribe to the statements of those grievances that we read in the press—such as the frequent assertion . . . that college students are the most exploited class in our society. It may be that college students are miserable. At the same time, they are one of the most favored groups in our society. They are fairly wealthy; and they are the largest leisure class in America—our mass consumers of culture, the advance guard of the great owning and managerial orders into which they will move at graduation. Far from being exploited, they ride on the backs of all of us—and sometimes they use spurs.

True, the college student's future, though rosy and assured in general, is unknown in detail and perhaps therefore frightening. But "exploitation"? Youth is exploited by its own ambitions, its own contradictions, its own hopeless passions, its own destructive violence—and certainly *not*, in middle-class America, by an intervening, destructive society. . . . Doubtless the draft, with its inequities, does cramp youth somewhat. It is true also that the student is under pressure—to get into a first-rate college and, later, graduate school. Most students work harder than their parents ever did in college. But is the pressure intolerable? If it were, the activists on the campus would all flunk out.

As for worries, students today are better off than their parents were. The latter were plagued by money worries; they looked forward to a world of unemployment or, later, to a war—of considerably larger size than the current phase of the cold war. Today's students and younger faculty members have never known a time when the country was not affluent. . . .

Society's hypocrisy is the great weapon in the hands of youth in its war with age. The older generation is bad, youth says, and only youth can be relied on to act with pure motives. From that

notion stems the moral arrogance so noticeable in the pronounce-
ments of youth leaders. For example, a high-school editorial
writer, protesting a school regulation, says that opposition to
the rule is a "peaceful method of rebellion, by a generation that
has watched its parents solve problems by atomic bombs, napalm, civil-rights murders and genocide." Such a statement
ought to be astonishing, but it is generally accepted with the
reply, "Well, it's true that the older generation has made a
mess of things." I imagine that the younger generation would
become indignant—and properly so—if an editorial writer said
that youth solves problems by pouring kerosene over Bowery
derelicts and igniting them, desecrating Jewish graves, filling the
jails and hospitals with addicts, and murdering a President. . . .

We must have lost our moral nerve if we cannot say, at east
to ourselves, that such accusation comes with poor grace from a
generation saved by its parents from Dachau and Belsen; a generation saved from physical destruction in World War II and
political destruction in the cold war; a generation in which the
diseases that slowly killed Schubert and Keats . . . can be arrested.

What I am really concerned about is the addled pates of the
older generation. We don't believe the incredible generalizations
that youth makes about age, and we should have the grace not
to pretend that we do. We also don't have to believe the generalizations that youth makes about youth. The majority of college students [have supported] the U.S. purpose in the Vietnam
war; and though students are more permissive about sexual
norms, there is no real evidence that sexual behavior has changed
significantly in 30 years. . . . The vast majority of young people
are Men at Work. They have their enormous sorrows and world-
weariness and hopeless love affairs. But, by and large, they do
not seem rootless and alienated. . . .

There is, however, a small but significant portion of the
younger generation that is at open war with society. And we
cannot automatically condone their acts or abdicate moral judgment. . . . When we tell youngsters that whatever they do is for-

given (in fact, approved in advance), we are making them all as anonymous as a company of angels. . . . The crisis of identity —if it does exist in any form different from the personal crises of the past—must reside in this absence of moral judgment. . . .

Thus, youth has come to expect institutions such as our courts and universities to have similar built-in forgiveness. Thus, they have arrogated to themselves that sense of moral superiority which no human being has a right to. Thus, they raise their present forms of hell.

In short, we have been had. We have been had by a number of adults who gain cheap approbation from young people by turning traitor to their own wisdom. They have loudly assumed that right-wing extremism is the product of "the authoritarian personality" and neurosis, while left-wing activism is altruistic. They have hurt the young by teaching them not that good ends excuse bad means, but that bad means are a good end in themselves; that mere action is somehow virtuous; that anger is wisdom.

All of us, I think, and not only the professional camp followers of youth's army, have spent too much time flattering our children. We have abdicated the roles of teachers and parents. We wish to be colleagues and brothers and sisters, forgetting that youth is more likely to condemn us than to love us for such disrespect of ourselves, for this refusal to take them seriously enough to tell them what we really think.

The young *will* grow up, and they will do so more quickly if we refuse to play their games. They have a right to look to us for balance, common sense and a sense of humor. With these unspectacular but indispensable qualities we can call off the war between the generations and proceed with the job of trying to improve society through education.

STEVEN KELMAN

you force us to rebel

**Adults often like to pretend the real
world doesn't exist. Kids can't.**

On both high-school and college campuses, the official
statements about almost any subject are so widely distrusted
nowadays that citing them is the best way to have yourself
marked as a dupe or a simpleton. Adults might understand how
serious this problem is if they'd listen to the words of the songs
of somebody like Bob Dylan. His most popular songs are talking
about skepticism, about what's really going on in the world as
compared to what we're being taught is going on in the world.
When we take a look for ourselves, the facts we see are so different from what we've been taught that we have no choice but
to turn into rebels or at least skeptics. Kids grow up "tryin'a
be so good"—in the words of one Dylan song. When we fall
from this "good" innocence it's like going through an earth-
quake; the ground under you just isn't solid anymore. . . .

Most parents don't want to accept this explanation. It's said
that we're know-it-alls, though we're really know-nothings, and
it's said that an affluent society produces spoiled brats who have
no sense of values and no appreciation of all the things being
done for them.

There are a number of facts that show this isn't true. For instance, philosophy courses in almost every college are in unprecedented demand. . . . At Harvard, where I am now, the
Phillips Brooks House, which does all sorts of social service and
community-assistance projects, is the largest organization on
campus. . . .

Even if some sort of reaction of young people against their

parents is inevitable, the revolt is now taking a particular form
—skepticism. It took the same form, by the way, in 19th-cen-
tury Russia. When youth gets skeptical, it does not indicate that
anything is wrong with youth, but rather that something is wrong
with adults. And that "something" is the way you usually look
at and react to what's going on in the world. "Hypocrisy" is a
big word with us, and it's a mortal sin in our moral code, dooming the sinner to our version of hell—permanent eclipse of any
moral influence he might have on us. . . .

It all starts in first grade. There we are treated to a candy-
cane world where all the children in the textbooks are white tots
living in suburbia with a dog running around the lawn. When
suburban kids find out about slums, they're apt to get skeptical.
When slum kids are taught about a world that has nothing to do
with the world in which they live, they have to do the same. . . .

No teen-ager can escape knowing that love and sex are part of
the real world. So how does society's agent, the school, present
this part of reality? It ignores it. . . . Health teachers reduce
puberty to a section of an inane chart on "stages of human development." When we find out the facts and feel the emotions,
how can anyone expect us not to be skeptical about an adult
world which tries to act as if none of this existed? And the moral
code that we have developed, "sex with love," seems to us to be
more logical than anything you've put up.

The whole idea the school seems to try to get across is that if
you don't teach it to us, it doesn't exist. . . . In junior high school
we had a thing called a "Reading Record Card." This was supposed to be a list (and brief discussion) of all the books you
had read each year. But "all the books" actually meant all the
books that were in the school library. And when students protested against the refusal to allow listing of books like *1984*
and *The Grapes of Wrath*, we were treated like people in China
who try to whisper that Mao Tse-tung is not the only recognized
writer in the world. And what are we taught about literature?
We are often required to memorize such details as "What color
was Ivanhoe's horse?" and "What hotel did Gatsby and the

Buchanans meet in?" rather than talking about how a book means something in helping us to figure out ourselves or other people. So kids often give up the classics. . . .

And how about student government? I was active in it during high school, but the majority attitude of indifference was a pretty good instinctive reaction. In most schools the "governments" must restrict themselves to planning social extravaganzas. When they try to do something—as when ours voted to fast for a lunch in sympathy with the people of India—the administration vetoed our plans. . . .

It sometimes seems to us that myths are peddled to us about *everything* we are taught. For example, the quaint myth of the American family farm . . . obscures the reality of giant agricultural industries and underpaid migrant labor. The history of American cities as it is generally presented comes to a screeching halt at the turn of the century. American history textbooks I've seen are at least 30 years behind the latest historical investigations. Thus one widely used junior-high history text states that the sole purpose of American intervention in Latin America in the early part of the century was to "lend a helping hand" to the people by building roads, bridges and hospitals. This is a little hard to believe. More than one kid I know has reacted by taking the position that our only motive in Latin America was financial greed. From my experience, American-history courses generally produce more anti-Americanism than understanding of history.

And what about the presentation of the one problem which concerns kids most of all—race? Well, one junior-high-school civics book devotes a total of four paragraphs to the history of the Negro in the United States. The last hundred years of Negro history are summed up like this:

During the War Between the States, all Negro slaves were set free. Since then American Negroes have got through a difficult period of adjustment to new ways of life. They have made remarkable progress in a short time.

Now, when we . . . look at the world, it is entirely natural that we think someone has been trying to put something over on us. Our world includes Watts and also suburbia, grape pickers as well as family farms, Latin Americans whose memories of American troops often center on the two-bit dictators the troops installed rather than the roads they built. And why would you teach us unreality if you didn't accept it?

In the world presented in most "Communism" courses, "Democracy" and "Communism" fight each other out on a wooden stage. After going through one of these courses, it takes someone with a vivid imagination to realize that these things are ideas millions of people around the world are living and sometimes dying for. . . .

Take this example from [a book by J. Edgar Hoover]:

COMMUNISM: There is a total disregard for the inherent dignity of the individual.
FREEDOM: There is a deep and abiding respect for the inherent dignity and worth of the individual.

We only have to look at the pictures of the Alabama police dogs to know that things are not that simple at all. So a lot of kids react by concluding that there's no difference between "Communism" and "Freedom" in this respect. . . .

As we go through school, we are subjected to lots more of this evidence that the real world and the world being taught us aren't the same. Of course, some of us never rebel. They will form the shock troops of the older generation and in our vocabulary are "finks." Or, they will just "cop out" to boredom.

But for the others, an overdose of unreality, just like an overdose of anything else, can produce crazy results—even a sickness. Flirtations with things like LSD and "pot" are merely escaping reality, not trying to refuse to adapt to it. It is, for example, a tragedy that anti-Communism is becoming a dirty word on the American campus. It is also a tragedy that the political activism of a generation concerned with the world is in

danger of being wasted in the pursuit of semi-anarchist dreams.
And the refusal to believe anything people in authority say is
only a reaction to the fact that last time we believed we were
deceived. . . .

What is really needed is a revamping of the way we are
taught. One suggestion might be to drop our fetish with "objectivity" in subjects toward which we are not objective. Politics
are not objective. Love is not objective. People are not objective.
Instead of objectivity, the guiding word in our schools should be
democracy—which is, as far as I can tell, the prevailing philosophy in our country. Democracy means trusting us to make up
our minds. Using democracy in a course about Communism, for
example, could mean matching a text that defends a free society
with one defending Communism. To the nervous Nellies who
recoil, I ask, "Don't you think that the case for Democracy is
the better one?" Don't you realize that in the Vietnam war we
are given absurd analogies to European history and opponents
tend to view the Viet Cong as 20th-century versions of Robin
Hood? . . .

The point is this: Adults often like to pretend the real world
doesn't exist. Kids can't. We might want to *escape* from it, but
we can't *forget* about it. And we know the difference between
the world we're taught and the world we experience. And if we
blame you for trying to put something over on us, it's only because we're taught what, alas, most Americans seem to think.
If the school is trying to turn its back on reality, it only represents an America that's doing the same thing. And that's what
really worries us.

DANIEL P. MOYNIHAN

nirvana now*

**Who are these outrageous young people? . . .
they are Christians arrived on the scene
of Second Century Rome.**

We have been seeing in the flamboyance of the hippies,
the bitterness of the alienated college youth, the outrageousness
of the New Left, little more than mutants of the old bohemianism, the never-ending conflict of generations, and perhaps the
persistence of neo-Marxist radicalism. We may be wrong. Just
possibly, something more important is abroad. We may be witnessing the first heresies of liberalism. . . .

It will seem odd to use ["heresy"] to describe such assertively nonreligious phenomena as the Students for a Democratic Society. [But] to the youth of this time secular liberalism
presents itself as every bit as much a system of "established
and commonly received doctrine" as did Christianity, for example, when it was the legally prescribed belief of the Holy
Roman Empire, or the Massachusetts Bay Colony. To be sure,
the doctrines of liberalism can be elusive. It is a conviction,
Learned Hand might say, that is not too sure of itself—save on
the point that it is vastly to be preferred to any creed that is.
Liberals are not without tracts—hardly—but tend more to look
to institutions as repositories of their beliefs, liberalism being
in every sense as much a *way* of doing things, as it is a set of
propositions as to what is to be done. It is not without its
schisms and assuredly not without its confusions. But in all its
essentials of an optimistic belief in progress, in toleration, in
equality, in the rule of law, and in the possibility of attaining a

* From a longer address.

high and sustained measure of human happiness here on earth, liberalism is the nigh universally accepted creed of the ruling elites of the Western world. . . . Not surprisingly, then, given especially the great value liberalism places on skepticism and inquiry, liberalism itself is beginning to be questioned. . . .

The liberal present is the only world [American youth] know, and if it is not to their liking, as for many it is not, their only alternative is to consider how it might evolve into something new, there being no possibility of reverting to something old. What follows is very like a spiritual crisis, and in the manner of individuals and communities that have confronted such in the past, some lapse into indifference and quietism, others escape into varied forms of stabilized hysteria, while still others turn to confront doctrine itself, and in a mood of intensely felt revelation reject the very foundations of orthodoxy.

What indeed is most striking about the [recent] surge of protest is the degree to which it reenacts in matters of style and structure the great heresies that have assailed the religious establishments of other ages. "The sun shone," Samuel Beckett writes in the opening passage of *Murphy*, "having no alternative, on the nothing new."

The forms of youthful protest at this time are many, and not all, of course, visible. . . . The most familiar-seeming, and for that reason possibly the most deceptive of the new tendencies, is that of the New Left itself. It is familiar because it has taken a familiar form: the organization of a group defined by political objectives. Yet in truth something profoundly new may be present here, for the object of the New Left is not to capture the system but to transform it. The older radicalisms were inextricably involved with things-as-they-are, and, owing especially to Marx's view of economic determinism, they largely deprived the radical challenge to liberal capitalism of any *moral* basis: the system had a destiny that was working itself out regardless of any intentions, good or evil, on the part of mortals so innocent of the laws of economics as to suppose they, rather than things, were in the saddle. The Old Left was so utterly "mate-

rialistic" and "realistic" as to use those very terms to describe
one of its defining dogmas. As Richard Blumenthal [Harvard
'67] observed in the *Nation,* it is precisely this "crass materialism" that [S.D.S.] reject. It is precisely the "dehumanizing" of
modern society that they resent. Society's "main and transcending" concern, Tom Hayden writes, "must be the unfolding and
refinement of the moral, aesthetic and logical capacities of men
in a manner that creates genuine independence." However that
is to be achieved, Blumenthal adds, it is not likely to be by way
of "a house in the country and a two-car garage." The movement is purposely "anti-ideological, even anti-intellectual." It
is precisely that rational commitment to logic and consistency—
of the kind that can lead from game theory at the RAND Corporation to the use of napalm in Vietnam—that these young
persons abhor.

Of late they have set about building things called "independent power bases" among the poor (a concept one fears may have
been borrowed from the Strategic Air Command), but the striking fact about the famous Port Huron Statement adopted by
S.D.S. in 1962 is that it barely, and then only indirectly, touches
on problems such as poverty. It is addressed exclusively to middle-class intellectuals and college students: the "people of this
generation, bred in at least modest comfort, housed now in universities, looking uncomfortably to the world we inherit." The
world about them was so content with material affluence as to
suppose it had attained stability, where in truth there was only
stagnation. The theme of the Port Huron Statement is that men
must *live,* not simply exist. "Some would have us believe that
Americans feel contentment amidst prosperity—but might it not
better be called a glaze above deeply felt anxieties about their
role in the new world?" Man, they declared, had acquired a
role of consumer rather than creator. His capacity for love, for
creativity, for meaningful relations with others was being lost
amidst the machinery of government. S.D.S. proclaimed a social
system in which men would not only share one another's fate,
but participate, each one, in shaping that destiny: "We believe

in generosity of a kind that imprints one's unique individual
qualities in the relation to other men, and to all human activity."
For such a goal the Gross National Product is indeed a crude
indicator of success.

Who are these outrageous young people? I suggest to you
they are Christians arrived on the scene of Second Century
Rome. . . . The second century was not unlike the twentieth, and,
leaving aside the somewhat gratuitous assumptions of Europeans that they are the Greeks of this age, let there be no doubt
that we are the Romans. It was a world, Froude writes, in which
"Moral good and moral evil were played with as fancies in the
lecture-rooms; but they were fancies merely, with no bearing
on life. . . . "Into the midst of this strange scene of imposture,
profligacy, enthusiasm and craving for light," Froude continues,
"Christianity emerged out of Palestine with its message of lofty
humility."

Who were these Christians? They were first of all outrageous.
They were "bad citizens, refusing public employment and avoiding service in the army; and while . . . they claimed toleration
for their own creed, they had no toleration for others; every
god but their own they openly called a devil. . . ." They had no
temples, no altars, no images, and boasted just that. "Fathers and
tutors, they say, are mad or blind, unable to understand or do
any good thing. . . ." Of learning they had little and cared less.
Nor had they any great interest in respectable people who observed the rules of society and tried to keep it running; they
cared only for the outcast and miserable. To be a sinner, they
seemed to say, was the one sure way to be saved. They were altogether of a seditious and revolutionary character. . . .

God commanded that the world provide that which is needed
by man: as he is weak there must be compassion; as he is sinful
there must be the forgiveness of sins; and above all, as he is
Godlike, his life must be seen as sacred. If that condition has
never been achieved, neither has the Western world ever been
the same since first embracing the belief that it should be. Can
there be any mistaking that the New Left speaks to the rational,

tolerant, reasonable society of the present with the same irrationality, intolerance and unreasonableness, but possibly also the same truth with which the absurd Christians spoke to Imperial Rome? ... [A truth spoken now to the] liberal doctrines of the American Empire, with its panoply of technical assistance, constitutional conventions, mutual assistance treaties and development loans, accompanied as it seems to be by the untroubled, or at least willing, use of astonishing degrees of violence to help others perceive the value of going along?

The young people of the New Left know what they want; a larger, more diffuse group can best be described as knowing what they do not want, which is what they have. These are so-called alienated students of the present generation. The psychiatrist Seymour L. Halleck recently described them as "existing in a state of chronic identity crisis. ... [their] constant cries of 'Who am I, I don't know what I believe, I have no self' are accompanied by anxiety which while subdued is nevertheless pervasive and relentless." Affluence means nothing, and the increase in personal freedom that comes with growing up is as much as anything a threat to which the individual responds with "a peculiar kind of apathy and withdrawal. ... Having failed to develop an internalized value system which allows him to determine his direction in life, he is paralyzed when the external world removes its guidelines and restraints." Such persons, Dr. Halleck reports, will occasionally involve themselves in campus protest movements and sustain the interest for a short while, but not long, which is perhaps just as well, as "When he does become involved with the activist groups he can be characterized as the most angry and irrational member of that group." Sex and drugs are outlets, but joyless ones. They have everything, but nothing works.

Have we not seen this person through history, turning away from a religion that was failing him, rejecting its laws and opting instead for standards of conduct derived wholly from internal personal resources? The object of a liberal secular society being to induce human happiness, it more or less follows that those who reject it will choose to be unhappy and evoke their spirituality more in despair than in ecstasy, but *mutatis mutandis*, are we not witnessing the emergence of secular antinomianism?

Not a precise but an interesting parallel is to be seen in Sabbatianism, the mystical Jewish heresy that sprang up in the Holy Land in the seventeenth century and spread through large sections of Sephardic and then Ashkenazic Jewry. . . . Judaism faced a series of crises at this time: persecution, apostasy and, for some reason, a sudden impatience with the Lord: how long were the Jews to wander in exile? [Gershom G.] Scholem writes: "Doctrines arose which had one thing in common: That they tried to bridge the gap between the inner experience and the external reality which had ceased to function as its symbol. . . . The religious . . . and moral nihilism of the radicals is after all only the confused and mistaken expression of their urge towards a fundamental regeneration of Jewish life, which under the historic conditions of those times could not find a normal expression.". . .

Nathan M. Pusey has voiced his own serious doubts about "the idea that the way to advance civilization is to start over," but one cannot deny the attraction of just this view for persons who find themselves inexplicably not getting from society exactly those satisfactions society most confidently promises them.

Of course, far the most visible of the new protestants are those who do not protest at all, who simply smile, wave daffodils, cover the walls of their *quartiers* with graffiti suggesting we "Legalize Living," and wear their own variety of campaign buttons the quintessential of which demands with purest obstinacy, "Nirvana Now.". . . Lilies of the field, bearded and sandaled, they live on air and love and, alas, drugs. They seek not to change our society, but simply to have nothing to do with it. They are in quest of experiences wholly mystical and internal on the one hand, and tribal on the other. The modern American style of the effective individual functioning in a coherent but competitive society is not for them. Hunter S. Thompson in *The*

New York Times Magazine . . . reported an interview with such a young woman living in the Haight-Ashbury section of San Francisco: "I love the whole world," she said, "I am the divine mother, part of Buddha, part of God, part of everything." How did she live? "From meal to meal. I have no money, no possessions, money is beautiful only when it's flowing; when it piles up it's a hang-up. We take care of each other." Did she use drugs? Yes: "When I find myself becoming confused I drop out and take a dose of acid. It's a shortcut to reality; it throws you right into it." Did she pray? "Oh yes, I pray in the morning sun. It nourishes me with its energy so I can spread love and beauty and nourish others. I never pray *for* anything; I don't need anything. Whatever turns me on is a sacrament: LSD, sex, my bells, my colors . . . that is the holy communion, you dig?"

Perhaps not. Yet those assertions would have seemed perfectly clear and altogether admirable to a member of the Brethren of the Free Spirit (or the Spiritual Libertines), a mystical Christian heresy that permeated vast areas of medieval Europe, notably the teeming cities of Flanders and the lowlands, from the twelfth century onward almost to our time. . . . In their mystical craving for an immediate experience of God, their antinomianism, and emphasis on ecstasy, the Brethren of the Free Spirit were not unlike the Jewish Sabbatians, or for that matter the early Christians. . . . Sexual promiscuity became a matter of principle, and marriage was denounced as an impure state. Eroticism and ecstasy were valued beyond all things as symbols of having achieved what was in truth a state of self-deification. In an age when wealth suddenly appeared in Europe, these heretics characteristically preached a communism of property, and chose to be utterly penniless: in [Norman] Cohn's words [from his *The Pursuit of the Millennium*], an elite of amoral supermen. . . .

Documents from Cromwell's England, a time when the Brethren, known as Ranters, were flourishing, leave no doubt, again in Cohn's words, that the " 'Free Spirit' really was exactly what it was said to be: a system of self-exaltation often amount-

ing to self-deification; a pursuit of total emancipation which in
practice could result in antinomianism and particularly in an-
archic eroticism; often also a revolutionary social doctrine
which denounced the institution of private property; and aimed
at its aboliton.". . . . A comedy of 1651 by Samuel Sheppard describes the "Character of the roaring Ranters of these Times"
in terms that are familiar to say the least:

. . . .

> All lie down, as in a swown,
> To have a pleasing vision.
> And then rise with bared thighs,
> Who'd fear such sweet incision?

. . . .

It is said the youth of Haight-Ashbury are not much addicted
to scholarship, and they may be pardoned for giving to their
service corps the name of "Diggers," after the primitivist community established near Cobham in Surrey in 1649-50. . . . But
they are nonetheless mistaken. Hippies are Ranters.

Supposing all this to be so, does it matter? I believe it does.
In the first place these persons matter: they number some of the
fine spirits of the age. A liberal must regret the loss of belief in
another as much as a decent churchman would. In the second
place, these youths are trying to tell us something. It was Ches-
terton, surely, who described heresy as truth gone astray. Seen
in large terms, it is clear that these protests have been generated
by at least three problems facing our society, each one of which
can be said to arise from tendencies that are distinctively those
of secular liberalism.

The first tendency is that our optimism, belief in progress,
and the possibility of achieving human happiness on earth, combined with our considerable achievement in this respect at home,
have led us to an increasingly dangerous and costly effort to
extend our system abroad. We are in the grip of what Reinhold
Niebuhr has called "The Myth of Democratic Universality," the
idea that democracy is a "universal option for all nations." The

irony, of course, is that it is just because our own history has been so unique that we are led to suppose that the system that has emerged from it can be made worldwide. It is an effort doomed to fail.

No civilization has ever succeeded in doing anything of the kind, and surely none whose qualities are as historically conditioned as ours should even try. . . . As our efforts repeatedly fall short of their pronounced goals, we begin covering up, taking shortcuts, and in desperation end up doing things we would never conceivably start out to do. Princes of the Church, modest sons of small-town grocers, begin proclaiming holy wars in Asia, while the man in the street acquires an appallingly troubled vision of those who protest. In the words of a Columbia student, describing the mood of a crowd watching a peace march: "War is virility; love of peace is bohemianism and quite probably a sexual perversion."

Liberals have simply got to restrain their enthusiasm for civilizing others. It is their greatest weakness and ultimate arrogance. Bertrand Russell suggests that the great Albigensian heresy, with its quest for personal holiness and cult of poverty, was due at least in part to "disappointment of the failure of the crusades." Very likely it will be the success rather than the failure of *our* crusades that will most repel youth. Nathan Glazer has suggested that this generation is already marked by the belief that its government is capable of performing abhorrent deeds.

Not the least reason the American commitment to the diffusion of liberal democracy abroad has become a corrupting enterprise is that those values are not yet genuinely secure at home. This is an ugly fact we somehow never finally confront. At just those moments when we seem about to do so, something, somehow, comes along to distract us. Yet there persists in American opinion a powerful component that is illiberal, irrational, intolerant, anti-intellectual, and capable if unleashed of doing the most grievous damage to the fabric of our own society. A cen-

tury of universal education has not destroyed this tendency; it
has only made it more articulate. . . .

  We have not been able to get rid of racism, or to secure an
equal place for Negroes in our society. . . . And we begin to
perceive that Negroes are not immune to some of the less attractive qualities of their persecutors. We have not been able to get
rid of poverty, and begin to perceive that some of our more
treasured liberal reforms may have had unanticipated consequences that may even make it more difficult to do so. (Thus,
having destroyed the power of the working-class political-party
organization in our cities, we now pour millions of dollars of
federal funds into projects designed to overcome the psychic
effects of "powerlessness" among the poor.) And we have not
rid ourselves of a brutal streak of violence. If the [Johnson]
Administration escalated the conflict in Vietnam, remember that
the largest body of opinion in the United States would bomb the
yellow bastards into the stone age, and a solid quarter specifically favors using the atom bomb. Cohn reports that the Ranters
really began to flourish after the execution of Charles I.

  A third problem that has contributed to the rise of youthful
protest is . . . that, as the life of the educated elite in America
becomes more rational, more dogged of inquiry and fearless of
result, the wellsprings of emotion *do* dry up, and in particular
the primal sense of community begins to fade. As much for the
successful as for the failed, society becomes, in Durkheim's
phrase, "a dust of individuals." But to the rational liberal, the
tribal attachments of blood and soil appear somehow unseemly
and primitive. They repress or conceal them, much as others
might a particularly lurid sexual interest. It is for this reason,
I would suggest, that the nation has had such difficulties accepting the persistence of ethnicity and group cohesion as a fact both
of domestic and of world politics.

  Thus it is possible not only to sympathize with the new protest, but to see much that is valid in it. At the same time we are
required to note that which is dangerous. The protest movement
is likely to grow rather than otherwise, for the educated middle

class from which it draws its strength is growing, and will soon be the dominant American social group. Moreover, the forms of protest are likely to have a striking impact for the very reason that their object is not to redirect the system, but to disrupt it, and this is never a difficult thing to do. It is entirely possible that this disuption could bring to power the forces of the right, and this is indeed an avowed strategy. *Nach Hitler uns.* . . . At Harvard, when a member of the Cabinet came as an invited guest, but under arrangements that did not suit them, the students of the New Left took possession of his person. Such tactics in the early days of Fascist Italy appalled civilization. . . . [Tom] Kahn has described the New Left as "panic disguised as moral superiority" and others have noted how that panic subtly induces a fascination with violence—the most grievous of all possible liberal heresies.

To see history as an earnest evolution from the peat bogs to John Stuart Mill, or to the 1964 Democratic platform, is a simplicity that will not much commend itself to anyone any longer. [But] neither would I reject the theme of J. H. Plumb's new series, *The History of Human Society*, "that the condition of man now is superior to what it was." Things are better, and where they are best is in the liberal industrial democracies of the North Atlantic world. I hold these regimes to be the best accommodation to the human condition yet devised, and will demand to know of those who reject it, just what they have in mind as a replacement. By and large the central religious and philosophical traditions of the West have led us to where we are now. Some of the heresies against that tradition have helped, and some indeed have been incorporated into it. But just as many have evidenced ugly and dangerous tendencies, of which a terrible certainty about things is surely the foremost. . . .

To protect dissent, no matter how noxious, is one thing. To be indifferent to its growth is another. Men who would undo the system may speak: but they must be answered. The less than soul-stirring belief of the liberal in due process, in restraint, in the rule of law is something more than a bourgeois *apparat:* it involves, I argue, the most profound perception of the nature of human society that has yet been achieved, and, precisely in its acknowledgment of the frailty of man and the persistence of sin and failure, it is in the deepest harmony with the central tradition of Judeo-Christian theology. It is not a belief to be frittered away in deference to a mystique of youth.

What we must do first of all is listen. Young people are trying to tell us something. They are probably right in much of what they say, however wrong their prescriptions for righting matters. Then we must respond. American liberalism needs to bring its commitments in balance with its resources—overseas and at home. . . . What is asked of us is honesty: and what that requires is a great deal more rigor in matching our performance to our standards. . . .

If we do this we shall find, of course, that there is altogether too much that is shoddy and derivative, and in a final sense dishonest, about American life. I suspect we will also find that the awareness of this fact is more diffused within the American electorate than it will have suited the mildly dissenting liberal *cognoscenti* to imagine. It is one thing to read in Richard Rovere's "Letter from Washington" in the *New Yorker* that "This city is awash with lies and deceptions. . . ." It is another to learn, as Rovere with his unmatched toughness of mind would insist, that two-thirds of the American people believe the assassination of President Kennedy to have been part of a broader conspiracy. . . .

These are signs of danger, as much as are the rioting cities and turbulent campuses. The foundations of popular confidence in the American system are proving to be nothing like so solid and enduring as the confident liberal establishment has supposed. . . . If we respond well to these signs of danger—and if we find a meaningful role in helping to transform the system for those who now attack it—we are likely to evolve a society of considerable nobility. But the first requirement is to acknowledge that what we have so far made of our opportunity is very much less than we should have.

The story is told of the building of the great Catholic Shrine of the Immaculate Conception in Washington: generations of truck drivers, coal miners, and cleaning women contributed their pittances to the coffers of the American hierarchy which slowly amassed the fortune required to construct this most fabulous edifice. It was a building that had everything. Nothing was spared of precious metal and lustrous stone. Nothing was spared by way of design: elements of every architectural tradition in the world were skillfully incorporated in the soaring façade and billowing dome. At last it was finished, and there followed a triumphant week of procession and ceremony, chorus and sermon. Then silence fell. The next morning a child was praying in the crypt when a vision of Our Lady appeared. Smiling that most beatific of all smiles, She looked down and said, "Build a beautiful church on this site."

MARGARET MEAD

growing up in america*

With rapid social change, the remembered behavior of parents no longer provides a possible model.

Young people today reach adulthood in a period of very rapid change. New standards of educational and vocational adjustment, earlier onset of puberty, earlier ages of marriage and parenthood, compulsory military service for many, great economic prosperity [with increasing structural unemployment and deep] uncertainty about the future of mankind in general and of the United States in particular—all these conditions have altered the manner in which young peple meet the age-old problems of shifting from the contradictions and unevenness of physical puberty, dependency upon parents and teachers, and juvenile status before the law, to the status of responsible adults.

EDUCATIONAL ENVIRONMENT. . . . The increasing number of young people attending high school has resulted in [an extremely heterogeneous] high-school population . . . which includes those who are capable of absorbing higher education and those who are impatient and incapable of profiting by education at the moment. In this latter group are boys . . . chafing

---

* These were some of Dr. Mead's views in 1961 and are excerpted from a longer essay. Many basics still hold. Where shifts are now discernible, this analysis helps put them in sharper relief and perspective.—A.K.

to become independent, and girls whose attention is focused primarily upon marriage.

In large cities where the recent urban migrants are rural Mexicans, Puerto Ricans, and Negroes from the rural South— all with educational backgrounds which fail to fit them for urban schools, and with types of precocious maturity which make them especially intolerant of educational restraints and imposed dependencies—the American high schools have become quite different from the . . . image in the minds of the older teachers . . . of what high schools should be.

The rapid spread of junior high schools has accentuated some of these qualities of the recent urban arrivals, isolating, as it does, groups of boys and girls who range from those with the physique of children to those who have fully attained [adult] stature . . . and leaving them without the leadership and corrective example once provided by the older . . . high-school [youth] of former years. Here the anxieties about relative growth, forced association with the opposite sex at a period when it is not physiologically appropriate, the discrepant rate of maturation of boys and girls, are all intensified. The junior high school has become a forcing ground for inappropriate and socially maladjusted attitudes in both boys and girls, laying the basis for hostility to females on the boys' part and, on the girls' part, pressure toward marriage combined with contempt for males. Although these deficiencies are widely recognized, the temptation of using new junior high schools as a quick solution to the population pressures on the school system makes it probable that junior high schools will increase. . . . A presently available corrective is to locate junior high schools [near] senior high schools and community junior and senior colleges. These can provide models of late adolescent behavior on the one hand and, on the other, can relieve the pressure on the younger and less developed boys for precocious mating behavior.

CULTURAL AND SOCIAL TENSIONS. The past decade witnessed an increasing access on the part of juveniles to those mechanical aspects of urban and suburban living which make the practice of antisocial behavior easier; they can range farther afield, acquire and manufacture weapons, and so forth. The spread of gang behavior into prepuberty, into a period in which the young are least accessible to ethical and moral appeals, has played a part in the establishment of styles of antisocial behavior characterized by heartlessness and impersonality.

Correctives here lie particularly in those educational and recreational institutions which can utilize the curiosity and activity patterns of the prepubertal boys, and which can give the girls accessibility to mimetic maternal behavior. There has appeared also, in many religious groups, an attempt to shift religious choice and membership downward to an age earlier than the traditional period of expected spiritual awakening at puberty. So, while the restraints and requirements of formal education have spread upward in the age range by increased pressure upon all young people to attend high school—which turns many schools into places where young people respond either as prisoners, or as the irresponsible members of a drafted peacetime army whiling the time away—many other behaviors have shifted downward in the age range. We therefore find high school combined with gainful employment. We find active mating behavior, organized antisocial behavior, and attempts on the part of religious and youth groups to create countervalues.

The pseudo-permissiveness of the last twenty years, which has combined some recognition of the physical problems of puberty, a distrust of any absolute pedagogical or parental imperatives, a relaxation in school discipline very often unaccompanied by genuine changes in the content of classroom learning or in parental and pedagogical expectation, has encouraged the development of an adolescent generation more than usually dependent upon the mores of the peer group, and unresponsive to the efforts of responsible elders. The commercialization of the styles and fads of various subcultural groups, and the continuous publicizing in the mass media of teenage behavior styles in their more extreme forms, have created a mass adolescent culture pattern, available to high-school students, of a sort that was not available even to college students twenty years ago. . . .

The survival of adult expectations of an entirely different order, among adults to whom marriage while in high school appears as monstrously inappropriate, serves to confuse the issue further. Young people whose education will terminate upon leaving high school find themselves in a world in which they are treated, depending on regulations in various states, as mechanically incompetent to obtain a driver's license, liable to military service, excluded from those branches of industry in which more rapid advance is possible, and by child labor laws which also serve to restrict competitive membership in many occupations. They are forbidden to buy beer and cigarettes, tempted by the illicit traffic in narcotics, denied orderly information available to the same age group in the armed services about protection from venereal disease, pressured to display precocious mating behavior, and excluded from daytime education if they become parents.

CONFORMITY. . . . The increased conformity which is demanded of those high-school students who will go on to [higher] education is in part a reaction against the high-school styles that have been set by this newer group of young people [whose] immediate family background, previous educational training, neighborhood mores, and occupational goals contrast strongly with the more traditional image of high-school students. . . .

So we have conferences on "nondelinquent youth," emphasis upon an unspotted school record even in elementary school, tremendous pressure on young people . . . to present a career line which shows even and continuous conformity to existing educational and social standards. . . . Experimentation and pursuit of imaginative bypaths is discouraged. High school and college have become progressively vocationalized, and statistics on successes and failures in national contests for scholarships and for admittance to specially desirable institutions have increased the widespread sense that to succeed today it is necessary to conform and to compete in terms of national norms.

There are various counteractive forces here, also. Witness the frequency with which the children of college-bred parents rebel, not during puberty but during their college years, and the number of able young people who never look to higher education for themselves and are content with truncated, low-level goals, who later come to form the group that sees the American scene as a complex, bureaucratically controlled "rat race," in which the attainment of rewards is capricious and corrupt. . . .

SHIFT FROM LONGTIME GOALS. There has been a marked shift throughout this generation from the pursuit of longtime goals, once regarded as characteristic of the educated portions of the community, to the "more, more, more now" philosophy once regarded as characteristic of economically underprivileged groups with an uncertain present and a dark and deprived future. Immediate sex gratification as represented by early marriage, early attainment of full adult status including parenthood, and the possession of the material attributes of economic independence, such as house and car, TV, a full and complete way of life bought on the installment plan rather than saved for—this has become the style for young professional and business people. . . .

The widespread dissemination of information on the preferred style of living which has been greatly accelerated by TV . . . has increased the extent to which all Americans live on a single scale of values. Each defines his success not in relation to his immediate neighbors alone, but in terms of a national image of the good life. While this condition increases productivity and prevents stagnation and plateaus (as in the United Kingdom) because of the image which differing classes and groups share of their consumption potential, it also tends to create an enormous group of people who may define themselves as failures, as "nobodies," as "people who don't count."

These self-definitions are reflected . . . in the way in which college students think of themselves as helpless to affect society in any way, and in the comments of many highly educated and highly placed persons on the hopelessness of attempting to influence anything as complex as the modern world. . . .

With rapid social change, the remembered behavior of parents no longer provides a possible model. Instead, the conspicuous consumption patterns of young couples just a few years older and a few income notches higher, as pictured in the mass media, become the only recognized models. As young people are made aware, by the distance between their parents and themselves, of the unprecedented nature of present-day life, their need to catch at the present is reinforced. They feel that there is no other way of life except the here and now. . . .

Paralleling the shift to immediate goals and immediate economic gratifications has come a shift in attitudes towards sex which places an increasing burden on the late adolescent, especially the boy, at a time when his sex impulses are most urgent and he has least experience in managing them. While the American insistence upon marriage as the only moral and appropriate framework for sex gratification has not altered, the general acceptance of sex activity for everyone between puberty and senility, as conducive to normality, health, and adjusted personality, has enormously increased. Accompanying this is an uneasiness, a lack of faith in single blessedness, whether secular or religious.

Young people are confronted by an adult world which warily watches them lest they get in trouble and prods them towards the earliest possible establishment of permanent and suitable sexual ties. The social anxieties found in the poor and disorganized parts of our society a quarter of a century ago have spread upwards, and parents heave sighs of relief when both sons and daughters are "safely married." The age at which marital choices are expected to be made makes the adolescent girl of fourteen to sixteen responsible for obtaining and holding a suitable mate, pushing him towards the amount of vocational education which will support early marriage and parenthood, subordinating abilities and ambitions of her own to further this marriage by foregoing advanced education herself, and working to facilitate his. The parents who place such great importance on their children's behaving normally have become increasingly willing to underwrite marriages in which the young husband is unable to support his wife and children. . . .

THE SEARCH FOR IDENTITY. The search for the testing out and selection, and final acceptance, of a satisfying identity within which the individual personality can pursue a creative life with freedom and dignity is a task which is appropriate to late puberty. The adolescent becomes accustomed to the changes which have taken place within his body, to the new balance that must be established between his inner perceptions of an emerging adult self and the new responsibilities thrust upon him. It is here, during the rapid swing between a return to the dependencies of childhood and a precocious reach for the independence of adulthood, between impulse newly realized and controls only partly developed—it is in this period of shift and flux that ideals can be grasped and kept with an intensity which seldom appears at other stages of growth. The great, burning faiths of the past and blazing hopes for the future of mankind can be presented to the adolescent and embraced by him. Talents and special gifts can be tried out, tentatively, and some measure established of the amount of commitment that can be made to art or science, to politics or business or other vocation, without consideration of its simple economic value. . . .

But such search and such commitments are possible only if the society is willing to extend to young people, in their late adolescence, a kind of psychological moratorium (as Erikson has called it) during which they can experiment without being called upon to succeed; an *as if* period in which heights of aspirations and depths of despair can both be experienced with-

out final economic, social, or personal psychological consequences.

In those periods of history which we think of as golden ages,
such a time of freedom from immediate consequences of any
act was permitted to a small number of youth—at least to the
males—of privileged classes. A few years without pressure, exposed to all the best that had been thought and said in the
world, a chance to travel and to assay the world around them,
freedom from insistent importunity to marry, to make a living,
to settle down, was given them. There was time to form intense
friendships with the like-minded of the same sex, time for strong
teacher-student ties to develop, time for the growing mind to
find models among the great of the past and of the emerging
present, time to sleep, to grow, to experiment, to change, and
to choose. In such periods the fiercest political idealism, the
hardest religious choices, the acceptance of stringent artistic
disciplines belonged to youth; and these demands upon the
privileged were reflected in turn in a greater tolerance towards
the young people with less education, who were expected to
sow their wild oats even while settling down to a life of premature toil.

During the past quarter century we have enormously widened
the possibilities offered by society to [most] children. . . . But
at the same time there have been certain losses. One of the
most striking is the loss of a period when youth can find itself.
The educational period which was once tentative and experimental is now quite as directly functional as the life of a
weaver's apprentice in the Middle Ages. . . .

TIME

let it be vivid, let it be now!

Look at you, making it with your neighbor's wife just to prove that you're really alive. . . . screwing up the land and the water and the air for profit. . . . And you're gonna tell us how to live?

The Man of the Year ran the mile in 3:51.3, and died under mortar fire at An Lao. He got a B-minus in Physics I, earned a Fulbright scholarship, filmed a documentary in a Manhattan ghetto, and guided Gemini rendezvous in space. He earns $76 a week with Operation Head Start in Philadelphia, picks up $10,800 a year as a metallurgical engineer at Ford, and farms 600 acres of Dakota wheat land. He is a whole generation: the man—and woman—of 25 and under. . . .

In the U.S., citizens of 25 and under . . . nearly [outnumber] their elders; by 1970, there will be 100 million Americans in that age bracket. . . . Never have the young been so assertive or so articulate, so well educated or so worldly. Predictably, they are a highly independent breed, and—to adult eyes—their independence has made them highly unpredictable. This is not just a new generation, but a new kind of generation. . . .

Cushioned by unprecedented affluence and the welfare state, he has a sense of economic security unmatched in history. . . . Science and the knowledge explosion have armed him with more tools to choose his life pattern than he can always use: physical and intellectual mobility, personal and financial opportunity, a vista of change accelerating in every direction.

Untold adventure awaits him. He is the man who will land on the moon, cure cancer and the common cold, lay out blight-proof, smog-free cities, enrich the underdeveloped world and, no doubt, write finis to poverty and war.

For all his endowments and prospects, he remains a vociferous skeptic. Never have the young been left more completely to their own devices. No adult can or will tell them what earlier generations were told: this is God, that is Good, this is Art, that is Not Done. Today's young man accepts none of the old start-on-the-bottom-rung formulas that directed his father's career, and is not even sure he wants to be A Success. He is one already. . . . One thing is certain. From Bombay to Berkeley, Vinh Long to Volgograd, he has clearly signaled his determination to live according to his own lights. . . .

Sociologists . . . call them "alienated"or "uncommitted"; editorial writers decry their "noninvolvement." In fact, the young today are deeply involved in a competitive struggle for high grades, the college of their choice, a good graduate school, a satisfactory job—or, if need be, for survival in Viet Nam. Never have they been enmeshed so early or so earnestly in society. Yet they remain honestly curious and curiously honest. Far from "disaffiliated," they are more gregarious than any preceding generation.

. . . Despite its vast numbers and myriad subspecies, today's youth is most accurately viewed through the campus window: nearly 40% of all American youth go on to higher education, and more will soon follow. Despite their vaunted hang-ups, Yale's Kenneth Keniston, . . . who has concentrated on student psychology, concludes that most of today's college students are a dedicated group of "professionalists." In the meritocracy of the '60s and '70s, he says, "no young man can hope simply to repeat the life pattern of his father; talent must be continually improved." According to Keniston, only about one student in ten deviates from the spartan code of professionalism. "Few of these young men and women have any doubt that they will one day be part of our society," he concludes. "They wonder about where they will fit in, but not about whether."

. . . For all the attention won (and sought) by their picket lines, petitions and protest marches, political activists on campus number at best 5% of the student bodies at such traditionally cause-conscious universities as Chicago, Columbia or California. At the majority of colleges and universities, there have been no student demonstrations against anything. . . .

In nearly all their variants, the young possess points of poignant common interest. From activists to acidheads, they like to deride their elders as "stick-walkers" and "sellouts." Fond of such terms as "fragmentation" and "anomie" in sketching their melodramatic self-portraits, many of them assume an attitude that borders on nihilism. To the standard adult charge of youthful irresponsibility, a young Californian can reply, as authors J. L. Simmons and Barry Winograd show in *It's Happening*, with the emotional outrage of a John Osborne character:

"Look at you, brainwashing a whole generation of kids into getting a revolving charge account and buying your junk. (Who's a junkie?) Look at you, needing a couple of stiff drinks before you have the guts to talk with another human being. Look at you, making it with your neighbor's wife just to prove that you're really alive. Look at you, screwing up the land and the water and the air for profit, and calling this nowhere scene the Great Society! And you're gonna tell us how to live? C'mon, man, you've got to be kidding!"

Few organized movements of any description, from the John Birch Society to the A.F.L.-C.I.O. to the Christian church, have the power to turn them on. "We're not going to get in Wrigley Field and 'put one over the plate for Jesus baby,' " says a Georgia coed. Even union members have little sense of militancy. Having little fear that they will ever lack material comforts for their own part, the young tend to dismiss as superficial and irrelevant their elders' success-oriented lives. "You waited," sniffs a young Californian. "We won't." Nonetheless,

today's youth appears more deeply committed to the fundamental Western ethos—decency, tolerance, brotherhood—than
almost any generation since the age of chivalry. If they have
an ideology, it is idealism; if they have one ideal, it is prag-
matism.

Theirs is an immediate philosophy, tailored to the immediacy
of their lives. The young no longer feel that they are merely
preparing for life; they are living it. "Black Power now!" cries
Stokely Carmichael. "Action now!" demands Mario Savio.
"Drop out now!" urges Timothy Leary. As Buell Gallagher,
president of the City College of New York, sees it: "This generation has no utopia. Its idea is the Happening. Let it be concrete, let it be vivid, let it be personal. Let it be *now!*"

. . . It esteems inventiveness, eloquence, honesty, elegance
and good looks—all qualities personified in the Now Generation's closest approximation of a hero, John F. Kennedy. "Heroism and villainy begin with fantasy," says Stephen Kates, 23,
a brilliant concert cellist. "This generation has no fantasies."
In fact, as Harvard sociologist Seymour Lipset observes, they
are "caught up in the myth that J.F.K. was a radical President,
and would have done all sorts of things, bypassing the older
generation.". . .

. . ."We're the Bomb Babies," says Los Angeles City College
student Ronald Allison, 23. "We grew up with fallout in our
milk." The hyperbole may sound sentimental, but because of
the Bomb, some Now People reach their teens feeling that they
are trying to compress a lieftime into a day.

Despite unprecedented academic and social pressures, the
young on campus are carefully keeping their options open. . . .
From Columbia to U.C.L.A., the shift is away from specialized
subjects such as engineering and business administration and
toward the humanities: English, history, political science. . . .
A new field of interest is urban planning, for today's young are
committed as was no previous generation to redeeming the
social imperfections that have ired and inspired the New Muck-
rakers: Ralph Nader *(Unsafe at Any Speed)*, Richard Whalen

(A City Destroying Itself), Michael Harrington *(The Other America)*.

For the most altruistic, there are the Peace Corps and the 14 domestic service programs. "Here is a real, positive outlet," says Gibbs Kinderman, 23, who with his wife Kathy, 24, daughter of historian Arthur Schlesinger Jr., directs a poverty program in Appalachia. Laurance Rockefeller Jr., 22, great-grandson of John D., obliquely justifies his work as a $22.50-a-week VISTA volunteer in Harlem: "Beyond affluence, what?" Answers co-worker Tweed Roosevelt, 24, great-grandson of Teddy: "Individualism."

. . . The search for individual identity is as old as the generational gap. Athens and Rome both fondly cosseted and firmly curbed their children. Youth did not achieve a degree of social and political freedom until the 12th century. A rebellious band of University of Paris students decamped to Oxford and established a new and freer university; soon their idea spread throughout Europe, along with an entire youth subculture of drinking, wenching, dueling. . . . In Italy, students formed guilds and hired professors . . . dictated the curriculum, and at Bologna even insisted that their teachers speak at the double in order to get their money's worth. . . .

The transition from the free university of the Middle Ages to the disciplined college of the Renaissance heralded the birth of a new concept: the prolonged and protected childhood. "The adolescent," writes British sociologist Frank Musgrove, "was invented at the same time as the steam engine. The principal architect of the latter was Watt in 1765; of the former, Rousseau in 1761." Rosseau extolled puberty as "the second birth; then it is that man really enters upon life; henceforth no human passion is a stranger to him."

. . . In the century after the French Revolution, new youth movements throughout Europe were the harbingers of change: Mazzini's "Young Europeans" in Italy; Russia's czar-bombing nihilists; the Balkan *Omladina* (rejuvenation); Germany's *Wandervögel* (birds of passage). . . . That youth movements

can be perverted and captured by dictators and demagogues became all too clear: the successor to Germany's *Wandervögel*
was the Hitler Youth, which the Communists took over intact
in East Germany after 1945, changing only the name. Mao Tse-
tung and his heir, Marshal Lin Piao, have shown that China's
youth, steeped for millennia in a tradition of respect for their
elders, can be turned in a moment into marauding anarch-
ists. . . .

In the U.S., the leftist causes of the Depression remained
inert in the immediate postwar years. Then the "Silent '40s"
spawned the Beat Generation of the '50s, which reached deeply
into such existentialist authors as Camus, Heidegger and Sartre,
and cultivated a keen sense of social dislocation along with
its beards. But their *Zeitgeist* was intellectual and stylistic; the
1960s brought a revival of true political dissent. Civil rights
was the trigger, civil disobedience their weapon, marches and
sit-ins the strategy.

. . . Because the nation endorsed the civil rights movement,
America's youthful activists tasted victory in their pioneering
cause. . . . and a New Left was born: a grass-roots populist
mélange of organizations and splinter groups that struck in
all directions—antipoverty, anticensorship, antiwar, antiestablishment. . . .

Harvard-based Lutheran Chaplain Paul Santmire, 29, finds
that "these kids have been fed a Milquetoast gospel in a modern world; they view religion with a certain anthropological
sophistication. Yet they are past Nietzsche, because they really
would like to believe." More than 250,000 students are helping tutor children in depressed areas. A more immediately
fruitful area for social involvement is the campus itself—a
malleable microcosm of an existing and perfectible world. . . .

What the Now Generation possesses in every stratum is a
keen ability to sense meaning on many levels at the same time.
In its psychological armory it counts a powerful array of
weapons—both defensive and offensive. Foremost among them:

a built-in bunk detector for sniffing out dishonesty and double standards. . . .

"LSD is like Ban deodorant," says a University of Michigan acidhead. "Ban takes the worry out of being close; LSD takes the worry out of being." The National Student Association's Chuck Hollander, 27, who has written extensively on the subject, estimates that 20% of college students use drugs, ranging from pep pills to marijuana, the amphetamines to the psychedelics (LSD, mescaline, and Psilocybin).

In the two major population centers of California, the use of marijuana (alias "boo," "grass," "tea" or "Mary Jane") is so widespread that pot must be considered an integral part of the generation's life experience. Insiders say that no fewer than 50% of Los Angeles high school students have tried marijuana at least once, and that 25% use it regularly once or twice a week.

. . . The generation shows the same empirical approach to love as many do to drugs. Says Billie Joe Phillips, 23, a Georgia coed who writes a twice-weekly column for the Atlanta Constitution: "For most of the girls in my age group who are married, it would have been better if someone had given them a gross of prophylactics, locked them in a motel room for two weeks, and let them get it out of their systems." Boys and girls have exorcised sexual inhibitions. They are monogamous only if they choose to be; they claim to find the body neither shameful nor titillating, and sneer self-righteously at the adults who leer at "topless" waitresses. "Hung up on sex," is the put-down.

Many adults fear that the long-hair kick among boys, the pants-suit fancies of girls, indicate a growing transferal of roles. Max Lerner warns darkly that homosexuality is on the rise among the young throughout the world. Not so, says the Now People: "It's just that we talk about it more openly."

Another adult worry is that the pervasive Pill will give rise to mindless, heartless promiscuity among the young. They do, it is true, subscribe to a more tolerant morality than their elders, but their mating habits have changed little. "The old submarine—the girl who's under all the time—that's wrong," says a Southern coed. "So is being a professional virgin." Reasons Elizabeth Crosby, a sophomore at New College in Sarasota, Fla.: "Our attitudes are more an emphasis on relationship, and sex is bound up in this."

. . . For all their skepticism and hedonism, the Now Generation's folk art reflects a uniquely lyrical view of the world. Music is its basic medium, having evolved from the brassy early days of rock 'n' roll into the poignant, pithy beat of folk-rock (or "Rock-Bach" as the West Coast enthusiasts call it). From the controlled venom of the Beatles in a song like *Eleanor Rigby* ("Wearing the face that she keeps in a jar by the door") to the Eliotesque elegance of Simon & Garfunkel's *Dangling Conversation* ("Like a poem poorly written/We are verses out of rhythm/Couplets out of rhyme . . ."), the subject matter goes far beyond the moon-June lyrics of the past in pop. . . .

The generation's other folkways are equally expressive. The no-touch, deadpan dances that so intrigue and sometimes repel adults are, to the Now People, not a sex rite but a form of emancipation from sex. "After all," says Jordan Christopher, "the beginning of dance was self-expression. It began without physical contact, and it wasn't for centuries that dancing went into the drawing room and became stiff and formal.". . .

Can the Now Generation accommodate their own parents? "The generational gap is wider than I've ever seen it in my lifetime," says Harvard's David Riesman. Predicts Britain's Leslie Paul, whose autobiography gave the phrase "angry young man" to the world in 1951: "The relations of the generations may become the central social issue of the next 50 years, as the relations between the classes have been for the past half-century."

The questing, restless majority of the young may already be ahead of that issue. By the existential act of rejecting *cogito, ergo sum* for *sum, ergo sum,* they have taken on, willy-nilly, a vast commitment toward a kindlier, more equitable society. The young often seem romantics in search of a cause, rebels without *raison d'être*. Yet in many ways they are markedly saner, more unselfish, less hag-ridden than their elders. . . .

Henry David Thoreau would have felt at home with the young of the '60s; they are as appalled as he was at the thought of leading "lives of quiet desperation." Indeed, for the future, the generation now in command can take solace from its offspring's determination to do better.

They will have to. For better or for worse, the world today is committed to accelerating change: radical, wrenching, erosive of both traditions and old values. Its inheritors have grown up with rapid change, are better prepared to accommodate it than any in history, indeed embrace change as a virtue in itself. With his skeptical yet humanistic outlook, his disdain for fanatiscism and his scorn for the spurious, the Man of the Year suggests that he will infuse the future with a new sense of morality, a transcendent and contemporary ethic that could infinitely enrich the "empty society."

MARILYN SWARTZ

an under-twenty-five reply to "time"

The media has headlined protest, but ignored . . . the beneficial results.

Ever since the mass media discovered students in the century A. B. (After Berkeley), it has portrayed them most inaccurately. It has stressed student anger "against," but neglected their ideas and actions "for." The media has headlined protest, but ignored the deeper reasons behind student upheavals and the beneficial results protest brought. While playing up noise and dancing in the streets, it has played down the reforms young people have achieved by reasoning and working with adminstrators and the "establishment.". . .

Time magazine saw fit to award its "Man of the Year" title to the under-twenty-five generation. Although *Time* gave praise to youth, it did so with a typical, small degree of thoughtful analysis, leaving a reader with little comprehension of this generation. Not only did *Time* think those under twenty-five were a "new kind of generation" (which every generation is), but the generation that would "land on the moon, cure cancer and the common cold, lay out blight-proof, smog-free cities, enrich the underdeveloped world, and, no doubt, write tmis to poverty and war." *Time* evidently thought it was writing a review of the successful sequel to *Don Quixote*.

The *Time* article was a hodgepodge of fact and fiction; it followed the practice now customary in the press of characterizing the young along the exceedingly narrow spectrum of "activists to acid-heads," and in so doing applied the outspoken views of a minority to the bulk of the generation. The article predicted a changing era, but beyond a pethora of platitudes did not define what or how it would change. . . .

Psychologists and sociologists and educators and politicians . . . looked at the problems activists and discontents were causing on campuses and the White House lawn, and seemed to come to the not too earth-shaking conclusion that students were alienated. Some even hinted that this alienation was due to faults in society. . . .

The current wave of student alienation dates at least back to 1960. Not only are people years late in recognizing that this alienation exists, but they are only beginning to think they should listen to the alienated. Listening, however, only seems to be a prescription to make the young and alienated happy. It doesn't. One of the characteristics common to those under twenty-five that *Time* did catch is that they have a "built-in bunk detector for sniffing out dishonesty." Young people know it is dishonest to listen to someone and not take seriously what he says. . . .

It is a minority that colors a generation. A minority sat in the Constitutional Convention, initially worked toward the abolition of slavery, developed large industry, internationalism, the New Deal, and progressive education. When we speak of a generation, we often mean a small group of innovators and leaders. Some of the leaders of the young generation today are alienated and some are not; some are working within the establishment and some outside it. All want something different. . . .

Side by side with students who have opted out, become hippies, and take LSD, are young men and women gathering forces and working to change existing institutions. They are seeking changes because the institutions they see are not relevant to the world they see developing or to the way they will live in it. Students want their brief years of education to be a process that encourages curiosity, repsonsiveness, involvement, and theoretical and practical judgment—the qualities that can make life useful. But on many campuses students are taught only to listen, take notes and obey rules handed down by an undemocratic body.

Students want to be included in the administrative and educational process. They want to make educational institutions a part of their lives, so they can relate to them as part of a world they want to understand. The campus is a societal microcosm where young people may search for the answer to "Who Am I" and for the relationship of "Who I Am" to "What Is." When students are not able to relate to their surroundings, to relate the "I" to the "Is," they become irresponsible or withdrawn; or they work like hell to make the system relevant.

Reed Whittemore, who taught at Carleton College for twenty years, says that students are often disloyal to institutions because there is so little to be loyal to. He suggests that the way to develop loyalty is to be part of something. Let the students start teaching themselves, he says; participating in education will make people believe in whatever education is trying to do.

One young woman intensely involved in, and loyal to, the educational process is Rita Dershowitz, a Hunter College graduate [who] has been director of the Higher Education Seminars sponsored by the United States Student Press Association with a grant from the Carnegie Corporation. U.S.S.P.A. set up the program to make college editors aware of all aspects of education. . . .

Rita has arranged weekend seminars for student newspaper editors and six-week summer sessions on a college campus. The weekend sessions are not structured as the usual conference would be: there are discussions rather than speeches. . . . The subject matter changes as participants change their ideas of knowledge. [Noted] educators, writers and thinkers . . . have attended meetings. They do not lecture . . . they are there for the curious to question. The editors learn from the specialists, from each other, and from themselves. . . . Some people are confused by the method, or upset to learn that they are not very intellectually creative or self-reliant. Most of them do become interested in the process of learning. They do think about what a classroom should be, and by thinking up ways to change the existing structure, they become loyal to the process of learning.

The learning process is as important as what is learned, says Rita. Whether schools are explicit about it or not, they are teaching values and attitudes as well as transmitting information. . . . The [educational] system assumes people are in the classroom to absorb rather than create and rediscover. Rita is not interested in overturning the educational system tomorrow. She is interested in setting up a model that can be adapted by other institutions. Returning to their schools . . . college editors are writing about educational issues . . . setting up their own seminars . . . confronting faculty so that they rethink their ideas on education, and . . . constantly seeking involvement in the educational process. . . .

The tyranny of the lecturn, the coldness of the lecture, and the impersonality of the classroom situation have led students at several colleges to create [auxiliary] Free Universities where groups meet at arranged times and discuss agreed-upon topics. . . .

One of the first such universities is the Experimental College at San Francisco State College. [In 1967] students, faculty and interested outside specialists [were teaching] about seventy courses, which [included] a seminar in mass communication, organized by the staff of a local noncommercial radio station; classes in nonobjective literature, the college and war, meta-Hamlet, the historical development and social significance of black power, propaganda, brainwashing and the political metaphor, gestalt therapy, conscientious objector counseling, [and so forth]. . . . The Experimental College has . . . made its impact on San Francisco State. The State College has absorbed some of its courses and methods into the curriculum, including a full-credit seminar in the education department on higher education where ten students and a professor, distinguishable only by age, decide together what they are going to learn. . . .

Professor Richard Axen . . . said that the Experimental College has "activated a guilt that faculty members have felt for a long time, for their authoritarianism and for having mistreated students for so long."

Those who start experimental colleges, Rita Dershowitz suggests, as well as the hippies and close-knit civil rights groups, are trying to create a subculture of gentleness, concern for one another, and an escape from man-made tensions, commercialization and materialism. Not tomorrow or the next day, but in the not-too-distant future, a more personal and relevant education that takes the ideas of students into greater consideration will become more and more prevalent. Students . . . are willing to work harder and in a different way, for the sake of a more rounded experience. They are willing to spend time working with administrators and faculty in setting up requirements and courses, and in determining together educational values. In confronting the administrative process, they learn why some things must be done in a university and why others cannot be. Perhaps thus they will become as loyal to their accredited universities as they are to their free universities—and they could become part of a process leading to citizen involvement and responsiveness rather than apathy or resignation.

Some colleges and universities are reexamining their institutions in terms of the student. They not only are giving him a chance to relate to what "Is," but are asking . . . students either to participate in college decision-making or to form committees of their own, parallel to faculty committees, to make tentative proposals. . . . .

Young people are [also] beginning to ask the same consideration of social values and involvement from other sectors as they demand in their education. And others are beginning to listen. . . . The conservative National Association of Manufacturers [has] sponsored a panel for its membership at which student leaders discussed their occupational preferences. Most of them definitely did not include business as a possibility. A senior editor of *International Science and Technology,*

David Allison, writes that a typical member of this generation will choose that job that offers high social value. Young scientists, he says, are asking, "What is this company for?" Corporations depend on these young scientists for growth, and they can change the corporation by refusing to work solely for profit [by joining companies which apply science to human, social needs]. . . .

Not all the leaders of the under-twenty-five generation are college derivatives. . . . Because of night wanderings, noise, scuffles and riots, the Nashville city government imposed an evening curfew on teen-agers. To the dismay of the adult community, the curfew only increased activity. Teen-agers were led by a young social protester, who had been arrested nearly a hundred times, and had been the mascot of racial demonstrations since he was twelve. As he began another jail sentence, he and his friends sent the mayor an eight-page letter reflecting the general protest and frustration of the young people, and making positive recommendations on how the government and the young could work together. . . . Mr. Robert Horton, chief administrative officer to the mayor, met with them and listened for two hours in an open meeting at a high-school auditorium. The high-schoolers said that to keep off the streets, they needed a place to go. They asked that community centers be turned over to them on Saturday nights. The city complied. The youngsters drew up their own code of conduct (stricter than the city would have required), chose chaperones and made their dances interracial. The students also sought regular meetings with government officials, and now these officials discuss with avid high-schoolers subjects ranging from a better-educated police force to air pollution to the war in Vietnam.

One young leader who [unlike many] believes that working within the system produces greater results than fighting it is Sanford Greenberg . . . at twenty-six an Assistant to the White House Science Adviser. . . . "I was very interested in social change and improvement," he says, "and could have ended up fighting the system . . . I've found, however, that people will listen to your ideas when you back them up. Outsiders who feel frustrated about the system have not learned to be persuasive. They have good intentions, but do not understand or face the practical problems." Greenberg says that when you work within the system, you can compromise the superficials, and still hold onto your individualism and idealism. . . . Young people . . . have the will and energy to devote to making a better world, even when told, "it can't be done.". . . "When we assume leadership, the country will be different because we will continue to try, to change, to improve.". . .

[Gerald Moore, however, in an article in *Life*, claimed that] the attitudes of this generation have not changed from those of the generation ten years ago. . . . Moore chose to write about Indiana because it is a typical large university of twenty-six thousand students from all economic levels, geographic areas and religious backgrounds. Just as at many colleges and universities, students at Indiana University have marched against the war in Vietnam and in particular during the Cuban blockade turned out a thousand strong to demonstrate both against United States policy and against the demonstrators. The changes I.U. is making are typical: . . . curfew was abolished for many women students. Juniors and seniors will soon be allowed to take four courses without receiving grades for them, simply pass or fail. . . . Interracial dating is common although not accepted by a majority. Seven years ago, the student body elected a Negro as president. Marijuana, LSD and various stimulants are present on campus, but most students are not interested, believe them harmful and immoral. . . .

On the whole, Moore found that Indiana students wanted to get ahead socially and financially, and looked down on intellectuals, beardniks and beatniks. Those who had worked in Head Start centers, hospitals, orphanages and anti-poverty programs had done so without humanitarian motives. "Many of us want to be teachers," Moore reported one girl explaining. "The experience will make us better teachers, that's all.". . . The campus is still wild with football cheers rather than fiery political debates, and professors are still complaining of student apathy and dullness. [Moore] was able to find, however, campus leaders, unlike those in his day, he said, who are able to disrupt the status quo by fighting for student power and participatory democracy.

[The key point Moore overlooked is that it is precisely] these student leaders who will establish a new societal framework in which the majority of students will [in due time] want to succeed. The leaders will temper their aims; they will not achieve all they seek, but society will be changed by them. . . .

Many people of the young generation are really quite different from the image carried in the media. [Their protest takes different forms depending upon the acceptance and understanding of those within the order that young people seek to change. Communications, however, as a] business that caters to the tastes of its buyers, entertains them and educates them with as little pain as possible. But if we are to know more about students than their fornication rates, the length of their beards, the shortness of their skirts, and the number involved in [riots], we have to demand, as buyers of the media, that it perform with more conscience and honesty than it does now. . . . And in order that the economic impact be made, many more individuals must be taught to be searching and analytical. This is a hundred-year plan, at least. For the plan to succeed, we need the kind of values and education that young people are demanding for the sake of everybody's world.

CHRISTOPHER JENCKS
and DAVID RIESMAN

---

perspectives on the
campus arena

The dissident minority will continue to grow.

Among the many myths which afflict contemporary thinking about American colleges, none is more persistent than the one which maintains that in the good old days, when colleges were small, faculty and students had intimate personal contacts on a day-to-day basis. This myth has several sources. One is the assumption that because the faculty were not busy with research or consultations, they had time and energy for their students. A second reason for this myth is the general American tendency, perhaps the human tendency, to assume that if things are presently bad, they were once better, rather than realizing that they are likely to be *considered* bad precisely because they are getting better.

Whatever its origins, the myth does not square with the facts. Even a cursory reading of academic history makes clear that eighteenth- and nineteenth-century colleges, while small enough, were neither harmonious nor intimate. The students were continually struggling with the faculty, whom they almost all regarded as the enemy. The faculty reciprocated in kind, devoting itself mainly to the enforcement of academic and social rules, often of the most trivial kind. There was always a somewhat autonomous and rebellious student culture, just as there was a somewhat autonomous juvenile culture in many of the large families chronicled in Victorian novels.

The conflicts which inhibited faculty-student communication about non-disciplinary issues should not surprise us. Colleges have always been institutions through which the old attempt to impose their values and attitudes on the young. They have therefore taken over from parents the tension-filled and affect-laden tasks of socialization. This was particularly difficult in a frontier society where many parents were fearful lest their children lapse into the seeming barbarism of the ever-visible Indians. They therefore clung tightly to small as well as large manifestations of their inherited tradition. These parents and their clerical spokesman saw colleges as a device for protecting them against the danger of losing their precarious ties to an Eastern or even European past. It was therefore natural for the colleges to resist all compromise with the interests and predilections of the young. There could not but be conflict in such institutions, just as there could not but be conflict (however well repressed) in such families.

This conflict was intensified by the fact that most colleges also took over from the adult intelligentsia the task of transmitting some version of High Culture—in the narrow literary as well as the broad anthropological sense—to the semi-civilized young. It is true that adult versions of High Culture have never had the same authority in America as in countries like France and Japan, and perhaps this is true of adult culture in the broad sense as well. Nonetheless, nineteenth-century American educators believed in the value of what they had to teach, and sought to impose it on the young, whether the young enjoyed it or not. They seldom succeeded very well, but the mere attempt was often enough to keep the young on the warpath and produce continuing guerrilla resistance.

STUDENT AUTONOMY. One of the attractions of a college, even in nineteenth-century America, was that it enabled its students to find at least a small measure of freedom from adult control. The students were very closely regulated on paper, but they gained strength from numbers and were often quite successful in resisting the intent (and often even the substance) of college rules. The young man who would otherwise have had to stay on the family farm or go to work under the watchful eye of an office supervisor therefore found a kind of freedom in college. He had co-conspirators in breaking the rules, and while he could be punished by expulsion, this was a common and far from serious fate in an age where records seldom followed a man from one place to the next.

So while colleges were designed to familiarize the young with the best that had been thought and said by their elders, to give them a sense of continuity between their own problems and those of previous generations, and thus hopefully to spare them learning everything again by trial and error, they sometimes had precisely the opposite effect. Even when the college was in no sense a university, and its faculty was fully committed to transmitting the conventional wisdom rather than questioning or expanding it, the autonomy of the student culture could make the college a *de facto* instrument of cultural change. Whether it wished to or not, a college could become the crucible in which the younger generation shaped its distinctive values and acquired a sense of separate identity, rather than one in which the young were shaped by those who had gone before and acquired their predecessors' sense of history and purpose. . . .

CHALLENGING ADULT LEGITIMACY. The lack of intimacy and harmony between young and old is, then, hardly a twentieth-century novelty. Nor are youthful efforts to meet adult pressure by sabotage and selective inattention a uniquely modern phenomenon. Nonetheless, we are convinced that nineteenth-century conflicts between the generations differed from today's in some important respects. Nineteenth-century young people seldom challenged the legitimacy of their elders' authority. They merely claimed that it had been abused in a particular case, or even more commonly, they defied it without creating any ideology to bolster them. Even the riots which marked the nineteenth-century college life were more like peasant revolts against tyranny than like revolutionary movements. In the twentieth century, on the other hand, the increasing separatism of teen-age culture and the massing together in high schools and colleges of very large numbers of young people of identical age and social condition have gradually led to a new atmosphere in which the basic legitimacy of adult authority has been increasingly called into question. . . .

FROM PSEUDO-PARENT TO SCHOLAR. There was a time, as we have already said, when most college instructors saw themselves, however reluctantly, as policemen whose job was to keep recalcitrant and benighted undergraduates in line, exacting a certain amount of work and imposing a measure of discipline. These men were more often clergymen than scholars, even though a few were both. They found it natural to justify their work in terms of improving the social and moral character of the young rather than in terms of their intellectual attainment. This cast them in a quasi-parental role.

Today's college faculty seldom sees itself this way. In the better universities and university colleges, professors are usually scholars or at least pseudo-scholars and have much less emotional investment in their students' social and moral development than did professors a century ago. Today's scholars are still willing to monitor the academic lives of the young, at least by proxy, insisting that students take certain courses, pass certain examinations, and so forth. But few have any interest in dominating the non-academic lives of the young—in shaping what is no longer even called the students' moral character. In part this is because they think the role of moral tutor (or worse, policeman) would interfere with their ability to work with students on academic matters. In part it is because while they often disapprove of hedonism and athleticism and shower sarcasm on young people who indulge in such heresies, they do not care enough to invent or supervise alternatives.

AMBIVALENCE ON PRINCIPLE. Many professors and administrators are also less certain than they once were what students *ought* to be or become, and are reluctant to go the mat with the young over principles in which they themselves only half believe. Then, too, even those professors and administrators who are individually sure of their ground and opposed to permissiveness in their personal dealings with the young sometimes find that it is politically expedient to avoid collective regulation of student behavior. If the adult community is divided on those matters, as it often is, any effort to impose adult standards on the young inevitably deepens and intensifies divisions within faculty and administration. Thus it often turns out that the wisest course is to avoid the issue. The easiest way to do this is to deny the need for any rules in a controversial area, leaving it to the students' discretion.

The result of all this is that many faculty and some administrators develop a Veblenian deal. They want undergraduates to act like graduate apprentices, both socially and intellectually, and when a particular undergraduate deviates from this norm they tend to say that he "doesn't belong at a university." Since only a minority of undergraduates have either the talent or the motivation to act like apprentice scholars, many professors disclaim responsibility for the majority, urge more selective admission, and hope for the best. They view the faculty and its apprentices as the "heart of the university," and the still uncommitted undergraduates as an expendable penumbra. The easiest way to ensure that the penumbra does not interfere with the main business of the university is to let its members go their own way relatively undisturbed, hoping that they will educate one another or pick up something in the library or from lectures.

There are, of course, exceptions. Some faculty, perhaps especially in the humanities, are more eager to have their students adopt a particular cultural style than to become imitative and not very capable scholars, while some, especially in the social sciences, look to students to carry out political mandates, either in alliance with them or in compensation for their defections.

Some who have become professors in recent years see themselves as ever young, hedonistic, and hep, and revel in the more anti-intellectual manifestations of student rebelliousness even when it is directed at themselves. Even in a scholarly faculty some are ambivalent about their own scholarship and nurture other and contrasting qualities in the young. Transference obviously enters all these cross-generational transactions. There are occasionally deviant academicians who are willing to participate at the adolescent level in both the make-believe and the reality of student life. Such men are sometimes frivolous but often dedicated. On the most academic campuses they sometimes protect the young from becoming too adult too soon. The danger is that they will also reenforce the incompetent amateurism and the self-indulgent or self-pitying protective cults by which young people so often counteract adult expectations.

THE RISE OF THE TEACHING ASSISTANT. Nonetheless, the character of most faculties *has* changed, not only over the past hundred years but even over the past thirty. Until World War II even senior scholars at leading universities did a good deal of what they defined as scut work, teaching small groups of lower-level students, reading papers and examinations, and so forth. Their labors were supplemented by ageing but unscholarly instructors and assistant professors, who were not given tenure, status, or high salaries, but were kept around precisely because there were lots of routine teaching jobs to be done and they were willing to do them. Today, however, few well-known scholars teach more than six hours a week, and in leading universities many bargain for less. Even fewer read undergraduate examinations and papers. At the same time the [American Association of University Professors] and other faculty groups have pushed through "up or out" rules on faculty promotion, so that the permanent assistant professor is now practically unknown at leading universities. The routine problems of mass higher education have therefore fallen by default to graduate students. These students have assumed the role of shop stewards, mediating between the highly professionalized faculty who run the curriculum and the still amateur undergraduates who pursue it. Graduate teaching assistants handle quiz sections, read examinations, listen to complaints, and generally protect the professors from over-exposure to the ignorant.

CHANGING STUDENT OUTLOOKS. . . . Today's students are quite different from those who entered college a generation or two ago. They have lived in a very different sort of adolescent sub-culture before matriculating, and college occupies a different place in their overall life cycle. There was a time in the not-so-distant past when a middle-class high-school boy could goof off in class or get in trouble on his block with almost complete confidence that his misadventures would not be held against him. If he decided to go straight he could do so simply by applying to a reputable college. If his parents could pay the tuition his other failings would usually be forgotten. No more. Today's high-school student is told that his future position in life depends on getting good professional training, that this depends on his getting into a good college, and that this in turn depends on his performing well in high school. A misstep in high school may, in other words, count against him forever. (Or so the myth says. In reality America still offers a great many second chances, explicitly as at Parsons College, covertly elsewhere.) This does not, of course, mean that high-school boys always *act* as if they will be held permanently answerable for the mistakes they made in high school or as if they will get permanent credit for their triumphs, though girls often do act this way. But even the boys are more inclined than in the past to feel that this is the case, at least with regard to their work. This is especially true in the East, where gradations of college prestige are finer and fear of not making the right college is correspondingly enhanced.

The effect of such assumptions is difficult to chart, but they appear to hasten a kind of maturity. High school students seem to feel that they are more on their own, and that their fate depends more on what they do and less on what their parents do for them. Success seems to depend on what they have in their heads, not what kinds of property their parents have in the bank. Partly as a result, many children feel relatively little obligation to maintain strong ties with their parents or to conform to their parents' standards. Some begin relating almost exclusively to their peers by the time they are twelve or thirteen. They also become involved with the opposite sex earlier than their parents did, partly because physical maturity comes sooner and partly because post-Freudian parents are ambivalent in their opposition to adolescent sexuality, perhaps partly because the greater flexibility of sexual identities has heightened anxiety about the possibility of being homosexual and has thus made it more important to prove one's heterosexuality.

SELF-DETERMINATION IN HIGH SCHOOL. Breaking out of the family circle has always left the young uncertain where their loyalties lie and what limits still restrict their behavior. They become involved in all sorts of quasi-familial groups which arouse at least temporary faith in something larger than themselves. The residential college, with its fraternities, football games, and general emphasis on school spirit, was once such a group. Today the suburban high school plays this role, at least among the middle classes, just as the junior high school is now the scene for many early adolescent dramas once associated with high school. By the time today's young people reach college they have therefore already partly broken away from their families and are ready for a more mature role. Whether one looks at the books they have read, their attitudes towards the opposite sex, their allergy to mickey-mouse extracurricular (or curricular) makework, or their general coolness, today's entering freshmen seem older than those of the 1920's and 1930's. . . .

At the same time certain kinds of responsibility come later and later. While young people still hold various kinds of temporary jobs during adolescence, they find it hard to embark on a career in the traditional sense before they reach 22. The most interesting work usually requires professional training beyond the BA and often is not begun in earnest until 25 or older. This means not only that the young usually are denied the kinds of responsibility which go with many jobs, but that they often depend on their families for money until at least 21 and often even later.

Thus, while adolescence begins earlier, it also continues longer. Students must begin making good records sooner, yet these records bring tangible results later and later. This combination of precocity and enforced dependence encourages students to create a make-believe world in which it is as if they were grown up. To achieve this they must organize their own lives, define their own limits, set their own ideals, and deny the authority and legitimacy of the adult world which they cannot join.

DISSIDENT MINORITIES. As in all class struggles, the actors in the war between the generations often take positions contrary to what an outside analyst would regard as their class interest. Just as the civil rights movement had to fight Negro apathy as well as white supremacy for many years, and depended in many ways on white liberals for both money and legitimacy, so too students who oppose adult discrimination and segregation have found that they are a minority among their agemates and that both their political success and their internal morale depend on finding adult supporters. (Their political successes seem to depend mainly on the tacit support of the faculty; their morale depends more on overt support from graduate students and from non-students of that age.)

Broadly speaking, undergraduates assert themselves in one of two ways. Some temporarily repress the fact that they will eventually become adults themselves, and act like "permanent students." Others construct visions of the adult world which are in some sense harmonious with the student culture in which they are currently immersed. Many, of course, do both things, either simultaneously or sequentially.

The attitudes of the scholarly faculty, and the ways in which these encourage unscholarly students to create a counter-reality, have already been touched on. Feeling guilty about their neglect of unscholarly undergraduates, some professors talk about the importance of students' taking responsibility for their own education and about the impossibility of anyone else's doing the job for them. The faculty justify their neglect of the students by pointing to the students' neglect of them. Some precocious and sophisticated students welcome such talk, arguing that students are indeed mature and responsible, and that the university should recognize this and treat them accordingly. The net result is often that both sides conspire to encapsulate the undergraduates in their own world.

ENCOUNTERS WITH FACULTY. It is important to recognize the mutuality of this relationship. Students, for example, often complain about "lack of faculty-student contact" and tell horror stories about professors who have office hours once a month in an ill-publicized place. But the professors rightly counter by noting that few students come to whatever hours they keep, and that those who do come usually argue about grades. Similarly, students complain that they have no unofficial, personal contact with their nominal mentors. Professors respond by pointing out that when they ask students to their homes many make excuses and the rest seem uncomfortable and eager to go. While we think this latter observation underestimates the significance of such encounters to some students, it is certainly true that they seldom provoke significant communication, much less rapport. What the students really need is a sense that an adult takes them seriously, and indeed that they have some kind of power over adults which at least partially offsets the power adults obviously have over them. In order to be taken seriously and exercise power they must, despite their youth, contribute in some way to the world which they are about to join. They seldom get this sense directly from their professors, for the academic enterprise in which professors are engaged seldom excites them. Even if the academic world does excite them, they seldom find any way to contribute to it, even at the margins. It is true that imaginative faculty members, especially in the less fully organized fields, have found ways to bring eager undergraduates into research, so that some have published papers, with or without their mentors, in leading specialized journals. In microbiology it has been possible until recently for an undergraduate to come to the frontier by the time of his junior year; this has also been possible in sociology and in some areas of psychology. It is evidently more difficult in most branches of economics or physics. Whether it is attempted seems to depend in part on whether faculty members feel they stand to gain from success. In highly selective colleges such as Reed, Swarthmore, or Amherst, scholarly professors have long made do with undergraduate research assistants and have organized seminars for advanced undergraduates; but where graduate students and postdoctoral fellows are available as subordinates and colleagues, the greater effort needed to bring undergraduates along is generally less common. Nonetheless, it seems clear that the possibility exists, at least for a minority of students. When we look, for example, at the work published by undergraduates at the University of Kansas in the annual volume sponsored by that institution, or at the work published by Harvard undergraduates in the volumes of papers done for the second author's undergraduate course, it seems to us that undergraduates should be taken seriously as colleagues by even distinguished scholars. . . .

[But] the academic profession like almost all others has been very reluctant to admit . . . the possibility that amateurs could make significant contributions. Such an admission would imply, for one thing, that all its training and certification machinery were superfluous and that those who had fought their way through had wasted their time. Euphoric but untalented amateurs can, moreover, often do considerable damage—though this is far less of a danger in academic life than in, say, medicine or engineering. Whatever the merits of the case, however, the academic profession is at least as elitist and exclusive as the American professional norm. This makes it in some ways very unsuited to the socialization of young people who are by definition outside the charmed circle. While some students nonetheless identify with their professors, the majority cannot afford to take the professorial model too seriously, for they have no reason to think they could approximate it if they tried.

SYMPTOMS OF ANTI-ORGANIZATION. Feeling excluded from the world of work in which their professors participate, many students retreat to a more hedonistic world of football and fraternity parties, or sex and drugs. Since today's students are increasingly anti-organizational in outlook, the latter have gradually displaced the former as a focus of interest. The appeal of sex and drugs is compounded by the bitterness of adult opposition, for anything which evokes such hostility from adults becomes almost by definition "grown up." The decline of the double standard has also made sex more important to undergraduates, for male undergraduates no longer have to depend on lower-class partners and therefore find it easier to blend sex with sociability and even study. The availability of coeds has not only driven the old campus prostitutes out of business but encourages proto-marital relationships which consume far more time and emotional energy than was once common. These relationships occupy such a central place in many undergraduates' lives that they are no longer willing to endure the inconveniences and humiliations adults have traditionally imposed on pre-marital sex. There are few campuses on which the rules surrounding relations between the sexes are not under attack, both as irritations and as hypocrisies.

When one turns from the external forces which drive students to seek a self-contained sub-culture to the internal forces which give this sub-culture strength to resist adult pressure, the role of the graduate student assumes considerable importance. There was a time when undergraduates were almost as remote from graduate students as from professors. Undergraduates were often from more affluent families than graduate students on the same campus, and they were almost always less committed to intellectual values. The graduate students, in turn, felt that undergraduates were a frivolous lot, and had little or nothing to do with them. Today, however, undergraduates are more mature and more thoughtful, and the gap seems narrow at some points. It is true that graduate students in professional schools like law and medicine still keep pretty much to themselves. They have no institutional contact with undergraduates, and they already identify to some extent with their future professions.

GRADUATE DOUBLE AGENTS. Graduate students in the arts and sciences, on the other hand, often seem somewhat less professionalized. While many of them make strenuous efforts to emulate their professors rather than undergraduates, others become double agents, maintaining ties with their past as well as their future. These dissident graduate students often become the leaders and legitimizers of undergraduate discontent— a phenomenon well documented at Berkeley in recent years but increasingly common elsewhere too. . . .

The mere existence of this sort of graduate student has an effect on the self-conception of many undergraduates. Graduate students are not yet quite adults, but they have many of the adult prerogatives to which undergraduates aspire: somewhat responsible jobs, reasonably satisfactory incomes which do not depend on parents, the right to live where and how they please, sexual liberty, and fairly long academic tethers. They are, moreover, committed to this way of life for a more or less indefinite period, which they are often in no hurry to end. A graduate student may therefore look to his juniors—and sometimes to himself—like a perpetual student in the Latin American tradition. For the undergraduate who finds himself unable to identify with any of the career alternatives he knows about, this life may seem a lesser evil—avoiding a difficult choice, preserving a measure of youthful noncommitment, and yet not exacting the

full price usually demanded of those who remain dependent on
their elders. . . .

Graduate students of this kind, along with the undergraduates
who identify in whole or in part with them, form a semi-stable
occupational group. Unlike those undergraduates and professional students who expect to be on campus for a fixed period
and then depart for something better, these students see no immediate prospect of changing their status. They are therefore
far more interested than other students in trying to improve
their present circumstances. Most students have what might be
called a white-collar mentality, which assumes that if they conform to their superiors' demands they will be rewarded and rise
to a new role in the world. The dissident minority, on the other
hand, has what might be called a blue-collar mentality. This
outlook excludes promotion as remote or unlikely, and focuses
on improving the conditions associated with its present work.
While this dissident group is small, it includes many of the most
competent and articulate students.

SUB-CULTURES IN PERSPECTIVE. Looking at undergraduate sub-cultures in historical perspective, we are inclined
to predict that the dissident minority will continue to grow. It
represents a natural response to the extension of adolescence,
both back into what was once childhood and forward into what
was once adulthood, and extension in both directions is likely
to continue. Psychologically if not chronologically, college
therefore comes later in the overall life cycle, and its role *in
loco parentis* is increasingly subject to challenge. . . . Given the
appealing Continental example, the growing logistical difficulties of enforcing rules made *in loco parentis*, and the increasing
moral and emotional doubts of the administrators and faculty
who must make most of these rules, it seems likely that undergraduates who demand an end to the doctrine will slowly get
their way on most campuses. . . .

There are colleges, public and private, where undergraduates'
impatience for such changes threatens the very survival of the

institution, by arousing the ire of powerful adults who regard student pranks as funny but cannot laugh off student solemnity. We have talked to students on such campuses who say that if the college authorities would frankly admit that the rules exist to protect the college from community reprisal, they would co-operate; what they say they cannot abide is being told that the rules are for their own good. Whether most would in fact coop-erate we are not sure. Some among the current student genera-tion are in revolt against all authority, obsessively testing all limits. Clothes are a constraint; razors are a constraint; courses and examinations are constraints; intervisitation hours are a constraint; refined language is a constraint. This revolt is sup-ported by developments in the arts and also in the bohemias of the world—developments which are readily visible to under-graduates. It is a revolt which has also won a measure of long overdue support in the courts. On many campuses the rebels can also count on the tolerance of their fellow students, who fear to be thought square or chaste or fearful or finks. In this situation there may be some students who will inhibit themselves in order to save the institution, but there are likely to be others who relish the prospect of the institution's succumbing to community dis-approval, thus revealing the community's rottenness for all to see.

Nonetheless, despite some students' refusal to present a clean-cut fact to the public, virtually all the colleges which now feel threatened will survive and even prosper. The real question is therefore how the increasing autonomy of many undergraduate sub-cultures will affect the individual participants' long-term growth and development—and thus how it will affect the larger society. We find it hard to imagine, for example, that students who spend four (sometimes ten) years in the more alienated Berkeley hippie scene will slip easily into the established adult institutions within which the middle classes now earn their liv-ing. Even four years in Cambridge can develop a set of assump-tions and habits rather poorly suited to the occupations for which Harvard has traditionally prepared its alumni. Some of these alumni may be permanently out of tune with the world of work.

HIPPIES AND ACTIVISTS. In examining this question, one must distinguish between students whose estrangement from adult life is so complete that they withdraw into passivity and privatism (often nourished by drugs) and students who, while alienated from the adult society they observe around them, still have enough hope for the future to make an active effort at political change. The activists may seem almost wholly committed to anti-organizational ideologies and behavior, but they can often change their views quite suddenly, especially if institutions they had defined as hopelessly rigid and square take them seriously, adopt their rhetoric, and toy with their program. The relations between some radicals and the federal poverty program illustrate this. But even the hippies who have no political program may find a place in the corporate state if they have technical competence. Thus one finds industries employing computer programmers whose dress and demeanor remain aggressively bohemian and who often continue to live in colonies of like-minded souls on the fringe of some ethnic or academic ghetto. . . .

It could be argued, however, that as students acquire more freedom their world may become more like that of adults—as, for example, the world of graduate students in some ways already is. One of the distinguishing features of student life is that its participants are allowed to make mistakes without paying too heavy a price. They can, in other words, be somewhat irresponsible. If students do not do their work they may get a bad grade, and if they get enough bad grades they may be fired, but the amount of absenteeism, indolence, and sheer incompetence permitted students is far greater than that permitted almost any other sort of worker. Similarly, if a student gets arrested for smoking marijuana his parents will usually go to bat for him, find lawyers, pay bail, and the like. Not only that, but the civil authorities are likely to be relatively lenient, chalking up his failings to youthful excess rather than moral turpitude. Radicals and idealists often deplore all this, saying that students should have no greater privileges than other members of society. Yet if this were really to happen students would probably become far more cautious in their outlook, taking fewer risks and supporting fewer radical causes, both moral and political. Look, for example, at those students who plan professional careers. These are the students whose work is "real" in the sense that their failures count heavily against them. And these are by and large soberly professional as undergraduates even in their dress. . . .

THE ADULT BACKLASH AND THE "SAFE" COLLEGES. The customs and concerns of student sub-cultures vary enormously, but all are in one way or another at odds with the adult sub-cultures from which they spring. The growing autonomy of such sub-cultures has therefore been greeted with less than universal enthusiasm by responsible adults. Fearful parents believe that if they let their children immerse themselves in one of these sub-cultures, the children may never outgrow it. This fear flourishes especially among parents who have not themselves been to college. Not having been undergraduates themselves, these parents have not had the experience of passing through this particular phase and slipping into the post-collegiate adult world. This may make them exaggerate the difficulty of the transition and underestimate the probability that it will eventually take place. But even college-educated parents worry about whether their children will prove as resilient as they themselves did. They worry doubly when they see that the distance between many student sub-cultures and adult society is wider than it was a generation ago. And even we ourselves, while less anxious about these matters than most parents and professors, are not sure that such fears are wholly unfounded.

Parental worries are compounded by ambiguities. Parents and other adults usually conform to the achievement ethic of the highly organized society in which they work, but many are also attracted by more spontaneous, hedonistic, impractical, and pre-industrial possibilities. As David Matza has pointed out, this means that there is a kind of secret sharing between many adults and those adolescent sub-cultures which defy adult ambition, taste, and sobriety. Adults may patronize teenagers whose immaturity finds symbolic expression in panty-raids, but only the most puritanical are alarmed by them. When frivolity turns to defiance, however, the adults' response changes correspondingly. Even those who view themselves as liberals are frequently upset by long hair, marijuana and LSD, miscegenation, and seemingly unpatriotic anti-militarism. There is, in other words, some point at which almost every parent wants to draw the line, even though not every parent dares to try. [Some who try] seem to succeed at least in part. . . . All over America there are children who want to eschew the youth sub-culture and move with maximum safety and minimal delay into some kind of adult world. A number of otherwise undistinguished colleges have been able to attract substantial numbers of students by catering to these hopes and fears. These safe colleges fall into two general categories: the closely regulated residential colleges, most of which are church-controlled, and the commuter colleges, most of which are publicly controlled. . . .

LEGITIMACY AND STUDENT REVOLT. We do not see how adults can indefinitely contain the generational revolt. In the long run undergraduates are almost certain to win increasing autonomy, and the doctrine of *in loco parentis* is likely to be abandoned in post-secondary institutions. The minority which is officially charged with such work, usually concentrated in the dean's office, has little more chance of success than a colonial administration confronted with a determined guerrilla movement. The dissident students are only a small minority on most campuses, as the administration constantly emphasizes. But the young troublemakers swim in a sea of relatively tolerant fellow travelers, many of whom will protect student rights against the adult administration even if they themselves feel little impulse to exercise such rights. While there are also many conservative students sympathetic to adult values, they tend to be apathetic and cannot be counted on to play an active role in defending the status quo against youthful defiance. Likewise, while there are many adult faculty nominally allied with the administration who are put off by student insolence, dissidence, and resistance, they have mixed feelings about the time-consuming tasks of enforcing *in loco parentis,* and in a crisis the administration cannot count on them. . . .

All metaphors can, of course, be pushed too far. We do not expect the generational revolt to achieve victory in the same sense that the Algerian revolt did. Neither legislators nor trustees are ready to haul down the banner of adult responsibility and turn over the regulation of student affairs either to the students themselves or to the police who regulate other citizens. College administrators eager to be loved, or at least not abused, by the young may in some cases want to abandon the struggle to impose their will on undergraduates, retrenching to the "neo-colonialist" position they now take vis-à-vis graduate students. But they will seldom feel free to go this far, even if they want to. Adults will therefore continue to regulate and restrict undergraduate life in a variety of ways for many years to come, making periodic attacks on the students' sense of maturity and dignity. But as in guerrilla warfare, the occupying powers may win all the battles while gradually losing the war. The problem is at bottom one of legitimacy, and the claims of adults on undergraduates seem to achieve this less and less.

Nonetheless, the metaphor of guerrilla warfare and colonial liberation suggests another side to our prophecy. It is one thing for undergraduates to win the same actual rights as other adults; it is quite another thing to win the freedom which they *imagine* goes with adult status. The waning of formal adult control over the social aspects of undergraduate life is unlikely to be accompanied by comparable waning of control over undergraduate work. Today's graduate students are after all nominally free, but they are actually very much constrained by the fact that adults control their future status in society. This will probably be the case with tomorrow's undergraduates. Generational revolt, in other words, will probably bring the appearance of victory, but it will also lead to neo-colonialism, for the young can no more afford to go their own way independent of adults than Ghana or Cuba can get on without making peace with at least some of the Great Powers.

ARTHUR M. SCHLESINGER, JR.

students and the velocity of history*

We are eaten up with an intensity that we cannot name.

[We] admire the . . . willingness to be vulnerable.

Let there be born in us a strange joy.

Today, more than ever before in any country in history, the indispensable climax of the children's preparation—and the parents' hope—is college. "Going to college" is now considered to hold the key to life—the key not only to intellectual training but to social status and economic success.

In 1900 one out of every twenty-five young people from 18 to 21 was in college; in 1939, one out of seven; in 1968, almost one out of two. In California four out of every five high-school graduates now go on to college. The United States today has nearly 6 million college students—46 per cent of all young people from 18 to 21. By 1970 we are expected to have 7.5 million college students—which means that our student population will have more than doubled in the single decade of the sixties.

Yet, the more college students we have, the more baffling they seem to become. Many adults look on college students today as spoiled and ungrateful kids who don't know how lucky they are to be born in the greatest country on earth. Even men long

* From a longer essay.

identified with liberal views find the new undergraduate, in his extreme manifestations, almost unbearable. Yet the very magnitude of student discontent makes it hard to blame the trouble on individual malcontents and neurotics. A society which produces such an angry reaction among so many of its young people perhaps has some questions to ask itself.

Obviously most of today's students, in spite of the tantrums, came to college to prepare themselves to earn a living in our present society. Most still have the same political and economic views as their parents. Most, until 1968, supported military escalation in Vietnam. Most believe safely in God, law and order, the Republican and Democratic parties and the capitalist system.

Yet something sets this generation of college students apart from their elders—both in the United States and in much of the developed world. For this college generation has grown up in an era when the rate of social change is faster than it has ever before been in human experience. This constant acceleration in the velocity of history means that lives alter with startling and irresistible rapidity—that inherited ideas and institutions live in constant jeopardy of technological obsolescence. For an older generation, change was still something of an historical abstraction, dramatized in occasional spectacular innovations, like the automobile or the airplane; it was not a daily threat to identity. For my children, it is *the* vivid, continuous, overpowering fact of everyday life, suffusing every moment with tension and therefore, for the sensitive, intensifying the individual search for identity and meaning. The very indispensability of a college education for success in life compounds the tension; one has only to watch high-school seniors worrying about the fate of their college applications. And college itself, in a society which is beginning to value academic grades more than social status, may determine the student's future and is therefore grimly competitive as never before.

This, too, is the first generation to have grown up in the electronic epoch. Television affects our children by its rapid and early communication to them of styles and possibilities of life, as well as by its horrid relish in crime and cruelty. But it affects the young far more fundamentally by its creation of new modes of perception. "The instantaneous world of electric informational media," McLuhan has argued, alters basically the way people perceive their experience. Where print culture gave experience a frame, viewing it in logical sequence and from a distance, electronic communication is simultaneous and collective; it "involves all of us all at once."

Another factor distinguishes this generation—its affluence. The post-war rise in college enrollment in America, it should be noted, comes not from any dramatic increase in the number of youngsters from poor families but from sweeping in the remaining children of the middle class. "This is the first generation of students," says the president of the Harvard *Crimson*, "which is not going to school for purely economic reasons." Status and affluence, in the words of Tom Hayden, a student radical leader, become "facts of life, not goals to be striven for." This puts many students in the position to resist economic pressures to buckle down and conform. As another radical has written, "Our minds have been let loose to try to fill up the meaning that used to be filled by economic necessity.". . .

The velocity of history, the electronic revolution, the affluent society—these have given today's college students a distinctive outlook on the world. And a fourth fact must not be forgotten: that this generation has grown up in an age of chronic violence. My generation has been through depressions, crime waves, riots and wars; but for us episodes of violence remain abnormalities. For the young, the environment of violence has become normal. They are the first generation of the nuclear age—the children of Hiroshima. The United States has been at war as long as many of them can remember—and the Vietnam war has been a particularly brutalizing war; for most students have come to feel that the insensate destruction we have wrought in a rural Asian country ten thousand miles away has far outrun any rational assessment of our national interest. Within the United

States, moreover, they have lived with the possibilty, as long
as many of them can remember, of violence provoked by racial
injustice. Even casual crime has acquired a new dimension.
Some of them have never known a time when it was safe to
walk down the streets of their home city at night. Above all,
they have seen each of three men who, in their own experience,
most effectively embodied the idealism of American life shot
down; and the impact of this can hardly be overstated. And—
let us face it—our national reaction to these horrors has only
strengthened their disenchantment: a brief orgy of remorse
followed by business as usual and the National Rifle Association triumphant.

The combination of these factors has given the young both
an immediacy of involvement in society and a sense of individual helplessness in face of the social juggernaut. The highly
organized modern state undermines their feelings of personal
identity by threatening to turn them all into interchangeable
numbers on IBM cards, not to be bent, folded, spindled or
mutilated. Contemporary industrial democracies stifle identity
in one way; contemporary communist states in another; but the
sense of impotence is all-pervasive among the young. So too
therefore is the desperate passion to re-establish identity and
potency by assaults upon the system. . . .

American undergraduates first fixed on racial justice as the
emblem of a corrupt society. Until recently, most college students supported the war in Vietnam—so long as other young
men were fighting it. It used to exasperate Robert Kennedy when
he asked college audiences in 1966 and 1967 what they thought
we should do in Vietnam—hands waving for escalation—and
then asked what they thought of student deferment—the same
hands waving for a safe haven for themselves. At last, as the
draft began to cut deeper, the colleges began to think about
the war; and, the more they thought about it, the less sense it
made. In the last two years resistance to the draft has provided
a main outlet for undergraduate revolt.

No one should underestimate the magnitude of this resistance. In 1968 I have not encountered a single student who still supports military escalation in Vietnam. Not all students who hate war burn draft cards or flee to Canada. Many—and this may be as courageous a position as that of defiance—feel, after conscientious consideration, that they must respect laws with which they disagree so long as the means to change these laws remain unimpaired. Yet even they regard their friends who choose to resist with sympathy.

Still, the draft and the war, however appalling they are to the young, remain not so much causes as symptoms of the profounder disquietude. If we Americans blame the trouble on the campuses just on the war, for example, or (to take another popular theory) on permissive child-rearing ideas, we will not understand the reasons for student turbulence. After all, the students of Paris were not rioting against a government which threatened to conscript them for a war in Vietnam; nor are the students of Poland, Spain and Japan in revolt because their parents were devotees of Dr. Spock. As Stephen Spender has observed, the militant students of Paris and West Berlin think they want to be proletarianized; the militant student of Prague to be bourgeoisified. What exists in common is a deeper disquietude, the character of which was well explained the other day by, of all people, General de Gaulle. The "anguish of the young," the old General said after his own troubles in June with French students, was "infinitely" natural

in the mechanical society, the modern consumer society, because it does not offer them what they need, that is, an ideal, an impetus, a hope, and I think that ideal, that impetus, and that hope, they can and must find in participation.

Not every American student exemplifies this anguish. It appears, for example, more in large colleges than in small, more in good colleges than in bad, more in urban colleges than in rural, more in private and state than in denominational institutions, more in the humanities and social sciences than in the physical and technological sciences, more among bright than among mediocre students. Yet, as anyone who lectures on the college circuit can testify, the anguish has penetrated surprisingly widely—among chemists, engineers, Young Republicans, football players and into those last strongholds of the received truth, Catholic colleges and fundamentalist colleges in the backwoods.

How to define this anguish? It begins with a profound dislike, aggressive among the activists and muted, but none the less essential, among the quieter majority, for the society which produced them. The world, as it roars down on them, seems a series of impersonal structures lying in wait to suppress their individualities and computerize their futures. They see it as a conspiracy against idealism in society and identity in themselves. The System, one student cried out in a television interview,

hits at me through every single thing it does. It hits at me because it tells me what kind of a person I can be, that I have to wear shoes all the time which I don't have on right now. . . . It hits on me in every single way. It tells me what I have to do with my life. It tells me what kind of thoughts I can think. It tells me everything.

Another student added, with rhetorical bravado: "Regardless of what your alternatives are, until you destroy this System, you aren't going to be able to create anything."

The more typical expression of this mood is private and quiet. It takes the form of an unassuming but resolute passion to seize control of one's own future. My generation had the illusion that man made himself through his opportunities (Franklin D. Roosevelt); but this era has imposed on our children the belief that man makes himself through his choices (Jean-Paul Sartre). They now want, with a terrible urgency, to give their own choices transcendental meaning. They have moved beyond the Bohemian self-indulgence of a decade ago—Allen Ginsberg and Jack Kerouac. "We do not feel like a cool swinging generation," a Radcliffe senior said this year in a commencement prayer,

—we are eaten up by an intensity that we cannot name. Somehow, this year more than others, we have had to draw lines, to try to find an absolute right with which we could identify ourselves. First in the face of the daily killings and draft calls . . . then with the assassinations of Martin Luther King and Senator Kennedy.

The contemporary student generation can see nothing better than to act on their own impulses of truth: *"Ici, on spontane,"* as a French student wrote on the walls of his college during the Paris insurgency. One student said to me:

Basically, the concept of this "do your thing" bit (as ludicrous as it sounds) may be the key to the matter. What it means is similar to Mill's *On Liberty* because it alows anybody to do what he wants to do as long as it does not intrude on anyone else's liberty. Therefore, nobody tries to impose anything on anybody, nor do they not accept a Negro, a hippy, a clubby, and so forth. I really believe that today we see beyond superficial appearances and thus, in the end, will have a society of very divergent styles, but that will be successfully integrated into a really viable whole. . . . We test out old thoughts and customs and either dispose of them or retain them according to their merits.

Along with this comes an insistence on openness and authenticity in personal relationships. A 1968 graduate—a girl—puts it clearly:

I think in personal conduct people admire the ability to be vulnerable. That takes a certain amount of strength, but it is the only thing which makes honesty and openness possible—it means you say the truth and somehow leave open a part of your way of thinking—of course you cannot be vulnerable with everyone or you would destroy yourself— but it is the willingness to be open, not just California cheerful open, which is almost a mask, since it is on all the time, and therefore cannot be truthful—it is a little deeper than that. . . . It means being strong enough to reveal your weaknesses. This willingness to be vulnerable— and those you are vulnerable with are your friends—coupled with ability to be resilient—to be strong but supple—those are good qualities, because inherent in them are honesty and humor, and the good capacity to love.

This is the ethos of the young—a commitment not to abstract pieties but to concrete and immediate acts of integrity. It leads to a desire to prove oneself by action and participation—

whether in the Peace Corps and VISTA or by meeting local tests
of college and community existence. The young prefer performance to platitude. The self-serving rhetoric of our society
bores and exasperates them, and those who live by this rhetoric
—e.g., their parents—lose their respect.

It is understandably difficult for parents, who have worked
hard for their children and their communities, to see themselves
as smug and hypocritical. But it is also understandable that
the children of the sixties should have grown sensitive to the
gap between what their parents say their values are and what
(as they see it) their values really are—the gap made so vivid
in the way the land of freedom and equality so long, so un-
thinkingly and so shamefully condemned a tenth of the population to tenth-class citizenship. "It is quite right that the young
should talk about us as hypocrites," Judge Charles E. Wyzan-
ski, Jr., recently said at Lake Forest College. "We are."

And, more often than they know, parents themselves unconsciously signal to their children a cynicism about the System
or a disgust for it. Every father who bewails the competitive
tensions of life, who says he "lives for the weekend," who conveys to his children the sense his life is unfulfilled—they are all,
as Professor Kenneth Keniston of Yale has put it, "unwittingly
engaged in social criticism." There is even what one observer
has described as the "my son, the revolutionary" reaction of
proud parents, like the mother of Mark Rudd, the Columbia
student firebrand who emerged briefly in the spring of 1968 as
the Che Guevara of Morningside Heights.

Today's students are not generally mad at their parents.
Often they regard their father and mother with a certain compassion as the victims of the System which they themselves are
determined to resist. In many cases—and this is even true of
the militant students—they are applying the values which their
parents affirmed; they are not so much rebelling against their
parents' attitudes as extending them. Revolt against parents is
no longer a big issue. There is so little to revolt against. Seventy-
five years ago parents had unquestioning confidence in a set of

rather stern values. They *knew* what was right and what was wrong. Contemporary parents have been too much swept along themselves by the velocity of history to be sure of anything.

No, the boys and girls of the 1960s, unlike the heroes and heroines of Dreiser, Lewis, Fitzgerald and Wolfe, are not targeted against their parents. Their determination is to reject the set of impersonal institutions—the "structures"—which also victimize their parents. And the most convenient structure for them to reject is inevitably the college in which they live. In doing so, they construct plausible academic reasons to justify their rejection—classes too large, professors too inaccessible, curricula too rigid, and so on. One wonders, though, whether educational reform is the real reason for student self-assertion, or just a handy one. The biggest troubles happen not at the worst but at the best insitutions, and generally involve not the worst but the best students. One sometimes suspects that the fashionable cry against Clark Kerr's 'multiversity' is a pretext, and one doubts whether students today would really prefer to sit on a log with Mark Hopkins.

This does not mean that "student power" is a fake issue. But the students' object is only incidentally educational reform. Their essential purpose is something different—it is to show the authorities that students exist as human beings and, through a democratization of the colleges, to increase control of their lives. For one of the oddities about the American system is the fact that American higher education, that extraordinary force for the modernization of society, has never modernized itself. . . .

While spreading professionalization has made American higher education better than ever before, it has also produced professors more concerned with colleagues than with students, and it has increased discontent among undergraduates—especially among those who do not have their professional or vocational future all worked out by their freshman year—and a longing, in the words of Riesman and Jencks, for "a sense that an adult take them seriously, and indeed that they have some kind of power over adults which at least partially offsets the power adults obviously have over them." An eastern undergraduate puts it this way:

Students want more excitement from their courses and, especially, more courses which have something to do with their life. They want to align the universities with their new concepts of freedom and their new interests. The pettiness, traditional values, useless regimen that we feel we are removing from our lives is more difficult to remove from bureaucratized, self-interested universities.

Academic government, in most cases, is strictly autocratic. . . . As a Columbia student recently put it, "American colleges and universities (with a few exceptions, such as Antioch) are about as democratic as Saudi Arabia." The students at Columbia, he adds, were "simply fighting for what Americans fought for two centuries ago—the right to govern themselves."

What does this right imply? At Berkeley students boldly advocated the principle of *co-gobierno*—joint government by students and faculties. This principle has effectively ruined the universities of Latin America, and no sensible person would wish to apply it to the United States. However, many forms of student participation are conceivable short of *co-gobierno*— student membership, for example, in boards of trustees, student control of discipline, housing and other non-academic matters, student consultation on curriculum and examinations. These student demands may be novel, but it is a little hard to argue that they are unreasonable. Yet most college administrations for years have rejected them with about as much consideration as Sukarno, say, would have given to a petition from a crowd of Indonesian peasants. The situation of college students today is like that of organized labor before the Wagner Act.

[As the docile] student generation of the fifties was passing away, John F. Kennedy and the civil rights freedom riders, then the Vietnam war stirred the campuses into new life. Still college presidents and deans, like Tom Girdler and Ernest Weir in face of the CIO in the thirties, ignored the signs of protest. The result inevitably has been to hand the initiative to student extremists who seek to prove that force is the only way to make complacent adminstrators and preoccupied professors listen to legitimate grievances.

The present spearhead of undergraduate extremism is that strange organization, or non-organization, called Students for a Democratic Society. Its Port Huron statement of June 1962, an humane and interesting if interminable document, introduced "participatory democracy"—that is, active individual participation "in those social decisions determining the quality and direction of his life"—as the student's solution to contemporary perplexities. In these years SDS performed valuable work in combatting discrimination and poverty; and this work generated a remarkable feeling of fellowship among those involved. But the Port Huron statement no longer expresses official SDS policy; and SDS itself has become an excellent example of what Lenin, complaining about left-wing communism in 1919, called "an infantile disorder."

This is not to suggest that SDS is communist, even if it contains Maoist and Castroite (or Guevaraite) factions. The official American Communist Party detests it—a feeling cordially returned by many SDSers, who regard the Communist Party as itself part of the System. . . . The basic thrust of SDS is, if anything, syndicalist and anarchistic, though the historical illiteracy of its leadership assures it a most confused and erratic form of anarcho-syndicalism. The anarchistic impulse extends to its organization—the infatuation with decentralization is so great that there is none (the joke is "the Communist can't take over SDS—they can't find it")—as well as to its program— the infatuation with the creative power of immediate action is so great that there is none.

Anarchism, with its unrelenting assault on all forms of authority, is a natural adolescent response to a world of structures. As a French student scribbled on the wall of his university at Nanterre, *"L'anarchie, c'est je."* But the danger of anarchism has always been that, lacking rational goals, it moves toward nihilism. The strategy of confrontation turns into a strategy of provocation, intended to drive authority into acts of suppression supposed to reveal the "hidden violence" and true nature of society. Confrontation politics requires both an internal sense of infallibility and an external insistence on discipline. Soon the SDS people began to show themselves, as one student put it to me, "exclusionary, self-righteous and single-minded. I feel that they (along with certain McCarthy people) are the one group that does not think that everybody should do their thing, but rather do the SDS thing." The Marcusian contempt for tolerance became in time a virtual rejection of participatory democracy. Professor William Appleman Williams of Wisconsin, whose own historical writing stimulated this generation of student radicals, ended by calling them "the most selfish people I know. They just terrify me. . . . They say, 'I'm right and you're wrong and you can't talk because you're wrong.' ". . .

At Columbia the SDS leaders displayed even less interest in negotiating the ostensible issues than the university administration. Their interest was power. Said Mark Rudd, the SDS leader,

If we win, we will take control of your world, your corporation, your university, and attempt to mold a world in which we and other people can live as human beings. Your power is directly threatened, since we will have to destroy that power before we can take over.

For the sake of power they were prepared, as a liberal Columbia professor put it, to "exact a conformity that makes Joe McCarthy look like a civil libertarian." After the Columbia putsch, Tom Hayden set forth the revolutionary future. The goal, he said, mimicking Che Guevara's pledge to "create two, three, many Vietnams in Latin America," was to "create two, three, many Columbias . . . to expand the strike so that the U.S. must change or send its troops to occupy American campuses. . . ."

As the SDS leaders get increasing kicks out of their revolutionary rhetoric, they have grown mindless, arrogant and, at times, vicious in their treatment of others. Their effect is to betray the function of the university, which is nothing if not a place of detached and unfettered inquiry, and to repudiate the western tradition of intellectual freedom.

Now SDS membership is an infinitesimal fraction of the 6 million students enrolled for degrees in American colleges. Yet this fact should not induce undue complacency in the country clubs. Many students who would never dream of joining SDS or of approving its tactics nevertheless share a sense of estrangement from American society. The number of student activists is very much larger than just the membership of SDS. This spring the Gallup poll reported that one student in five had taken part in protest demonstrations—a statistic which suggests not only that a million students may be counted as activists but that the proportion has probably doubled since the estimates of student rebels in the spring of 1966 as one in ten (Samuel Lubell) and one in twelve (the Educational Testing Service). All studies, moreover, indicate that the activists are good students, that they abound in the best universities and that they are, in the main, the sons and daughters of the relatively affluent.

What is significant is not just the rather large number of student activists today but their success in winning the tacit consent of the less involved. . . . For the activists very often appear to mirror the real if unspoken desires, or at least concerns and anxieties, of the majority on a wide range of issues, social and political as well as academic. . . . And when the activists turn on, the administrators at last begin to do things which, if they had any sense, they would have done on their own long since—as Columbia is revising its administrative structure for the first time (*The New York Times* tells us) since 1810. Commissioner Howe says: "Perhaps students are resorting to unorthodox means because orthodox means are unavailable to them. In any case, they are forcing open new and necessary avenues of communication." Both Berkeley and Columbia will be wiser and better universities as a result of the student revolts. One can hardly blame the president of the Harvard *Crimson* for his conclusion:

All the talk in the world about the unacceptability of illegal protest, all the use of police force and all the repressive legislation will not change the fact that attention is drawn to the evils in our universities in this way. As long as students have no legitimate democratic voice, attention is drawn only in this.

The students' demand for a "legitimate democratic voice" in the decisions which control their future is part of a larger search for control and for meaning in life. The old sources of authority—parents and professors—have lost their hold. Nor does organized religion retain much power either to impose relevant values or to advance the quest for meaning. Nominal affiliation has not faded away as much in American colleges as, say, at Cambridge University in England, where a recent poll showed 37 per cent agnostic or atheist, 35 per cent Christian and 27 per cent indeterminate. But religious belief in the traditional sense is no longer widespread in American colleges. A Catholic girl recently said that among students she knew "there definitely is no interest in any doctrine about the supernatural. The interest is in human values." The Radcliffe commencement prayer this June began: "We pray that You will hear us as we think about our graduation, even though we have trouble using the traditional language for talking to You and though many of us no longer feel a part of a religious community."

Finding so little sustenance in traditional authorities, students today have to evolve their own values. The determination of the most thoughtful is to live according to their own standards of authenticity. It is hard, however, to fix these standards with great confidence, because undergraduate mores are in a state of such constant flux. Students, like everyone else, are rushed along by the velocity of history. The electronic age produces, consumes and discards with extravagant speed. Television in particular accelerates certain forms of growth, or at least of knowing sophistication. As the Dean of Students at Northwestern put it, if Booth Tarkington were writing *Seventeen* today, he would have to call it *Eleven*. So, in contemporary colleges, students fresh from high school may become the pacemakers, with things to teach to seniors.

The search for meaning in life often takes forms which an older generation can only regard as grotesque or perilous. Thus drugs: a device by which, if people cannot find harmony in the world, they can instill harmony in their own consciousness.

The persons attracted to drugs [writes a student] were looking for a new dimension in life which, they believed, would expand their powers of creativity and enable them to pursue more fulfilling lives. They wished to leave an ugly and destructive society for a more beautiful, significant environment among people of non-competitive, non-political, non-material tastes.

To some it will seem blasphemous to regard drugs as a substitute for religion. Yet one can hardly doubt that William James, if alive today, would have included ecstatic states induced by drugs in his *Varieties of Religious Experience*. For many young people drugs offer the closest thing to a spiritual experience they have; their "trips," like more conventional forms of mysticism, are excursions in pursuit of transcendental meanings in the cosmos. This is why the young so much admire the conclusion of Stanley Kubrick's *2001: A Space Odyssey*—a conclusion which only bewilders the older generation.

The invasion of the life of the young by drugs is relatively recent; and it provides a good illustration of the intra-generational conflict. A venerable figure of 25, just out of law school, tells me,

When I was a freshman in 1960, drugs were really a fringe phenomenon. Today pot is *the* pervasive form of nightly enjoyment for students. How can parents understand this if a person like myself, hardly four years older than my sister, isn't able to understand it?

And a college junior says:

The newest generation of college students I already feel somewhat cut off from and scared of. Whereas we may be uncommitted, they have absolutely no conception of being committed and therefore don't worry about it. The problem is that they got into drugs while they were in high school, or even earlier. They may have lacked certain of the reser-

vations that we had. They may have lacked the sense of responsibility
which is so necessary in tackling serious problems. Perhaps therefore
they went too fast too soon. Anyway, I wonder what is left for them
when they get into college—what will be their kicks?

As for the drugs themselves, marijuana is a staple. It causes
little discussion in its purchase, use or non-use. On the large
campuses "everybody" has smoked it at one time or another;
or at least this is a common student impression. A more precise
estimate—from Dr. S. F. Yolles, director of the National Institute of Mental Health—is that about 2 million college and high
school students have had some experience with marijuana. Fifty
per cent of those polled said they had no effects. Presumably
most of the rest find in the chemical expansion of consciousness
an occasional means of relaxation or refreshment, as liquor is
for their parents. It is hard to persuade students (and many
doctors too) that "grass" is any more lethal than tobacco or alcohol; and parents achieving a high on their fourth martini are
advised not to launch a tipsy tirade against marijuana. Dr.
Yolles says of the student drug taker, "The academic standing
of the occasional user was better than average, while the heavily
involved drug user had lower than average scholastic grades."

LSD, on the other hand, is quite another matter, and its vogue
has notably waned in the last year or so. Students, reading about
its possible genetic effects and hearing about the "bad trips" of
their friends, simply reject it as too risky. College students, it
should be added, are very rarely hippies; when drugs begin to
define a whole way of life, students drop out, and studies go by
the boards. . . . But an interesting departure, reported from
Cambridge, Massachusetts, is the resurgence of simple, old-fashioned drinking. "Younger kids who really started right off with
grass often missed the whole alcoholic thing, and now they stop
you on the street and say wow they got drunk and what a trip
it was." No doubt this development will reassure troubled parents.

Love is another medium in which the young conduct their
search for meaning. Against Vietnam they cried: "Make love,

not war." "The student movement," one girl observed, "is not a cause. . . . It is a collision between this one person and that one person. It is a *I am going to sit beside you.* . . . Love alone is radical." The culmination of love is personal relations (or, as students, corrupted by their professors of sociology, prefer to say, "interpersonal" relations).

Here attitudes have relaxed, though it is not clear how much the change in sexual attitudes has produced a change in sexual behavior—to some degree, certainly, but not so much as some parents fear. A poll this spring at Oregon showed that 40 per cent of the unmarried women students had (or claimed) sexual relations. Dr. Paul Gebhard, who succeeded the late Dr. Alfred Kinsey as director of the Institute for Sex Research at the University of Indiana, observes that sexual relations among college students are "more fun nowadays," especially for women, and create less guilt. Unquestionably the pill has considerably simplified the problem.

No longer is it [again a girl is speaking] Oh, I can't sleep with anyone because sex is sinful or risky or whatever; it is, rather, Do I want to sleep with this person and, if I do, how will it affect me or the relationship? . . . The emphasis is on satisfying whole, friendly, honest relationships of which sex is only a part. Where sex is accepted as an extension of things, then nobody really talks about it that much, except as a pleasant thing.

The new naturalness has encouraged the practice known to deans as "cohabitation" and to students as "shacking up" or "the arrangement"—that is, male and female students living together in off-campus apartments. Rolling with the punch, colleges are now experimenting with coeducational student housing. Nearly half the institutions represented in the Association of College and University Housing Officers now have one form or another of mixed housing. What may be even more shocking to old grads is the vision of the future conveyed by the report that at Stanford the Lambda Nu fraternity proposes next year to go coed.

The new freedom of sex and drugs may be less depraved than it seems:

> We might take drugs and cohabitate and do other things which may have been looked down upon ten years ago [a junior says], but I think they are all done within a similar-type Puritan ethic. Action within this ethic has been enlarged while the ideology remains the same . . . the responsibility factor remains the same.

Though students today no longer find models, if they ever did, in parents, professors or pastors, though many seek fulfillment in their personal code of authenticity or in drugs or love, they have not abandoned heroes entirely. Nearly all regard John F. Kennedy with admiration and reverence. Many followed and then mourned his brother; many others followed Eugene Mc-Carthy (and cut their hair and beards in order to be "clean for Gene"); many like John Lindsay. . . . The testimony is general, however, that the old don't count for very much in the colleges. "The models for today's students," a sophomore writes, "probably come more from their contemporaries than any other group —the latest draft card burners, people with the guts to live the way they want despite society's prohibitions, etc.—or from older people who sympathize with them and give intellectual prestige to their feelings."

Above all, students find in music and visual images the vehicles that bring home reality. "THE GREAT HEROES OF THIS DAY AND AGE," a girl affirms in full capitals, "ARE BOB DYLAN AND THE BEATLES." Dylan "gave us a social conscience and then he gave us folk-rock and open honest talk about drugs and sex and life and memory and past."

As for the Beatles, "Well, they taught us how to be happy. We evolved with the Beatles." The evolution was from a simple happiness to a more complex form of sensibility—from the first Beatle songs, with their insistent beat, to the intricate electronic songs of today and their witty, ambiguous lyrics. "When you really listen to *Sergeant Pepper*, it can be an exhausting, amazing, frightening experience. Especially 'A Day in the Life' which is a hair-raising song because it is about our futures too and death."

What these heroes stand for, in one way or another, is the determination to affirm the integrity of the private self against the enveloping structures and hypocrisies of organized society. They embody styles of life which the young find desirable and admirable and which they seek for themselves. "Let there be born in us," the Radcliffe commencement prayer this year concluded, "a strange joy, that will help us to live and to die and to remake the soul of our time."

Yet college students have no easy optimism about the future. "When people talk about the future," one remarks, "they either talk of utopias, desert islands populated by their chosen friends, or revolution."

For the moment they are determined, in the words of the student orator at the Notre Dame commencement this year, not to be satisfied to "play the success game." More college graduates every year hope for careers of public and community service. The acquisitive life of business holds less and less appeal.

Mostly students [says one of them] know what they *don't* want to be: they don't want to be tied down to a hopeless, boring regimen; they don't want to give in to the establishment, after spending most of their youth avoiding it; they don't want to profit through special interest groups and to the detriment of people in need. Mostly they want to make the society they live in better, richer for all, more fun. The problem is that they lack the plans to accomplish the ends.

One can hardly doubt that a good many—perhaps most—of these defiant young people will be absorbed by the System. Hal Draper, an old radical musing on the 800 sit-inners arrested at Berkeley at the height of the Free Speech Movement, wrote, "Ten years from now, most of them will be rising in the world and in income, living in the suburbs from Terra Linda to Atherton, raising two or three babies, voting Democratic, and wondering what on earth they were doing in Sproul Hall—trying to remember, and failing."

One must hope for the sake of the country that some of this

fascinating generation *do* remember—not the angry and sense-less things they may have done, but the generous hopes which prompted them to act for a better life. But who can say?—certainly not their elders. Yet the attempt at understanding may even be a useful exercise for the older generation. I discovered this in talking to students for the purposes of this piece. And I treasure a note from one who patiently cooperated. "Even as I distrust anybody of the older generation who tries to write about the younger," the letter said, "I think it will be interesting to see how you figure it out."

HENRY STEELE COMMAGER

students in rebellion

**Neither an expression of original
sin nor the product of a conspiracy. . . .
they love the chains that bind them.**

. . . At its best, student revolt in America is characterized by idealism, at its worst by bad manners and violence, and
almost everywhere by an exasperating combination of logic and
irrationality. This is because it is directed not so much against
academic as against public grievances, not against ostentatious
injustices and oppression as against authority, traditionalism
and complacency.

At Columbia University it takes the form, largely symbolic,
of resistance to the building of a university gymnasium with
facilities for Negro children in a public park—a gesture which
the university itself had imagined to be one of friendship and
cooperation; at Northwestern it endorses the segregation of
blacks in their own dormitories—an arrangement contrary to
state laws against segregation; at Wisconsin and elsewhere it
is a protest against allowing military and corporation recruiters
on campus; at Rochester, and scores of other universities, it is
directed against the mindless acquiescence of the university in
the importunate demands of the military for the exploitation of
university resources and facilities. None of these issues is so in-
transigent that it might not yield to reason or to compromise;
none certainly seems pernicious enough to justify, scarcely even
to explain, the use of force. All of them have a common denominator: resentment against the readiness—indeed the eagerness—of the university to forget its traditional commitment to

the great commonwealth of learning, and to enlist in and assimilate to the political and military establishment.

Irrational as is the outburst of student discontent, the explosion of public disapproval is equally irrational and may be
more dangerous. To the public, as to the academy, the student
revolt is a traumatic experience, and the public reaction to it is
just as emotional as is the student reaction to university mal-
practices. What possesses the young, their elders ask. . . . We
have given them everything, parents assert—an expensive education; a four-year exemption from toil and responsibility, and
even from the military; a guarantee of a privileged position in
the American society and economy. And to what end? One segment of adult society sees in the student revolt nothing but ingratitude. Another looks upon it as somehow a rejection of law
and order and morality and a surrender to irresponsibility—a
wholesale license to indulge in LSD and sex. Still others darkly
suspect a Communist or a Black Power conspiracy. And everywhere there is angry resentment that the young should so shatter
our dream of happy and carefree college years, our vicarious
enjoyment of a youth we never had. And along with this is a
sense of guilt that somehow we have forfeited the confidence of
the young. . . .

Yet the student revolt is neither an expression of original sin
nor the product of a conspiracy, but an overvigorous and overdue assertion of a discontent that has been brewing for years,
and that has come to a head—as many things have come to a
head—with the Vietnam war.

First, it is a revolt against the anachronistic notion that the
university stands *in loco parentis* to students who are physically,
sexually, politically and perhaps even intellectually like any
other segment of adult society. There is considerable justice in
this complaint and logic in this protest. The university has persisted in the habit of acting *in loco parentis* long after the justification for it has disappeared. Yet if little is to be said for the
current practice, something is to be said for patience with the
liquidation of that practice and the working out of some new

formula. Universities do not, after all, act as parents out of sadistic instincts. The institution of *in loco parentis* is an ancient one, rooted in two centuries of our own experience with students who were, indeed, children and who required parental care. Thirteen or 14 was the customary age of entrance to college in the 18th century—and after. . . .

Gradually during the 19th century the age of students crept upwards, but colleges were not prepared to abandon the habits of generations and treat them as adults, nor were parents, who confessed a passion for the prolongation of youth unique to our own country. That passion lingers on: every politician speaks of "our boys" in Vietnam, and it never seems to occur to us that if they are indeed boys they shouldn't be there but in school.

Not only are college students kept in a state of pupilage; they are subjected to the indignity of being treated like high-school pupils, hedged in for four years by requirements of courses, credits, majors and minors, attendance, examinations, all of which are, in a sense, vestigial remains from the high school. They are fobbed off with professors who do not teach, or who teach not gladly but badly. They are often denied an effective voice—sometimes any voice—even in the conduct of their own affairs: the organization of student life, discipline, newspapers and journals, the choice of speakers, even the games they play.

Student reaction to all this is just as irrational as university policy. Students reject the parental role of the university but they reject, with equal vigor, the intrusion of the civil authority onto the campus. They defy university limitations on their drinking habits, sexual freedom, use of drugs, or privacy, but they are outraged at the notion that in all these matters they should be subject to the same disciplines, the same laws and the same penalties that apply to all other members of society.

Nor do most of them know what to do with student freedom when they have it. We have, in a sense, so corrupted them that they love the chains that bind them. They do not want freedom from the tyranny of courses, but more courses—courses, now, in sociology, now in the ghetto, now in Negro history, now in the

Vietnamese war. . . . They want to be part of the university enterprise, even to have representatives on board of trustees, but show little interest in the scientific and intellectual functions of the university—the library, for example, or laboratories—and little initiative in the cultivation of music and the arts.

Second, students are revolting against bigness—bigness which reduces the individual student to a computerized number, denies him access to professors, or even to his fellow students, weakens instead of strengthening his sense of individuality, and threatens to fit him into a kind of benevolent academic Brave New World. They are revolting against the university which . . . subjects them to inferior instruction from graduate students; which houses them in glorified barracks, or worse yet, houses some of them in fraternity and sorority houses and others in barracks—and wraps all of them in a cocoon of rules and regulations. Here, again, some of the fault is their own making. Students could insist on good instruction—or stay away from bad. They could, but do not, clamor to be housed in cluster colleges that are somehow manageable. They could certainly do away with the inequities and anachronisms of fraternity and sorority which mirror and even exaggerate the inequities and discriminations of secular life.

Third, students are protesting against what seems to them the irrelevance of much of the education imposed upon them—education justified chiefly by tradition, or by habit, or by the convenience of professors or, still more dubious, by the supposed requirements of the business community or of a government whose standards students do not respect.

So much for the discontents that concern the students themselves, discontents with the internal character and operations of the academy. But these, though they may be most pervasive, are not the most profound. Be it said to the credit of our students that what disturbs them most deeply are public rather than private wrongs; what chiefly alienates them from the university is not its failure as an educational institution, but as a public institution; not its intellectual miscellaneousness, but its moral obtuseness.

A great many students are indeed, in the fatuous phrase of their critics, alienated intellectuals, and they have much to be alienated from. They are alienated by the spectacle of the deep inequalities in a society dedicated to equality, and they are convinced that the academy shares responsibility for creating and perpetuating these inequalities. Now they demand, with a kind of desperate impatience, that the university make up for past sins and lost time: that it admit twice as many blacks as ever before, that it provide special tutoring and social facilities for them and concede them special privileges and power. They do not seem to realize that all this is a form of racism, nor that in their passion to do justice to the blacks they forget the many other neglected victims of our society and our economy.

They are ashamed that great urban universities have, for the most part, been content to go about their business without giving thought to their neighbors or neighborhoods, and they ask that the university abandon its isolation and its aloofness and take an active part in slum clearance, neighborhood rehabilitation, improvement of schools, legal aid and similar things.

To the argument that preoccupation with current and immediate problems will distract the university from concentration on future and general problems, they answer that the university is already using a large part of its resources on current problems—but on the wrong ones. For they are outraged by the readiness of the university to ally itself with the business, political and military establishment, to train businessmen and scientists prepared to serve corporations on almost any terms, to lend their intellectual resources and their academic facilities to almost any branch of the government or the military. . . . They remember that it was John Gardner who said that "when a government agency with money to spend approaches a university, it can usually purchase any service it wants," and they quote president Wallis of the University of Rochester to the effect that "universities have become important wheelers and dealers . . . (Their) role is in danger of becoming something like that of hotel keeper for transient scholars and projects.". . . They distrust, as well, professors who go whoring after lucrative contracts of power or prestige, who are prepared to serve almost any governmental agency . . . prepared even to accept limitations of secrecy in scientific research. . . .

Students know that their universities are under no more obligation to help the CIA recruit employes or to help Dow Chemical make money than they are to help authorities license cars or help *Playboy* get advertisements. And they listen, with undisguised cynicism, to university authorities invoking high-sounding principles like "an open campus" or "freedom of information" to defend policies that have no relation to either. Because they are young they cannot remember, and do not know, that in World War II every university cooperated with military and with government . . . and that no one then argued the impropriety of academic participation in the Manhattan Project, in radar, in the Office of War Information, the Office of Strategic Services, or in military government, nor, for that matter, the propriety of government recruiting on campus. They should be reminded of this.

[But] university authorities should not have to be reminded that they are not prisoners of precedent, and that there is a difference between a war which the entire community regards as involving the very survival of civilization and one which a major part of the community—certainly the academic community— regards as hateful and immoral.

Student rebellion, then, takes on a pattern quite different from that of most rebellions with which we are familiar. It is primarily a rebellion against conditions outside the campus—against practices which students regard as immoral: the war in Vietnam with its accompaniment of napalm and potentially lethal gas and concentration camps; vast expenditures for future wars at a time when the nation is starved for essential social services; the power of the military-industrial-labor-university complex which seems unlimited; racial discrimination and urban decay and police brutality; the cruel waste of human and of natural resources.

In other circumstances we would call this an idealistic protest. But the methods with which it is conducted are far from idealistic. What shall we say of these methods—the bad manners, the stridency, the destructiveness, of the student protest—but that it is deplorable, and not only deplorable but absurd. Students deplore violence violently; they use the arguments not of reason but of force to persuade the university to abandon the sponsorship of force and return to the path of reason. In the name of freedom they deny freedom of speech or of conduct to the majority of their fellow students. They call impatiently on government to cultivate patience and yet they champion tolerance with brutal intolerance. They are in short tiresomely inconsistent.

But let us keep in mind the wise words of the Rev. William Ellery Channing about the abolitionists: "The great interests of humanity do not lose their claims on us because sometimes injudiciously maintained." Injudicious may seem what Theodore Roosevelt once called a "weasel word," but the principle is the same, and students can retort that most of the words that come from trustees and university presidents are weasel words. Besides, those who are most vociferous in charging students with lawlessness and violence do not come into court with clean hands. Students can, and do, retort that it is their elders, and betters, who have set the examples that they now follow.

Who are you, they fairly ask, to counsel reason and moderation? Is it reason and moderation you have displayed in your policies toward Vietnam? Who are you to deplore violence, you who have poured more bombs on little Vietnam than were rained on either Germany or Japan during the last war! Who are you to plead the cause of law and order, you who are even now waging a lawless war with lawless weapons, violating the Charter of the United Nations and flouting international agreements on the uses of gas and of weapons of indiscriminate destruction!

Who are you to counsel patience, you who have displayed so little patience with Communist China, and who were so impatient to plunge into Santo Domingo with your Marines before there was any evidence of danger there! Who are you to counsel judiciousness, you who launched the Bay of Pigs attack on a sovereign nation, and who were prepared to condemn the world to a nuclear war at the time of the missile crisis!

Who are you to deplore with such anguish the flouting of civil laws, you who have flouted the provisions of the Fourteenth and Fifteenth Amendments for a century! Who are you to decry student intransigence about the draft, you who stood idly by while one half the states of the Union openly nullified almost every civil rights act on the statute books! Who are you to bustle about arresting draft resisters with such a show of outraged patriotism, you who failed so conspicuously to arrest Governors Barnett or Wallace when they resisted the decisions of the Supreme Court by force, and who have failed to enforce those decisions against a thousand others who defy them!

One violation of the law does not excuse others, but it is hypocritical of our society to insist on a double standard of morality—one for students, and another and very different one for government itself—and to deplore student violence as a prelude to revolution while standing idly by when local and state officials indulge themselves in open violence.

The answer to student protest and revolt is not hysteria and it is not suppression. Students have something to say—something important for all of us, and we should not deny ourselves the benefit of their protest or their advice because we do not approve of their manners. Nor should we take refuge in that habit of bewilderment and outrage that is the professional mark of the middle-aged. Let us take reassurance, rather, from the reflection that when older and more respectable elements of society were silent, students spoke up. . . .

IRVING KRISTOL

what's bugging them?

**A logic which proceeds from the
most exemplary democratic premises to
the most illiberal conclusions.**

No one, except perhaps a few college administrators, mourns the passing of "the silent generation." But it must be said in its favor that at least one knew what the American university students of the 1950s were silent about, and why. They were conformist for plain, indeed, obvious and traditional, conformist reasons. We may have been distressed and vexed by this conformism; we were not mystified by it; where as we are very much mystified by the nonconformism of the students of the sixties.

Many of the same middle-aged critics who so fervently and eloquently condemned the silent generation are now considerably upset and puzzled at the way students are "misbehaving" these days. One wanted the young to be idealistic, perhaps even somewhat radical, possibly even a bit militant—but not like this! It used to be said that the revolution devours its children. It now appears that these children have devoured this revolution.

What is it all about? One thing is fairly clear: the teach-ins, the sit-ins, the lay-downs, the mass picketing, and all the rest are not *merely* about Vietnam, or civil rights, or the size of classes at Berkeley, or the recognition of Red China. They are about these issues surely, and most sincerely. But there is, transparently, a passion behind the protests that refuses to be satisfied by the various topics which incite it. This passion reaches far beyond politics, as we ordinarily understand that term.

Anyone who believes the turbulence will subside once we reach
a settlement in Vietnam is in for a rude surprise. Similarly,
anyone who thinks of present-day campus radicalism as a kind
of overzealous political liberalism, whose extremism derives
from nothing more than youthful high spirits, is deceiving himself. What we are witnessing is an event *in* American politics,
but not *of* it.

Indeed, one of the most striking features of the new radicalism on the campus is that it is, in one sense, so apolitical. It
is a strange experience to see a radical mood in search of a
radical program; it is usually very much the other way around.
These young American radicals are in the historically unique
position of not being able to demand *a single piece of legislation*
from their government—their "platform" is literally without
one legislative plank. Their passion for "freedom now" co-
exists with a remarkable indifference to everything the United
States government is doing, or might do, in this direction.

If one read every campus leaflet published . . . and attended
every campus or off-campus demonstration, and knew only
what one learned from these sources, one would hardly be aware
that the Johnson Administration had enacted in the area of
civil rights the most far-reaching reforms in a century of legislative history. There has been no campus meeting to celebrate
the passage of the Civil Rights Act or the Voting Rights Act.
There has not even been any meeting criticizing these laws for
"not going far enough." It's as if nothing had happened—or,
to put it more precisely, as if whatever happens in Washington
has nothing to do with the world the students live and act in.

The same sort of thing is to be seen with regard to the war
on poverty, a topic upon which students will declaim passion-
ately and with unquestionable sincerity. But it seems that their
passion is so pure, their sensibility so fine, that these would
be violated by a consideration of anything so vulgar as how
to get more money into poor people's pockets. The recent increase in social security and the medicare bill made their way
through Congress without the benefit of so much as a benevolent

nod from the campuses. Whenever I have mentioned this legislation in conversation, I have received an icy stare of incomprehension and disdain, as if I were some kind of political idiot
who actually believed what he read in the New York *Times*.

Even in the single area where one would most except specific
and tangible proposals of reform, the organization of the multiversity, these have not made their appearance. For an entire
year the students of the University of California at Berkeley
have given dramatic evidence of dissatisfaction with their university experience—and does anyone know specifically what
they would like, by way of improvement? The university officials certainly don't know, nor do the regents, nor do the faculty.
Some outsiders *think* they know. Berkeley is too large, they
say, too anonymous; there is no possibility of a face-to-face
community of scholars, young and old. This is true enough.
But the Riverside branch of this same university is a small
liberal arts college, with great intimacy and comfort, and for
the past decade it has had much difficulty in attracting enough
students. They all want to go to Berkeley, and the reason, they
will explain, is: "That is where the action is."

The denunciations of the multiversity suspiciously resemble
the way New Yorkers excoriate "megalopolis"—having come
there in the first place, and determinedly remaining there, for
no other reason than that New York *is* a megalopolis. All
Americans will always insist that they adore small towns and
detest great cities, but the movement of population from towns
to cities remains strangely unaffected. And Berkeley, even today, has far more student applications than it can handle; one
might even say, *especially* today, for I understand that the
number of applications has, in fact, slightly increased.

No, the upsurge of left-wing sentiment and left-wing opinion
on the American campus today is not the sort of thing progressive parents and educators had in mind ten years ago when they
benevolently urged students to become "socially committed"
and "more idealistic." They naïvely wished them to have intelligent discussions of Vietnam, not to hurl insults and epithets

at Averell Harriman (as happened at Cornell), or tear up their
draft cards, or laud the Viet Cong. They wished them to be urbane and tolerant about sex, not to carry placards with dirty
words, or demand the sale of contraceptives in the college book-
store. They wished them to be concerned for civic and social
equality for the Negro, not to denounce "white America" as a
pious fraud, whose "integration" did not differ essentially from
South Africa's apartheid, or express sympathy with a mindless
(if occasionally eloquent) black nationalism. They wished—
they wished, in short, that their children be just like them, only
a wee bit bolder and more enlightened. Instead, these children
are making it very clear that being just like their parents, progressive or not, is the fate they wish most deperately to avoid.

And this, I think, is the crux of the matter. The new student
radicalism is so fundamentally at odds with our conventional
political categories because it is, above all, an *existentialist*
revolt. The term is unfortunately chic, and ambiguous, too. But
in this context it has a fairly definite meaning: the students are
in rebellion, not so much because things are bad for them, or
for others, but because things are what they are for them and
for others.

Clues to the meaning of this rebellion may be found in two
phrases that now appear ever more commonly in the left-wing
campus vocabulary. The first is "organized America." The second is "participatory democracy."

"Organized America" is, quite simply, America, and not, as
one might think, some transient bureacratic excrescence on the
body of America. As a matter of fact, today's students are immensely skillful in coping with bureaucracies and their paper
work. They fill out forms and applications with a briskness and
competence that startle the middle-aged observer. (I would
guess that no one over the age of forty could properly fill out
a college application form unless he received guidance from
some kindly youngster.) What bugs the students is not these
trivia but the society they emanate from—the affluent society,
welfare state and all. The liberalism (and the radicalism, too)

of the 1930s and 1940s has borne its fruit, and it tastes bitter to the children, setting their teeth on edge. That is why American students, amidst reasonably general prosperity and under a liberal Administration that is expanding the welfare state more aggressively and successfully than anyone had thought possible, feel more "alienated" than ever before. So many college students "go left" for the same reason that so many high-school students "go delinquent." *They are bored.* They see their lives laid out neatly before them; they see themselves moving ahead sedately and more or less inexorably in their professional careers; they know that with a college degree even "failure" in their careers will represent no harsh punishment; they know "it's all laid on"—and they react against this bourgeois utopia their parents so ardently strove for.

One of the unforeseen consequences of the welfare state is that it leaves so little room for personal idealism; another is that it mutes the challenge to self-definition. All this is but another way of saying that it satisfies the anxieties of the middle-aged while stifling the creative energies of the young. Practically every college student these days understands what is meant by an "identity crisis": it is one of the clichés of the sixties. It is not, perhaps, too much to say that mass picketing on the campus is one of the last, conclusive twitches of a slowly expiring American individualism.

American youth, however, has had one grand idealistic experience: the civil rights movement. This has been the formative experience for the activists of the 1960s; it is this movement that gave them a sense of personal power and personal purpose; and it is the civil rights movement which instructed them in the tactics of civil disobedience that are now resorted to at the drop of a hat. Unfortunately, the civil rights movement has had one great drawback: so far from being a proper "dissenting" movement, it had behind it the President, Congress, the courts, the laws of the land, and a majority of public opinion. This fact helps explain why the younger militants have constantly pushed the movement toward "extremes"—for example, demanding

utter, complete, and immediate *equality of condition* for the
Negro, as against mere equality of opportunity. Such equality
of condition is what "freedom now" has come to mean. And
since this demand cannot be fulfilled without repealing three
centuries of history . . . there is some satisfaction in such a
maneuver. The trouble is that the students do not know how
to fulfill this demand either, and are even running out of extremist slogans; which is why so many of them are receptive to
the idea of switching their attention to Vietnam, where they can
be more splendidly, less ambiguously, in "the opposition."

A second theme of student radicalism today . . . is the idea
of "participatory democracy." This is a vague notion, but a
dynamic one. It expresses a profound hostility toward, and
proposes an alternative to, everything that is impersonal, manipulative, "organized" in the American political process. Indeed,
many of these students simply dismiss American democracy as
a sham, a game played by the "power structure" for its own
amusement and in its own interests. *True* democracy, they insist,
can only mean direct democracy, where the people's will is expressed and legislated by the people themselves rather than by
elected representatives, most of whom achieve office by deceit
and retain office through the substantial support offered them
by the vested interests.

One is reminded by this of nothing so much as the Russian
Narodniki ("populists," our textbooks call them) of the end of
the nineteenth century. They, too, were largely middle-class
students who selflessly turned their backs on the careers the
Czarist bureaucracy offered them. They, too, "returned to the
people," leaving the fleshpots of Petrograd for the villages of
the interior, much as our students leave their comfortable homes
in New York or Chicago for Southern ghettos and slums. And
they, too, were hostile to the nascent liberal institutions of their
day, seeing political salvation only in a transformed and re-
deemed people rather than in improvements in any kind of system of representative government. It is also interesting to recall
that, though they were as individuals the gentlest and most

humane of their time, they nevertheless believed in the justice and efficacy of terrorism against the status quo and assassination against its spokesmen.

The analogy is, of course, very superficial: the United States today is not Czarist Russia of yesterday. But it is nevertheless illuminating, because it helps reveal the inner logic of the idea of "participatory democracy," a logic which proceeds from the most exemplary democratic premises to the most illiberal conclusions. Though few students these days learn it in their social studies course, the Founding Fathers of the American republic were exceedingly familiar with the idea of "participatory democracy"; as a matter of fact, this was what the word "democracy" usually meant prior to 1789. They rejected "participatory democracy" (they called it "direct democracy") in favor of "representative government" for two reasons. First, they didn't see how it could work in so large and complex a nation, as against a small city-state. Second, and more important, they thought it inconsistent with the idea of free government—that is, a government that respected the liberties of the individual. For participatory democracy requires that all people be fit to govern; and this in turn requires that all people *be made* fit to govern, by rigid and uniform educational training, constant public indoctrination, close supervision of private morals and beliefs, and so forth. No legislator can be as free as a private citizen, and to make all the people legislators is willy-nilly to abolish the category of private citizen altogether.

This, of course, is exactly what the Communists do, after their own fashion. They claim to exemplify a truer, more "direct," more "participatory," more "popular" democracy than is to be found in the representative institutions of the bourgeois West. The claim has a certain plausibility, in that regimes established by mass movements and mass revolutions certainly "involve the people" more than does any merely elected government. The semblance of "involvement" is perpetuated, as we know, through the mass organizations of the Communist state, and the fact that it is done under compulsion, and becomes more of a farce with every passing Communist year, is one of the inner contradictions both of the Communist system and of the myth of direct democracy itself.

These contradictions our left-wing students are not entirely unaware of. Though many of them are, to one degree or another, either pro-Communist or belligerently "neutralist," theirs is a very qualified and unconventional version of this attitude; which is why conventional anti-Communist propaganda tends to pass them by. They are, for instance, extraordinarily uninterested in the Soviet Union, and they become ever less interested to the degree that the Soviet Union liberalizes its regime —that is to say, to the extent that the Soviet Union becomes merely another "organized" system of rule.

What they seek is a pure and self-perpetuating popular revolution, not a "planned economy" or anything like that. And this is why they are so attracted to Castro's Cuba and Mao's China, countries where the popular revolution has not yet become "bourgeoisified." As for mass terror in Cuba and China—well, this actually may be taken as a kind of testimony to the ardor and authenticity of the regime's revolutionary fervor. Our radical students, like other radical students before them, find it possible to be genuinely heartsick at the injustices and brutalities of American society, while blandly approving of injustice and brutality committed elsewhere in the name of "the revolution."

Like other radical student generations before them, they are going to discover one day that their revolution, too, has been betrayed, that "organized society" is what revolutions establish as well as destroy. One hopes they will not be made too miserable by their disillusionment. One also hopes, it must be added, that they won't make *us* too miserable before that day arrives.

TOM HAYDEN

two, three, many columbias

Authentic opposition to the middle-class world of manipulation . . . and careerism. . . . The U.S. must either change or send its troops to occupy American campuses.

The goal written on the university walls was "Create two, three, many Columbias"; it meant expand the strike so that the U.S. must either change or send its troops to occupy American campuses. . . .

The American student movement has continued to swell for nearly a decade: during the semi-peace of the early '60s as well as during Vietnam; during the token liberalism of John Kennedy as well as during the bankrupt racism of Lyndon Johnson. Students have responded most directly to the black movement of the '60s: from Mississippi Summer to the Free Speech Movement; from "Black Power" to "Student Power"; from the seizure of Howard University to the seizure of Hamilton Hall. As the racial crisis deepens so will the campus crisis. But the student protest is not just an offshoot of the black protest —it is based on authentic opposition to the middle-class world of manipulation, channeling and careerism. The students are in opposition to the fundamental institutions of society.

The students' protest constantly escalates by building on its achievements and legends. The issues being considered by seventeen-year-old freshmen at Columbia University would not have been within the imagination of most "veteran" student activists five years ago.

Columbia opened a new tactical stage in the resistance movement . . . from the overnight occupation of buildings to permanent occupation; from mill-ins to the creation of revolutionary
committees; from symbolic civil disobedience to barricaded
resistance. Not only are these tactics already being duplicated
on other campuses, but they are sure to be surpassed by even
more militant tactics. In the future it is conceivable that students
will threaten destruction of buildings as a last deterrent to police
attacks. Many of the tactics learned can also be applied in
smaller hit-and-run operations between strikes: raids on the offices of professors doing weapons research could win substantial
support among students while making the university more blat-
antly repressive.

In the buildings occupied at Columbia, the students created
what they called a "new society" or "liberated area" or "commune," a society in which decent values would be lived out even
though university officials might cut short the communes through
use of police. The students had fun, they sang and danced and
wisecracked, but there was continual tension. There was no
question of their constant awareness of the seriousness of their
acts. Though there were a few violent arguments about tactics,
the discourse was more in the form of endless meetings con-
vened to explore the outside political situation, defense tactics,
maintenance and morale problems within the group. Debating
and then determining what leaders should do were alternatives
to the remote and authoritarian decision-making of Columbia's
trustees. . . .

The striking students were not holding onto a narrow conception of students as a privileged class asking for inclusion in
the university as it now exists. This kind of demand could easily
be met by administrators by opening minor opportunities for
"student rights" while cracking down on campus radicals. The
Columbia students were instead taking an internationalist and
revolutionary view of themselves in opposition to the imperialism of the very institutions in which they have been groomed
and educated. They did not even want to be included in the

decision-making circles of the military-industrial complex that runs Columbia: *they want to be included only if their inclusion is a step toward transforming the university.* They want a new and independent university standing against the mainstream of American society, or they want no university at all. They are, in Fidel Castro's words, "guerrillas in the field of culture."

. . . it is clear that the demands of black students for cultural recognition rather than paternalistic tolerance, and radical white students' awareness of the sinister para-military activities carried on in secret by the faculty on many campuses, are hardly confined to Columbia. Columbia's problem is the American problem in miniature—the inability to provide answers to widespread social needs and the use of the military to protect the authorities against the people. This process can only lead to greater unity in the movement.

Support from outside the university communities can be counted on in many large cities. A crisis is foreseeable that would be too massive for police to handle. It can happen; whether or not it will be necessary is a question which only time will answer. What is certain is that we are moving toward power—the power to stop the machine if it cannot be made to serve humane ends.

American educators are fond of telling their students that barricades are part of the romantic past, that social change today can only come about through the processes of negotiation. But the students at Columbia discovered that barricades are only the beginning of what they call "bringing the war home."

RUSSELL KIRK

beginning in doubt

Anyone who has done much boating [understands] that "Don't rock the boat" is a most necessary axiom.

Where will the present ferment among college students end? If one were to consider only outward phenomena, one probably would reply, "In private and public anarchy." Yet, as St. Paul put it, those who begin in doubt shall end in certitude.

Friends at Stanford University sent me a copy of a booklet or magazine entitled *Freshman Voices: Student Manners and Morals.* The contributors to this little volume all are first-year students at Stanford, and most of them (they write rather well, by the way) exhibit the attitudes of rebellion with which everyone has become familiar. Institutionalized rebellion, indeed, is the new conformity on many a campus.) One encounters among these essays the usual shallow preoccupation with experiment in sex, with LSD, and the like. But also one encounters something a great deal more nearly original: a serious questioning of the present intellectual domination of liberalism and rationalism. There is significant passage in a well-reasoned essay, "The Two-Culture Trap," by Mr. Jeffrey Harris:

". . . In all industrialized nations, but especially in the United States, rationalism is gradually becoming outmoded. By this I don't mean that the amount of knowledge is decreasing, or that the average IQ is slowly dropping; if anything the opposites are true. But I do believe that rationalism, as a single directive force in daily life, is becoming less important. This change is not due solely to human reactions against the

dehumanizing forces in rationalism and technology. Rationalism, having been too successful, is destroying itself."

Now the principal function of college and university, necessarily, is to develop the rational faculty. As Pascal said, nevertheless, "The heart has reasons that the reason does not know."
And a doctrinaire Rationalism, preached by latter-day Enlight-
eners as limited in their imagination as were many of the eigh-
teenth-century *philosophes,* offers little enough to the mind and
the heart of the generation now rising. So Mr. Harris, for one,
begins to perceive that rationalism and right reason are not
synonymous.

Another contributor to *Freshman Voices,* Mr. Don Farrow,
discusses "Influence of the Liberals." From a pre-college conservatism of complacency, he appears to have been converted,
in some degree, to the cause of protest. Still, he is not quite
satisfied that latter-day liberalism really possesses the answers:

"The protestors, by presenting the concepts most alien to us,
have made us understand ideas that before we would have flatly
condemned; we learn to overcome our initial prejudices, to
listen to the unusual. But because we are seldom challenged by
conservative arguments, and because we are detached from the
influence of our parents, we sometimes hold in contempt anyone who is traditional, or patriotic, or socially popular, and
we see ourselves as enlightened and our parents as ignorant.
It is easy to condemn society in college, and think yourself a
liberal. There are few people who will argue back. . . .

"The liberal stance is convincing, and most of us are convinced by it, but for many there is often the feeling that we are
being inundated with one point of view, that the more conservative side of each question is being hidden."

This is a canny surmise. Mr. Farrow seems to imply that the
questing intellects among the freshmen are not at all happy to
abide in the shadow-world of doubt for doubt's sake, of negation
for negation's sake; he recognizes that his generation may be
conceited:

"Our morals, or lack of morals, show our increasing conviction that there is nothing absolute or dependable in this world, that nothing is real and no purpose is valid unless we make it so and believe in it. There is no God, or if there is, the code that people attribute to him is only an invention of man. There is no country in itself worthy of patriotism, unless its ideals coincide with what we personally feel is just. And since Nuremberg, we even feel that a person must decide whether the laws are good and should be followed, or bypassed because they contradict what he believes is right."

Well! However naive some of these attitudes may be, the mood reminds this writer of St. Augustine's pursuit, through all the schools, of certitude—which at last he attained. (Augustine, so neglected today, perhaps has more to teach this age than has any other philosopher.) Justice cannot be apprehended by what one "personally feels"; it is necessary to know the norms of justice if one is to say anything sensible about the crimes which led to Nuremberg, for instance, or about the unjust character of the trials themselves.

Some degree of revolt against Daddy and Mommy must be expected among college undergraduates, nor is it unhealthy; but such skepticism, in the true university, should lead to normative understanding. Mr. Terry Barnett, in an essay called "Growing Up," remarks that "parents and other adults seem often to sacrifice moral objectives for material (and thus social) security. The warning, 'Don't rock the boat,' seems to be taken as axiomatic."

College students naturally challenge platitudes. Yet most platitudes are true: that is why they have become platitudinous. Anyone who has done much boating, for instance, comes to understand that "Don't rock the boat" is a most necessary axiom. Test all things, says St. Paul. But only a liberal ideologue, smug in his secular dogmas, will think it well to remain forever unmanned by Doubt as an end.

HAROLD TAYLOR

riots, wars and american education*

**Universities have . . . lost their
intellectual and moral identity.**

The universities have become corporations for producing, transmitting, and marketing knowledge, and in doing so
have lost their intellectual and moral identity. At the time that
they should have been creative centers for the development of
strategies for peace, disarmament, and world unity, they were
busy with Defense Department contracts. When the educational
problems of the Negro were getting worse by the day, they were
busy making admission requirements more and more favorable
to the white middle-class student from privileged environments.
It is no wonder that a new generation of students, trained by
the mass media to detect events in the world of affairs and
conscious of the visible flaws in their society and its educational
system, has risen to challenge the aimlessness and the intellectual lethargy of the big university in America.

I do not see how the university president and the university
faculty member can . . . absolve themselves from responsibility
for defining the aims of their society and the function of their
institutions. Where were the university presidents when Joseph
McCarthy was terrorizing the country with his lies, charges, and
threats? They were closeted with their trustees, working out
the most efficient ways to get rid of radicals and liberals in the
faculty. Where were they when their students, the clergy, the

* From an address.

scientists and the citizens, and the intellectuals of the world, were resisting the war policy of the United States in Vietnam? They were closeted with their deans, working out the best way of getting rid of the students who burned their draft cards and demonstrated against the war. . . .

A 1968 statement by President [Grayson] Kirk of Columbia University, a former professor of international relations, was the first we have seen from a university president suggesting that there was anything wrong with our war policy. But even this statement was flawed at the center, where its moral impulse should be, when Dr. Kirk argued that "it is not possible for us to derive from this conflict, no matter how it is finally settled, enough long-range benefit to the security and welfare of our country to justify the effort we have made or may be called upon to make."

What an argument! Apparently if we could gain more benefits by killing more people, devastating more villages and destroying more of Vietnam, we should go right ahead with the war.

But then, Dr. Kirk's argument extends to the faults of the younger generation which is protesting against his kind of thinking. "Our young people," he says, "in disturbing numbers appear to reject all forms of authority, from whatever source derived, and they have taken refuge in a turbulent and inchoate nihilism whose sole objectives are destructive. . . ."

If the university and its present leadership fails to act, to [try to] stop the war, to reform the archaic curriculum, to grant legitimate student rights, to take its students seriously, to take a stand against racism and racial injustice, then what else can serious people do, students or anyone else, than to move beyond acquiescence into protest and resistance? This country is lucky to . . . have a strong and vocal body of young activists who understand the nature of their society and who won't put up with it.

The power of the social and intellectual force within the new generation of students has been greatly underestimated by educators and the public, who have tended to think of . . . activists . . . concerned with civil rights and world affairs as a general nuisance, a motley group of radical dissidents, draft-dodgers, or young rebels who will soon get over it. On the contrary, what we have is a new and significant national asset. . . . The core of the student protest movement is composed of a serious and informed body of young people who act out of a sense of personal commitment to each other and . . . compassion for those who have been blocked from a place in society. They care very much for the quality of their own lives and are sensitive to the effects of their acts on the lives of others. They are responsible critics of the society and its educational system, and the best of them have a political sophistication and social energy which is in advance of many of those appointed to educate them. . . .

WILLIAM F. BUCKLEY, JR.

the responsibilities of the student*

Self-control is one of the most exhilarating of pleasures.

At a recent national convention of the Young Americans for Freedom, a boisterous and happy gathering of the kook-free right wing (which is where my own heart is) advanced several brave resolutions, in the spirit of the general radicalism of the day, one of them calling for the repeal of the minimum wage laws on the grounds that they can be demonstrated to be anti-Negro in effect. The other calling for the repeal of the progressive feature of the income tax, on the grounds that it can be shown to violate the spirit of the Fourteenth Amendment. Such proposals tend to shock those who have been brought up in the certitudes of the New Deal. But there is a lot of ice being broken these days, and it isn't by any means a foregone conclusion—is it?—that the great thaws will bring only left-minded reforms. Who would have thought only a few years ago, when everyone was called upon to laugh out loud at Barry Goldwater, that the Postmaster General in a Democratic Administration would be calling, as Mr. O'Brien has now done, for turning over the postal system, in effect, to private enterprise?

Then there was the meeting of the National Students Association. The earlier revelation that over the years the NSA had taken funds *sub rosa* from the CIA put its young officials in an agonizing position, it being generally assumed that when the

* From an extemporaneous speech.

government puts up money, it expects a *quid pro quo*. Could it be that during all those years the NSA had done something— *patriotic?* The thought was too horrible to live with, and it was widely expected that as an act of expiation, the NSA would hurl itself into extinction.

It did not do that, to the apparent regret of the Students for a Democratic Society, who feel that the NSA is not sufficiently revolutionary. The conservative caucus also desired to put an end to the NSA. Its point was that the NSA is unrepresentative of the American student community—for which demonstration I believe I speak for the entire non-student community in expressing profound gratitude—and that the original purpose of NSA was to furnish services for students, whereas in fact NSA tends to get its kicks from wandering around the world big-thinking about America's shortcomings.

The third position prevailed: that NSA would continue, that its ambition is to "work out a style of life that lets you stay honest and revolutionary and eating and effective after the first hot flushes of puppy radicalism." As I understand it, NSA hopes to make the world safe for radicalism. And a spokesman made it very clear that the exclusivist radicalism of the SDS is, somehow arrogant; in a way, undemocratic. "Man," he said to an SDSer, "I'd like to work with you. But if you think you are more radical and noble and pure and incorruptible than I am, forget it."

The NSA is thus seen by one student organization as having become bourgeoisified. And that even though the NSA endorsed black power as "the unification of all black peoples in America for their liberation *by any means necessary.*" By any means necessary" was understood by *The New York Times* and by me —and that makes a solid majority—as including force and violence if necessary, which makes it of course interesting that there hasn't been any such resistance to that phrase as for instance was summoned against the relatively modest suggestion of Mr. Goldwater at San Francisco that extremism in defense of liberty is no vice. . . .

Some students wish to express their contempt of the policies of the NSA by that conclusive disdain of ignoring it even to the point of declining to agitate for its reform or elimination. Now the primary responsibility of the student, surely, is intellectual. On that proposition most liberals and most conservatives would unite. But have you noticed the arresting similarity in the positions of radical leftists and conservatives on the proposition that mere positivist educational attainments are not enough, that they do not describe the *ultima* ratio of education? The old, and still serviceable formulation is: Education for what? The radicals at the University of California go so far as to say, even as the Marxists do, that education unharnessed to revolution is pure frivolity, that the university is merely the place where one happens to be at a particular moment in one's personal history, whence to wage revolution, and that therefore the sophisticated student is the student who turns to the advantage of the revolution whatever special weapons he finds himself able to dispose of in virtue of his situation at a university. The university, to the radical leftist, is less a place where one pauses to learn the imperatives of humility than a place where organization is easy because of the general congestion and the exploitability of idealistic impatience and, most of all, a place where one can reasonably expect that all one's revolutionary posturings will be faithfully recorded by local TV and, if the PR is right, by *Life* magazine's inquiring photographers.

The conservative student, as I understand it, agrees with the revolutionary to the extent of insisting that there must be a purpose in education that goes beyond the acquisition of intellectual skills and knowledge. The purpose of education, Mr. Russell Kirk has said, is to enable us to apprehend moral norms —what is enduringly right and enduringly wrong—by intellectual means.

There was a day, but it is past now, and is likely to be forever behind us, when social units were small enough to permit the individual an effective withdrawal from the life of the community. . . . Politics, it has been said, is the preoccupation of the quarter-educated, and I do most solidly endorse that observation, and therefore curse this century above all things for its having given all sentient beings very little alternative to occupying themselves with politics. It is very well to say that we will ignore the Great Society. But will the Great Society repay us our courtesy by ignoring us? How is it possible, therefore, for a man sensitive to the sufferings of others to devote himself wholly to his and his family's private concerns?

No such freedom exists nowadays, which is the exclusive reason, surely, to deplore this century's most distinctive aggression, which is against privacy, publicly understood. Move your ashtray from here to there, and in this century there are vibrations born that rattle the bones of other men far, far away. Fail to bestir yourself in foreign policy, and you fail to bring hope to desperate people. Decline to talk back to the editor of your newspaper, and you will find before long that he is reaching into your very living room to regulate the temperature of your life. Students who accept passively the strictures of their textbooks will find that they are indulging not abstract arguments relating to other people in other times, but terribly concrete arguments binding on their own life and their own thought. Mr. Norman Mailer can counsel us to an existentialist permissiveness; but soon we recognize that thrill-seeking is a tedious, strategic substitute for the headier pleasures of duty and restraint, of order and peace, of self-discipline and self-cultivation. Mr. Jack Kerouac and his apostles at Haight-Ashbury and Millbrook, New York, can counsel us to go on the road and to drop out and anesthetize our senses; but to do that is right away to acknowledge that we are refugees, seeking the privacy of the Flying Dutchman.

What, then, are the responsibilities of the American student? My list is not comprehensive, but any list should, I think, touch on the following points.

1. In his book, *The Revolt of the Masses,* Ortega identified the distinguishing feature of modern man, which is his utter incomprehension of the extent of his indebtedness to other people. Ortega's point is platitudinously recalled here and there,

mostly in an economic context, as when the local bore from the
NAM reminds us of the iniquitous reliance by the few on the
sweat of the many—a point worth making, mind you, but a
point so often made without reference to the fuller implications
of it. There is every reason for the weak relying on the strong.
Who else are they expected to rely upon? But why is it that the
strong feel the need to rely upon the weak? In purely economic
terms, that is what the monopoly labor unions do when they
drive up wages at the expense of those who are not competitively
equipped to rise with the union scale. At an economic level that
touches on education, you see the students in New York and
California angrily denouncing proposals that they contribute
to the cost of their own education, even when it is demonstrated
that taxi drivers and elevator operators would be thus relieved
of a part of the burden of supporting them. At another level, a
law student writes: "Too often we have thrust upon us the notion that society owes us something, the notion that we must do
nothing, accomplish nothing to justify our existence." That is to
finger, surely, the first responsibility of the student, to give back
not as good as he gets—in this sense he is, providentially, the
eternal beneficiary, who cannot possibly give back as good as he
gets. In a single library shelf, students have access to the work
of Aristotle and Plato; of Milton and Shakespeare; of St. Augustine and St. Thomas, and Eric Voglen. How can any of us expect
to repay in kind? We repay not by suggesting that what we can
contribute to our culture is equal to what our culture has vouchsafed to us. We contribute most by recognizing the extent of our
patrimony. The principal contribution we are in a position to
make as individuals to the commonweal is the recognition of
other individuals' superiority to ourselves. The mere acknowl-
edgement of that superiority is ennobling; sets us apart, paradoxically, from our bumptious fellow men. Gives us the vantage
point whence, simultaneously, to judge our own limitations, and
our own potentialities, and the acutest needs of the world we
live in.

2. Concerning their teachers, the student does owe them, I

think, (a) the respect which is due them in virtue of their academic achievements; and (b) a courteous skepticism concerning the ideological pretensions of those who have ideological pretensions. The best way for a student to treat an arrogant teacher is to patronize him. The teachers who most need patronizing are those who patronize the ideals of this country. I suggest that students train their ears to distinguish between criticisms which are reformist in character, and those others which suggest an ignorance of, or even a hostility to, the essential American propositions; between those teachers whose criticisms are less in the spirit of Martin Luther than in the spirit of Lee Harvey Oswald, whose hatred of America is finally justified only by the ineradicable fact that America did, indeed, produce Lee Harvey Oswald.

The point I make should be stressed if only because (3) I do think that it is among the responsibilities of students to meditate on the fact of their being Americans. As distinguished from, say, Chinese, or Yugoslavs, or even Frenchmen. This presupposes a knowledge of history. The abstraction that, in search of higher education, students are catapulted from any bonds to their fellow Americans and graduated into a supra-national elite is UN talk, i.e., silly. Our culture is not merely a drag upon our intellectual development. It is the likeliest source of our intellectual animation as believable human beings. It isn't parochial for us to proceed with the conviction that it makes a *difference* that the blood of Thomas Jefferson and James Madison, of Lincoln and Emerson, of Thoreau and Theodore Roosevelt runs through our veins, as indeed it does even in those of us who arrived only yesterday as immigrants from Transylvania. There is no such thing as a universality of outlook so total as to deprive us of the meaning of our own experience as Americans. The more we know, the more greatly relevant we will discover our nationhood.

4. It is students' responsibility to insist as best they can that reason be reintroduced to all discussions, especially those most highly vexed by passion. It might be contended that here is the

principal contribution of conservatism, as formally understood, to the commonweal. And that is true even though conservatism sharply distinguishes itself from Rationalism, which is a fanatical application of one, but only one, of the strengths of conservatism, namely reason. Rationalism, as Professor Oakeshott says, is making politics as the crow flies.

The principal problems of our time are, paradoxically, political, rather than natural; i.e., man-made, rather than nature-made. If the time and capital currently being spent on the manufacture of bullets were spent instead on food and education, there would be no hunger, no illiteracy. But who would surrender his bullets for an extra loaf of bread when the barbarians are on the prowl? Politics is the great spendthrift of human energy, and yet it may be said to have done more harm than good. It took government to transform *Mein Kampf* into Buchenwald, *Das Kapital* into concentration camps.

To some people [Oakeshott observes], "government" appears as a vast reservoir of power which inspires them to dream of what uses might be made of it. They have favorite projects, of various dimensions, which they sincerely believe are for the benefit of mankind, and to capture this source of power, if necessary to increase it, and to use it for imposing their favorite projects upon their fellows, is what they understand as the adventure of governing men. They are, thus, disposed to recognize government as an instrument of passion; the art of politics is to inflame and direct desire.

Now, the disposition to be conservative in respect of politics reflects a quite different view of the activity of governing. The man of this disposition understands it to be the business of government not to inflame passion and give it new objects to feed upon; but to inject into the activities of already too passionate men an ingredient of moderation; to restrain, to deflate, to pacify and to reconcile; not to stroke the fires of desire, but to damp them down. And all this, not because passion is vice and moderation virtue, but because moderation is indispensable if passionate men are to escape being locked in an encounter of mutual frustration.

Twenty-year-old Rachelle Diner writes in the daily bulletin issued during a National Student Association congress:

The Purple Gang has come to the Congress. Have you heard them? They came in from Detroit to show us just how angry they are, and just how impossible it is for us to help them. I said to them: "Just *tell* us what to do. Tutorials? Organize white folks." And they say: "Don't push us in that trick bag, man." "*What* trick bag?" I asked them. "Should we pass a 'let's run guns to the ghetto' resolution?" You really ought to talk with the kids from Detroit, check it out, check it out a couple of times. They've got opinions about just about everything, and they know what they want, and they want it *now*. Try to persuade them that things are going to change—"I've been waiting 200 years, baby. I been praying, and picketing, and sitting-in and legislating, and getting on school boards, and nothing changes. But now I'm going to burn. Burn down my side of town. And they're going to come in with their housing projects and shuffle me around. They'll build it *up* again and I'll tell you something, baby, we'll burn it down again."

"And," the perceptive young lady of the NSA concludes, suggesting that sense of helplessness with which the whole country is stricken, these people "don't sit around and talk. They walk around, and shout, and put you down, and run you through changes, and you come out excited. Maybe you're turned off. But let's try to talk truth, shall we? Our tutorials are nice. And all our programs, from Upward Bound to JOIN and back are nice. . . . But there's a war on in this land."

That's right, there is, and Professor Oakeshott, who wrote away back before Watts, in 1962, knows why. Even as St. Augustine knew why when he wrote, in his own less hectic context, about the limitations of the City of Man. Surely among the responsibilities of students is not merely to enlist in crusades for the benefit of mankind, but also to enlist in crusades for the advancement of knowledge concerning the limitations of crusades. "Where activity is bent upon enterprise," Oakeshott brings his analysis to a sublime analytical climax, "the indispensable counterpart is another order of activity, bent upon restraint. . . . Rules about which we are not disposed to be conservative are not rules, but incitements to disorder; the conjunction of dreaming and ruling generates tyranny."

And(5) I suppose my remarks must mention, under the strain

of the stimulations of the day, the necessity not only to regulate our political appetites, but also our other appetites. There are the conventional temptations. Sex, booze, drugs, iconoclasm, each one of them potentially a killer, emotionally, physically, intellectually, unless practiced with reference to standards defined outside the demands of our senses. Don Giovanni died not only painfully, but a nervous wreck, for the knowledge that there was someone somewhere whom he had not seduced. A student pusher writes that he lives in nervous apprehension lest the drug exists which he has not tasted. I lie sleepless at night worrying that I might die before having the opportunity to incur just one more disapproval from *The New York Times*. It is all quite pointless, isn't it? And one has, at a university, a chance precisely, as Russell Kirk tells us, to stock up on the intellectual arguments with which to apprehend the moral norms, one of them being that self-control is one of the most exhilarating of pleasures. I can't say that I envy students—so much to do, so many confusing people like myself to hector them along the way. And so very necessary to enjoy themselves as they go, and this surely (6) is a paramount responsibility: their responsibility to find pleasure; and there is nothing to match the sensation of discovering one's own powers, of sensing some of the magic excitement that generated the very idea of America, of feeling a little of the spiritual consolation that comes with the knowledge that we are not alone, that the Lord of Hosts is with us yet.

EDWARD SCHWARTZ*

what we want—
and why

**Exclusion from responsibilities
is a poor way of encouraging us to
accept them. . . . the essence of . . .
our sense of defining ourselves may be
the taking of risks.**

. . . We have been weaned on two paradoxes: Our
affluence enables us to assume less responsibility for our lives
than did our parents for theirs in the Depression, but our freedom encourages us to demand more responsibility; the questions
which are the most critical to our lives, to the lives of all people,
are those over which individual men in a mass society can exercise little control. The attempt to resolve these paradoxes—of
obtaining responsibility in a context of freedom; of asserting
power in a climate of powerlessness—has been the central thrust
of all major student movements. . . .

To begin, how do our elders relate to us? If there is anything
which unites students of all persuasions, it is the college administrator or public official who challenges the sense, the responsibility, the interest, or the ability of the student himself. I have
seen college presidents whose political positions were in substantial agreement with those of a student body lose all support
from students simply because they talked down to them, or tried
to pander to them, or refused to listen to them. . . . Conversely,
I have seen administrators whose public and political positions
differed markedly from those of their students win enormous

* Formerly President, National Student Association.

student support by demonstrating a willingness to take students seriously, to listen to their demands, to present clear statements of disagreement, to convey a sense that they were trying to learn from what the students are saying. . . .

A society which worships youth inevitably will produce people who are afraid of the young—afraid of not "making it" with the young. The rest is defense—assertions of legal authority, polemical attacks on irresponsibility, snide references to appearance and dress; or, as often, feeble attempts to ingratiate, to play Boy Scout leader, to use "hip" language which the elder does not really understand. When a student encounters either specimen of elder, he turns himself off. If the elder is a tyrant, he spawns a revolution; if he becomes a boy scout leader, he is ridiculed. . . . The elders who "make it" with students are those without hang-ups in dealing with them, those who look upon a student as a potential friend and who are willing to open relationships with students on that basis. . . .

Students are aware of the fact that . . . not every professor can be a Demosthenes. What they do expect, however, is that some sense of the scholar's enthusiasm for his subject be transmitted in the particular way in which the individual teacher is capable of presenting it. When professors read verbatim from ancient lecture notes, or when they refuse to discuss material with their students, they reinforce an impression that while the professor may care deeply about his subject, he does not care about his students. . . .

Most students do not view "education" as being simply the time spent memorizing somebody's lectures for an exam. The period between eighteen and twenty-three years is fundamentally a time of clarifying who we are, how we behave, what our relationship is to other people, what kinds of responsibility we can handle, what our functional roles can and will be. Classrooms, at best, are resource banks for this exploration—centers to obtain information; to learn tools of evaluation; to reflect on what others have said about the inherent qualities of nature, man, and society.

Yet the process of integration, of developing selfhood, is the critical process, and we feel that this can proceed only in a climate of personal testing. The university may be a special sort of community, but it is, nonetheless, a community, and we like to feel that we play "adult" roles in shaping its environment and policies. Insofar as forces inhibit our freedom, or prevent our participation, opportunities to test our capacities as citizens are lost.

However, demanding that option to make our own decisions—and our own mistakes—runs counter to the educational theory which holds that young people are not "ready" to do certain things, are not "ready" to play certain roles. Yet even if we are not "ready"—whatever that means—most of us feel that exclusion from responsibilities is a poor way of encouraging us to accept them. University administrators often say, "Wait until you leave here." Yet we know that those who do not demand responsibility at a college level will not demand it later in life. . . . Consequently, the student power cry is a cry for selfhood. Although the dormitory issues, the curfews, student finances, the independent student press, the boy-girl questions seem trivial issues in their own right, they are important as symbols of areas in our lives which test selfhood and self-expression. . . .

Students used to say, "Liberalize rules." Now they demand, "Let us make the rules.". . . The former shows no concern for community decision-making—it is a cry for personal freedom; the latter presumes that the right to make the decision is the goal. Both demands involve a quest for greater responsibility, but "student power" is much more an existential plea for self-respect and for respect from the establishment.

On those campuses where educational policy has become an issue, invariably the conflict has been between those who confine education to transmission of knowledge, development of analytical skills, and those who view the process as being necessarily broader. . . . Most students are not demanding a curriculum dealing entirely with current problems or social issues. What "relevance" means, more often than not, in student curricular theories, is personalization: How does the curriculum fit in with my personality development, with my ability to solve problems, with the questions which I am asking about myself and the world around me? Do professors care about these things? These concerns spring from classrooms in which students are not challenged, or engaged in the subject, and in which subjects are not related, even peripherally, to human enterprise.

Students are doers, and we want to learn to act more effectively. We need power in the extra-curriculum; we need involvement in the curriculum. It is useless to tell a young person not to take risks; the essence of our youth, of our sense of defining ourselves, may be the taking of risks, of assuming new roles, of testing ourselves in different environments, of experimenting with new ways of changing others. The institution of the university is our laboratory for these experiments. It either accords the space and resources for them, or it does not. When the university does not, we will attempt to free the space for ourselves, even if this means challenging the institution itself.

The involvement of students in political and social causes must be seen in this framework as well—that of freeing space for learning and action; of defining rules; of asserting selfhood and responsibility. A basic question is: Should students participate in politics at all? For those who think the answer is an obvious "yes," it may come as a surprise to learn that this has been a hotly contested issue on many campuses. [And] it will still be years before the majority of American colleges and universities call themselves "activist.". . . The student who does become involved politically has chosen a new identity for himself; he is functioning in an unexplored area in which fresh information, untried skills, and new energy are needed. If he is serious about his new interest, the route to political activity will mean an extensive reading list, a change in his course schedule, and a willingness to expose himself to the risks of argument, debate, attack. Students take politics seriously, and if there are those who remain uninvolved, fear of failing to meet understood prerequisites of political action often is the cause. Our elders often do not ask such questions; their political activity more frequently reflects personal interests than it does any conscious decision to undertake a new position in society.

Despite conflicts over the "role" of students in politics, there are few issues which will unite students. . . . Most students support lowering the voting age to eighteen; students have been united around maintenance of free tuition in New Jersey, New York, and California; students oppose state interference in local university affairs and will demonstrate surprising unity when such interference produces loss of university funds, repression of political groups on campus, or bans on speakers. Indeed, on some of these questions, the unwillingness of students to "dirty" themselves in politics contributes to their hostility to political interference in the university. There may be as great an underlying sense that "these dumb politicians shouldn't muck around with our lives" as there is an intuitive loyalty to their institution or to civil liberties. . . .

The two central issues of the decade—civil rights and Vietnam—have both involved America's response to cultural deviation, at home and abroad. For the student who himself is engaged in self-definition, the culture's repression of those who do not "toe the middle-class line" is seen as directly related to the culture's attitude toward him. One rarely hears students talk of "poverty" with the same fervor as they talk of the "black people," or the "Vietnamese people." Stokely Carmichael to the contrary, students have not tried to organize among whites, rich or poor.

This willingness to defend those who deviate from mass oppression creates its own standard for political leadership. The liberal-left knows that dissidents are powerless, but the important criterion is the sustenance of the dissident community. . . .

After all the rhetoric, extensive ideological bombast, the fellow on the left will tell you that he is dreadfully afraid of becoming "co-opted," of being sucked up by the suburbs, by IBM, by the machine. He fights this with fervor. Those who "play ball with the system"—who work for candidates, who talk to government officials, who dress up occasionally—are untrustworthy. In the end, the left argues, the liberal will sacrifice his battle for cultural freedom, for himself, the blacks, and the Vietnamese in exchange for a comfortable position in society. Indeed, the left may feel that the liberal cannot understand the people for whom he presumably fights, since the liberal does not deviate from cultural norms himself. . . .

When the debate is applied to specifics, it becomes quite brutal. The left will strive to differentiate itself from the mass; the liberal will try to point out areas within the American tradition which support his case and try to build upon them. The left will use confrontation tactics almost on principle, with the goal of "shocking" the mass; the liberal will try to avoid these tactics, almost on principle, from fear of "antagonizing" the mass. The left talks of "destroying" the system; the liberal talks of rebuilding it. . . .

The liberals are, indeed, products of their own tradition. They are responding to failures of American society to cope with the problems of the cities and with the emerging nations around the world, and hoping for the "right" leadership to influence public policy in the "right" directions. The left sees America's response to the problems of cities and developing nations as being generically related to America itself—to its culture, its values, its attitudes, which may coerce the majority as effectively as its own minorities, and minorities elsewhere.

If electoral politics seems inadequate to the left, it is because the nature of the problem which they perceive cannot be solved simply through new leadership; it will involve a transformation of institutions from the ground up. That the radicals have not found a coherent strategy to effect this transformation reflects as much the nature of the problem as it does their own emotional hang-ups. For some, moreover, outlines of a strategy of long-term organizing in ghettos, universities, suburbs, and corporations are developing, which might pull the liberal community along with it.

These, then, are the concerns—developing relationships with

adults based on attitudes of mutual respect; developing communities of learning in which people's ability to act and experience is deemed as important to growth as their ability to absorb information and to decide; and developing a tolerance for cultural pluralism in this country and abroad. While the issues—as well as the tactics—vary from year to year, the themes have been constant, and probably will remain so as long as our mass institutions remain mass. . . .

I have not even used the traditional terms of liberalism—jobs, education, housing, welfare—because these are not the problems which students face. The problems are deeper than that, involving the structure and values of mass culture, and if we cry out, it is because the beast is difficult to move. . . .

McGEORGE BUNDY

---

faculty power*

**The heart of the matter today is
political.**

... The man who would describe the American university today must share with W. S. Gilbert's major general a pretty taste for paradox. It is richer and stronger than ever, holding a role of constantly growing importance, both as an institution and through its members, in determining the course of society. Yet it is also poor and weak; its financial requirements have never been greater, and both from inside and outside it is subject to pressures without precedent. The academic profession has never been more highly rewarded or more divided. The eagerness of the student to get in is matched only by his energetic discontent after he makes it. The government itself at every level appears to alternate between lavishness and callous unconcern —and also between hostility and dependence. Policemen may vent their frustrations on uncivil and disobedient students in the same season that their superiors are seeking the help of the university for new patterns of police education.

These are not merely surface phenomena. Behind all these paradoxes there is a deep uncertainty among us about two fundamental elements in the structure of the university—its economics and its politics. ...

In economic terms the American university is as certain to grow and to flourish as the best growth stock of the best-managed company. Within that great certainty, of course, there are hundreds of doubts, at least one for each institution and a dozen others that are more general. Moreover, when I say that the

* From a longer essay.

money will be found, I assume unending effort by those who will have to find it. Obviously the university president must be one of these men and the university presidency must have the powers that will let him play this part. But when we speak collectively, we can say with conviction that the economic future of the American university is a sure thing.

The heart of the matter today is political. In saying that, I of course do not intend a foolish assumption that economics and politics can be wholly separated, nor do I think that I am simply indulging the prejudices of a retired political scientist. What I am trying to say is simply that the distribution of authority and responsibility among the various members of a university is now in question as it has not been for generations. The traditional patterns of the past are under attack, I think correctly. The problem of politics in the contemporary university is to come to terms with new requirements, and to make right judgments on the reshaping of the political process.

The most visible of the contemporary concerns is the question of the role and responsibility of the student. The high visibility of this question is justified by its importance, although it is far from clear that those who make the most noise are also making the most sense. At the far edge of the movement of student activists there is a group which would rather destroy the university than reshape it for peaceful progress. Moreover, this small group has reached a conscious and carefully calculated decision that its object must be to discredit the present management of universities by means whose only test is whether they work to this specific end. Where these conspirators have been skillful in their choice of issues and targets, they have been able to draw upon a reservoir of student and even faculty support which is much wider and much more significant than they are. Some of their methods strike me as contemptible, and some of their rhetoric as ridiculous. But they are good politicians in two fundamental respects which deserve our attention: they rightly regard the university administration as the political center of their attack, and they rightly regard the general opin-

ion of the faculty as the decisive judge of any action against
that center.

The student radicals, in short, have understood what too
many of the rest of us have either failed to understand or forgotten—the real political relation between the presidency and
power in a university [:] . . . the university president, on academic matters, is the agent and not the master of the faculty.
It is the faculty which is the necessary center of gravity of the
politics of the university for teaching, for learning, for internal
discipline, and for the educational quality and character of the
institution as a whole.

There is, indeed, only one field in which the faculty is not
decisive, and that is the field of resources—of economics. This
is a big exception, and its consequence is that a major role remains for trustees, but only a Marxist would conclude that this
exception destroys the argument. In a great American university one kind of man should find the money and another kind
of man should set the policy, and when this rule is broken, the
result is disaster. Only the president and his chief lieutenants,
for their sins, have to be both kinds of man.

The growth of faculty responsibility and power in academic
matters is obvious to all who see the daily give-and-take of
academic bargaining. . . . Before the Second World War there
were only a few places where tradition, excellence, and administrative restraint had combined to give the faculty great
strength. Now that strength has been conferred on the academic
profession as a whole by the massive authority of the law of
supply and demand. The economic force of this law has been
matched by a new level of social and political prestige for men
of learning as a class. The fact that a few professors are offensive in asserting their own importance should not blind us to the
interesting point that by and large they are right.

So far, unfortunately, professors have used their new powers
more for themselves as individuals than for their profession as
a whole, let alone for the institutions in which they live. . . .
It is neither surprising nor wicked that professors should have

behaved in this fashion. It is in the nature of power that most men use it first to meet their own most urgent needs. . . . It is not only necessary but in a deep sense right that a profession which has this new and growing importance should seek [first] to ensure its own necessary and legitimate rights. Nothing in the corporate claim of the institution can outweigh the preeminent requirement that its teachers and scholars should be free to do their own best work as they themselves determine. It is surely no accident at all that the best of our universities are those in which this freedom is most plainly and steadily assured.

Moreover, faculty . . . committees on instruction and on educational policy have labored in good faith and with great concern from generation to generation over the shape and direction of the academic curriculum. In stretching out to new disciplines and fresh subjects initiative has come as often from the faculty as from the management. And in some lucky places the faculty has kept a continuous and active role in such critical activities as admission, student discipline, and even athletics. Each such effort has had its constructive effect upon the fabric of the academic community.

But . . . by and large, the members of university faculties as a class have accepted the assumption that the institutions in which they had won their place or to which they have been called by their achievements were institutions whose fundamental structure was sound and whose daily management could properly be left to others. More than that, the internal state of mind of the average professor has led him somehow to the further belief that those who did this job of management were lesser men than he. There is a paradox here, of course. The same men who look down on management have often harbored a certain envy for the managers. . . .

I believe that this ambivalence gives a clue both to present misunderstanding and to future understanding between the faculty and the president, but first let us note that, even at its most ordinary, administration has its good and proper value. Someone must attend to the parking problem. . . . Moreover, faculty members who sneer at growing adminstrative staffs have wholly misconstrued their own true interest. It would be a great improvement if professors as a class would give the same respect to all administrators that they give to rare-book librarians.

But it is one thing to delegate power to administrators and quite another to neglect one's own final responsibility. Too many professors in too many of our universities—even some of the very best—have done just that in recent years. Having secured their own academic freedom—and here the record of most institutions is very good indeed—the faculties have tended to assume that the internal strength and health of their universities were self-sustaining, and their government a matter of little moment. They have thus left the field open both for insensitive administrators and for student agitators. . . .

[Indeed,] one of the characteristics of the power of the faculty in the great American universities is that in most cases that power has not been formally recognized. Both the law and the mythology of the university run against the view that the faculty is the vital center. By the terms of their charters our universities belong to their governing boards, either as self-perpetuating private bodies or as agents of the state. This legal authority of trustees is as unquestionable as it is misleading. And what the law puts on trustees, the myth puts on the president. . . .

But a retired political scientist may be pardoned if he finds it pleasant to tilt a little with the windmills of law and mythology. It is a fact of history and a necessity of academic politics that no board of trustees has ever made a university great, and that where a president has done so it has been always and without exception through his faculty. Seen in its true color, the age of greatness among university presidents was an age in which very able men gave proper honor to scholars and teachers. . . .

In many places which call themselves universities, of course, the faculty has no such power as I have described. Where a heavy majority of professors really have no other place to go, where the economic survival of the institution is in question, or where traditions of professorial independence are weak, the faculty may well fail to occupy the center of politics. But the fact that the procession of academic institutions is long and varied does not change the importance of the political reality which exists at the best and strongest ones; indeed, it only makes it more important, for what is true at the head of the line today will be true elsewhere in time. In our foremost universities today it is the faculty which is central.

I am far from suggesting that the faculty can have any absolute authority. It is the nature of a university that no power is ever absolute, and that a high measure of negative power is shared at all times by all parts of the institution. To take a simple example with present relevance, it has always been in the power of the student to strike. What has held him back has been a complex set of forces among which his own internal sense of purpose has been the most important. If a majority of students should come to believe that the disruption of the university is more important than their own education, there will be no future for the institution as we know it. That outcome, I think, is as unlikely as it is undesirable, but the residual power of the student body as a whole is plain. That power is a proper constraint upon the power of administrators, and even on the power of the faculty.

Our current turmoil at its noisiest—and I think also at its most significant—concerns the role of the student. This is a hard topic and in a fundamental sense a new one. In the few fast years since the first demonstrations at Berkeley, it has moved from the basically easy question of the freedom of the student (the question is easy because the student will insist on his personal freedom and will get it) to the much more interesting question of the student's role in the political process of the university. When I was in academic life in the 1950s, the problem was a student unconcern that was reflected in a great lack of respect for things like student government. Only among a handful of graduate students was there active concern with the policies of the Harvard administration, and that concern was nine-tenths economic. I remember, in passing, that we were much distressed by the fact that the more we did for the graduate students the louder they complained; we found it hard to accept in our own community one of the fundamental political laws of any revolution of rising expectations.

In the short decade since then the pressure of students for a larger role has become a major force. It may change in its shape and direction; it may become less strident in tone as it becomes stronger and more confident of its own reality. It will not go away. And the record of its life thus far is the best possible present-day demonstration of my central proposition. When it comes to a crunch, in a first-class university it is the faculty which decides. Time after time when students have carried their point against a dean or a president or a board of trustees, the underlying and validating force in their success has been the opinion of the faculty. Just as often and just as plainly, where an administration has held its ground or won its case, it has succeeded because it had the support of dominant faculty opinion. Most important of all, where there has been a reasonable reconciliation of the new and the old—a responsible recognition of the rights and interests of all—the solution has rested securely upon the will of the faculty. . . .

If the faculty is really the fountain of power, why should it bother with a president at all, or at a minimum, should it not elect him? The answers to these questions are pragmatic and not philosophic. The faculty needs a president because like any large group of people it needs an agent and a spokesman for much of its business. . . .

I myself think that it is historic accident and not sound policy which has made the trustees and not the faculty the prime movers in choosing presidents. . . . I am far from supposing that a secret ballot of all professors would invariably produce good results, but trustees have not been infallible either. Yet I think it doubtful that a sudden revolution in customary procedures is either necessary or desirable. The trustees have their own right to a major role, because of their financial and sometimes their public responsibilities, and within the present standard processes of choice there is ample room for an effective faculty role. The best single test for the appointment of a president is still the question whether over the long pull he is the man the faculty would most wish to have. Trustees and their committees, if they respect this criterion and seek out faculty sentiment accordingly, are as likely to make reasonable judgments as the faculty itself. What they lack in firsthand knowledge may be balanced by their absence of firsthand ambition. . . .

The constitutions of our leading universities, written and unwritten, are very different from one another. In some institutions there is evident need for formal change. In particular cases it may even be wise to move toward strong faculty membership in the board of trustees itself, a notion recently revived by John Kenneth Galbraith. But the readiest and the most powerful instrument of reform is still the presidency, in the university as in the federal government. . . .

The university [however] is not and should not be a simple democracy, not even a democracy of scholars. Its politics are much more subtle, and the rights and responsibilities of its members more varied. There is [for example] a necessary and important difference between senior and junior faculty members, and one of the most difficult and urgent of the present needs of the university world is to improve the connection between them. If there must be a choice between the two, the political center belongs to the senior faculty—to those who hold permanent appointments. But it is better if that choice can be avoided by giving an effective role to the younger faculty too. When the younger faculty is alienated, there is a danger much greater than any posed by disaffected students.

At last we come to the presidency itself. . . . It is a commonplace of academic gossip that it is harder to get good men to serve as presidents of colleges and universities than it used to be. Certainly presidents themselves—all volunteers when they took their jobs—have recently shown a disturbing fondness for the mood of Thomas Jefferson: they do indeed perceive their presidency as a "splendid misery." Moreover they use the noun with feeling and the adjective with irony. To a degree this weariness is the product of the economic struggle whose eventual success I have so casually assumed. In major measure it is the consequence of irritation and even stronger feelings in the face of a constant battle of wits with student radicals who are often outrageous but seldom stupid. In still larger part it is the consequence of the unending effort to interpret one kind of man to another: the professor to the legislator, the student to the trustee, the treasurer to the dean, the old to the young, and oneself to every man. How can I claim to bring comfort to these men by the assertion that in all these troubles they are the agents of the faculties for which they work?

I submit that the comfort, while cool, is considerable. It is the comfort that comes from the replacement of legal fiction and mythology by reality. The president who sees himself either as the unmoved mover or as the agent of his board is doomed, in this generation, to disappointment and perhaps also to destruction. The president who sees himself as the agent of his faculty is at least in the world of reality.

[And] this world is not only real; it is good. . . . In my own experience no group of men in America offers richer opportunities for the man who would make himself their agent. He must of course share their basic convictions himself: . . . he should believe in and understand the university as a community of learning.

[But] let us make no mistake about it: this presidency, like the greater one in Washington which has so sorely tried its occupants, is a political office. No man who lacks a zest for political action should accept the presidency of a university. . . .

So let us assume a president who sees himself as the instrument of his faculty colleagues, who understands and believes in the purposes of the university, and who knows and likes the arts of politics. What then? To such a man there opens an opportunity for service and for action which has few equals and

no superior in the processes of modern American life. Such a
man can satisfy his interest in management by ensuring the
skillful and expeditious dispatch of all the hundreds of lesser
things which a modern university requires and which a modern
faculty prefers to ignore. He can also satisfy his taste for inquiry and imagination by searching out the unexpressed desires
and the still unshaped needs of his faculty colleagues. The
president in that sense should act for his faculty as any effective
political executive acts for his constituency. . . .

Whatever is most urgent in his university, at any given time,
becomes his business. . . . He may say today that he did not
take the job to be a policeman. But if the most important question before the university is to preserve or to re-establish the
condition of ordered liberty, then the faculty's chief agent will
have to take the lead on that issue—he cannot take refuge in
depreciation of the policeman's role; he or his qualified representatives had better get there before the cops, or at least with
them. Where major trouble has been avoided in these recent
crises, there has almost always been alertness and concern on
the part of the president or his responsible representatives.

Of course we must all hope that riot prevention will not be
the president's permanent preoccupation. I myself am a cautious optimist on this point, precisely because I believe that
where faculties and presidents work together on the basic premise I have described, they will prove to have not only the power
but also (and more important) the wisdom that the situation
demands.

If I am right, then the president will be able to enjoy still
other kinds of critical political action, some of them more
familiar and less startling. He will usually have the task of
finding the deans of the several schools, always in the most
intimate consultation with the faculty. I think he should also
have a watchful and occasionally a decisive role in the choice
of the faculty itself, either by his own action or in larger universities by action of the faculty deans. It is an amiable illusion
that the community of scholars is immune to narrowness or

error in the co-option of its peers, and one of the president's most important obligations to his faculty is to try to save it from its tendencies toward folly—this is a task which the faculty as a whole will honor and praise even while individual professors are complaining violently about a particular presidential or decanal decision. The academic administrator never serves the faculty more faithfully than when he looks past its present desires to its future judgment. Of course this is a hard and dangerous game, but I remain convinced that it is a necessary part of the good government of a great university. To put it on no higher level: a faculty that expects the president to act as its strong and perceptive agent on all the other tough problems had better let him in on some of the fun too, if it wants a good man on the job.

And the professors do want a good man on the job. They want a man who speaks their languages and hears them talking. They want a man who is just as good as they are—a man who deserves ungrudgingly the grudging respect they already give to his office. They need a man who is their kind of man, to act for them and for their colleagues. If they get that kind of man, they will welcome his activities in the politics of appointment and promotion because most of the time he'll do more good than harm. If he goes too far, or makes too many mistakes, they have their remedy. . . .

The professors can do still more: they can join in the hard work. They can help with the necessary committees, and can help to get rid of the unnecessary ones. They can accept administrative assignments themselves or respect those colleagues who do so for the right reasons. In short, they can and should join in the process of government, always accepting the same rule they ask the president to accept—the principle of accountability to the faculty as a whole. Faculty members who accept this kind of responsibility reinforce the faculty even as they reinforce the administration. . . .

I believe trustees will continue to have a major role in the institution, and the readiness of students for a greater share of responsibility, whatever its immediate and temporary explosiveness, should be a gain for the university as a whole. But in the end, and unrepentantly, I insist on the faculty as the center. Trustees give time and money and advice and external support of all sorts; students spend some years here. But for members of the faculty the university is life itself. This central commitment is what justifies their central role, and in their effective relations with the presidency is the center of the politics of the modern university.

RICHARD POIRIER

the war against
the young*

**We have used youth as a revenge
upon history, as the sacrificial expression of our self-contempt.**

The social systems which organize and rationalize contemporary life have always been ingeniously armed for the day
when youth would rebel against the essentially pastoral status
assigned to it. Despite pamperings until recently unimaginable,
despite economic briberies and various psychological coercions,
the rebellion has broken out. Predictably, the response to it is a
gradual escalation involving a more naked use of the tactics
that were supposed to prevent, but which also helped to provoke, the crisis in the first place: patronizations, put-downs, and
tongue-lashings, along with offers of a place in the governing
system if only the system is left intact and promises that in
any case the future itself holds the solution to whatever now
seems to be the trouble. If this technique sounds familiar in its
mixture of brutality and pacification, in its combination of aggression and absorption, noted by Edgar Friedenberg in his
brilliant analysis of the adult treatment of the adolescent minority, if it sounds vaguely like methods used in other and related
domestic and foreign conflicts, then the point is obvious: our
society is unfortunately structured, in the prevalent forms of its
language and thinking, in ways designed to suppress some of
the most vital elements now struggling into consciousness and
toward some awareness of their frustrated powers.

* From a longer essay.

This struggle is essentially a cultural one, regardless of the efforts by older people to make political use of it or to place it, unflatteringly, within the terms of traditional politics, particularly cold-war politics. The intellectual weapons used in the war against youth are from the same arsenal—and the young know this—from which war is being waged against other revolutionary movements, against Vietnam, against any effective justice, as distinguished from legislative melodrama, in matters of race and poverty. These weapons, as I've suggested, are by no means crude. They scarcely look at times like weapons at all, and many of the people most adroit in handling them, writers and teachers as well as politicians, aren't even aware that they are directing against youth arguments of a kind used also to rationalize other policies which they consider senseless and immoral. Aside from the political necessities of candidates, why is it that people who can be tough-mindedly idealistic in opposition to our actions in Vietnam, or to our treatment of the powerless, talk about youth and think about the rebellion of youth in a manner implicit in the mentality that produces and excuses these other barbarities? The reason, I think, is that most people don't want to face the possibility that each of these troubles grows from the same root and can be traced back to the same murky recesses within each of us and within the social organisms to which we have lent ourselves. They prefer isolated and relatively visible sources for such difficulties, along with the illusion that each of them is susceptible to accredited forms of political or economic cleansing. By contrast, it is the conviction of the most militant young people, and of some older ones, that any solutions will require a radical change in the historical, philosophical, and psychological assumptions that are the foundations of any political or economic system. Some kind of cultural revolution is therefore the necessary prelude even to our capacity to think intelligently about political reformation.

Oddly enough, the young are proved right, in this supposition at least, by the nature of the attacks made against them,

[not by] the likes of Reagan and Wallace, but . . . from be-
calmed and sensible men, whose moderation is of a piece with
their desire to increase the efficiency of the present system. At
work in these attacks are the same tendencies of thought and
language that shape the moderate, rationalizing analyses of the
other nightmares I've mentioned. They help us to sleep through
them during the night and during most of the day.

Maybe the most prevalent of these tendencies is the insistence
on a language that is intellectually "cool," a language aloof
from militant or revolutionary vocabularies, which in their
exclusion sound excessive, exaggerated, and unserviceable. This
cool language is not at all dull or plodding. On the contrary,
it's full of social flair; it swings with big words, slang words,
naughty words, leaping nimbly from the "way out" to the "way
in"—it really holds the world together, hips and squares
alike. . . . With the suave observation that writers "who prefer
rationality to revolution are by no means conservative," [*Time*]
honored three distinguished commentators on youth and other
scenes. One of the three, Benjamin DeMott . . . had earlier
written . . . of what he called the "spirit of over-kill" among
some of his fellow writers, especially those of the revolutionary
fringe like Paul Goodman, Andrew Kopkind, and Susan Sontag.

According to DeMott, the verbal violence of this decade
"was" (and I'll get to the significance of this past tense in a
moment) "pressed not at new 'enemies' but at old ones already
in tatters." Just at a glance one had to wonder why "enemies,"
new or old, were assigned the unreality of quotation marks.
Has the semblance of negotiations made the war in Vietnam
disappear as an "enemy"? Does he mean racial injustice? the
horrors of urban life? the smothering effects of educational
institutions of which he is himself one of the most active critics?
I'm afraid these enemies aren't so easily dispelled. The degree
to which they press against DeMott's own "cool" dismissal of
them is in fact made evident, with engaging innocence, in the
very form of his essay. In order to find a requisite dispassion

for his own style, as against what he mistakenly takes for the dominant style of this decade, he must project himself to the end of the century and then look back at us. Like other critics of our violence, he is himself already visiting the famous year 2000, programming for which, as we are cautioned by a number of distinguished economists, sociologists, and technicians, will only be disrupted by people who fail to remain politely soft-spoken amid the accumulating squalor, blood, and suffering of their lives.

This peculiar form of address, by which we are asked to hear our present as if it were our past, suggests yet another and more subtle method of repression—the futuristic—now especially popular in the social sciences. A notably unembarrassed practitioner . . . commended by the article in *Time* magazine, Zbigniew Brzezinski, director of the Research Institute on Communist Affairs at Columbia . . . lets us know that, like it or not, we are already becoming a "technetronic society," and any old-fashioned doctrinal or ideological habits—as if ideology wouldn't be inherent in his imagined social systems—will get us into real, permanent troubles instead of temporary ones. We'll fail to adapt, that is, to "the requirements of the metamorphic age," and thus miss the chance of creating a "meritocratic democracy" in which "a community of organization-oriented, application-minded intellectuals [can relate] itself more effectively to the political system than their predecessors." We need only stay calm, and admittedly such language is not designed to excite us, since "improved governmental performance, and its increased sensitivity to social needs is being stimulated by the growing involvement in national affairs of what Kenneth Boulding has called the Educational and Scientific Establishment (EASE)." . . .

It's symptomatic of how bad things are that many of those who want the young and the rebellious to be more quiet follow the advice of Hubert Humphrey: they speak to the young not about the past, not even about the present, but about some future, which, as prognosticators, they're already privileged to know. They are There; the revolutionists are living in the Past. And who is here and now, living, suffering, and impassioned in the present? Apparently no one, except maybe a few of what Brzezinski likes to call the "historical irrelevants.". . . Such arguments and such uses of language—almost wholly abstracted from the stuff of daily life as it is lived in this year, these months, this week—do not define but rather exemplify the cultural and linguistic crisis to which the young are responding with silence even more than with other demonstrations of their nearly helpless discontent. "Power, or the shadow cast by power, always ends in creating an axiological writing," as the French critic Roland Barth puts it, "in which the distance which usually separates fact from value disappears within the space of a word." To prefer "rationality" to "revolution" is good *Time* magazine language. It can't be faulted except by those who feel, as I do, that a revolution is probably necessary if rationality is to be restored to a society that thinks it has been operating rationally. If the young are "revolutionary," and if this is the reverse of "rational," what, then, is the nature of the rationality they're attacking? Quite aside from science fiction passing for history in the writings we've just looked at, are the practices of the United States government with regard to most issues of race, poverty, the war, the gun laws, or even the postal service rational? Is it rational to vote an increase of money for Vietnam, and on the same hot day in July, cut appropriations for the summer employment of young Negroes and Puerto Ricans, thus helping to encourage a bloody summer at home while assuring one abroad?

These are all, as Brzezinski would point out, complex issues, and according to him, they will not be solved by "historical irrelevants," by those who, with revolutionary fervor, are yearning, as he would have it, for the simplicities of the past and who therefore "will have no role to play in the new technetronic society." But what has decided, since I know no people who have, that we want his "technetronic society," that it is desirable or inevitable? Who decides that it is necessary or even good for

certain issues to be construed as complex and therefore susceptible only to the diagnosticians who would lead such a
society? Why have certain issues become complex and who is
served by this complexity? Why is the life we already lead,
mysterious and frightening as it is, to be made even more so
by the ridiculous shapes conjured up in Brzezinski's jaw-break-
ing terminologies? Some issues are not simple, which does not
mean that some others are not unnecessarily complex. It is
clear to everyone that Vietnam is "complex." But it is equally
clear that it need not, for us, have become complex; that it
might not even have existed as an issue, except for those members of EASE who helped justify our continued presence there.
Maybe the secret is that it is really "easy" to be complex.

. . . In a way the most innocent example of this kind of
no-thinking passing in sound and cadence for responsible,
grown-up good sense is offered by George Kennan, the third
figure heralded for his rationality [by] *Time.* . . . Kennan's
speciality is what might be called "the argument from experience," easily slipping into "the argument from original sin."
"The decisive seat of evil in this world," he tells us in *Democracy and the Student Left,* a just-published debate between
him and nearly forty students and teachers, "is not in social and
political institutions, and not even, as a rule, in the ill-will or
iniquities of statesmen, but simply in the weakness and imper-
fection of the human soul itself." No one can deny a proposition
so general, but surely only someone who likes for other reasons
to plead the inescapable complexity of issues could propose
such an idea to people wondering how the hell we got into
Vietnam or why millions of poor in a country so rich must go
hungry every day. . . .

"I have heard it freely confessed by members of the revolutionary student generation of Tsarist Russia," Kennan rather
huffily reports, "that, proud as they were of the revolutionary
exploits of their youth, they never really learned anything in
their university years; they were too busy with politics."
Earlier, from Woodrow Wilson at his prissiest, he describes an

ideal "at the very center of our modern institutions of higher
learning": it is a "free place" in Wilson's words, "itself a
little world; but not perplexed, living with a singleness of aim
not known without; the home of sagacious men."

Was it such sagacious men, one must ask, since it surely was
not the rampaging students, who assumed that this ideal place
should also house ROTC units, defense projects, recruiters from
Dow Chemical, and agents of the CIA? An ideal institution
freed of *those* perplexities—which evidently do not bother Mr.
Kennan—is precisely what the students have been agitating
for. It is not possible to think about learning now without being,
as he pejoratively puts it, "busy with politics." The university
officials and the government have seen to that. But again, Kennan probably doesn't regard ROTC as a political presence on
campus, and students are "busy with politics" not in the precious hours wasted on drill and military science, but only while
agitating against these activities, which are mostly useless even
from a military point of view. Out of this mess of verbal and
moral assumptions, the finest and stiffest blossom is the phrase
"freely confessed": imagine having the gall to tell someone
outright that as a student you hadn't even done your assignments while trying to overthrow a corrupt and despotic government. Doubltless that government also preferred its universities
"not perplexed" by anything related to the conduct of public
affairs.

Compared with the futuristic modes of Brzezinski and De-
Mott, Kennan's mode of argument is at least honest about seeing the present only as if it were the past. In its rather ancient
charm it isn't nearly so dangerously effective as still other less
explicitly theological, less passionate, more academically sys-
tematized methods now in vogue for abridging youthful radicalism or transcendentalism. Consider for example what might be
called the tight-contextual method. This is particularly useful
in putting assassinations in their place, or rather in no-place
("it was not Dallas that curled a finger round that trigger and
pulled it; it was a sad and sick individual," one informant irre-

futably told me), and in explaining why we cannot withdraw from Vietnam. That country gets reduced, in this form of argument, to some thousands of vaguely identified friends whom we cannot desert, even though their worth is even more difficult to locate than is their presence during combat operations. Of course this kind of analysis works wonders on anything as worldwide and variously motivated as student or youth protest. Unanswerably the students at Columbia are not the students in Paris or Czechoslovakia or even Berkeley. Like the leaders in any generation, the rebellious students are only a small minority of the young, a minority even of the student bodies they belong to. There are local, very special reasons not only for the motivations of each group but for each of the different acts of each group. What is astonishing, however, is that they all do act, that they are all acting now, that the youth of the world almost on signal have found local causes—economic, social, political, academic ones—to fit an apparently general need to rebel. So universal and simultaneous a response to scarcely new causes reveals in the young an imaginative largeness about the interconnection of issues, an awareness of their wider context, of a world in which what in former decades would have been a local war is now symptomatic, as is poverty and the quality of life in our cities, of where the dominant forms of thinking have taken us. . . . The young are in effect rebelling against precisely the kinds of analysis that are inadequate to explain what the young are up to. More terrifying than the disorder in the streets is the disorder in our heads; the rebellion of youth, far from being a cause of disorder, is rather a reaction, a rebellion against the disorder we call order, against our failure to make sense of the way we live now and have lived since 1945.

Yet another form of restrictive or deflationary analysis—and appropriately the last I'll consider—is a special favorite of literary critics and historians as well as politicians: the anti-apocalyptic. Implicit in some of the methods we've already looked at, this one dampens revolutionary enthusiasms with the

information that history has recorded such efforts before and
also recorded their failure—the Abolitionists, the young Bol-
sheviks, the Luddites. All claims to uniqueness are either tarnished by precedent or doomed to meaninglessness. We've been
through it all, and are now doing the best we can, given—and
here we're back at the borders of Original Sin—our imperfect
state of being. In the treatment of militant youth, this type of
argument is especially anxious to expose any elitist or fascist
tinge in the young, with their stress on a chimerical "participatory democracy" or their infantile assumption that the worst
must be allowed to happen . . . if ever the inherent horrors of
the "System," and thus the necessities of revolution, are to become apparent to everyone. . . . But only a minority of the articulate and protesting young lend themselves to anything so
politically programmatic. Such arguments are wholly peripheral to the emergence of youth as a truly unique historical force
for which there are no precedents. Youth is an essentially non-
political force, a cultural force, that signals, while it can't by
itself initiate, the probable beginnings of a new millennium,
though hardly the one described in the Book of Revelations. If
only because of its continuously fluid, continuously disappear-
ing and emerging, membership, it is incapable of organizing
itself into shapes suitable to the political alliances that can be
made by other, more stable minority groups like the blacks. It
has no history; it may never have one, but it is that shared experience of all races which may come finally to dominate our
imagination of what we are.

What is happening to the youth of the world deserves the
freest imagination, the freest attention that older people are
capable of giving. It requires an enormously strenuous and,
for most people, probably impossible intellectual effort. Working within the verbal and conceptual frames—a sadly appropriate word—against which the rebellion of youth is in large part
directed, we must try to invent quite different ways of seeing,
imagining, and describing. So complicated is the task linguisti-
cally that it is possible to fail merely because of the vocabulary

with which, from the best intentions, we decide to try. It is perhaps already irrelevant, for example, to discuss the so-called student revolt as if it were an expression of "youth." The revolt might more properly be taken as a repudiation by the young of what adults call "youth." It may be an attempt to cast aside the strangely exploitative and at once cloying, the protective and impotizing concept of "youth" which society foists on people who often want to consider themselves adults. Is it youth or is it the economic and sexual design of adult society that is being served by what Erik Erikson calls the "moratorium," the period when people under twenty-one are "allowed" to discover their identities without at the same time having to assume adult responsibilities? Quite painfully, the young have suddenly made us aware that the world we have been seeing isn't necessarily the world at all. Not only that France wasn't France, but that even the young weren't necessarily that thing we call "young." It is no longer a matter of choice, therefore: we must learn to know the world differently, including the young, or we may not know it until it explodes, thus showing forth its true nature, to follow the logic of Marx, only in the act and at the moment of breakdown.

Before asking questions about the propriety and programs of young militants who occupy buildings, burn cars, and fight the police, let's first ask what kind of world surrounds these acts. Let's not conceive of the world as a place accidentally controlled by certain people whose wickedness or stupidity has been made evident by disaster, or as the scene of injustices whose existence was hidden from us. Because to do so implies that we are beguiled rather than responsible even for specific things that we do not know are happening. We're in danger of becoming like the Germans before the war who afterward turned to their children with dismay, then surprise, then amnesia. Such analogies to our present situation, and even more to an anticipated one, are not exact, but neither are they remote.

The world we now live in cannot get any better merely by changing its managers or improving some of its circumstances.

It exists as it does because of the way we think about one another and because of our incapacity, so far at least, to learn
to think differently. For those who fought in it and who are now
the middle generation and parents of the young, World War II
gave absolutely the worst kind of schooling. It trained us to
think in extraordinarily simplistic terms about politics and history. . . . We were convinced that evil resided in Nazism and
Fascism, and that against these nothing less than total victory
was acceptable. The very concept of total victory or uncondi-
tional surrender was part of a larger illusion that all wickedness was entrenched in certain places, circumstances, and persons, and very subtly these were differentiated from the people
or the nations where they found hospitality. . . .

World War II blinded us to the conditions at home that
required our attention, and so did the cold war that followed:
for nearly twenty-five years we looked at foreign devils rather
than domestic ills. The consequences were even worse in our
thinking, however, or rather in our not thinking, about the
true sources and location of our trouble. They are within ourselves and within the mechanisms of our own society. One
reason why those in the parental generation cannot understand
the rebellion of the young is that our own "rebellion" was
managed for us, while for the young now it is instinctive and
invented and unprogrammed. Our protest movement was the
war itself, the crusade against Nazism, Fascism, and Japanese
imperialism. . . .

If the war absorbed and homogenized the political feelings
of the millions like me who are now the parents of people
nearly old enough to be drafted for a quite different kind of
war, the G.I. Bill of Rights . . . allowed the first huge influx
into colleges, universities, and later into the academic profession, of people who for financial and social reasons weren't
before recognized as belonging to the group which represents
youth as our society likes to imagine it—the students. But,
given their backgrounds, which made them poignantly anxious
to take advantage of an opportunity they never thought avail-

able, much less a right, given their age, service experience, sexual maturity, and often marriage, this influx of a new kind of student had a stabilizing rather than a disrupting effect. We were maybe the first really serious mass of students who ever entered the academy, designed up till then, and still designed, to prolong immaturity until the ridiculous age of twenty-one or later.

If we were serious, it was in a bad sense, I'm afraid: we wanted so much to make it that we didn't much question the value of what we were doing. I'm not surprised that so few people my age are radical even in temperament. My fellow academicians who came through the process I've described have fitted all too nicely into the Anglophilic gentility of most areas of academic life, into the death-dealing social manners promoted by people who before the war could afford the long haul of graduate as well as undergraduate education. . . . Much more than the reputed and exaggerated effect of television and other media in creating a self-conscious community of the young (effects shared, after all, by people in their thirties and early forties), it is the peculiar nature of World War II and of subsequent schooling experience which separates the older from the younger but still contiguous groups. . . .

I suggest that people my age think not so much about the strangeness of the young but about their own strangeness. Why is it "they" rather than "we" who are unique? By what astonishing arrogance do people my age propose to themselves the program described recently in *The New York Times Book Review* by a critic who wrote that during the summer he would support McCarthy and that "beyond that, full-time opposition to radical or reactionary excesses in the arts and criticism strikes me as proper and sufficient activity for a critic. And political enough, too, in its ultimate implications." The ultimate implications are dead center. Dead because what can anyone mean now by an "excess," and from where does one measure it unless, like the person in question, he entertains, as do most of my contemporaries, the paranoiac illusion that he has emerged a representative of True Nature?

Only when the adult world begins to think of itself as strange, as having a shape that is not entirely necessary, much less lovely, only when it begins to see that the world, as it has now been made visible to us in forms and institutions, isn't all *there*, maybe less than half of it—only then can we begin to meet the legitimate anguish of the young with something better than the cliché that they have no program. Revolutionaries seldom do. One can be sick and want health, jailed and want freedom, inwardly dying and want a second birth without a program. For what the radical youth want to do is to expose the mere contingency of facts which have been considered essential. That is a marvelous thing to do, the necessary prelude to our being able, any of us, to think of a program which is more than merely the patching up of social systems that were never adequate to the people they were meant to serve.

Liberal reformers, no matter how tough, won't effect and might even forestall the necessary changes. In our universities, for example, there is no point in removing symptoms and leaving the germs. It is true, as the young have let us know with an energy that isn't always convenient even to sympathizers like myself, that our universities are too often run by fat cats, that renowned professors are bribed by no or little teaching, that a disproportionate amount of teaching is done by half-educated, miserably underpaid, and distracted graduate assistants, that, as a consequence of this imbalance, research of the most exciting kind has very little immediate bearing on curriculum, which remains much as it has for the past fifty years, and that, as Martin Duberman eloquently showed in a recent issue of *Daedalus,* authoritarianism in curriculum and in teaching, not to be confused with being an authority in a subject, is so much a part of our educational system that university students arrive already crippled even for the freedom one is prepared to give them. These conditions exist in a pattern of idiotic requirements and childish, corrupting emoluments not simply because our universities are mismanaged. The mismanagement has itself a prior cause which is to be found in the way most people think about scholarship and its relation to teaching—a question which is a kind of metaphor for the larger one of the relations between the generations: what conditions permit the most profitable engagements between an older mind that is trained and knowledgeable and a younger one anxious to discover itself but preconditioned by quite different cultural circumstances?

These circumstances have, of course, always differed between one generation and another, but never so radically as now. Never before have so many revered subjects, like literature itself, seemed obsolete in any strict compartmental form; never before have the divisions between such subjects as anthropology, sociology, and languages seemed more arbitrary and harmful to intelligent inquiry; and seldom in the history of modern civilization has there been a greater need felt by everyone for a new key to our mythologies, a key that we nervously feel is about to be found. For if we are at a moment of terror we are also at a moment of great expectation and wonder, for which the young have a special appetite. To meet this challenge, the universities need to dismantle their entire academic structure, their systems of courses and requirements, their notion of what constitutes the proper fields and subjects of academic inquiry.

Most people who teach have in their heads some ideal university, and mine would be governed by a single rule: there is nothing that does not need to be studied in class. . . . nothing must be taken for other than "strange," nothing must be left alone. . . . Above all, those working in advanced research sponsored at any university would also let capable students study that research and ask questions about it. . . . [Also] the university would be a place where curricula are discovered anew perhaps every year or so. The argument that the demands of an existing student body cannot be allowed to determine policy for succeeding ones would mean the reverse of what it now means: not that changes are difficult to effect, but that they would be effected year after year, if necessary, to meet the combined changes of interest in student and faculty. Given the sluggishness of most people, the results of such a policy would not be nearly as chaotic or exciting as one might imagine. Indeed, what would be hoped for is *more* disruption, and therefore more questioning and answering than one would ever get. . . .

The now not uncommon proposition that our problems are no longer manageable within existing political systems, and that we need an Authority empowered to decide what is best for us, cannot be ascribed merely to youth, Herbert Marcuse, Vietnam, race, violence, or any combination of these. The emerging failure of confidence in our way of managing ourselves and our interests in the world is the consequence of a political process now overwhelmed by the realities it has tried to hide, realities that have grown like cancer cells treated by pain-killers. Instinctively, the militant young are involved less in a political rebellion, where demands for their "program" would be relevant, than in an attack on the foundations of all of our current political programming. The issues they raise and the issues they personify are essentially anthropological, which brings us to the cultural rather than the political importance of [President Johnson's] proposal to move the voting age back from twenty-one to eighteen. The importance can be dramatized, with no intention of melodrama, by predicting that within twenty years or so it will be necessary to propose, if not to pass, a voting age of sixteen. Like other mere changes of policy, changes in voting age should not be taken as a sign that we are suddenly to be governed by new or radical modes of thinking. Rather, such reforms signal the accumulated power of forces which our operative modes of thinking have before tried to ignore and which they will now try to make invisible by absorption.

But with the mass of youth—nearly half the population is now under twenty-five—our society is faced with an unprecedented difficulty in the application of this essentially social technique. For when it comes to the young, society is not simply absorbing a group who, like the Irish or labor, duplicate in their social organization each part of the dominant group. To give something like adult or historic identity to a mass that has up to now been relegated to the position of "youth" means a disruptive change in the concept of human identity, of when that identity is achieved, of what it properly should contribute to history. The time scheme that governs our ideas of adolescence, youth, and maturity has changed many times in history since the sixteenth century—Juliet was fourteen, and early in the eighteenth century the age of consent was ten—but it was adjusted to the convenience of an extraordinarily small ruling minority which was in turn submissive to familial regulations. For the first time in history a change of this kind is being made on demand from a powerful mass of young people freed of familial pieties, and never before has a society worked as strenuously as ours, through a mesh of mythologies, to hold these young people back, in an unmercifully prolonged state of adolescence and of what we call "youth." Especially in the United States, the representative and most talented young—the students—have for generations been forced *not* to take themselves seriously as men and women. (So far, the rebellion has accomplished at least one thing; it has succeeded in demoting "collegiate types"— and the sickly reminiscent values that they injected into later life—from glamour to absurdity.). . .

The shattering of this pattern has been the work of a complex of forces that include students within the larger power bloc of youth, with its enormous influence on dress and mores, and, perhaps above all, its success in the fields of entertainment. By force of numbers and energy alone, the young have created images which older people are now quite anxious to endow with a sexual-social significance that they before refused to find in the activity of "kids." Put another way, youth has ceased to fulfill the "literary" role which American society has been anxious to assign them. They no longer supply us with a pastoral, any more than the "darkies" do. . . . By a pastoral I mean any form of life that has, by common consent, been secured from the realities of time and history, [that] helps stabilize the cycles of individual lives and of civilizations. Its function is an idealizing, simplifying one: it secures certain elemental human attributes from the contaminations of time and of historical involvement. But if the logic of pastoral is to protect certain attributes, its ulterior motive is to keep the human embodiment of these attributes in their proper place, servants rather than participants in daily business where real men really face complex reality.

Insofar as America's imagination of itself can be inferred from literature, from popular entertainment, from fashions, conventions, and educational theory, it can be said that we have used youth as a revenge upon history, as the sacrificial expression of our self-contempt. Youth has been the hero of our civilization, but only so long as it has remained antagonistic to history, only so long as it has remained a literary or mythological metaphor. War, the slaughter of youth at the apparent behest of history, is the ultimate expression of this feeling. The American hatred of history, of what it does to us, gets expressed in a preposterous and crippling idealization of youth as a state as yet untouched by history, except as a killer, and in a corresponding incapacity to understand the demand, now, by the best of the young, to be admitted into it. More hung up on youth than any nation on earth, we are also more determined that youth is not to enter into history without paying the price of that adulteration we call adulthood. To justify what grown-ups have made of our young, virgin, uncontaminated land, it's as if we are compelled to show that what happened was necessary. Exceptions would prove our human culpability for what is otherwise ascribed to history, and so all that is best in our land must either be kept out of history or tarnished by it. Like our natural wonders, youth will be allowed to exist only on condition that it remain, like some natural preserve, outside the processes that transform everything else into waste.

Surely the destination of our assets needn't be so bleak, so inexorable, so neurotically determined. It will now be seen whether or not we are to exhaust our youth, whether or not in its vulnerability, its continually evaporating and exposed condition, it can resist being made grist for the mill. Because youth is not a historically grounded pressure group, aware of its history, jealous of its progress, continuous and evolving. It is rather what we, all of us, sometimes are. I have avoided any precise definition of youth because it refers to the rare human condition of exuberance, expectation, impulsivensss, and above all, of freedom from believing that all the so-called "necessities" of life and thought are in fact necessities. This condition exists most usefully, for the nation and the world, in people of a certain age, specifically in those who have attained the physical being that makes them wonderfully anxious to create life, to shape life, to enter into life rather than have it fed into them. It is the people of this age, members of what Friedenberg calls the "hot-blooded minority," who are in danger of obliteration as representatives of youth. It is impossible for them to remain youth, in any sense that would profit the rest of society, and also enter into history on the hateful terms now offered them by our political, economic, and technological system. . . .

So, what I'm saying is that if young people are freeing themselves from a repressive myth of youth only to be absorbed into a repressive myth of adulthood, then youth in its best and truest form, of rebellion and hope, will have been lost to us, and we will have exhausted the best of our natural resources.

NORMAN COUSINS

what are they telling us?

**The ability of the older generation
to be open to learning may well be
what is the most essential.**

The basic purpose of a university education has always
been not solely to provide an encounter with stockpiled knowledge but to enable the young to discover and pursue new questions, to develop a spirit of critical inquiry, and to test accepted
propositions. This theoretical definition of the university's function should now become, as students see it, the literal one; and
the results are as unsettling as they are promising and enormously exciting.

The significant thing about many of today's young people is
not that they are in revolt but that they are in search of workable
guidelines for their lives, their work, and their relationships.
Their break with the university and with their society in general
has less to do with the declared philosophy of the university and
the society than with the caricaturing of that same philosophy
by those who profess to venerate it. The new young "radicals"
are not the affiliated or labeled radicals of the Thirties. They are
unwilling to make out blank checks to anyone—whether ideol-
ogists or organizations or both. They are hypocrisy-spotters.
They are less impressed with resounding aims than with direct
acts of unquestionable integrity. They react sharply against de-
personalization and quantification. They are less impressed, for
example, with statistics showing the high average annual income
of the American family than with the day-to-day experiences of

those who live largely outside the benefits of abundance. They are not quite sure what it is they themselves want of life but they fight shy of the profusion of encumbrances that appear to keep their elders from standing erect and thinking straight.

And so they want a larger share in the decision-making about their lives. However much regard they may have for the superior learning of their teachers, they believe they themselves have something of value to offer in the determination of what it is they should be taught and even how they are to be taught. They see themselves not just as receptacles for instruction but as essential participants in the educational experience. They mirror the central tendency of the age—which is the quest for individual respect. Finally, they see themselves as thinking people in contrast to many of their elders whom they tend to regard as reflexive rather than reflective, and increasingly subject to computerized decisions.

The sudden, drastic outbreaks of violence that disfigure the visible life of some of those young people are a grim contradiction of their own stated contempt for violence and the irrational. Here, however, any careful study of the rapidity with which student demonstrations and protests have degenerated into violence will have to consider the extent to which the society itself has become a school for violence. Does it mean nothing to expose a child to thirty hours or more of television each week in which people are constantly beaten up or kicked around? A President of the United States and a great civil rights leader are killed with guns that can be bought through the mail or over the counter, yet it is impossible to get enough support to prohibit the sale of such weapons. Does such a fact say nothing about the casual public approach to violence? Villages in Vietnam have been systematically destroyed and countless thousands of people have become homeless; the reasoning is that this will save them from marauding Vietcong. What kind of deformed thinking is it that can conceive of such nonsense? Does this have no part in the growing atmosphere of desensitization? Is it possible, in short, to detach completely the eruptive actions of young people from the violence that surrounds them and that indeed is fed to them with the blessings of their elders?

The student demonstrations—violent or otherwise—will not be put down by charging police on or off horseback. A great deal more knowledge than has been in evidence thus far must be brought to bear. One suspects that the basic causes of violent protest are to be found in the mirror and will not yield to dismay, disgust, or despair. The ability of the older generation to be open to learning may well be what is most essential in making education work.

LIONEL TRILLING
(Interviewed by Stephen Donadio)

columbia: symbol and substance*

I find that, contrary to my first expectations, I have great respect for them.

DONADIO: Have your feelings about the Columbia situation changed a great deal during the course of events?

TRILLING: It's amazing to me how difficult I find it to answer that question. . . . The nearest thing to a feeling that I can now recall or experience is my puzzled preoccupation with what the students are and want. I'm not in the dark about the hard—core radical students, the SDS—I think I quite understand them. It's the relatively moderate but still militant students that make the puzzle for me. I can't in the least draw upon my own attitudes as a student to help me toward comprehension. Like all my friends at college, I hadn't the slightest interest in the university as an institution: I thought of it, when I thought of it at all, as the inevitable philistine condition of one's being given leisure, a few interesting teachers and a library. I find it hard to believe that this isn't the natural attitude and when I hear about present student attitudes and demands, as it were in the abstract, they seem to me to be chiefly incomprehensible, even absurd, or, sometimes, merely willful and mischievous. But it has almost never failed that when I meet the students themselves . . . I find that, contrary to my first expec-

* From a longer interview.

tations, I have great respect for them and that their demands at least begin to make sense. I think that what happens is that when I confront them personally I see them in their cultural and social situation, and since I understand why this should arouse their antagonism and rebelliousness, I am the better able to see why they should direct their protest at the university, which they take to be representative of the society, as the part of the society with which they are most immediately involved and which is most accessible to their protest. My seeing this doesn't prevent me from thinking that they are wrong in dealing with the university as if it were perfectly continuous with the society, or as if it were the microcosm of the society. Both Noam Chomsky and Stuart Hampshire tried to correct this view in speaking to student audiences here. If it should persist, if students conduct themselves toward the university as if its shortcomings and anomolies produced the same kind of effect as the shortcomings and anomolies of the society, or of a particular government, the academic life will soon be made impossible. . . .

The most radical students were expressing their doctrinaire alienation from and disgust with the whole of American culture. The less radical but still militant students were attempting to reach a new definition of what a young person is in relation to the institutions he is involved with. It is often remarked that maturation in our society comes much earlier than it used to even a few years ago, not intellectual maturation but cultural maturation. This circumstance is of crucial importance. Our colleges and universities were designed for students who were in certain respects considerably less developed than students now are, and one way of coming to an understanding of the students' dissatisfaction with the university is to perceive that they are pressing for the recognition of their maturity, for the right to participate in decisions about their lives in a way that is consonant with their sense of their development. . . .

Perhaps as an element of this new early maturation, there has developed among young people an appetite for gratuitous political activity. In speaking of their political activity as gratuitous, I don't mean to say that it has no relation to actuality, but quite apart from all actual and practical ends in view, there is, I think, the desire to be politically involved, in some extreme and exciting way. . . . It seems to me, the gratuitous element is considerably greater than it was in the thirties. For young people now, being political serves much the same purpose as being literary has long done—it expresses and validates the personality. In saying this, I don't mean to question the authenticity of their emotions and motives, but I do mean to suggest that many —not all—of the issues they raised were adventitious or symbolic. . . .

It is obvious that there will have to be a greater participation by the students in the affairs of the University. Just how far that participation should go I'm not yet prepared to say. It seems to me that some of the demands made even by the moderate (but militant) students are extravagant and impracticable. At the same time I must say that the students from this group with whom I have talked were very impressive in point of their seriousness, intelligence and responsibility.

A chief difficulty in carrying out the delicate work of defining the kind and extent of the participation that is appropriate to students will of course be the injection into the deliberations of the views of the radical students, which I believe not to be in good faith. Among considerable sections of public opinion, I seem to observe, there is a tendency to believe that the satisfaction of the demand for "student power" must inevitably lead to the improved health of universities. This is a mere sentimentality. An excess of student power, we are told on reliable authority, has virtually ruined the universities of Japan.

It's plain that the faculty will have to be much more involved in the practical life of the University than it has hitherto been. There are disadvantages in this of which everyone is aware— the possibility of a politicalized faculty, rancorous in endless debate, the time that scholars and teachers will have to give to ever-multiplying committees. But these dangers and discomforts must not be exaggerated.

SHERMAN B. CHICKERING

how we got that way*

We knew instinctively what a "behavioral sink" was before Tom Wolfe applied the term to New York.

We have our own America, our own bag. We all participate to a greater or lesser extent in a common youth culture. The culture is homogeneous, integral and pervasive. We are part of it because we were born into it. We differ only in how much we identify with it, not whether. . . . We who were born after, say, 1940 grew up in an environment radically different from that of our parents. We were able to see the environment, and our parents couldn't. Our parents could see only that we were different, not why we were different. . . .

Youth culture is the way we affirm the existence of a totally new environment; it is our response to it. The religion of the youth culture is the cult of experience; campus chaplains tailor their ministry to helping students become involved in "meaningful human relationships." The sex is not so much a revolution as it is a relationship; it is a ritual, a shared experience consecrated by the engagement of the whole person. The education is action-oriented; it makes of society a laboratory for the humanities and breaks down the walls between disciplines and classrooms. The politics is crisis-oriented, a "participatory democracy" founded on confrontations between youth and the leaders of the prevailing culture. The arts are "action arts," notably folk singing, jazz and abstract films. Leisure activity is kinesthetic, characterized by discothèques, "happenings," psyche-

---

* Twenty-seven-year-old Sherman Chickering, editor-publisher of *Moderator*, considers himself neither an activist nor a hippie.—A.K.

delia, and the omnipresent motorcycle. The economics is self-imposed poverty, the hallmark of which is exploitation of the consumer economy (for example, theft, "borrowing," living off the land, "scarfing" of leftovers). The hero of the culture is the man of "sincerity," whether he be the hedonistic Jean-Paul Belmondo, the strident Fidel Castro, the scrofulous Bobby Dylan, or the David Merrick who said, *"Holly Golightly* was my Bay of Pigs."

The culture is of a piece. All the elements reflect a central thrust, which is why the New Left radical and the seemingly traditional fraternity "jock" are on common ground. Although some young people express most of the manifestations of the culture, and others very few, all express at least some elements of the common culture. . . . Those who participate *most* in youth culture, the ones who are not "well-adjusted" to society, are often the ones who are the most at peace with themselves. As John Leo reported in the New York *Times* of June 19, 1967, "Psychologists and social scientists, operating independently on various campuses and with varying research methods, agree [that] . . . activists as a group are . . . psychologically more stable than non-activists."

The [other] true believer within youth culture . . . is the "hippie," the complete dropout from organized society. . . . The activist is most likely to be the child of liberal Democratic parents; the hippie is most likely to be the child of conservative Republicans. The one considers his father a New Deal sellout, but adopts his father's Constitutional ideals; the other considers his father irrelevant, and rejects the prevailing culture entirely. Nevertheless, the common ground between the activist and the hippie is considerable. Professor Richard Flacks of the University of Chicago singles out at least three common traits: "romanticism," "moral purity," and rejection of conventional career opportunities. All are characteristic of youth culture generally, and all are logical responses to the postwar environment.

Youth culture seems to provide the necessary matrix within which a young person can find an entire, well-integrated iden-

tity. Those . . . who do not partake of the entire youth culture
because they are attracted to the traditional culture (for example, parental values, career patterns) are the ones who appear
to suffer the most acute and prolonged identity crises.

At one extreme there are those who accept the traditional culture completely, and are somehow able to resist the psychic implications of the new environment. In the middle is a vast and
growing group of young people who are torn between the
starkly different alternatives posed by the two cultures. At the
other extreme are a growing number of young people who identify themselves in the way Stokely Carmichael does, embracing
"blackness" rather than trying to become "white."

This celebration of youth culture as a complete answer to
every human need undoubtedly appears bizarre to anyone over
the age of thirty. . . . Younger generations in times past seem
to have latched onto experiences they called their own . . . only
to find more lasting satisfaction within the prevailing culture.
The difference today is that the new experiences of the young
are no longer confined to a response to new *fragments* of reality.
For the first time, in recent history at least, youth culture is a
response to a *totally new environment.* . . .

There are four elements, or forces, which I find most crucial
to a definition of the new environment, and most responsible
for the new youth culture. . . . The first was our peculiar parents. Ours was an Oedipal childhood, especially if we were war
babies. Father was away, or dead. Mother was independent,
working, worried, and looked to us for affection. A sense of perpetual siege was built into us, and hence a sensitivity to potential or actual human loss. While the experience was probably
similar to that of a World War I or Depression baby in this respect, the enormity of the conflict and yet the state of relative
economic abundance fostered in us a sensibility peculiar to the
times. We absorbed the impression that economic security could
not replace or compensate for emotional insecurity.

If we were postwar babies, we absorbed much the same impression, although for somewhat different reasons . . . docu-

mented by Kenneth Keniston in *The Uncommitted.* Our mothers were the dominant figures in our lives because our fathers were so involved in "making it" with the drive, and sense of time lost, left over from the war. This situation deepened and exacerbated the split already evident between the educated, emancipated woman frustrated in her attempts at role definition and her somewhat shadowy, elusive husband whose energies were spent somewhere off in the anonymous void of the economy. Our mothers often felt insecure about their self-fulfillment in marriage and so invested an inordinate amount of emotional capital in their children. . . . The parents set the stage. Their children, especially the boys, became uprooted. Boys tended to identify more with the "emotional" qualities of their mothers rather than the principles and practices of their fathers.

The most important, and most multidimensional, of the forces shaping youth culture was mass communications—the second crucial element of the new environment. . . . Signs, billboards, store displays, supermarkets, the traditional media, and finally the new, all-consuming, substitute environment, television, enveloped us in a cocoon of sensory information. I think it is doubtful that anyone who did *not* grow up in this postwar period can appreciate how much the senses of the young were bombarded, as they are today, by messages. Indeed, the media—in the broadest sense of the word—provided a new environment. To those who grew up in the new urban complexes, it virtually *was* the environment. . . .

We felt like members of a global village; indeed we were exposed to instant news, the Top Ten and Westerns with a worldwide audience of two hundred million. Our common experience was our media experience. So, to set Marshall McLuhan aside for the time being, the *content* of the media made us feel at home in a world of jingles, jungles and juggernauts. In turn, this environment impressed upon us the presence, and the all-consuming importance, of *people.* Our ideas had arms and legs. (Especially when we figured out our chances of winning a trip to the Howdy Doody Show—about one in ten million?) Hence, unlike our parents, we thought of principles, programs and power in terms of personalities and clever phrases.

We were also massaged. McLuhan has it right. Sights, sounds, bombardments—the little boxes turned in on our aural and tactile senses, and activated them the way print never did, or could. Sensory "information" seemed to go through our *bodies* to our brains, or central nervous systems, rather than almost directly into cognitive perception. Our perceptions were throbbing, pulsating. Ours were participant perceptions. Experience rather than knowledge became the wellspring of our motivation. And the only permanent feature of our affluent, static society that provided us regularly with stimulating experience was television, and the related aural/tactile media. No wonder I have difficulty with the word "media"; I can't consider television and the media environment generally as an intermediary; I consider it—feel it, perceive it—as a beginning and end, a constitutive feature of everyday experience.

Both content and medium conspired to make us more sophisticated than any amount of heritage, tutelage or erudition could have. The world as a global village taught us to see people in the nakedness of deeds that contradicted words. The message of the media taught us to leap into life with all five senses. The result was that we learned to see right through to the quick; we learned to distinguish thought from action in others, and learned to mesh thought and action in our own lives. We learned that Ipana toothpaste was better than Crest if it felt better, not if it claimed to be, and learned that Captain Video was sometimes more for real than toothpaste. The media made hypocrites, squares, finks and fnerds of the world's big shots, and made hippies and swingers of us little boys. . . .

The new media is one reason, the main one, why we took so well to social criticism, especially in its comic-book form. *Mad* comics became our Word. As Laurence Wylie writes, "*Mad's* symbol, the insipidly smiling Alfred E. Neuman, who maintains his ghoulishly cheerful expression while the most appalling things go on around him, stands for American culture itself as the adolescent experiences it." He also stands for the adolescent who says, "What, Me Worry?—I've got it all figured out." Which he did: when we read the serious literature of social criticism we knew all about it already. . . .

Our first environment was our peculiar parents. Our second was the synthetic one, the new, all-pervasive media and the primers for it such as *Mad*. Our third was the affluent, populous, classless society and, with it, the absence of tomorrow.

Most of us either grew up in sizeable cities or were at least exposed to them regularly. . . . We knew instinctively what a "behavioral sink" was before Tom Wolfe applied the term to New York. We became used to fighting for our classroom, transport or theater seats. We were no longer a people brought up with the luxury of a fence separating us from our "good neighbors." We had to face up to interpersonal confrontations. . . .

Whether we were the sons of union organizers or corporation presidents or civil servants, we [whites] had relatively equal chances for survival in the new postwar technocracy. We no longer felt predestined to a place high or low in the social hierarchy. By the same token, we no longer felt so deeply the internal compulsion to fulfill the promise of that high or low place. We were aided and abetted in this lack of the traditional drive by the new economic facts of life.

We were the first generation born into widespread affluence. . . . For us the economic incentive, as well as the class/status incentive, had largely disappeared. This condition was fostered considerably by our peculiar fathers (not to be confused necessarily with my own). Children of the Depression, our fathers did not wish to see their own children go through similar deprivation. Thus we were weaned on "the good things in life," all of which were costly. In this frame of reference, the habit of solving sibling problems with money was, of course, congenial to shadowy Depression-bred Dad. His parental responsibilities could be discharged financially rather than paternally. Hence, when son came to father with a "How do the stars work" question, Dad could feel confident, or at least complacent, in saying, "Here, kid, take five bucks and go see a movie." As it were.

So, What Me Worry? The question of tomorrow became considerably less pressing. Money was at hand. And father was not to be listened to for advice on the big questions later on because he didn't bother with our little questions earlier. The rewards available through playing the Tomorrow game—Dad's game— were evaporating. This situation was fine by us, for we were more tuned in on Today anyway by our electronic media, and the manifold seductions of the new environment. The old secular eschatology had been shattered.

The fourth element, aside from the new home, media and marketplace, was provided by The Bomb. . . . We were, in one respect, the most unravaged generation that has ever lived. Yet, almost by contrast, we felt deeply the ghoulish presence of the mushroom cloud. . . . The Bomb became for us the equivalent of knowing at night that Boris Karloff really *was* hiding under the bed. After all, we saw the doumentaries of the Bikini blasts, and we had to wear name tags around our necks back there in the late forties. And we had to lie under our desks during air raid drills, wondering whether the wooden top of our desk was strong enough to keep out the blast. For kids this is not a game or a functional necessity; it is a reality. It is a tangible fear. It is a nightmare. . . .

We feel the absurdity represented by The Bomb, and react in at least two observable ways: We have one more reason to live for Today rather than Tomorrow, and the fact that The Bomb exists becomes an absolute gauge, an ultimate proof, by which to consider our leaders misguided at best, and, at worst, sick. (*Mad* magazine once carried a sequence that showed two land masses on the planet hurling I.C.B.M.'s at each other until the missiles were finally being launched from tiny fragments of orbiting terra firma.) The generation gap again: There are evidently those who can read Herman Kahn and take him seriously. We can't take Kahn seriously because we *can* take The Bomb seriously. Hence the popularity among us of sick jokes, horror film revivals, the theater of the absurd, Hobbits, trivia games, *Dr. Strangelove*, the *Realist* magazine, *Marvel* comics, and C-grade movie heroics.

Our peculiar parents, our new media, our marketplace, our Bomb: They bring us face-to-face with a prevailing culture that does not respond to the new environment. So we become alienated, and take up exclusively with each other.

Youth culture gains its hold over us through our confrontation with institutional America as well as through our response to the new environment. The confrontation becomes most acute when we reach college, for college is the gateway through which we are invited to participate fully in the major institutions of society. We discover after we settle into college that we are not really there to learn but to get good grades and acquire a passport into the economy. To a generation raised on person-to-person peer group experience and heightened sensitivities (if not sensibilities), this sort of higher Pavlovian encampment is frustrating. We chafe for less grading and more individualized professorial attention not out of a desire for license but out of a need for the chemistry of interpersonal confrontation. We consider the old education a sybaritic appurtenance of the Industrial Revolution, class privilege and a hardship-oriented society. It does not answer to our needs.

The ultimate frustration for the college man, prior to freak-out or sellout, comes from the sizeable time span between vocational choice and actual application. A virtual galaxy of forces conspires to keep young men, as Harold Taylor puts it, huffing and puffing on the sidings of higher and higher education: the specialized requirements of the "knowledge explosion"; an antiquated, book-oriented curriculum rather than an experience-oriented one involving work-study programs; the convenience offered recruiters by the designation "Ph.D.," over "M.A.," over "B.A." . . .

We are not allowed to go to work in a job that uses our education until we have had too much education for our own good. We lose our executive drive drying up over economics textbooks.

When we finally enter the economy, if we haven't fallen out of it first, we have become too old to take chances. We have moved from farm club to clubhouse without our turn at the plate. The massive institutions into which we move are generally too big to offer us our turn at bat while we're in our twenties anyway— even if we still had enough stuff left to handle it. No wonder an increasing number of young people embrace youth culture not only as a logical response to the environment but also as an alternative preferable to waiting for action until it's too late to act.

The new environment creates a new response, and the response bears a striking resemblance to the culture of Negro youth in the ghetto. Parents: In the ghetto, children often grow up with a mother but no father. Media: The truncated ghetto family has a television set and a transistor radio if it has anything. Marketplace: The psychological function of enforced deprivation is strikingly similar to that of affluence in eliminating the success drive. The Bomb: For the ghetto child, "Whitey," or The Man, is The Bomb. Because the ghetto child's environment in many ways functions like the middle-class youth's new environment, the two youth cultures resemble each other. As a result many middle-class youths find it easier to identify with ghetto children than with their own parents. . . .

We are made in America, a hundred percent American. Yet we are a foreign country on American soil. Older Americans are just beginning to realize we are something else. . . . *The new environment makes us an experience-oriented generation; the prevailing culture makes us experience-starved.*

The radicals and youth cultists deserve a hearing. The outspoken and outrageous few are saying a great deal about the relatively quiescent multitude. The vast majority of young people shares the experience, if not the logical response. The majority is simply unprepared to respond logically and integrally to the new environment. They perceive existing institutional patterns, and try to fit in. They are governed by the objectives of getting a job and raising a family. . . . But this majority, like the militants and dropouts, has been conditioned by forces that deny the logic of the existing institutional environment. As a result, the majority is troubled. It is a susceptible majority, open to the suasions of the motivated minority. [Thus] vast institutional change is inevitable, and will be forthcoming.

LESLIE A. FIEDLER

the new mutants*

Freud is a fink!

. . . The "mutants" in our midst are non-participants in the past (though our wisdom assures us this is impossible), drop-outs from history. The withdrawal from school, so typical of their generation and so inscrutable to ours, is best understood as a lived symbol of their rejection of the notion of cultural continuity and progress, which our graded educational system represents in institutional form. It is not merely a matter of their rejecting what happens to have happened just before them, as the young do, after all, in every age; but of their attempting to disavow the very idea of the past, of their seeking to avoid recapitulating it step by step—up to the point of graduation into the present.

Specifically, the tradition from which they strive to disengage is the tradition of the human, as the West (understanding the West to extend from the United States to Russia) has defined it, Humanism itself, both in its bourgeois and Marxist forms; and more especially, the cult of reason—that dream of Socrates, redreamed by the Renaissance and surviving all travesties down to only yesterday. . . .

With Dada the notion of an anti-rational anti-literature was born; and Dada became Surrealism, i.e., submitted to the influence of those last neo-Humanists, those desperate Socratic Cabalists, Freud and Marx—dedicated respectively to contriving a rationale of violence and a rationale of impulse. The new irrationalists, however, deny all the apostles of reason, Freud as well as Socrates; and if they seem to exempt Marx, this is be-

* From a longer essay.

cause they know less about him, have heard him evoked less
often by the teachers they are driven to deny. Not only do they
reject the Socratic adage that the unexamined life is not worth
living, since for them precisely the unexamined life is the only
one worth enduring at all. But they also abjure the Freudian
one: "Where id was, ego shall be," since for them the true rally-
ing cry is, "Let id prevail over ego, impulse over order," or—
in negative terms—"Freud is a fink!"

The first time I heard this irreverent charge from the mouth
of a student some five or six years ago (I who had grown up
thinking of Freud as a revolutionary, a pioneer), I knew that
I was already in the future; though I did not yet suspect that
there would be no room in that future for the university system
to which I had devoted my life. Kerouac might have told me
so, or Ginsberg, or even so polite and genteel a spokesman for
youth as J. D. Salinger, but I was too aware of what was wrong
with such writers . . . to be sensitive to the truths they told.
It took, therefore, certain public events to illuminate (for me)
the literature which might have illuminated them.

I am thinking, of course, of the demonstrations at Berkeley
and elsewhere, whose ostensible causes were civil rights or
freedom of speech or Vietnam, but whose not so secret slogan
was all the time: *The Professor is a Fink!* And what an array
of bad anti-academic novels, I cannot help reminding myself,
written by disgruntled professors, created the mythology out of
which that slogan grew. Each generation of students is invented
by the generation of teachers just before them; but how different they are in dream and fact—as different as self-hatred and
its reflection in another. How different the professors in Jeremy
Larner's *Drive, He Said* from those even in Randall Jarrell's
Pictures from an Institution or Mary McCarthy's *Groves of
Academe. . . .*

Many of the thousands who resisted or shouted on campuses
did so in the name of naïve or disingenuous or even nostalgic
politics (be careful what you wish for in your middle age, or
your children will parody it forthwith!); and sheer ennui

doubtless played a role along with a justified rage against the hypocrisies of academic life. Universities have long rivaled the churches in their devotion to institutionalizing hypocrisy; and more recently they have outstripped television itself . . . in the institutionalization of boredom.

But what the students were protesting in large part, I have come to believe, was the very notion of man which the universities sought to impose upon them: that bourgeois-Protestant version of Humanism, with its view of man as justified by rationality, work, duty, vocation, maturity, success; and its concomitant understanding of childhood and adolescence as a temporarily privileged time of preparation for assuming those burdens. The new irrationalists, however, are prepared to advocate prolonging adolescence to the grave, and are ready to dispense with school as an outlived excuse for leisure. To them work is as obsolete as reason, a vestige (already dispensable for large numbers) of an economically marginal, pre-automated world; and the obsolescence of the two adds up to the obsolescence of everything our society understands by maturity.

Nor is it in the name of an older more valid Humanistic view of man that the new irrationalists would reject the WASP version; Rabelais is as alien to them as Benjamin Franklin. Disinterested scholarship, reflection, the life of reason, a respect for tradition stir (however dimly and confusedly) chiefly their contempt; and the Abbey of Theleme would seem as sterile to them as Robinson Crusoe's Island. To the classroom, the library, the laboratory, the office conference and the meeting of scholars, they prefer the demonstration, the sit-in, the riot: the mindless unity of an impassioned crowd (with guitars beating out the rhythm in the background), whose immediate cause is felt rather than thought out, whose ultimate cause is itself. . . .

The choice has been extended beyond what the earlier laureates of the new youth could imagine in the novel: the nervous breakdown at home rather than the return to "sanity" and school, which was the best Salinger could invent for Franny and Holden; or Kerouac's way out for his "saintly" vagrants, that "road" from nowhere to noplace with homemade gurus at the way stations. The structure of those fictional vaudevilles between hard covers that currently please the young *(Catch-22, V., A Mother's Kisses)*, suggest in their brutality and discontinuity, their politics of mockery, something of the spirit of the student demonstrations; but only Jeremy Larner, as far as I know, has dealt explicitly with the abandonment of the classroom in favor of the dionysiac pack, the turning from *polis* to *thiasos*, from forms of social organization traditionally thought of as male to the sort of passionate community attributed by the ancients to females out of control.

Conventional slogans in favor of "Good Works" (pious emendations of existing social structures, or extensions of accepted "rights" to excluded groups) though they provide the motive power of such protests are irrelevant to their form and their final significance. They become their essential selves, i.e., genuine new forms of rebellion, when the demonstrators hoist . . . the sort of slogan which embarrasses not only fellow-travelers but even the bureaucrats who direct the initial stages of the revolt: at the University of California, the single four-letter word no family newspaper would reprint, though no member of a family who could read was likely not to know it. . . . The prophetic literature which anticipates the movement, [suggests] that the logic of their illogical course eventually sets the young against language itself, against the very counters of logical discourse. They seek an anti-language of protest as inevitably as they seek anti-poems and anti-novels, end with the ultimate anti-word, which the demonstrators at Berkeley disingenuously claimed stood for FREEDOM UNDER CLARK KERR.

Esthetics, however, had already anticipated politics in this regard; porno-poetry preceding and preparing the way for what Lewis Feuer has aptly called porno-politics. . . . Of course, [after a] while, there will be no [one] left to shock—anti-language becoming mere language with repeated use and in the face of acceptance; so that all sense of exhilaration will be lost along with the possibility of offense. What to do then except to choose silence, since raising the ante of violence is ultimately self-defeating; and the way of obscenity in any case leads as naturally to silence as to further excess? Moreover, to the talkative heirs of Socrates, silence is the one offense that never wears out, the radicalism that can never become fashionable; which is why, after the obscene slogan has been hauled down, a blank placard is raised in its place. . . .

When the Town Council in Venice, California, was about to close down a particularly notorious beatnik cafe, a lady asked to testify before them, presumably to clinch the case against the offenders. What she reported, however, was that each day as she walked by the cafe and looked in its windows, she saw the unsavory types who inhabited it "just standing there, looking—nonchalant." And, in a way, her improbable adjective does describe a crime against her world; for non-chaleur ("cool," the futurists themselves would prefer to call it) is the essence of their life-style as well as of the literary styles to which they respond: the offensive style of those who are not so much *for* anything in particular, as "with it" in general. But such an attitude is as remote from traditional "alienation," with its profound longing to end disconnection, as it is from ordinary forms of allegiance, with their desperate resolve not to admit disconnection. The new young celebrate disconnection—accept it as one of the necessary consequences of the industrial system which has delivered them from work and duty, of that welfare state which makes disengagement the last possible virtue, whether it call itself Capitalist, Socialist or Communist. "Detachment" is the traditional name for the stance the futurists assume; but "detachment" carries with it irrelevant religious, even specifically Christian overtones. The post-modernists are surely in some sense "mystics," religious at least in a way they do not ordinarily know how to confess, but they are not Christians.

Indeed, they regard Christianity quite as the Black Muslim (with whom they have certain affinities) do, as a white ideology: merely one more method—along with Humanism, technology,

Marxism—of imposing "White"or Western values on the colored rest of the world. To the new barbarian, however, that
would-be post-Humanist (who is in most cases the white offspring of Christian forebears) his whiteness is likely to seem
if not a stigma and symbol of shame, at least the outward sign
of his exclusion from all that his Christian Humanist ancestors
rejected in themselves and projected mythologically upon the
colored man. For such reasons, his religion, when it becomes
explicit, claims to be derived from Tibet or Japan or the ceremonies of the Plains Indians, or is composed out of the non-
Christian sub-mythology that has grown up among Negro jazz
musicians and in the civil rights movement. . . .

It is all part of the attempt of the generation under twenty-
five, not exclusively in its most sensitive members but especially
in them, to become Negro, even as they attempt to become poor
or pre-rational. . . . [And] what starts as a specifically American movement becomes an international one, spreading to the
yé-yé girls of France or the working-class entertainers of Liverpool with astonishing swiftness and ease.

What interests me more particularly right now is a parallel
attempt of young men in England and the United States to
assimilate into themselves (or even to assimilate themselves
into) that otherness, that sum total of rejected psychic elements
which the middle-class heirs of the Renaissance have identified
with "woman." To become new men, these children of the
future seem to feel, they must not only become more Black than
White but more female than male. . . . Surely, in America,
machines already perform better than humans a large number
of those aggressive-productive activities which our ancestors
considered man's special province, even his *raison d'être*. Not
only has the male's preorgative of making things and money
(which is to say, of working) been pre-empted, but also his
time-honored privilege of dealing out death by hand, which
until quite recently was regarded as a supreme mark of masculine valor. While it seems theoretically possible, even in the
heart of Anglo-Saxondom, to imagine a leisurely, pacific male,

in fact the losses in secondary functions sustained by men appear to have shaken their faith in their primary masculine function as well, in their ability to achieve the conquest (as the traditional metaphor has it) of women. . . .

Literary critics have talked a good deal during the past couple of decades about the conversion of the literary hero into the non-hero or the anti-hero; but they have in general failed to notice his simultaneous conversion into the non- or anti-male. Yet ever since Hemingway at least, certain male protagonists of American literature have not only fled rather than sought out combat but have also fled rather than sought out women. From Jake Barnes to Holden Caulfield they have continued to run from the threat of female sexuality; and, indeed, there are models for such evasion in our classic books, where heroes still eager for the fight (Natty Bumppo comes to mind) are already shy of wives and sweethearts and mothers.

It is not absolutely required that the anti-male anti-hero be impotent or homosexual or both (though this helps, as we remember remembering Walt Whitman), merely that he be more seduced than seducing, more passive than active. Consider, for instance, the oddly "womanish" Herzog of Bellow's . . . best seller, that Jewish Emma Bovary with a Ph.D., whose chief flaw is physical vanity and a taste for fancy clothes. Bellow, however, is more interested in summing up the past than in evoking the future; and *Herzog* therefore seems an end rather than a beginning, the product of nostalgia (remember when there were real Jews once, and the "Jewish Novel" had not yet been discovered!) rather than prophecy. No, the post-Humanist, post-male, post white, post-heroic world is a post-Jewish world by the same token, anti-Semitism as inextricably woven into it as into the movement for Negro rights; and its scriptural books are necessarily *goyish.* . . . Burroughs is the chief prophet of the post-male post-heroic world; and it is his emulators who move into the center of the relevant literary scene, for *The Naked Lunch* (the later novels are less successful, less exciting but relevant still) is more than it seems: no mere essay in heroin-hallucinated homosexual pornography—but a nightmare anticipation (in Science Fiction form) of post-Humanist sexuality. . . .

The young to whom I have been referring, the mythologically representative minority (who, by a process that infuriates the mythologically inert majority out of which they come, "stand for" their times), live in a community in which what used to be called the "Sexual Revolution," the Freudian-Laurentian revolt of their grandparents and parents, has triumphed as imperfectly and unsatisfactorily as all revolutions always triumph. They confront, therefore, the necessity of determining not only what meanings "love" can have in their new world, but—even more disturbingly—what significance, if any, "male" and "female" now possess. For a while, they (or at least their literary spokesmen recruited from the generation just before them) seemed content to celebrate a kind of *reductio* or *exaltatio ad absurdum* of their parents' once revolutionary sexual goals: The Reichian-inspired Cult of the Orgasm.

Young men and women eager to be delivered of traditional ideologies of love find especially congenial the belief that not union or relationship (much less offspring) but physical release is the end of the sexual act; and that, therefore, it is a matter of indifference with whom or by what method one pursues the therapeutic climax, so long as that climax is total and repeated frequently. And Wilhelm Reich happily detaches this belief from the vestiges of Freudian rationalism, setting it instead in a context of Science Fiction and witchcraft; but his emphasis upon "full genitality," upon growing up and away from infantile pleasures, strikes the young as a disguised plea for the "maturity" they have learned to despise. In a time when the duties associated with adulthood promise to become irrelevant, there seems little reason for denying oneself the joys of babyhood—even if these are associated with such regressive fantasies as escaping it all in the arms of little sister (in the Gospel according to J. D. Salinger) or flirting with the possibility of getting into bed with papa (in the Gospel according to Norman Mailer).

Only Norman O. Brown in *Life Against Death* has come to terms on the level of theory with the aspiration to take the final evolutionary leap and cast off adulthood completely, at least in the area of sex. His post-Freudian program for pan-sexual, non-orgasmic love rejects "full genitality" in favor of a species of indiscriminate bundling, a dream of unlimited sub-coital intimacy which Brown calls (in his vocabulary the term is an honorific) "polymorphous perverse." And here finally is an essential clue to the nature of the second sexual revolution, the post-sexual revolution. . . . What is at stake from Burroughs to Bellow, Ginsberg to Albee, Salinger to Gregory Corso is . . . a radical metamorphosis of the Western male—utterly unforeseen in the decades before us, but visible now in every high-school and college classroom, as well as on the paperback racks in airports and supermarkets. All around us, young males are beginning to retrieve for themselves the cavalier role once piously and class-consciously surrendered to women: *that of being beautiful and being loved.* Here once more the example of the Negro—the feckless and adorned Negro male with the blood of Cavaliers in his veins—has served as a model. . . .

Watching young men titivate their locks (the comb, the pocket mirror and the bobby pin having replaced the jacknife, catcher's mitt and brass knuckles), we feel the same baffled resentment that stirs in us when we realize that they have rejected work. A job and unequivocal maleness—these are two sides of the same Calvinist coin, which in the future buys nothing. Few of us, however, have really understood how the Beatle hairdo is part of a syndrome, of which high heels, jeans tight over the buttocks, etc., are other aspects, symptomatic of a larger retreat from masculine aggressiveness to female allure—in literature and the arts to the style called "camp." And fewer still have realized how that style, though the invention of homosexuals, is now the possession of basically heterosexual males as well, a strategy in their campaign to establish a new relationship not only with women but with their own masculinity. In the course of that campaign, they have embraced certain kinds of gesture and garb, certain accents and tones traditionally associated with females or female impersonators; which is why we have been observing recently (in life as well as fiction and verse) young boys, quite unequivocally male, playing all the traditional roles of women: the vamp, the coquette, the whore, the icy tease, the pure young virgin. . . .

There is also a sense in which two large social movements that have set the young in motion and furnished images of action for their books . . . are connected analogically to the abdication from traditional maleness. The first of these is nonviolent or passive resistance (so oddly come back to the land of its inventor, that icy Thoreau who dreamed a love which ". . . has not much human blood in it, but consists with a certain disregard for men and their erections. . ."). The civil rights movement, however, in which nonviolence has found a home, has been hospitable not only to the sort of post-Humanist I have been describing; so that at a demonstration . . . the true hippie will be found side by side with backwoods Baptists, nuns on a spiritual spree, boy bureaucrats practicing to take power, resurrected socialists, Unitarians in search of a God, and just plain tourists, gathered, as once at the Battle of Bull Run, to see the fun. For each of these, nonviolence will have a different sort of fundamental meaning—as a tactic, a camouflage, a passing fad, a pious gesture—but for each in part, and for the post-Humanist especially, it will signify the possibility of heroism without aggression, effective action without guilt. There have always been two contradictory American ideals: to be the occasion of maximum violence, and to remain absolutely innocent. Once, however, these were thought hopelessly incompatible for males (except, perhaps, as embodied in works of art), reserved strictly for women: the spouse of the wife-beater, for instance, or the victim of rape. But males have now assumed these classic roles. . . .

The second social movement is the drug cult. . . . Only fiction and verse, however, have dealt with the conjunction of homosexuality, drugs and civil rights, eschewing the general piety of the press which has been unwilling to compromise "good works" on behalf of the Negro by associating it with the deep radicalism of a way of life based on the ritual consumption of "pot." The widespread use of hallucinogens . . . is not merely a matter of a changing taste in stimulants but of the programmatic espousal of anti-puritanical mode of existence—hedonistic and detached—one more strategy in the war on time and work. . . . With drugs we have come to the crux of the futurist revolt, the hinge of everything else, as the young tell us over and over in their writing. When the movement was first finding a voice, Allen Ginsberg set this aspect of it in proper context in an immensely comic, utterly serious poem called "America," in which "pot" is associated with earlier forms of rebellion, a commitment to catatonia, and a rejection of conventional male potency. . . .

Here . . . is where the young lose us in literature as well as life, since here they pass over into real revolt, i.e., what we really cannot abide, hard as we try. The mother who has sent her son to private schools and on to Harvard, to keep him out of classrooms overcrowded with poor Negroes, rejoices when he sets out for Mississippi with his comrades in SNCC but shudders when he turns on with LSD; just as the ex-Marxist father, who has earlier proved radicalism impossible, rejoices to see his son stand up, piously and pompously, for CORE or SDS, but trembles to hear him quote Alpert and Leary or praise Burroughs. Just as certainly as liberalism is the LSD of the aging, LSD is the radicalism of the young.

If whiskey long served as an appropriate symbolic excess for those who chafed against Puritan restraint without finally challenging it—temporarily releasing them to socially harmful aggression and (hopefully) sexual self-indulgence, the new popular drugs provide an excess quite as satisfactorily symbolic to the post-Puritans—releasing them from sanity to madness by

destroying in them the inner restrictive order which has somehow survived the dissolution of the outer. It is finally insanity,
then, that the futurists learn to admire and emulate, quite as
they learn to pursue vision instead of learning, hallucination
rather than logic. The schizophrenic replaces the sage as their
ideal, their new culture hero, figured forth as a giant schizoid
Indian (his madness modeled in part on the author's own experiences with LSD) in Ken Kesey's *One Flew Over the
Cuckoo's Nest.*

The hippier young are not alone, however, in their taste for
the insane; we live in a time when readers in general respond
sympathetically to madness in literature wherever it is found,
in established writers as well as in those trying to establish new
modes. . . . In any case, poets and junkies have been suggesting
to us that the new world appropriate to the new men of the
latter twentieth century is to be discovered only by the conquest
of inner space: by an adventure of the spirit, an extension of
psychic possibility, of which the flights into outer space . . .
are precisely such unwitting metaphors and analogues as the
voyages of exploration were of the earlier breakthrough into
the Renaissance, from whose consequences the young seek now
so desperately to escape. The laureate of that new conquest is
William Burroughs; and it is fitting that the final word be his:

This war will be won in the air. In the Silent Air with Image Rays. You
were a pilot remember? Tracer bullets cutting the right wing you were
free in space a few seconds before in blue space between eyes. Go back
to Silence. Keep Silence. Keep Silence. K.S. K.S. . . . From Silence re-
write the message that is you. You are the message I send to The Enemy. My Silent Message."

The Naked Astronauts were free in space. . . .

SUSAN SONTAG

as much an experience as an idea

**There is a profound concordance between
the sexual revolution, redefined, and the political revolution, redefined. The ordinarily
available options of character repress . . . the
deep experience of pleasure, and the possibility
of self-knowledge.**

About the only promise one can find anywhere in this
country today is in the way some young people are carrying
on, making a fuss. I include both their renewed interest in
politics (as protest and as community action, rather than as
theory) and the way they dance, dress, wear their hair, riot,
make love. I also include the homage they pay to Oriental
thought and rituals. And I include, not least of all, their interest
in taking drugs—despite the unspeakable vulgarization of this
project by Leary and others.

. . . Leslie Fiedler, in a remarkably wrongheaded and interesting essay . . . ("The New Mutants") called attention to the
fact that the new style of young people indicated a deliberate
blurring of sexual differences, signaling the creation of a new
breed of youthful androgynes. The longhaired pop groups with
their mass teen-age following and the tiny elite of turned-on
kids from Berkeley to the East Village were both lumped together as representatives of the "post-humanist" era now upon
us, in which we witness a "radical metamorphosis of the western
male," a "revolt against masculinty," even "a rejection of conventional male potency." For Fiedler, this new turn in personal

mores, diagnosed as illustrating a "programmatic espousal of
an anti-puritanical mode of existence," is something to deplore.
(Though sometimes, in his characteristic have-it-both-ways manner, Fiedler seemed to be vicariously relishing this development, *mainly* he appeared to be lamenting it.) But why, he
never made explicit. I think it is because he is sure such a mode
of existence undercuts radical politics, and its moral visions,
altogether. Being radical in the older sense (some version of
Marxism or socialism or anarchism) meant to be attached still
to traditional "puritan" values of work, sobriety, achievement
and family-founding. Fiedler suggests, as have Philip Rahv and
Irving Howe and Malcolm Muggeridge among others, that the
new style of youth must be, at bottom, apolitical, and their
revolutionary spirit a species of infantilism. The fact that the
same kid joins SNCC or boards a Polaris submarine or agrees
with Conor Cruise O'Brien *and* smokes pot and is bisexual and
adores the Supremes, is seen as a contradiction, a kind of ethical fraud or intellectual weak-mindedness.

I don't believe this to be so. The depolarizing of the sexes, to
mention the element that Fiedler observes with such fascination,
is the natural, and desirable, next stage of the sexual revolution
(its dissolution, perhaps) which has moved beyond the idea of
sex as a damaged but discrete zone of human activity, beyond
the discovery that "society" represses the free expression of sexuality (by fomenting guilt), to the discovery that the way we live
and the ordinarily available options of character repress almost
entirely the deep experience of pleasure, and the possibility of
self-knowledge. "Sexual freedom" is a shallow, outmoded
slogan. What, who is being liberated? For older people, the sexual revolution is an idea that remains meaningful. One can be
for it or against it; if for it, the idea remains confined within
the norms of Freudianism and its derivatives. But Freud *was* a
Puritan, or "a fink," as one of Fiedler's students distressingly
blurted out. So was Marx. It is right that young people see beyond Freud and Marx. Let the professors be the caretakers of
this indeed precious legacy, and discharge all the obligations of

piety. No need for dismay if the kids don't continue to pay the old dissenter-gods obeisance.

It seems to me obtuse, though understandable, to patronize the new kind of radicalism, which is post-Freudian and post-Marxian. For this radicalism is as much an experience as an idea. Without the personal experience, if one is looking in from the outside, it does look messy and almost pointless. It's easy to be put off by the youngsters throwing themselves around with their eyes closed to the near-deafening music of the discothèques (unless you're dancing, too), by the longhaired marchers carrying flowers and temple bells as often as "Get Out of Vietnam" placards, by the inarticulateness of a Mario Savio. One is also aware of the high casualty rate among this gifted, visionary minority among the young, the tremendous cost in personal suffering and in mental strain. The fakers, the slobs and the merely flipped-out are plentiful among them. But the complex desires of the best of them: to engage and to "drop out"; to be beautiful to look at and touch as well as to be good; to be loving and quiet as well as militant and effective—these desires make sense in our present situation. To sympathize, of course, you have to be convinced that things in America really are as desperately bad as I have indicated. This is hard to see; the desperateness of things is obscured by the comforts and liberties that America does offer. Most people, understandably, don't really believe things are that bad. That's why, for them, the antics of this youth can be no more than a startling item in the passing parade of cultural fashions, to be appraised with a friendly, but essentially weary and knowing look. The sorrowful look that says: I was a radical, too, when I was young. When are these kids going to grow up and realize what we had to realize, that things never are going to be really different, except maybe worse?

From my own experience and observation, I can testify that there is a profound concordance between the sexual revolution, redefined, and the political revolution, redefined. That being a socialist and taking certain drugs (in a fully serious spirit: as a technique for exploring one's consciousness, not as an anodyne

or a crutch), are not incompatible, that there is no incompati-
bility between the exploration of inner space and the rectifica-
tion of social space. What some of the kids understand is that
it's the whole character-structure of modern American man, and
his imitators, that needs rehauling. (Old folks like Paul Goodman and Edgar Z. Friedenberg have, of course, been suggesting
this for a long time.) That rehauling includes Western "masculinity," too. They believe that some socialist remodeling of institutions and the ascendance, through electoral means or otherwise, of better leaders won't really change anything. And they
are right.

Neither do I dare deride the turn toward the East (or more
generally, to the wisdoms of the nonwhite world) on the part of
a tiny group of young people—however uninformed and jejune
the adherence usually is. (But then, nothing could be more ignorant than Fiedler's insinuation that Oriental modes of thought
are "feminine" and "passive," which is the reason the demascu-
linized kids are drawn to them.) Why shouldn't they look for
wisdom elsewhere? If America *is* the culmination of Western
white civilization, as everyone from the Left to the Right declares, then there must be something terribly wrong with Western white civilization. This is a painful truth; few of us want to
go that far. It's easier, much easier, to accuse the kids, to re-
proach them for being "non-participants in the past" and "dropouts from history." But it isn't real history Fiedler is referring
to with such solicitude. It's just *our* history, which he claims is
identical with "the tradition of the human," the tradition of
"reason" itself. Of course, it's hard to assess life on this planet
from a genuinely world-historical perspective; the effort induces
vertigo and seems like an invitation to suicide. But from a
world-historical perspective, that local history which some young
people are repudiating (with their fondness for dirty words,
their peyote, their macrobiotic rice, their Dadaist art, etc.) looks
a good deal less pleasing and less self-evidently worthy of per-
petuation. The truth is that Mozart, Pascal, Boolean algebra,
Shakespeare, parliamentary government, baroque churches,

Newton, the emancipation of women, Kant, Marx, Balanchine ballets, *et al.*, don't redeem what this particular civilization has wrought upon the world. The white race *is* the cancer of human history; it is the white race and it alone—its ideologies and inventions—which eradicates autonomous civilizations wherever it spreads, which has upset the ecological balance of the planet, which now threatens the very existence of life itself. What the Mongol hordes threaten is far less frightening than the damage that Western "Faustian" man, with his idealism, his magnificent art, his sense of intellectual adventure, his world-devouring energies for conquest, has already done, and further threatens to do.

This is what some of the kids sense, though few of them could put it in words. Again, I believe them to be right. I'm not arguing that they're going to prevail, or even that they're likely to change much of anything in this country. But a few of them may save their own souls. America is a fine country for inflaming people, from Emerson and Thoreau to Mailer and Burroughs and Leo Szilard and John Cage and Judith and Julian Beck, with the project of trying to save their own souls. Salvation becomes almost a mundane, inevitable goal when things are so bad, really intolerable.

One last comparison, which I hope won't seem farfetched. The Jews left the ghetto in the early nineteenth century, thus becoming a people doomed to disappear. But one of the by-products of their fateful absorption into the modern world was an incredible burst of creativity in the arts, science and secular scholarship—the relocation of a powerful but frustrated spiritual energy. These innovating artists and intellectuals were not alienated Jews, as is said so often, but people who were alienated *as* Jews.

I'm scarcely more hopeful for America than I am for the Jews. This is a doomed country, it seems to me; I only pray that, when America founders, it doesn't drag the rest of the planet down, too. But one should notice that, during its long elephantine agony, America is also producing its subtlest minority generation of the decent and sensitive, young people who are alienated *as* Americans. They are not drawn to the stale truths of their sad elders (though these are truths). More of their elders should be listening to them.

ART BUCHWALD

buchwald's guide
to campus capers

It's appalling, absolutely appalling.

It is generally agreed that the student unrest going on these days is worldwide. It doesn't matter if the students live in a permissive society or a totalitarian one—they're still raising cain. And for that reason, those of us watching from the sidelines are divided as to whether the unrest is a good thing or a bad thing.

At the University Club the other day I was having a brandy and cigar with some very nice chaps when the question of student demonstrations came up.

"I see where they still haven't solved the problem at Columbia," Liverwhistle said.

"It's appalling, absolutely appalling," Cartwright sputtered. "The students should all be booted out on their ears. You can't have a university if you're going to have children running around locking up the faculty."

Conrad said, "Did you read what's going on in Paris? The students have tied up the city."

"Ah yes," said Cartwright. "One can't help admiring the French students' gumption. They've certainly put de Gaulle in his place."

"You have to respect their attitude," Liverwhistle said. "At lease the students can see through de Gaulle."

"I don't think things have cooled off at Stanford," Studsdale commented. "They're still holding the administration building."

"If you ask me," said Cartwright, "it's a Communist plot. These things don't just happen."

"Did you read where the students in Czechoslovakia not only demonstrated, but caused the downfall of the Soviet-backed regime?"

"God bless them," said Conrad. "If we're ever going to see the end of tyranny behind the Iron Curtain, it's going to be the students who accomplish it."

"I understand the same thing could happen in Poland," Liverwhistle said, "and perhaps even East Germany. They're a new breed, those students, and a credit to the human race."

"You know, of course," said Studsdale, "that the administration completely collapsed at Northwestern and gave in to every demand of the students there."

Cartwright said, "My blood boiled when I read the story. Those damn kids don't know up from down and they're telling us how to run the country. I say we have to act now and act firmly."

"The students in Franco's Spain have been agitating for a year now. No one knows how many are in jail," Conrad said.

"The poor kids," Liverwhistle said. "They're only trying to make a better world, and they're thrown in jail for it. I think we should get up a petition and send it to the Spanish Ambassador."

"I see they're having another sit-in at Berkeley," Liverwright commented.

"They're always having a sit-in at Berkeley," Studsdale said. "I'll tell you what's wrong with the kids today. They've got too much money. They don't even appreciate what we've gone through to give them an education. All they talk about is freedom. What kind of freedom?"

"It's the faculty," said Conrad. "They're the ones who egg the students on. Instead of jailing the students, they ought to lock up the faculty. Then we'd stop all this anarchy on campuses."

Cartwright, who was flipping through a newspaper, said, "It

says here that the students in Communist China are thinking about having another Red Guard revolution."

"Great," said Liverwhistle. "Old Mao won't be able to take another one of those."

Liverwright agreed. "I must say one thing for the students abroad. They sure have a lot of class."

NORMAN PODHORETZ
(Interviewed by Alexander Klein)

yes and no

There is a vast discrepancy between the ideals and objectives of a liberal education and the vocational realities in American society.

QUESTION: The New Left and the hippies, though they're small minorities, are considered to be two basic manifestations of youth today.

ANSWER: Yes, we're all of us very historically minded, so we tend to believe that generational changes are enormously significant; consequently the small minority which is most different from its immediate predecessor generation is always the center of attention. And it is always a small minority that is responsible, if not for making historical changes, at least for articulating or dramatizing them. Back in 1957 when the Beats appeared, they seemed to me very significant, not as a literary group, but as a social phenomenon. It was as though all the qualities of youthfulness which had been repressed among the youth of the 1950's had suddenly come bubbling to the surface and been turned into a kind of ideology by the Beats. In the fifties the magical words were maturity, responsibility, sobriety. There was no romanticizing of youth. On the contrary, there was a good deal of denigrating of youth, and insofar as there was a cultural ideal in vogue during the fifties, it was that of the adult—the mature, responsible, disciplined, intelligent adult. Salinger's *Catcher in the Rye* expresses perfectly this notion that youth was not only misunderstood but that in some sense

the world was in a conspiracy against it. The qualities of youth
—spontaneity, wildness, the quest for novelty, the interest in
experimenting with sensation—all that was frowned upon generally. Then the Beats came along and turned youthfulness itself into a kind of ideology. They were the first expression of
what has by now become the dominant notion in our culture, so
historically they're very important.

Now the Beats were, of course, non-political and in that sense
the ancestors of the hippies. But, I think the New Left was also
born out of the Beat movement. Because there was a certain
logic to the Beat movement which that movement in itself was
unable to fulfill. What the Beats were saying was that this society was sick, insane, was engaged in a conspiracy both conscious and unconscious to destroy, as Allen Ginsberg put it, the
best minds of the generation, to destroy youthfulness and spontaneity, and the only answer the Beats had to this was the strategy of withdrawal and of voluntary poverty.

Now a genuine artist, someone with talent, can, in fact, withdraw from the mainstream of a given social system and can
even flourish under those conditions. But people who have no
particular talent and no sense of vocation are in a dreadful
bind; I mean, what do they do when they grow up? It seems to
me that there was an implicit political logic in the Beat ideology.
This attack on the society had inevitably at some point to turn
political. The Beats were curiously of the fifties in the sense that
they never envisaged the possibility of changing society to make
it conform more closely to their notion of a good society. Most
people in the fifties assumed that American society was for all
practical purposes finished. You could tinker with it a little bit
here, a little bit there, but no radical changes could be made,
and the Beats accepted this view. Then came the sit-ins in the
South—a great surprise to most people—a sudden upsurge of
political energy among the Negroes in the late fifties. The beginnings of an active Negro movement crossed, or mated, with
this Beat sense of non-political disaffection to produce the New
Left. And of course there was in those days a very obsessive

preoccupation with the danger of nuclear war. Today people appear to have forgotten about the bomb.

There were other phenomena associated with the Beats. I think of the appearance of the so-called sick comics—most of them actually quite tame. But in the late fifties Mort Sahl seemed very daring, even Nichols and May seemed daring, because they brought a tone of irreverence into the public culture that had simply not been there for a long time. Then of course there were the black humorists in the novel, culminating in the best book in that tradition, *Catch-22*. All this helped in the generating of a new cultural and political atmosphere of which Kennedy was both a part and a cause. The Kennedy administration itself was more an atmosphere than anything substantive. It would be difficult to define Kennedy's impact in terms of legislative or foreign-policy achievements.

The New Left did not begin as an activist movement. As I recall, the first signs of its existence were in rather academic periodicals such as *Studies on the Left* put out by graduate students who were discovering a new interest in Marxism and were writing quite ponderous articles on the nature of American society as seen from a Marxist or neo-Marxist point of view. But there were no protests, no demonstrations. All those direct-action techniques were later taken over from the Negro movement in the South.

The difficulty of course with youth movements is that youth is an unstable condition, and nature is its enemy; with each passing year you get less young. And if you build a movement around the principle of youthfulness, you're almost dooming yourself to obsolescence in a very short time. The old left in America had its youthful auxiliaries, but it was not built around kids. Nor did it idealize youthfulness as a principle.

Q: David Riesman and many others believe that the generation gap has never been wider. Many view it with concern if not alarm.

A: I don't know whether it's true that the generation gap has never been wider. The most extreme expression of that

point of view is Leslie Fiedler's idea that today's youth are
"mutants," almost a new species. Others believe this is a normal
generation gap which has been aggravated by certain factors in
our society. I myself don't believe that the new generation are
mutants. I have children of my own and I have my troubles with
them, but they don't seem to be members of a different species.
It's even possible to talk to them sometimes.

The last time I lectured at a college, I told the students that
I was too young to be as intimidated by them as some older
people seemed to be, that I tended to not trust anyone *under*
thirty, that my own feeling was that I had more to say to them
than they had to say to me. I was being deliberately provocative,
of course; but instead of being provoked they were totally aston-
ished at being talked to this way. It was perfectly clear that no
one had talked to them like that before; some of them seemed
to like it very much.

Anyway, the idea of a generation gap is becoming a little
silly. We've reached the point now where a new generation pro-
claims itself every six months. I gather from Kenneth Keniston's
book, *Young Radicals*, that they now talk without any irony
about the Old New Left, the New Left, and the New New Left.
Three generations in eight years.

Q: What about the sexual revolution?

A: I suspect that revolution is more rhetorical than real. My
own notion of a true sexual revolution would be a world in which
girls hopped into bed with boys as casually as boys used to do
with girls. Complete promiscuity, in other words, and an acceptance of promiscuity as normal and right. By all accounts,
nothing of that kind has happened or is likely to happen. Love
is now thought to legitimize sex, but that idea has been around
for a very long time; it's not revolutionary.

Q: Yes, but I think there is one huge change: premarital sex
is regarded as a good by *most* of the kids, girls included. If a
girl has problems in enjoying sex now, she wants to overcome
them, not necessarily to jump in bed with every boy, but to be
able to enjoy sex when she wants to. And, in many cases, she

wants to be free to experiment a fair bit, both short-term and
longer-term, before settling into marriage. I wonder if the over-
forties aren't inordinately jealous of the hedonistic life youth
appears to be enjoying?

A: Certainly, there's a natural envy. But I think there's also
a protective sense operating. Parents may be total libertarians,
but as parents they don't allow their little children to cross the
street at will. And, to be a responsible parent—by which I mean
seeing to it that your children survive reasonably well into
adulthood—you're forced to submit yourself and them to a good
many rules which you yourself often wish you could disregard.
In relation to their children, parents necessarily speak and act
in the name of prudence. In this general area the generational
conflict is almost a part of the biological law.

Q: Turning to another area, thirty years ago youth faced
the problem of making a living. Today the ones at the bottom
are facing it worse than ever, psychologically in any event, because the majority don't need to face it. They can say: "We're
not living to make it, feverishly, to achieve middle-class comfort and material security. We have that made. So we look elsewhere for purpose and meaning in our lives."

A: Here, they're justified. What we're seeing is the creation
of a dependent class, young people who are no longer children,
but are kept in a state of dependency, partly because society
has nothing for them to do. It's not for nothing that the graduate
schools are overloaded and it's not just happenstance that the
youth movement draws the line at thirty, rather than, say, at
twenty-one or twenty-five. Thirty was chosen as the terminal
point because for well-educated young people who are not
driven immediately by urgent necessity for food and shelter,
there are fewer and fewer jobs to do, particularly jobs they
themselves want to do. So they stick around in graduate school,
or opt out and drift for a while. One of the reasons the college
kids identify so easily with the masses of the blacks in the
ghettos is that they are both disenfranchised economically and
politically, or feel themselves to be. The blacks are obviously

in infinitely worse shape, but there is a kind of parallel problem here. Part of the difficulty, I think, lies in the nature of liberal education. In student rebellions the vast majority are liberal arts students; not engineering students or science or medical students. And there's very good reason for this. Liberal education was originally conceived as the education of free men, free meaning people not bound by the need to make a living, free meaning a gentleman with an income who could afford to cultivate his mind and his sensibilities. And liberal education has certain biases built into it. So if you are subjected to a liberal education, the better an education it is, and the more intelligent and sensitive you are, the more you are, in effect, being unfitted to work in society as it is presently constituted. There is a vast discrepancy between the ideals and objectives of a liberal education and the vocational realities in American society, or perhaps any industrial society. You can do two things with a liberal education. You can teach, which in a way is like becoming the priest of a religious order. Or if you happen to be very gifted, as a writer, painter, critic or social thinker, you can make a living in the "world." Otherwise you're in trouble because you've been taught that the other ways and modes of making a living in this society are contemptible, dehumanizing, unworthy of the serious and good man. Whatever one may say about the truth or falsity of this view, I think it's one of the elements of the difficulty we're in. And there are no ready solutions. Can you scrap liberal education or totally change society overnight?

Q: This relates to: (1) the students seeking a voice in determing curriculum and their education generally; (2) the fact that many of the best students seem to be cutting themselves off from tradition and complaining about the fact that such education is irrelevant. "The past is a fink." They would like to make education "more relevant" to their lives, their actions.

A: It doesn't seem to me self-evident that students ought to have a voice in the curriculum. I would need to hear many better arguments than I've heard in order to be convinced. As to the question of relevance, that's a very tricky concept. What seems relevant this week may seem irrelevant next week. Surely we can afford to have a few acres of the country walled off from the immediate urgent concerns of the surrounding world, places where one's sense of history and one's true sense of relevance can be developed, one's mind cultivated, one's sensibilities refined. Insofar as student power is hostile to those objectives, I for one would be hostile to student power.

ALFRED KAZIN

the party of hope

**A whole generation has unexpectedly . . .
become the leaven in the lump . . . the
conscience of our time. . . . What I
notice most . . . is their essential
meekness.**

The other day on Fifth Avenue in New York I saw a
truck crammed with students from a Catholic university who
are volunteers on a "reclamation" project in Harlem. One of
the students held up a placard which read, "God is not dead.
We are." When a teacher of my age gets to remembering too
fondly his ideals, struggles, and hopes as a college student in
the 1930's, it is important for him to see a placard like that
on Fifth Avenue, to recognize—in the midst of so much money,
ostentation, and waste—that the extraordinarily widespread
feelings of moral outrage filling our students today are incom-
parably purer and are likely to be more lasting than those that
arose from the politics of deprivation in the thirties.

In the thirties, the economic and social order had visibly
collapsed, and between hunger at home and Fascism-Nazism in
Europe, a student had good reason to feel that there was no
way to elementary human sanity and satisfaction but through
a militant and wholesale reconstruction of society from top to
bottom. As I look back upon it now, it occurs to me that com-
paratively few students indeed were involved in whatever was
particularly "militant"—and this militancy was often more the
mark of a fanatical ideology than of any idealistic, generous,
feeling participation in the suffering of the time.

The political activists of the thirties usually regarded themselves as an intellectual élite, as "cadres" or organizers of the

abject masses. Most important, the students who did most of
the analyzing, sloganeering, and talking were under the spell
of revolution as *total* change. And this, perhaps the last and
most obstinate of all nineteenth-century romantic illusions about
creating a wholly new world on the basis of literature alone,
meant that the agent of this romanticism would have to be brutal
power.

The radical élite of the thirties was in fact committed to a
dream so lofty, so unreal, so perennially exciting to the craving for a mythically "new world"—where man himself would
be utterly different from what he had always been—that only
arrogant authoritarian power would be able to create it. And
in fact the radicals of the thirties were committed to a model
of power—on the Russian model—whose moral consequences
would not become fully visible to them until the full horror of
the Soviet-Nazi alliance and the Second World War were unleashed upon them.

In justice, it must be admitted that the 1930's were singularly
a period of what the psychoanalyst Bruno Bettelheim in a
German concentration camp learned to call "extreme situations," and that the dream of a wholly "new" human being, who
was indeed soon to be manufactured under totalitarianism, had
behind it a necessarily drastic vision of change. Among hunger,
Fascism, and the oncoming war, life in the thirties was so hysterical as often to seem unreal, and this is why it became so easy
to idealize in later years as a period of "faith." A few students
and intellectuals seemed to have nothing but their hopes, and
their hopes were unlimited—and in fact unshared by most
Americans.

By contrast, students today seem to me the visible conscience
of society. I have never known a time when students were so
regularly a jump ahead of their elders in reacting to the
horrors of napalm, the idiocy of making political war on a
whole people, the banalities of middle-class life, the intoler-
ability of so much aggression, hatred, and human inequality in
our national life. What is so exciting to me about the present

generation of students is the fact that concern about "society"
has sprouted up, seemingly unmotivated in the richest and most
powerful nation in the world, from moral awareness, moral
sensitivity, moral intelligence. Not power over everybody else
in the name of a cruelly unrealizable ideal, not power for the
sake of universal abstractions, but a creative unrest is what
distinguishes the thinking of so many young people today.
What they have, very simply, is a refreshing freedom from the
materialism that in one way or another drives so many middle-
aged Americans crazy.

It may be that as one gets older one becomes more property
conscious, more cautious, and so, by degrees, more and more
disenchanted with oneself. Certainly the "guilt" that is one of
the more insistent maladies of our time often springs from the
middle-aged man's dislike of what he has become, what he is
forced to do, by contrast with the joyous self-affirmation so
natural to feel in youth. Of course there is much more to say
about "guilt" than this, but anyone who has seen what adult
"responsibility" can do to one's youthful idealism must admit
that everything the young say about the old is only too true.
Though we all have understandable excuses to make on the
subject and the worst seem to have no "guilt" at all, it is a
fact that only youth is poor enough and "irresponsible" enough
to look life straight in the face and to see the anxiety and bad
conscience that weigh down so many "successes" in our society.

In any event, society is always the hub of the matter nowadays, and so long as you are not wholly preoccupied by your
career and are still relatively unconsumed by the pressures, you
can see how insane and unjust much of society is, you can still
compare the human potential with the sufferings of a very large
part of the human race. Above all, if you are young enough to
be drafted, you can admit what the leaders of government do
not, that "war is the health of the state," that most people are
more and more committed to any economy that rests on war
and on war as a necessary and permanent part of culture.

In the 1930's, the social order was certainly breaking up

and a "new" society was supposed to replace it, but even radicals did not really feel committed to *awareness* of every human victim in the world—in fact, radicals especially were strikingly indifferent to the victims of the G.P.U., the old Soviet secret police. But today students even in Russia, Poland and Czechoslovakia, France and other countries seem to be refreshingly free of totalitarian ideologies and are as skeptical about the wholly "new" man manufactured by Communism as our students are about the corrupt old politicians we always have right at home. There is a universalism about the thinking of students everywhere that is one of the few checkmates to the ever-recurrent dreariness of national pomp and power, national interests and national mythification. I have seen this at Stony Brook and at Berkeley, at Harvard, in Berlin, and even in Moscow.

A whole generation has unexpectedly (perhaps to its surprise more than to ours) become the leaven in the lump, the party of hope, the spirit of change, the conscience of our time. For the first time in many years one can see what it means to persist in that healthy criticism of society that makes alternatives seem possible, that makes human faith possible again.

When this faith goes, as it has for so many middle-class, middle-aged Americans, life loses its savor. When it goes, one becomes sick with the bad faith of people who are defending nothing but their own interests even when they talk of saving Vietnam from "Communism." But when the spirit of change is present, it lights up everything one is unconsciously striving for.

What I notice most about students today, and don't always approve, is their essential meekness. I am aware that after a certain age, one insists upon "quiet," control, submission, and that the exasperated line that depleted energies take is always to accuse young people of being noisy, irreverent, and generally aggressive. But looked at in terms of their very real expectations and attitudes, our students are indeed meek. I mean by this that they do not believe in egotism, dominance, aggression, exploitation, and war.

For the first time perhaps since Christianity arose, one sees what a concerted philosophy of peace, here and everywhere in the world, shared in and acted on by young people everywhere, could mean to a world sickened by its unending violence. So far as I understand anything about my students, I understand that they are saying this: Without peace and without brotherhood nothing from here on out is possible. The meekness also follows from a marked lack of interest in business and moneymaking, from a lack of the old aggressive "individualism," from a sense of solidarity with all people of a certain age and with all people on the firing line of social crisis.

After the age of caution has come upon you, it takes a certain effort to admit that there are people around who want more for the human race than they want for themselves, that nothing likely to be gained by them as individual citizens matters so much to them as checking the moral deterioration of our society. That is why I am on the side of students today. With such young people the external commotion is to be firmly disregarded in favor of admiration—and gratitude.

ERICH FROMM

in the name of life*

**People are taught [to] mistake the
finger for the moon.**

What is so important and so beautiful about this occasion is that it is not something specific to Columbia University, to New York or the United States. It is part of a movement
going on in the whole world. . . . The essence of this movement
is the fight, or, if you like, the revolution in the name of life.
Life today is threatened in two ways: at present by the events
in Vietnam; beyond that by the threat of thermonuclear war. . . .

But life is not only threatened physically, it is also threatened in another sense. The society in which we live is already,
and more and more becoming, a society of zombies . . . of
automatons . . . of people who do not respond to ideas any
more, who do not feel and do not think, but who are programmed. And very few of us are aware of the programming,
because it is the nature of computers that they don't know
what they are programmed *with*. They just *are* programmed.

Our current programming follows certain principles. First,
that what is technically possible ought to be done. Technique
becomes the originator of values, and thus no values, except
those of technical progress, exist any more. Second, that our
actions and activities should be geared to maximum efficiency,
which of course means minimal human friction, which of course
means minimal human individuality.

This new society has been described very profoundly in
Lewis Mumford's beautiful book, *The Myth of the Machine,*

* From a speech at Columbia University protest counter commencement exercises.

in which he termed it the "megamachine." It has also been described, with approval and less profundity, by Professor Brzezinski as the "technetronic society." Mumford believes we still have a chance to fight it and to avoid it. Professor Brzezinski, in spite of many soothing and comforting words, seems to believe it's already here, and we had better accept it. . . . Some people on the far side of the political spectrum from the Professor also seem to believe that it is here, or almost here, and that there is no hope left. But, if there is no hope left, why are we here? Why are we fighting? . . .

It seems that one of the essential features of that society which we are approaching is a state of chronic low-grade schizophrenia. . . . I mean by that that an essential characteristic of schizophrenia, the split between thought and feeling, truth and passion, mind and heart is becoming complete in our time. . . . It has become fashionable to write about the possible death of millions upon millions of Americans (never mind other people who are killed) in the same tone used to discuss the transportation of coal. . . . A certain number of killed is acceptable, and a larger number [is not] acceptable, the only criterion being whether our economy can be made as good as new within twenty or thirty years. This way of writing and of thinking, in which one speaks about human affairs without any corresponding emotion, without any corresponding . . . visceral thinking, is indeed madness. . . .

There are many low-grade forms of psychoses which permit a person to function very well socially, in some societies even better, in spite of having lost that sanity in which mind and heart remain in harmony. It is in this sense that "sick" and "insane" are not just psychiatric concepts, but social concepts as well. If enough people share a common craziness, the craziness becomes normalcy, just as long as it doesn't go beyond that threshold which would make the crazy people incapable of working. In such a society, the person who is not crazy is thought to have lost his mind. Nietzsche said it beautifully:

"Anyone who doesn't lose his mind over certain events has no mind to lose."

Let me say a word about the application of this concept of the split between affect and thought to the problem of education. . . . Our education becomes more and more cerebral. That can't be helped, I guess, in the natural sciences, but I think it could be helped in what used to be and still is called the humanities. People are taught concepts, but they are not taught or confronted with the experience which corresponds to these concepts. They see, as the Zen Buddhists say, the finger which points to the moon and mistake the finger for the moon.

I believe this explains why so many of our young generation have become fed up with tradition. I am not speaking about the famous hundred great books, a very conventional idea, but about the living tradition on the strength of which we are here. The vitality of a culture depends on a tradition which inspires men, which gives them courage to live, which gives them, most of all, hope. . . . The work of the human race, which has gone on in its self-creation for the last four thousand years, cannot be replaced by any one person; no one can combine in himself a Plato, a Thomas Aquinas, a Thomas More, a Spinoza, and an Einstein. If today's youth lose contact with this tradition—not with a dead tradition of words and concepts but with that life which this tradition represents—it is difficult to see where they will be when they are not twenty but thirty and forty. What program of life will they have? What direction? What hierarchy of values beyond that of phrasemaking and vaguely expressed and formulated ideas?

I hope very much that this movement for life going on in the new generation all over the world will not remain merely a protest against the deadening educational bureaucracy and the deadening use of concepts and words, but that it will relate itself to the living tradition, not simply by accepting it but by digesting it . . . and by creatively [building on it and] changing it.

PAUL GOODMAN

the new aristocrats

A phenomenon unique in history. . . .
[They] may well save us from 1984.

Predictions about the future of America during the next generation are likely to be in one of two sharply contrasting moods. On the one hand, the orthodox liberals foresee a Great Society in which all will live in suburban comfort or the equivalent; given a Head Start and Job Training, Negroes will go to college like everyone else, will be splendidly employed and live in integrated neighborhoods; billboards will be 200 yards off new highways, and the arts will flourish in many Lincoln Centers. On the other hand, gloomy social critics, and orthodox conservatives, see that we are headed straight for 1984, when everyone's life will be regimented from the cradle to the grave by the dictator in Washington; administrative double talk and Newspeak will be the only language; Negroes will be kept at bay by the police (according to the social critics) or will be the pampered shock troops of demagogs (according to the conservatives); we will all be serial numbers; civil liberties and independent enterprise will be no more.

Yet these predictions have much in common. They assume the continuation of the same trends and attitudes that are now in full sway. There will be increasing centralization in decision making, increasing mass education as we now know it, a stepped-up rate of technical growth and a growing Gross National Product, and more use of a technological style—of "planning" or "social engineering," depending on one's bias—with heavy use of computers. These same premises are seen by some as enriching and great, and by others as menacing and empty.

Oddly, however, both kinds of prediction describe the play and leave out Hamlet; namely, the next generation itself, the young people who are going to be the heirs to all this greatness or the slaves of this social engineering. I have not seen a single forecast that takes into account that present high-school and college students will be of some importance in shaping society 20 years from now. . . .

I do not intend to predict what the future might look like if we take young people into account. I don't know (althought I give plenty of advice, which they disregard). What I want to show, however, is that point by point, with remarkable precision, articulate students—and an indeterminate number of others—*live, feel and think in direct opposition to the premises on which both the rosy and the gloomy predictions are based.* It is so in their community life, their ethics and their politics. If only because of sheer numbers, the temper of young people must make a difference for the future. And it is whistling in the dark to think that their opposition is a "generational revolt" that will be absorbed as they grow older and wiser, for it is endemic in our system of things. If the planners continue to treat this temper as if it did not exist, the result will be still deeper alienation and worse ultimate disruption. My experience in Washington, as a Fellow of the Institute of Policy Studies, is that social and educational planners have about as much information of what happens on college campuses as the State Department has about Vietnam.

COMMUNITY. About 50 percent of all Americans are now under 26. Of the college-age group, nearly 40 percent go to college—there are 6,000,000 in 2000 institutions. Of the present collegians, it is estimated that five percent are in some activity of the radical youth movement, usually "left" but sometimes "right." This does not seem a big proportion, but it has increased at least tenfold in the last decade, and it and the number of its alumni will certainly increase even more rapidly in the next years. We are thus speaking of several million people.

More important, they are the leaders. Radical collegians are not only middle-class but they are also disproportionately the best academically and from the most prestigious schools. Unlike Negro youth, who are now causing such turmoil, collegians are a major economic force, looming large among the indispensable inheritors of the dominant power in society. And although—or perhaps because—they do not share a common ideology but rather a common sentiment and style, in showdown situations like the troubles in Berkeley, they have shown a remarkable solidarity and a common detestation for the liberal center, crossing even the apparent chasm between extreme right and extreme left.

A chief reason for their solidarity and their increase in numbers is mass higher education itself. For most, going to college has little academic value—indeed, one of their shared sentiments is resistance to being academically processed for the goals of the System. In my opinion, about 15 percent, instead of 40 percent, ought to be in colleges; the rest, including most of the bright, would be better educated in other environments. Nevertheless, *the major colleges and universities are, in fact, many hundreds of physical and social communities of young people, with populations of a few thousand to 25,000, sharing a subculture, propagandizing one another and learning to distrust anybody over 30. Such collections of youth are a phenomenon unique in history.*

Consider some details from San Francisco State College, where I was hired as a teacher by the Associated Students last spring. With 15,000 students, the Associated Students collect $300,000 annually in dues, more than half of which is free and clear and which they use for untraditional purposes. These purposes include organizing a tenants' league, helping delinquents in a reformatory, running a tutorial program for Negro and Mexican children (with 300 collegian tutors), sponsoring a weekly television program on KQED, running an "experimental college" with offbeat courses, and hiring their own professors. They apply on their own for institutional grants from the Ford Foundation and the Poverty Program. . . .

Or consider the college press, with its fairly captive audience of a couple of million, many of them daily. In a few cases, e.g., Harvard and Columbia, publication has gone off campus and is not under the tutelage of "faculty advisors." Increasingly, college papers subscribe to news services and print (and edit) national and international news. . . . Occasionally, the college paper is the chief daily of its town (e.g., the Cornell *Sun*). More important, there is a national student press service that could be a powerfully effective liaison for mobilizing opinion on common issues. Last winter I wrote a fortnightly column on student matters for a tiny college in Vermont, which the enterprising editor at once syndicated to 50 other college papers. On this model there could spring up a system of direct support, and control, of students' "own" authors, just as, of course, they now indirectly support them through magazines whose main circulation is collegiate.

Nor are these young people properly called "youth." The exigencies of the American System have kept them in tutelage, doing lessons, till 23 and 24 years of age, years past when young industrial workers used to walk union picket lines or when farmers carried angry pitchforks, or young men are now drafted into the Army. Thus, another cause of their shared resentment is the foolish attempt to arrest their maturation and regulate their social, sexual and political activity.

More than other middle-class generations, these young live a good deal by "interpersonal relations" and they are unusually careless, in their friendships, about status or getting ahead. I do not mean that they are especially affectionate or compassionate—they are averagely so—but they have been soaked in modern psychology, group therapy, sensitivity training; and as a style they go in for direct confrontation and sometimes brutal frankness. Add to this the lack of embarrassment due to animally uninhibited childhood, for their parents, by and large, were permissive about thumbsucking, toilet training, masturbation, informal dress, etc. They are the post-Freudian generation in this country—their parents were analyzed from 1920 to 1940. The effect of all this psychology—for example, long sessions of mutual analysis or jabber about LSD trips—can be tiresome, at least to me; but it is fatal to suburban squeamishness, race and moral prejudice, and to keeping up appearances. Still another cause of resentment at the colleges is the impersonality and distance of the teachers and the big classes that make dialog impossible. Students are avid for dialog. Sometimes this looks like clamoring for "attention," as our statesmen say about the demonstrators, but it is really insisting on being taken seriously as troubled human beings.

Middle-class privacy also tends to vanish. An innovation of the Beats was the community use of one another's pads, and this spirit of sharing has persisted in off-campus university communities, which are very different from paternalistic dormitories or fraternity row. In big cities there are rapidly growing bohemian student neighborhoods, usually—if only for the cheaper rent—located in racially mixed sections. Such neighborhoods, with their own coffeehouses and headquarters for student political clubs, cannot be controlled by campus administration. In the famous insurrection of Berkeley, Telegraph Avenue could easily rally 3000 students, ex-students, wives and pals. . . .

Inevitably, sexual activity and taking drugs loom overlarge in the public picture; for, whereas unkempt hair, odd company and radical politics may be disapproved, sex and drugs rouse middle-class anxiety, a more animal reaction. The statistics seem to show, however, that quantitatively there are not many more sexual goings on than since the Twenties. The difference is that the climate has finally become more honest and unhypocritical. Sexuality is affirmed as a part of life rather than as the Saturday religion of fraternity gang bangs covered by being drunk. Since there is more community altogether, sex tends to revert to the normalcy of back rural areas, with the beautiful difference of middle-class prudence and contraceptives. . . . In the more earnest meaning of sex, love and marriage, however, the radical young still seem averagely messed up, no better than their parents. There is no remarkable surge of joy or poetry—the chief progress of the sexual revolution, so far, has been the freer treatment of small children that I mentioned above. The conditions of American society do not encourage manly responsibility and moral courage in men, and we simply do not know how to use the tenderness and motherliness of women. The present disposition of the radical young is to treat males and females alike; in my observation, this means that the women become camp followers, the opposite of the suburban situation in which they are tyrannical dolls. I don't know the answer. . . .

The community meaning of the widespread use of hallucinogenic drugs is ambiguous. (Few students use addictives; again, they are prudent.) I have heard students hotly defend the drugs as a means of spiritual and political freedom, or hotly condemn them as a quietist opiate of the people, or indifferently dismiss them as a matter of taste. I am myself not a hippie and I am unwilling to judge. It seems clear that the more they take pot, the less they get drunk, but I don't know if this is an advantage or a disadvantage. (I don't get drunk, either.) Certainly there is a difference between the quiet socializing of marijuana and the alcoholic socializing of the fraternities, suburbs and Washington. Also, being illegal and hard to procure, the drugs create conspiracy and a chasm between those who do and those who don't. As usual, the drug laws, like other moral laws, fail to eradicate the vice they intend to eradicate, but they produce disastrous secondary effects.

The LSD cult, especially, must be understood as part of a wave of religiosity in young persons that has included Zen, Christian and Jewish existentialism, a kind of psychoanalytic yoga, and the magic of the Book of Change. On the campus, a young Protestant chaplain—or even a Catholic—is often the center of radical activity, which may include a forum for psychedelic theory as well as peace and Negro rights. Certainly the calculating rationalism of modern times is losing its self-evidence; and it is not the end of the world to flip. Personally, I don't like it when people flip, it is eerie; I like people to be in touch, and I think the heads are mistaken when they think they are communicating. Also, in our overtechnological society, I am intensely suspicious of Dr. Tim Leary's formula to "turn on, tune in and drop out" by chemical means. Yet by and large, the public repression in this field is grossly disproportionate to the occasional damage that has been proved; and frankly, the burden of proof is the other way: If we do not want young people to live in harmless dreams, we have to provide something better than the settled arithmetical delusions of Mr. McNamara, not to speak of Herman Kahn, author of *On Thermonuclear War*.

The shagginess and chosen poverty of student communities have nuances that might be immensely important for the future. We must remember that these are the young of the affluent society, used to a high standard of living and confident that, if and when they want, they can fit in and make good money. Having suffered little pressure of insecurity, they have little psychological need to climb; just as, coming from respectable homes, they feel no disgrace about sitting a few nights in jail. By confidence they are aristocrats—en masse. This, too, is unique in history. At the same time, the affluent standard of living that they have experienced at home is pretty synthetic and much of it useless and phony; whereas their chosen poverty is not degraded but decent, natural and in many ways more comfortable than their parents' standard, especially if they can always corral obvious goodies such as hi-fi equipment and motorcycles. Typically, they tour Europe on nothing, sleeping under bridges; but if they get really hungry, they can drop in at American Express to pick up their mail. Most of the major satisfactions of life—sex, paperback books, guitars, roaming, conversation, games and activist politics—in fact, cost little.

Thus, this is the first generation in America selective of its standard of living. If this attitude became general, it would be disastrous for the expanding Gross National Product. And there is obvious policy and defiance in their poverty and shagginess.

They have been influenced by the voluntary poverty of the beat movement, which signified withdrawal from the trap of the affluent economy. Finally, by acquaintance they experience the harsher tone of the involuntary poverty of the Negroes and Spanish Americans whose neighborhoods they visit and with whom they are friends.

. . . Robert Hutchins [has] pointed out that business can no longer recruit the bright young . . . that the universities are rich and can offer competitive rewards. But I do not think this is the essence, for . . . at Harvard, business cannot compete even with the Peace Corps. The essence is that the old drive to make a *lot* of money has lost its magnetism. Yet this does not seem to mean settling for security, for the young are increasingly risky. The magnet is a way of life that has meaning. This is a luxury of an aristrocratic community.

ETHICS. The chief (conscious) drive of the radical young is their morality. As Michael Harrington, author of *The Other America,* has put it, "They drive you crazy with their morality," since for it they disregard prudence and politics, and they mercilessly condemn day-to-day casuistry as if it were all utterly phony. When politically minded student leaders, like the Students for a Democratic Society, try to engage in "tactics" and "the art of the possible," they may temporarily gain in numbers, but they swiftly lose influence and begin to disintegrate. Yet indignation or a point of honor will rally the young in droves.

Partly, the drive to morality is the natural ingenuousness of youth, freed of the role playing and status seeking of our society. As aristocrats, not driven by material or ulterior motives, they will budge for ideals or not at all. Partly their absolutism is a disgusted reaction to cynicism and the prevalent adult conviction that "Nothing can be done. You can't fight city hall. Modern life is too complex." But mostly, I think, it is the self-righteousness of an intelligent and innocent new generation in a world where my own generation has been patently stupid and incompetent. They have been brought up on a literature of dev-

astating criticism that has gone unanswered because there is no
answer.

The right comparison to them is the youth of the Reformation,
of *Sturm und Drang*, and of Russia of the Seventies and Eigh-
ties, who were brought up on their own dissenting theologians,
philosophes and intelligentsia. Let us remember that those students did, indeed, ultimately lead revolutions.

The philosophical words are "authenticity" and "commitment," from the existentialist vocabulary. And it cannot be denied that our dominant society is unusually inauthentic. Newspeak and double talk are the lingua franca of administrators,
politicians, advertisers and the mass media. These official people
are not even lying; rather, there is an unbridgeable chasm between the statements made "on the record" for systemic reasons
or the image of the corporation, and what is intended and actually performed. I have seen mature graduate students crack up
in giggles of anxiety listening to the Secretary of State expound
our foreign policy; when I questioned them afterward, some
said that he was like a mechanical man, others that he was demented. And most campus blowups have been finally caused by
administrators' animal inability to speak plain. The students
have faithfully observed due process and manfully stated their
case, but the administrators simply cannot talk like human beings. At this point it suddenly becomes clear that they are confronting not a few radical dissenters but a solid mass of the
young, maybe a majority.

Two things seem to solidify dissent: administrative double
talk and the singling out of "ringleaders" for exemplary punishment. These make young people feel that they are not being
taken seriously, and they are not.

In principle, "authenticity" is proved by "commitment." You
must not merely talk but organize, collect money, burn your
draft card, go South and be shot at, go to jail. And the young
eagerly commit themselves. However, a lasting commitment is
hard to achieve. There are a certain number of causes that are
pretty authentic and warrant engaging in: Give Negroes the

vote, desegregate a hotel or a bus, commute Chessman's sentence to the gas chamber, abolish grading and get the CIA out of the university, abolish HUAC, get out of Vietnam, legalize marijuana and homosexuality, unionize the grapepickers. But it is rarely the case that any particular authentic cause can really occupy the thought and energy of more than a few for more than a while. Students cool off and hop from issue to issue, then some become angry at the backsliders; others foolishly try to prove that civil liberties, for instance, are not so "important" as Negro civil rights, for instance, or that university reform is not so "important" as stopping the bombing of Hanoi. Others, disillusioned, sink into despair of human nature. And committed causes distressingly vanish from view at the June vacation, when the community disperses.

Shrewder psychologists among the young advocate getting involved only in what you "enjoy" and gravitate to—e.g., don't tutor unless you like kids—but this is a weak motive compared with indignation or justice.

The bother is that, except with a few political or religious personalities, the students' commitments do not spring from their own vocations and life ambitions; and they are not related in a coherent program for the reconstruction of society. This is not the fault of the students. Most of the present young have unusually little sense of vocation; perhaps 16 continuous years of doing lessons by compulsion has not been a good way to find one's identity. And there *is* no acceptable program of reconstruction—nobody has spelled it out—only vague criteria. Pathetically, much "definite commitment" is a self-deceptive way of filling the void of sense of vocation and utopian politics. Negroes, who are perforce really committed to their emancipation, notice this and say that their white allies are spiritually exploiting them.

It is a difficult period of history for the young to find vocation and identity. Most of the abiding human vocations and professions, arts and sciences, seem to them, and are (to a degree) corrupt or corrupted: law, business, the physical sciences, social work—these constitute the hated System. And higher education, both curriculum and professors, which ought to be helping them find themselves, also seems bought out by the System. Students know that something is wrong in their schooling and they agitate for university reform; but since they do not know what world they want to make, they do not know what to demand to be taught.

POLITICS. It is not the task of age 18 to 25 to devise a coherent program of social reconstruction; for instance, to rethink our uses of technology, our methods of management, our city planning and international relations. They rightly accuse us of not providing them a program to work for. A small minority— I think increasing—turns to Marxism, as in the Thirties; but the Marxist theorists have also not thought of anything new and relevant to overripe societies. Most radical students, in my observation, listen to Marxist ideological speeches with polite lack of interest—"they are empty, man, empty"—and they are appalled by Marxist political bullying. On the other hand, they are disgusted with official anticommunism. By an inevitable backlash, since they think all American official speech is double talk, they disbelieve that Communist states are worse than our own.

What the American young do know, being themselves pushed around, itemized and processed, is that they have a right to a say in what affects them. They believe in democracy, which they have to call "participatory democracy," to distinguish it from double-talk democracy. Poignantly, in their ignorance of American history, they do not recognize that they are Congregationalists, town-meeting democrats, Jeffersonians, populists. But they know they want the opportunity to be responsible, to initiate and decide, instead of being mere personnel. Returning from their term overseas, the first thousand of the Peace Corps unanimously agreed that exercising responsibility and initiative had been the most worthwhile part of their experience, and they complained that back home they did not have the opportunity.

The primary area for seeking democracy would be, one would

imagine, the universities, for that is where the students are and are coerced. And the radical students, who, we have seen, are among the best academically, have campaigned for *Lernfreiheit*—freedom from grading, excessive examination, compulsory atendance at lectures and prescribed subjects—and also for the ancient privilege of a say in designing the curriculum and evaluating the teachers. But unfortunately, as we have also seen, the majority of students do not care about higher education as such and are willing to put up with it as it is. They are in college for a variety of extrinsic reasons, from earning the degree as a union card to evading the draft. There is no mass base for university reform.

So instead of working in their own bailiwick, activist students have mainly sought participatory democracy for poor people, organizing rent strikes, opposing bureaucratic welfare procedures, and so forth. But there is an inherent dilemma in this. Negroes claim, perhaps correctly, that middle-class whites cannot understand their problems; if Negroes are going to run their own show, they have to dispense with white helpers. The present policy of the Student Nonviolent Coordinating Committee is that Negroes must solve their own peculiar problems, which are the only ones they care about and know anything about, and let their young white friends attend to changing the majority society. There is something in this. Certainly one would have expected Northern students to get their heads broken in the cafeteria at Tulane or the University of Mississippi, where they could talk with their peers face to face, as well as on the streets of country towns. And white Southern liberals have desperately needed more support than they have gotten.

But pushed too far, the rift with the middle-class students consigns poor people to a second-class humanity. The young Negroes cannot do without the universities, for there, finally, is where the showdown, the reconstruction of society, will be—although that showdown is not yet. Consider: Some pressing problems are universal; the poor must care about them, e.g., the atom bomb. Many pressing problems are grossly misconceived if looked at short range from a poor man's point of view; only a broad human point of view can save Negroes from agitating for exactly the wrong things, as they have agitated for educational parks, when what is needed in schooling is a small human scale. Also, there is something spurious in Negro separatism, for a poor minority in a highly technological society will not engineer the housing and manufacture the cars that they intend to use. Finally, in fact, the Negroes are, perhaps unfortunately, much more American than Negro. Especially in the North, they are suckers for the whole American package, though it makes even less sense for them than for anybody else. The Negro subculture that is talked up has about the same value as the adolescent subculture; it has vitality and it does not add up to humanity.

As in other periods of moral change, only the young aristocrats and the intellectuals can *afford* to be disillusioned and profoundly radical. And in a high technology, only the students will be able to construct a program.

In their own action organizations, the young are almost fanatically opposed to top-down direction. In several remarkable cases, e.g., Tom Hayden, Bob Moses, Mario Savio, gifted and charismatic leaders have stepped down because their influence had become too strong. By disposition, without benefit of history, they are reinventing anarchist federation and a kind of Rosa Luxemburgian belief in spontaneous insurrection from below. In imitating Gandhian nonviolence, they do not like to submit to rigid discipline, but each one wants to make his own moral decision about getting his head broken. If the Army really gets around to drafting them, it will have its hands full.

All this, in my opinion, probably makes them immune to takeover by centralists like the Marxists. When Trotskyites, for instance, infiltrate an organization and try to control it, the rest go home and activity ceases. When left to their own improvisation, however, the students seem surprisingly able to mount quite massive efforts, using elaborate techniques of communication and expert sociology. By such means they will never get power. But, indeed, they do not want power, they want meaning.

PARALLEL INSTITUTIONS. The operative idea in participatory democracy is decentralizing, to multiply the number who are responsible, who initiate and decide. In principle, there are two opposite ways of decentralizing: either by dividing overcentralized organizations where it can be shown that decentral organization is more efficient in economic, social and human costs, or at least not too inefficient; or by creating new small enterprises to fill needs that big organizations neglect or only pretend to fulfill.

Obviously, the first of these, to cut the present structures down to human size, is not in the power of the young. But it happens that it does require a vast amount of empirical research and academic analysis to find if, where and how decentralizing is feasible; and in current American academic style, there is no such research and analysis. So on 150 campuses, I have urged students to work on such problems. They seem fascinated, but I do not know if they are coming across. . . .

The other way of decentralizing, by creating parallel enterprises, better suits the student zeal for direct action, and they have applied it with energy and inventiveness. They have set up a dozen little "free universities" that I know about—probably there are many others—in or next to established institutions, to teach in a more personal way and to deal with contemporary subjects that are not yet standard curriculum, e.g., Castro's Cuba, Psychedelic Experience, Sensitivity Training, Theater of Participation. Some of these courses are action sociology, like organizing labor or community development. In poor neighborhoods, students have established a couple of radio stations, to broadcast local news and propaganda and to give poor people a chance to talk into a microphone. They have set up parallel community projects to combat the welfare bureaucracy and channelize needs and grievances. In the South, they have helped form "freedom" political machines, since the established machines are lily white. They have offered to organize international service projects as an alternative to serving in the Army. . . .

Regarded coldly, such parallel projects are pitifully insignificant and doomed to pass away like so many little magazines. And, in fact, at present, the most intense discussions among student radicals, causing deep rifts, are on this theme. Some, following older thinkers like Michael Harrington and Bayard Rustin . . . want to engage in "coalition politics," to become effective by combining with the labor unions and leftish liberals in the Democratic Party, to get control of some of the Federal money and to campaign for A. Philip Randolph's . . . 185-billion-dollar [Freedom Budget] to eliminate poverty. . . . Others, for example one wing of SDS, say that the use of participatory democracy and parallel institutions is not for themselves but to consolidate people into a political party; it is not to provide models for the reconstruction of society but, as a kind of initiation rite, to get into the big game of numbers and power. This seems to me to give up on the authenticity, meaning and beautiful spontaneous motivation that have, so far, been the real power of the radical young and the source of what influence they have had. And it presupposes that the young know where they want to go as a party, rather than in what direction they *are* going as a movement. But they don't know; they (and we) will have to find out by conflict.

In my opinion, it is better to regard the parallel institutions as a remarkable revival of a classical American movement, populism, that seemed to have been dead. It is now reviving on the streets and among citizens who storm city hall because they feel they have been pushed around; in such a movement, the young are natural leaders. The principle of populism, as in 1880, is to get out from under the thumb of the barons and do it yourself. And perhaps the important step is the first one, to prove that self-help is possible at all. There may be hope of bringing to life many of our routinized institutions if we surround them with humanly meaningful enterprises. The most telling criticism of an overgrown institution is a simpler one that works better.

This was John Dewey's vision of the young 60 years ago: He thought of an industrial society continually and democratically renewed by its next generation, freely educated and learning by doing. Progressive education, free-spirited but practical, was a typical populist conception. And it is useful to regard the student movement as progressive education at the college and graduate-school level; for at this level, learning by doing begins to be indistinguishable from vocation, profession and politics. It is the opposite of the mandarin establishment that now rules the country, and of the social engineering that is now called education. Maybe this time around, the populist movement will succeed and change what we mean by vocation, profession and politics.

So, describing radical students—and I do not know how many others—we have noticed their solidarity based on community rather than ideology, their style of direct and frank confrontation, their democratic inclusiveness and aristocratic carelessness of status, caste or getting ahead, their selectivity of the affluent standard of living, their effort to be authentic and committed to their causes rather than merely belonging, their determination to have a say and their refusal to be processed as standard items, their extreme distrust of top-down direction, their disposition to anarchist organization and direct action, their disillusion with the system of institutions, and their belief that they can carry on major social functions in improvised parallel enterprises.

Some of these traits, in my opinion, are natural to all unspoiled young people. All of them are certainly in contradiction to the dominant organization of American society. By and large, this is as yet the disposition of a minority, but it is the only articulate disposition that has emerged; and it has continually emerged for the past ten years. It is a response not merely to "issues," such as civil rights or Vietnam, but to deeply rooted defects in our present system, and it will have an influence in the future. It will make for a more decent society than the Great Society and it may well save us from 1984.

KENNETH KENISTON

the alienated*

A profound pessimism about, and distaste for, politics. . . . Implicitly their philosophies emphasize . . . passion and feeling, the search for awareness, contact, intensity, the cultivation of responsiveness.

Statistical studies had suggested that distrust was a primary variable in the alienation syndrome. Clinical investigations confirmed this finding. For alienated students, distrust extends far beyond a low view of human nature; they also believe that intimacy ends in disillusion, that attachment to a group entails the loss of individuality, and that all appearances are untrustworthy. Nor can American culture be trusted: it is mechanical, boring, trashy, cheap, conformist, and dull. Any kind of positive commitment is viewed negatively. . . .

From middle adolescence on, alienated students had become increasingly aware of the darkness, isolation, and meaninglessness of life. The universe itself is dead, lacking in structure, inherently unpredictable and random. Individual life, too, is devoid of purpose and preordained form. Consequently, any meaning or truth that an individual finds is inevitably subjective and

* These excerpts from an address, "Alienation in American Youth," summarize highlights of the five-year study of *non*political, alienated students, upon which Keniston's book *The Uncommitted; Alienated Youth in American Society* was based. Keniston estimated that even at the universities with "progressive" reputations such students "constituted a small minority—at most five to ten percent." But he predicts this percentage will increase. He also points out that "alienation is a reaction *to* and *against* certain aspects of American (technological) society" and not "purely an expression of individual psychology." In these excerpts, however, the psychological aspects are stressed, since the societal factors are discussed in many other essays in this volume.—A.K.

solipsistic. Morality, too, is seen as egocentric, arbitrary, and individualistic. Given the unpredictability of the future, long-range ethical idealism is impossible; the present becomes overwhelmingly important.

Alienated undergraduates do not react stoically to this view of the universe. On the contrary, their response is scorn, bitterness, and anger. Love and hate, they insist, are inseparable. Their own hostilities are close to awareness, and their scorn is especially intense when they confront other students who are not alienated. Indeed, their anger is so corrosive that it extends even to themselves. True to the logic of their position, they maintain that the consequence of self-knowledge is self-contempt, and are quick to admit their own self-revulsion. Similarly, their resentment is expressed in their conviction that all men inevitably use each other for their own purposes. . . . Another distinctive outlook of these students is a profound pessimism about, and distaste for, politics and political action. . . .

They distrust all Positive Thinking and therefore find it almost impossible to agree with any questionnaire statement that clearly expresses an affirmative view. But despite the negative cast of their *explicit* views, the alienated share an *implicit* positive search in a common direction. Implicitly their philosophies emphasize the positive value of passion and feeling, the search for awareness, contact, intensity, the cultivation of responsiveness, the importance of solitude, and the need somehow to express their experience of life. Their positive values are therefore "expressive" or aesthetic, in that their main focus is the present, their main source is the self, and their main aim is the development of awareness, responsiveness, and sentience. Rejecting the traditional American values of success, self-control, and achievement, they maintain that passion, feeling, and awareness are the truest forces at man's disposal. For most of them, the primary objective in life is to attain and maintain openness to experience, contact with the world and spontaneity of feeling. Anything that might fetter or restrain their responsiveness and openness is opposed: the goal, as one student puts it, is "circum-

scribing my life as little as possible.". . . The unifying theme
in the ideology of alienation is the rejection of what are seen as
dominant American values, an unwillingness to accept the trusting, optimistic, sociocentric, affiliative, interpersonally oriented,
and culturally accepting values which are, or were in less troubled times, the foundations of the American world view.

When we turn from alienated views of the world to the everyday life of alienated students, we find much less surface distinc-
tiveness. Formal socioeconomic and demographic variables do
not distinguish these students from their classmates, nor does a
casual search through college records, high-school records, or
even police records. But if we examine not *what* they do, but
how they do it, we soon discover that the alienated have a characteristic life-style. One crucial feature of this style of life is
intellectual passion. They pursue their intellectual interests with
such single-minded dedication that they almost completely disregard the conventional distinction between "work" and "goof-
ing off," made by most of their classmates. When they are challenged in their work, and above all when their assignments strike
some deep personal or symbolic chord, they can become totally
absorbed in intellectual work. When they become involved in
extracurricular activities, alienated students are naturally drawn
to those that allow them to express their artistic and "aesthetic"
interests. And in whatever they do, the style of their participation characteristically involves a preference for the role of the
detached observer. As a group, they avoid positions of responsibility or, when accorded them, repudiate them immediately. . . .

Their favored stance as detached observers led these students
into systematic wanderings. Whenever they were confronted with
a problem or conflict, they were likely to "take off," sometimes
for a long walk at night, sometimes for a few years out of college. In all of these wanderings, they seem to be searching not
so much to escape as to immerse themselves in intense experience. Sometimes they found such experience. In their interviews
and autobiographies, there are occasional mentions of epiph-

anies, mystical experiences, and revelations of Everything in the garish pennants of a filling station, in the way the light of the setting sun falls through an archway, or in the smell of burning leaves.

But despite their outward appearance of detachment from others, alienated undergraduates are inwardly highly (though ambivalently) involved with them. They are often simultaneously attracted to, and somewhat fearful of, an admired person —tempted to emulate him, but afraid that emulation might mean the sacrifice of their inner integrity. Given such ambivalence, it is understandable that these students tend to ruminate, often obsessively, about all close personal relationships. No friendship escapes detailed analysis from every point of view. This ambivalent examination is especially pronounced with girls. Almost invariably, when they do become close to a girl, it is either to one who is described as passive, dependent, and subservient, or to one who is so totally unacceptable to their parents as to precipitate a complete break between the student and his family, as with the eldest son of a religious Jewish family who became enamored of a girl of Arab descent. In these relationships with girls, as in most of their relationships with other people, they combine an agonizing desire for closeness with a great fear of it.

In interviews, as on questionnaires, alienated students are quick to admit their confusions, angers, anxieties, and problems. Given a list of neurotic symptoms, they check them all, describing themselves as socially undesirable, confused, depressed, angry, neurotic, hostile, and impulsive. Yet the inference that these students are grossly disturbed can only be made with reservations. For one, they reject the value assumptions upon which most questionnaire measures of "maturity," "ego strength," and "good mental health" are based. Furthermore, they make a great effort to undermine any so-called "defenses" that might protect them from unpleasant feelings. For most of these students, openness to their own problems and failings is a cardinal virtue. . . .

But after we have made due allowance for the tendency of

alienated students to exaggerate their own failings, many of
them are, in fact, confused, disoriented, and depressed. . . . Se-
cretely, some harbor fears that this unhappiness may be of their
own making, rather than merely a consequence of the human
condition. Their sense of themselves seems precarious and dis-
unified; they often doubt their own continuing capacity to cope;
they have little positive sense of relatedness to other people; the
boundaries of their own egos are diffuse and porous. Strong in
opposition, these students are weak in affirmation; unable to
articulate what they stand for, they have little sense of self to
stand on. . . .

An examination of what alienated students tell us about their
families and their earlier lives shows a remarkable consistency
in their reports. . . . For example, they frequently emphasize
the renunciations and sacrifices their mothers have made. To
their sons, these women appear to have been talented, artistic,
intense, and intelligent girls who gave up promise and fulfillment for marriage. They also seem to their sons vivid, sensuous,
and magnetic; and alienated students often wonder aloud
"whether marriage was worth it" to their mothers. Throughout,
these students express their special sympathy for and identification with their mothers, and their sadness at their mothers'
lack of fulfillment. But the mothers of alienated sons have another set of common characteristics—dominance, possessiveness, excessive involvement with their sons, oversolicitude. The
typical alienated student tells of his mother's intrusiveness, of
her attempts to limit, supervise, and restrict his independence
and initiative. And although few of the alienated admit that
their mothers have been successful in controlling *them*, they do
on the whole believe that their mothers have succeeded in controlling their fathers. . . .

Fathers are . . . described as men who, often despite notable
public success, are "failures in their own eyes," "apostates,"
disappointed, frustrated, and disillusioned men. But often, in
addition, their college-age sons portray them as having *once* had
youthful dreams, which they were unable to fulfill, as idealists

whose idealism has been destroyed by life. The precise agent of this destruction varies: sometimes it was Mother; sometimes it was the father's own weakness, particularly his inability to stand up against pressures for social success and recognition. So despite their frequent scorn for their dominated fathers, alienated students retain some sympathy for the same fathers as they *might* have been—a kind of covert identification with the fantasy of a youthful idealistic father. In characterizing their fathers at present, however, the alienated again and again emphasize qualities like detachment, reserve, inability to express affection, loneliness, and withdrawal from the center of the family. Contrasted with the expressive, emotional, controlling, and dynamic mother, the father appears weak, inactive, detached, and uninterested. . . .

. . . There was no mention of overt alienation in the life histories of these students until mid-adolescence—about the age of sixteen. . . . [Their] growing sense of alienation usually contrasted sharply with continuing academic and social success; and the contrast between inner alienation and outer success led to increasing feelings of estrangement from all those who accepted them merely at face value. Their alienation usually developed in isolation and spontaneously; it was usually only *after* they became alienated that these students sought out books, ideas, and people that would confirm and support them in their views. Among the students studied, alienation could *not* be explained as the result of identification with an alienated parent; on the contrary, it always seemed to involve a sharp repudiation of perceived parental values. . . .

Unconsciously, alienated students seem to believe that they defeated their fathers, who are now seen as weak and inadequate models of male adulthood. Probably, like most small boys, they attempted a "revolution" within the family in order to overthrow the tyrannical father and gain the exclusive love of the mother. But, unlike most boys, these boys believe that their revolution *succeeded* in destroying male authority. Yet, paradoxically, their apparent victory did not win them maternal love but maternal control, possessiveness, and oversolicitude. Furthermore, by displacing their fathers, they lost the right of every boy to a father he can admire. . . .

Such a childhood experience would clearly leave a college student with the unconscious assumption that apparently admirable men were really weak and impotent; and that apparently nurturing and loving women were really controlling, possessive, and even emasculating. Conventional adulthood, as epitomized by the father, would also seem unattractive and have to be rejected. Adult closeness with women would be frightening, as it would evoke fears of being dominated, controlled, and limited. Similarly, competition and rivalry would be avoided in everyday behavior, not out of the fear of failure, but from a fear of another Pyrrhic victory. . . . Then, too, the repudiation of conventional adulthood, of the dominant values of American society, is closely related to their unconscious determination not to let what happened to their fathers happen to them. . . .

To oversimplify a relationship that is always complex and ambivalent, the activist seems determined to implement and live out his parents' values, whereas the alienated student is determined to repudiate them and find alternative values. [Also] most activists seem to me to possess an optimism, faith in human nature, belief in the efficacy of human action, and a capacity for co-operative endeavors that few alienated students manifest. Thus, on the whole, alienation [and] student protest seem to me two quite distinct, if not opposed, phenomena. . . .

I suspect that youthful alienation of the sort I have studied will be a continuing, if not an increasingly prevalant, phenomenon. The kinds of families these students came from, while not statistically typical, seem to me sufficiently close to the emergent norm of the American family so that we can expect at least some of their offspring to be predisposed to alienation in the coming decades. The simultaneous emergence of a similar family type in the etiology of male homosexuality, adolescent male schizophrenia, and intense identity diffusion, as well as its appearance of this same family type in a great number of current novels and plays, suggests that the alienating family may become an increasingly common variant in middle-class American society. As our society becomes ever more technological, more specialized, more highly organized, it seems to me likely that a continuing group of the most talented, sensitive, and suitably predisposed of our youth will be repelled by our society, and will experience a transient and, in many cases, an enduring phase of alienation. As Donald N. Michael has . . . put it . . . "A growing group . . . of the most talented, sensitive, and searching of young adults and adolescents will be repelled by what they interpret as politicking, commercialism, high-presure bureaucracy, and the 'big' society, and by logic-chopping, 'dehumanized' and 'hemmed in' experience of the devoted scientist." Cultural alienation among a segment of our most talented and sensitive youth is, I think, an almost inevitable consequence of the kind of society we live in. And it is important that we understand its psychological, social, cultural, and historical origins. For one, to understand alienation is to be better able to understand some of our most perceptive students . . . in order to help them find personally meaningful and culturally productive ways of focusing and expressing their alienation. More important . . . I suspect that *most* reflective men and women are somewhat alienated from our society and our culture—some of us more, most of us less, alienated than these college students. By trying to understand what it is in our modern world that contributes to the alienation of such young men, we may be led indirectly to an understanding of what is most dehumanizing, unjust, cruel, ugly, and corrupt in our society. And this understanding is a prerequisite to whatever cures we can create.

different childhood experiences of radical and alienated youth

Among both the alienated and young radicals, there is evidence of an unusually strong tie to the *mother* in early childhood. But for the alienated, this tie seems both more intense and less adequately resolved. Those who become alienated describe a mother-son relationship that is intrusive, overprotective, and close-binding: the mother frequently involves the son in an alliance against the father. Furthermore, alienated students usually describe their mothers as sensuous and/or neurotic. These qualities are far less frequently ascribed to their mothers by radicals. Radicals describe their mothers as especially encouraging of achievement, independence, and initiative: these qualities are rarely reported in mothers of the alienated. And male radicals as a group seem more genuinely fond of, and grateful to, their mothers than do the alienated. Above all, young radicals generally appreciate their mothers' educating and individuating influences.

It is in their attitudes toward their *fathers* that the alienated and young radicals differ most drastically. Despite the variability in radicals' attitude toward their fathers, a majority expressed a kind of affection for their fathers that was extremely rare among alienated students. All radicals indicated that whatever their fathers' weaknesses, their fathers had important strengths, especially in the areas of values, principles, and convictions. Conscious ambivalence toward their fathers was the rule for activists, in contrast to the negative alienated perception of fathers as weak, detached, absent, distant, remote, and sometimes as totally uninvolved in the upbringing of their children. Radicals more often described their fathers as expressive, warm, sympathetic, and highly involved.

The *parental relationships* described by these two groups also differed. The prevailing pattern in alienating families involved a schism between the parents, coupled with a mother-son alliance against the father. This alliance often led the son to believe or suspect that the mother preferred him to her husband. The predominant pattern in radical families, however, is a parental "united front" vis-à-vis children. Even in those radical families where parents were in conflict, a mother-son alliance did not develop, apparently because the mother was not seductive toward her son. . . . Furthermore, when parental quarrels occurred in radical families, the parents generally tried to conceal them from their children—an effort that is consistent with a general family emphasis on the inhibition of anger and the minimization of conflict. Alienated students, in contrast, reported that their parents (usually their mothers) confided frequently in their sons the sources of parental conflict and maternal discontent. . . .

The *family culture* or value milieu of the two types of families also differs. Both radical and alienating families were generally highly permissive with their children. But in radical families, permissiveness was combined with extremely high standards and expectations, and with strong support for the son's individuality and autonomy. In alienating families, permissiveness was more often combined with considerable parental confusion over principles and with reluctance—especially on the mother's part—to see the son become autonomous and independent of his family. Alienating families were most often oriented toward conventional goals of success and social status, while radical families emphasized values like responsibility, independence, societal involvement, expression of feelings, service to others, and self-fulfillment. . . .

KENNETH CLARK

black youth search for identity

Is it possible to struggle for desegregation and at the same time to assert. . . . positive [racial] identity. . . ?

. . . While there is a new breed of younger Negroes who seem more assertive and insistent upon their rights as American citizens and who are demanding either unqualified equality or insisting upon an extreme Negro separatism, the masses of Negro youth are either preparing themselves for inclusion in the main stream of American life or have already become casualties of American racial injustices. Some Negro youth are stridently rebelling against what they consider to be the acquiescence to racial injustices, the cowardice of their parents, while the majority of others appear content or choose to be replicas of their parents. Nonetheless, the minority of assertive, insistent, demanding, volatile Negro young people reflects a significant racial reality of the present which cannot be ignored and which may well determine the future of American race relations. . . .

Within the past 20 to 30 years, it was possible for psychologists and other social scientists to make the case against the continuation of racial segregation in American life by pointing to the damage which segregation and discrimination inflicted upon the personality of Negro youth. The . . . Supreme Court in its historic *Brown* decision of 1954 referred to the deep feelings of inferiority which affected the hearts and minds of Negro children as a result of being segregated. . . . With this interpretation it became clear that the conscious and unconscious intent of white racists who imposed rigid forms of segregation in all areas of American life was to damage the personality of Negroes—to create feelings of doubt, to impair the self-esteem, to impose self-hatred and general ineffectiveness in Negroes. . . .

One of the results of the public discussion [which followed] was the raising of the morale of the Negro and the beginnings of an open struggle to remove all of the conditions which reinforced the sense of personal and racial inferiority in the Negro. . . . It is significant that these early forms of organized resistance . . . were led for the most part by young Negroes. Martin Luther King was in his mid-20s when he emerged as the leader of the Montgomery nonviolent defiance. [SNCC] emerged out of the insistence by students on being treated as human beings at a Negro college in Greensboro, N.C. . . . The daring, courage and sense of urgency on the part of the Negro youth in the late 1950s rescued the civil rights movement from the doldrums of tokenism and stirred the conscience of white and Negro Americans. . . . These demonstrations and their limited successes reduced feelings of inferiority and stimulated in Negroes, young and old, a sense of positive worth and increased belief in their ability to influence positively their own destiny. . . .

This new surge toward a positive racial identity took many forms among Negroes. When the late Malcolm X was the most articulate spokesman of the Black Muslim movement, he insisted upon a Garvey-type deification of the value of being black. Indeed the present tendency on the part of militant Negro youth to use the term black rather than Negro seems to come directly from the Malcolm X form of Negro assertion of positive racial identity. The struggle toward affirmation of his humanity also led the American Negro to the vogue of Africanism, that is, to identify as closely as possible with the emerging nations of Africa. The cult of "Negritude," the fad wherein Negro females refuse to straighten their hair as a protest against imitating the hair texture of whites, the tendency of some young Negro males to affect the African haircut, must be seen as part of the larger pattern of the present struggle for positive racial identity. The American Negro seems now self-consciously insistent upon his right to be clearly and visibly a Negro and insists upon being accepted as a Negro.

Paradoxically, the struggle for a desegregated America and the rising signs of positive esteem in the Negro came out of the same social and psychological base as the rising tide of racial separatism and Negro nationalism. This conflict between the desire for racial integration [and the desire for] racial isolation—and the indecision as to which is the more direct path to positive self-esteem for the Negro—is not yet resolved and contributes to the present inner turbulence of American Negroes. Is it possible to struggle for desegregation and at the same time to assert racism? Does positive identity in the Negro demand that priority be given to racism rather than to desegregation? The answers to these questions raise many social and psychological imponderables which are not made easier to deal with by the Negro nationalists' assertion that positive Negro identity is inconsistent with demands for a desegregated society; nor are the answers made easier by the middle-class Negro's denial of the psychological reality and attractiveness, particularly in the face of continued racial frustrations, of the arguments of the nationalists.

Probably the most difficult, nonrational manifestation of the new quest of Negro youth for an assertive and positive racial identity is . . . the recent epidemic of riots or rebellions in Northern and some Southern urban ghettos. While it is clear that generally these riots involved only a small percentage of Negro youth, the majority of the individuals involved in them appear to be young people. Direct observation of the young Negroes reveals that they are not only destructive, but in the process of destroying are seeking to affirm. They are affirming their power to destroy. In the act of rebelling they appear to be asserting the ability to rebel. Beneath the random and clearly destructive and irrational behavior, there remains the pathetic logic of asserting self-esteem and searching for a positive identity by exposing oneself to danger and even inviting death. This is the quest for self-esteem of the truly desperate human being. This is the way those who have absolutely nothing to lose seek a pathetic affirmation of self even if it is obtained moments before death. If this interpretation has any validity, all attempts at riot control in urban ghettos—running the gamut from anti-poverty programs through more systematic and coercive police and militia action—will fail unless they [include] the development of a constructive basis for a positive self-esteem in Negro youth.

One of the more intriguing facts of the present struggle of Negro young people for positive self-esteem is that this struggle is no longer restricted to lower-class Negro youth. . . . A substantial proportion of middle- and upper-middle-class Negro youth have become a part of the pervasive psychological and ideological revolt against American racism and social hypocrisy. The development of small groups of Muslim and black-nationalist-oriented Negro students in predominantly Negro colleges and the increase in the number of Afro-American societies in predominantly white colleges are examples of a rising pattern of racial assertiveness. . . . The small number of Negro students in predominantly white colleges are for the most part no longer content to maintain an anonymous, wishful, protective denial of their race as they seek at times condescending acceptance by their white classmates. The day when a Negro student seeks self-consciously to avoid any prolonged contact or social or academic interaction with the few other Negro students at an Ivy League or Midwestern college seems to have passed. Negro students . . . have insisted, at times against the advice of their deans, upon their right to organize themselves as Negroes and to discuss among themselves their common problems and aspirations. This is a significant development [in] the serious struggle for positive racial and self-

identity. . . . It represents a transition from the period of denial
to a period of personal and racial effectiveness.

Again, the persistent question remains concerning the extent
to which self-conscious racial identification can be made consistent with the struggle against racial segregation and oppression. These two forces are not necessarily inconsistent. . . . The
past period of denial eroded the capacity of those Negroes
trained in predominantly white schools to contribute in proportion to their advantages and training to the difficult struggle
for racial justice in America. The present self-conscious racial
assertion cannot be less eroding and probably will increase the
pool of Negroes who will use their training and education for
the attainment of racial justice. . . .

Negro youth, like other youth, appear to be rebelling against
the moral hypocrisy and inconsistencies of their elders. In
this rebellion, they run the same risks of extremism, of fads, of
evasions. They are subject to rejection, ridicule and name-call-
ing by those whom they confront with moral inconsistencies.
And they sometimes seek to protect themselves from these
counterattacks by smart-alecky cynicism, self-indulgent nega-
tivism, random hostility, by apathy, diffidence and moral indifference.

In the struggle for self-esteem and positive identity, it seems
clearly easier to reject programs which require personal expenditure of energy and commitment and to embrace the fads
which justify personal retreat and escape. Some Negro youth,
like rebellious white youth, are content to verbalize their protests against society and thereby mask their personal unwillingness to become involved in constructive programs for change.
But Negro youth cannot afford the luxury of verbal ambiguity.
The injustices inflicted upon them are real and concrete. They
cannot escape into the oblivion of "hippie land" with the same
seeming equanimity of their white counterparts. They cannot
afford the vagueness of the anxiety of whites. The badge of their
rebellion is their color and it is always with them in America.
In the transition from the deep feelings of inferiority to the goal

of an effective, positive identity, they seem at times to be driven to extremisms, to the illogic of rejecting not only "whitey" but rejecting all other Negroes who do not share their present form of extremism. . . . Even as they insist upon Negro history as a firm foundation for positive Negro identity, they reject the recent history and the sacrifices of those Negroes who made it possible for them to reach this stage of realistic quest for personal and racial affirmation.

But these are the unavoidable symptoms of any positive transition. They are signs of health and the persistence of the struggle for life and justice. To understand the positives of these young people, one must understand that no group of human beings can move from being the victims of extremes of injustice and inhumanity to the goals of self-acceptance and positive personal and racial identity without a transition period being marked by [intense and profound] turmoil.

JAMES BALDWIN

from dreams of love
to dreams of terror

Stokely. . . . will not live the life I've lived.

I first met Stokely Carmichael in the Deep South, when he was just another non-violent kid, marching and talking and getting his head whipped. This time now seems as far behind us as the Flood, and if those suffering, gallant, betrayed boys and girls who were then using their bodies in an attempt to save a heedless nation have since concluded that the nation is not worth saving, no American alive has the right to be surprised—to put the matter as mildly as it can possibly be put. Actually, Americans are not at all surprised; they exhibit all the vindictiveness of the guilty; what happened to those boys and girls, and what happened to the Civil Rights movement, is an indictment, of America and Americans, and an enduring monument, which we will not outlive, to the breath-taking cowardice of this sovereign people. . . .

America sometimes resembles, at least from the point of view of the black man, an exceedingly monotonous minstrel show; the same dances, same music, same jokes. One has done (or been) the show so long that one can do it in one's sleep. So it was not in the least surprising for me to encounter (one more time) the American surprise when Stokely—as Americans allow themselves the luxury of supposing—coined the phrase, Black Power. He didn't coin it. He simply dug it up again from where it's been lying since the first slaves hit the gangplank. I have never known a Negro in all my life who was not obsessed with Black Power. Those representatives of White Power who are not too hopelessly brain-washed or eviscerated will understand that the only way for a black man in America not to be obsessed with the problem of how to control his destiny and protect his house, his women and his children, is for that black man to become in his own mind the something less than a man which this Republic, alas, has always considered him to be. And when a black man, whose destiny and identity have always been controlled by others, decides and states that he will control his own destiny and rejects the identity given him by others, he is talking revolution. In point of sober fact, he cannot possibly be talking anything else, and nothing is more revelatory of the American hypocrisy than their swift perception of this fact. The "white backlash" is meaningless 20th-century jargon designed at once to hide and to justify the fact that most white Americans are still unable to believe that the black man is a man—in the same way that we speak of a "credibility gap" because we are too cowardly to face the fact that our leaders have been lying to us for years. Perhaps we suspect that we deserve the contempt with which we allow ourselves to be treated.

The government would like to be able to indict Stokely, and many others like him, of incitement to riot; but I accuse the government of this crime. It is, briefly, an insult to my intelligence, and to the intelligence of any black person, to ask me to believe that the most powerful nation in the world is unable to do anything to make the lives of its black citizens less appalling. It is not unable to do it, it is only unwilling to do it. Americans are deluded if they suppose Stokely to be the first black man to say, "The United States is going to fall. I only hope I live to see the day." Every black man in the howling North American wilderness has said it, and is saying it, in many, many ways, over and over again. One's only got to listen, again, to all those happy songs. Or walk to Harlem and talk to any junkie, or anybody else—if, of course, they will talk to you. It was a nonviolent black student who told Bobby Kennedy a few years ago that he didn't know how much longer he could remain non-

violent; didn't know how much longer he could take the beatings, the bombings, the terror. He said that he would never take
up arms in defense of America—never, never, never. If he ever
picked up a gun, it would be for very different reasons.

That boy has grown up, as have so many like him—we will
not mention those irreparably ruined, or dead—and I really
wonder what white Americans expected to happen. Did they
really suppose that the tremendous energy and the incredible
courage which went into those sit-ins, wade-ins, swim-ins, picket-
lines, marches, was incapable of transforming itself into an
overt attack on the status quo? I remember that same day in
Selma watching the line of black would-be voters walk away
from the courthouse which they had not been allowed to enter.
And I thought, the day is coming when they will not line up any
more.

That day may very well be here—I fear it is here; certainly
Stokely is here, and he is not alone. It helps our situation not at
all to attempt to punish the man for telling the truth. I repeat:
we have seen this show before. This victimization has occurred
over and over again, from Frederick Douglass to Paul Robeson
to Cassius Clay to Malcolmn X. And I contest the government's
right to lift the passports of those people who hold views of
which the government—and especially this government—disap-
proves. The government has the duty to warn me of the dangers
I may encounter if I travel to hostile territory—though they
never said anything about the probable results of my leaving
Harlem to go downtown and never said anything about my travels to Alabama—but it does not have the right to use my passport as a political weapon against me, as a means of bringing
me to heel. These are terror tactics. Furthermore, all black
Americans are born into a society which is determined—repeat:
determined—that they shall never learn the truth about themselves or their society, which is determined that black men shall
use as their only frame of reference what white Americans convey to them of their own potentialities, and of the shape, size,
dimensions and possibilities of the world. And I do not hesitate

for an instant to condemn this as a crime. To persuade black boys and girls, as we have for so many generations, that their lives are worth less than other lives, and that they can only live on terms dictated to them by other people, by people who despise them, is worst than a crime, it is the sin against the Holy Ghost.

Now, I may not always agree with Stokely's views, or the ways in which he expresses them. My agreement, or disagreement, is absolutely irrelevant. I get his message. Stokely Carmichael, a black man under thirty, is saying to me, a black man over forty, that he will not live the life I've lived, or be corralled into some of the awful choices I have been forced to make. And he is perfectly right. The government and the people who have made his life, and mine, and the lives of all our brothers and sisters and women and children an indescribable hell have no right now to penalize the black man, this so despised stranger here for so long, for attempting to discover if the world is as small as the Americans have told him it is. And the political implications involve nothing more and nothing less than what the Western world takes to be its material self-interest. I need scarcely state to what extent the Western self-interest and the black self-interest find themselves at war, but it is precisely this message which the Western nations, and this one above all, will have to accept, if they expect to survive. Nothing is more unlikely than that the Western nations, and this one above all, will be able to welcome so vital a metamorphosis. We have constructed a history which is a total lie, and have persuaded ourselves that it is true. I seriously doubt that anything worse can happen to any people. One doesn't need a Stokely gloating in Havana about the hoped-for fall of the United States; and to attempt to punish him for saying what so many millions of people feel is simply to bring closer, and make yet more deadly, the terrible day. One should listen to what's being said, and reflect on it: for many, many millions of people long for our downfall, and it is not because they are Communists. It is because ignorance is in the saddle here, and we ride mankind. Let us attempt to face the fact that we are a racist society, racist to the very marrow, and we are fighting a racist war. No black man in chains in his own country, and watching the many deaths occurring around him every day, believes for a moment that America cares anything at all about the freedom of Asia. My own condition, as a black man in America, tells me what Americans really feel and really want, and tells me who they really are. And therefore, every bombed village is my home town.

That, in a way, is what Stokely is saying, and that's why this youth can so terrify a nation. He's saying the bill is in, the party's over, are we going to live here like men or not? Bombs won't pay this bill, and bombs won't wipe it out. And Stokely did not begin his career with dreams of terror, but with dreams of love. Now he's saying, and he's not alone, and he's not the first, if I can't live here, well, then, neither will you. You couldn't have built it without me; this land is also mine; we'll share it, or we'll perish, and I don't care.

I do care—about Stokely's life, my country's life. One's seen too much already of gratuitous destruction; one hopes, always, that something will happen in the human heart which will change our common history. But if it doesn't happen, this something, if we cannot hear and cannot change, then we, the blacks, the most despised children of the great Western house, are simply forced, with both pride and despair, to remember that we come from a long line of runaway slaves who managed to survive without passports.

from an interview

QUESTION: You made a remark about the Beat Generation. I can't remember the exact quote, I think it was something to the effect that when you were six years old you were beat, and any black person living in the ghetto knew he was beat—he didn't have to go to school and get out of college and run away to become beat. I was wondering if you had that same view now.

ANSWER: I'm afraid I must say I never paid very much attention to the Beat Generation. It never struck me as being very interesting or very relevant to me—I'd seen those kids before and it didn't matter what they were doing, because presently they would go home and take over the family business. And that's what they really do, unless they're hung up on junk or something, or unless they do grow up, which is extremely difficult to do in this country. This is another symptom of Western despair. It shows me how little people care about their children.

Q: How do you view the hippie scene?

A: Again, it shows me how unable people are to love their children. That's what's wrong with those kids. They just want someone to pay attention to them, and I can't blame them. Their mothers and fathers thought it was more important to become something else rather than to raise their children.

Q: Rap Brown made the statement that he thought the hippie movement—the hippie scene—was politically irrelevant.

A: Well, it is politically irrelevant—but so, in this country, is politics.

Q: Evidently not so to Rap Brown.

A: Politics? What do you mean by that?

Q: If he finds the hippies politically irrelevant, then he must find other forces that are relevant in this country.

A: Well, Rap and I are very different people. I'm much older than Rap, and Rap may know a lot that I don't know—but the political institutions of this country, as we see them now, are visibly unresponsive, let us say that, to the real needs of what we have to call the American community. It does strike me as occurring mainly in a vacuum. And it'll be a long time before that changes. You know, the most stunning collection of mediocrities ever seen are sitting in Washington. God knows how they got there. And I don't know what they're doing there. They could not be more dangerous, but they're also ignorant.

THEODORE BIKEL

jewish campus youth*

Why do I have to be Jewish to be good?

"I may not know who I am," as one student put it, "but I certainly do know who I'm not and what I don't want to become." In Jewish terms this means a rejection of father's identity because it derives its blessing from a middle-class group rather than from within, a rejection of the synagogue (not necessarily for its content but for its form; "somehow the ideals of brotherhood seem to have been lost in the Sisterhood"), and a mistrust even of the Jewish organizations with positive action programs (because of the seeming preoccupation with self-serving membership drives and institutional exclusivism).

All shades of hippiedom, from the drug-happy, tuned-out, world-weary to the equally divorced Eastern-meditation cultists, as well as all shades of the activists sensitive to social injustice, number in their ranks more young Jews than the general population ratio of Jews to non-Jews. But even if the hippie element and the radical element put together comprise only about 15 to 20 percent of college-age youth, little comfort can be derived from the strait-laced, unhip, and non-revolutionary element of young Jews.

For where the Jewish hippie is totally estranged ("I'm out of it, man") and the Jewish radical openly hostile to Jewry ("To me it's all part of the Establishment, and it's all rotten"), the "straight" young Jew is for the most part blandly indifferent both to the Jewish ethos and to the plight of the dispossessed; to hunger, to poverty, to war (until the draft threatens him per-

* From a longer report for the American Jewish Congress.

sonally); in short, to anything outside the scope of his own advancement. He worries not about the inequality of distribution but about getting his slice of the pie, the larger the better. Worst of all, he seems to have gone from babyhood to old age without the turbulence, the agonies and the joys of adolescence and young adulthood. The most discouraging picture that lingers in my mind is that of the smug members of a Jewish fraternity (in whose entire curriculum of activity not a single Jewish thing was practiced) who talked and behaved like miniature old businessmen.

There are pockets of committed Jewish youths in many areas, notably the big urban centers. Some derive their commitment from a religious orientation, others from an ideological or political motivation, chiefly Zionism. Both are sensitive to problems affecting the world Jewish community and will readily participate in action programs relating to, for example, Soviet anti-Semitism or the threat to Israel's survival. However, while the ethno-politically motivated tend to respond also to social action in areas not necessarily affecting Jews, the religious group, for the most part, fails to acknowledge the general fight against social injustice as falling within the realm of Jewish principle. Acknowledging a fair number of exceptions, the trend toward exclusivism is stronger among the more orthodox of the religious youth groups and less so among the liberal and reformed, mirroring the adult Jewish community.

As to the Zionist youth movement, there is no doubt that the June 1967 war revived a good deal of broader interest in the campus activities of a relatively small cadre of Israel-oriented youths. However, the rising emotionalism over the specter of yet another wave of genocide did not prove to be of an enduring nature. As the threat subsided the temporary solidarity of young Jews weakened. Such is the character of reactive emotions as distinct from basic, active commitments.

The task of battling for souls is not to be fought among the comfort-seekers, the accepters of the status quo, nor in any great measure among the tuned-out or dropped-out, although the latter do present a mounting challenge. (The Jewish hippie is as lost as a Jew to Judaism as he is lost as a human being to society. He can be "turned on" from time to time by the ecstasy of a Shlomo Carlebach or the soaring, freewheeling religious mysticism of a Zalman Schachter; but it is not the Jewish aspect which is meaningful to the hippie but the ecstasy and the mysticism for their own sakes. He seems willing to relate to the "kicks" without accepting the discipline within the framework of which—and only in which—these manifestations are made possible.) The most important, the most excruciating struggle is with the action-oriented youth, the SDS member, the Civil Rights–New Left-oriented young Jew; the one active in the peace movement, the draft resisters' movement, and so forth. It is among this group's ranks that tomorrow's leaders are to be found, and tomorrow's philosophers, too; hence it is they who must be convinced that Judaism is a living, positive and creative force rather than an institutional entanglement or a societal anachronism.

Of the most frequently recurring arguments put to me on the various campuses the most burning, the most accusatory, was the question of relevance. For him, declares one young man, "the phenomenon of middle-class moral hypocrisy is a Jewish one. The lip-service paid to tradition by our parents' intoning prayers hastily dredged up from their childhood at the 'important' holidays, the only holidays where attendance booms at synagogues; kids dropped off on either Saturday or Sunday morning at 'Sunday' school, 'Hebrew' school, or whatever the suburban term might be this year, while Daddy goes off to the golf club and Mother has her hair done, plays cards or something less taxing.

"And those important holidays . . . they serve the social needs of the community, they act as a fashion show for the ladies, a kaffee klatch for the men, a place in which to show off one's wealth in open bidding—pledges for the 'building' fund. The men doze off as soon as the Rabbi starts the sermon, the women preen and nod to each other, more aware of their new hats than the pulpit. The gold and glitter, the plushness of the wall-to-wall carpeting. And, what of the world? . . . That is for later when we are in college and find out that the rest of the world does not have gold and glitter and new hats and plush floor covering."

We are all guilty of the gross Jewish misconceptions and illusions . . . Jews don't drink, don't swap wives; that's for the others, not for us. Not so. We have assimilated to a greater extent in this country than ever before in our history, and, having assimilated the good of a free society, we have assimilated the evils of that society as well. As to social awareness, the young people say their parents—self-styled liberals—have a curious attitude towards civil rights . . . if they live on Long Island, civil rights is for New York City, if they live in Bethesda, then civil rights is for Washington, D.C., if in Beverly Hills, then for Los Angeles—and they are all for it.

But even to kids who look beyond suburbia and into the Jewish experience of the past, the picture is bleak, for their contact with the community is to them totally unsatisfying. They recognize that where the individual and his relationship to ethical values had been of paramount importance in Jewish life, where once dissent and non-conformity were normal and acceptable to Jews (at least on the intellectual level if not the ritualistic), things have changed radically with the process of acculturation (a euphemism for assimilation). Now, they maintain, Judaism is just like other institutions—stagnant, demanding conformism and status-quo adherence.

Then there is the question of duplicity with regard to violence. As they ask America, how can you maintain that violence in the streets is wrong while violence in Vietnam is right? so they ask their fellow Jews or their parents who have finally taken a dove position on Vietnam: if you are truly a peacenik, then why give money to buy arms for Israel?

The doubts were by no means dispelled when I demonstrated with some force that the Jewish ethos had indeed a unique contribution to make to all these questions; that a framework existed within which Jews made a constructive contribution to

civil rights, to peace, to defense against right-wingers and racists, a contribution made not only with at least as much vigor as
within the New Left, for example, but with far more knowledge
and historical perspective. Then I was hit with a charge of eth-
nocentricity, or parochial exclusivism. For the young activist
asks, "Why do I have to be Jewish to be good?" He believes in
the brotherhood of all people; he wants to seek vigorously the
cures to mankind's ills: disease, famine, war, avarice, corruption. And he says he has the tools, as part of the youth movement, to atempt to deal with them. As he discounts the belief in
God as unnecessary to the motivation to do good, so also does
he discount the identification with his ethnic background as a
motivation for personal morality, seeing no connection whatsoever between his commitment and his Jewishness.

He is, of course, radically wrong in maintaining a stance of
"human being" rather than "Jew." True brotherhood does not
seek to eradicate differences in mores or behavior or language
or tradition; it merely maintains that a mans's acknowledged
differentness makes him no less than his brother. Those who
maintain otherwise are on the road to becoming what Leonard
Fein calls "functional amnesiacs," people who will not acknowledge roots or history, who will not seek in their grandfather's
attic for valuables before they assert that it contains only useless
and cumbersome junk.

In the end the point had to be made also that relevance is
surely not the only determinant of value, even in the atomic age
(perhaps especially then). For, while I presented many valid
arguments for the relevance of Judaism and Jewish values, it
occurred to me that the irrelevance of Judaism to the age of
technology was just as important to consider. Judaism is surely
as irrelevant to issues and actions as are poetry and music. Yet
what self-respecting society could afford to be without those?
I managed to some extent to convince some of my youthful opponents—but for every student I reached, at least to the extent
of his being prepared to continue with the dialogue, there were

dozens I did not reach and thousands with whom contact has yet to be established.

Not all students in the movement are motivated by the noble standards of renovating society from the bottom up and creating a new order truly resting upon the ideals of democracy, equality and wisdom. There are those who are in it for the excitement of action, those who imagine that rebellion can be a short-cut to understanding. These, running as they do from inner obligations, are surely not equipped to deal with outer ones. Worse still, they are content to act without a blueprint, since rebellion is to them an end in itself. As Milton Mayer says, a social order can be overturned in the name of greater justice, but if those who take power are no more selfless or wise than those who are displaced, there has been no gain. We must separate in our minds the true idealistic youthful revolutionary from the phony revolutionary who is in love not with justice but with rebellion.

Dealing with the former is our main and most important task: proving to him, by the weight of our actions and by the spectrum of our involvement, that his allegation—namely that no Jewish institution is capable of activist response to the problems of the day—is false. But we will not be admitted to their councils until we learn their language and learn that their problems are not just the problems of the young but the problems of the living of any age. Ironically, where once the older generation despaired of the younger, the younger now despairs of us and gives us up for lost. Where once we were the teachers of morality and ethics to our young, we are now faced with youthful teachers and sterner critics than ever we could be.

catholic teen-agers debate adult critics

When they put rosaries in my hand they forgot to place love in my heart. . . . I only ask my elders to look our way. And if they won't lend a hand, not to break *our* fingers with their ways.

today's rebellious generation

The Constitution on the Church in the Modern World begins: "The joys and hopes, the griefs and anxieties of the men of this age, especially those who are poor or in any way afflicted, these too are the joys and hopes, the griefs and anxieties of the followers of Christ." Article seven of the same constitution adds: "A change in attitudes and in human structure frequently calls accepted values into question. This is especially true of the young people, who have grown impatient on more than one occasion, and indeed become rebels in their distress." The young, the document continues, are aware of their influence in society, and they want to assume a role in it now. Their more sophisticated and critical view of the world has purified religion of its magical and superstitious aspect and led to a more vivid sense of God. "On the other hand, growing numbers of people are abandoning religion in practice."

The main reason many young people now feel alienated from their religion—as well as from many values cherished by the older generation—may be that they have never fully grasped what Christianity is. They have never understood, perhaps, how much the Church, in all its variety and fullness, strives to fulfill the deepest human needs, both personal and social.

In the Constitution on the Church, the Church describes itself above all as the new People of God—emphasizing its human and communal aspects—and it reminds us that all are called to witness to the gospel and serve the needs of the brethren and the world. Many members of the younger generation do not recognize this as the Church they have been raised in. They remember only such drawbacks as an over-negative sex education; teachers who have lacked sympathy for the great scientific and political movements of modern times; the Church's slowness, in some instances, to cry out against injustice, to stand up—like the prophet Jeremiah—to what they call the "establishment" or the "power structure." These young rebels do not see faith as a free human response to God or as a rational reaching out to Christ, the source of love and strength. For them faith has been submission to an impersonal system demanding not so much love of neighbor as Friday abstinence and Sunday Mass.

What zealous young people of the "new left" really want is to establish a community of love and knowledge where citizens share concern with passionate responsibility. This, actually, is what the Church is—a community of love and knowledge, at once more human and more universal than any city founded by men. But the disaffected young do not recognize it as such a community. They are frightened by its structure—as if it were a monolithic corporation run by old men in Rome. They feel they grow closer to the experience of community in "the movement" than they do at the Sacrifice of the Mass.

It may be that this stage of rebellion is the same one every generation in history has gone through; or it may be that the Church in the United States is only now witnessing the same apostasy of the young that France and other European countries saw some years ago. Even so, there are important differences. Today's rebellious generation, unlike its American predecessors, is open and vocal. Some young people have stopped going to Mass, while their elders continue to conform outwardly to a Christianity they have given up in their hearts. Another difference is that the American Church possesses both the youth and the traditions, the resources and the imagination, to care about this problem and to face up to it.

First we must recognize that, paradoxically, a great many of the rebels, at the very same time they feel they are losing their faith, are actually crying out for faith. If this is so, it is up to pastors, teachers and parents to show in their own lives that the heart of the Christian message really is love of God and of neighbor. In the concrete, this will have to be translated into welcoming Negroes into the neighborhood; consulting young people on certain factors of parish administration (particularly concerning the liturgy); somehow bringing more democracy into the structures of the Church; setting up "little councils" in all the dioceses; listening patiently and with humility to the laity; and carrying out a long-range re-education in Scripture, ecclesiology and social morality for clergy and laity alike, so that this new growth of faith may be both intellectually well-founded and emotionally sincere. If we miss this opportunity at this rare moment in history, we shall be poor indeed, and the next generation will be poorer than we shall ever know.

youth replies

Who are you to say that we are a rebellious generation? Also, what do you define as rebellious? . . . My generation has just as many good and bad points as yours. But one thing must be noted: my generation has been much more involved than yours. Teen-agers sponsor many fund-raising drives, work in many aid programs, join the Peace Corps—unheard of in your day. . . .

We have been given much more freedom than any others before us. This is why we have questioned some of the points of religion. By questioning, we will get a fuller and better understanding of what Christianity is than your generation will ever hope to realize. By looking around on Sunday at Mass, I have come to the realization that my adult Christian brothers have little idea of what Christianity is. Maybe it is because today's youth sees what has become of its forebears that we question and seek to find answers and beliefs that will satisfy our consciences of what is right or wrong with Christianity.

Patrick ————

Perhaps the reason why young people never grasped what Christianity is, is because on the local level priests and religious have not grasped it sufficiently either. If they have, they may not have put it into practice. I disagree . . . that most of the blame rests with the younger generation. We only see what is being practiced—not the idealistic proposals of the Church. We are taking issue with facts, not theory.

Paul ————

While attending a lecture for CCD teachers' instruction, several young classmates and I listened with horror to the responses of solid Catholic adults to the query: "What are your ideas concerning the Church?" Immediately they rattled off a host of memorized catechism answers. As my companion so aptly put it: "What happened to good old Christ?" Please help us put Christ back into the spirit of our people. We don't want a structure. We need a God.

Mary ————

Please don't try to talk down to us. We "young people" are not impatient; we have come alive. We have realized that this monolithic corporation run by old men in Rome is not alive to the needs and desires of its stockholders. We are tired of money-grubbing pastors and Sunday Mass being just the big day to rake it in. We are tired of bored priests, who have built walls of "procedure" and "respect" and "propriety" around themselves. We are tired of frightened little men.

We are alive and unafraid of human contact and community sharing. We get this experience not in any "movement" (whatever that may be) but in our personal friendships. Perhaps Mass might mean more to us if it meant more to the priests. We realize we are crying out for faith. We have known that. It is you people who have misinterpreted us. We are never afraid to look into ourselves. . . .

My generation is calling for dedicated, committed and unafraid leaders to guide and channel our tremendous vitality. We don't want scared little men. Stop worrying about rebellion and start finding dynamic leaders for us. . . .

Louis ———

I found your editorial perceptive and at least a bit heartening. I am 17 and, as you said, am "crying out for faith." I do not see it in many of my teachers, or in my pastor, or in my parents. Their faith is often too granite, often too mired in unfaith. The faith I seek is not an "I believe"—it is an "I live accordingly." When they put rosaries in my hand, they forgot to place love in my heart. When I received my first Communion, they forgot to say: "Christ is in you in the playground, too."

I'll play my part. I'll open myself to explanations of faith. I'll listen. But my eyes cannot but see the half-truth of words. They want to see the fulfilled truth of actions. And my body wants to work to manifest my own flimsy faith. Please, I only ask my elders to look our way. And if they won't lend a hand, not to break *our* fingers with their ways.

James ———

We are two seventeen-year-old girls. The statement was made that perhaps we, the younger generation, have "never fully grasped what Christianity is." This is very true: yet is this our fault? All too often our religion courses have dealt with pure Baltimore Catechism-type material. . . . After having been force-fed these answers for 12 years, it is no wonder that . . . we have become restless and rebellious.

We want to be able to question and to think out answers for ourselves with the helpful guidance of the Church, so that when we have found the answers, we will have a much firmer basis for our beliefs. Vatican II, thank goodness, has opened the door for this questioning, and many teen-agers have taken up the challenge. It is also up to the older generation, though, to realize their responsibility and to change in their approach to religion with us, not to immediately condemn us for our views.

Kathy ———

Eileen ———

adults react

The teen-agers' answers to the "rebellious generation" editorial were great. . . . The future is in good hands. I think the "old men" who manage the church agree. You see, we love those young, lovely, lively rebels. We expect, hope and pray that they will do better than we did.

Rev. ———

My dear young men: There are many among your priests (of whom I am one) who feel more in common with you than you realize. Your passionate decrying of a tired "system" is well taken. I am constantly stimulated by . . . your love of life and its challenges: your desire to see created a renewed and fresh Church, relevant and sensitive to the need for love among men. . . . Help me and my brother priests by your prayers and by the benefit of your ability to arouse in us the desire to keep pace with the dynamic era into which we have been thrust.

Rev. ———

As a second-year Extension Volunteer, I too have felt many of the same frustrations that these young people feel right now. Rebellious? No, I wouldn't call our teen-agers that—unless

you're referring to the natural quality of impatience characteristic of our age. In this case the impatience is well founded. To
see "Christians" ignore or turn away from suffering, abuse and
indifference is good reason for impatience. But teen-agers are
not alone in their quest for a more humane, a more understanding Church. Many of us, clergy and laity alike, are also impatient and eager for a more Christ-like Church. But it is a useless
quest unless we do something about it. Informed action is the
key. Teen-agers, keep that restlessness and impatience until you
can look around and say: "Look at these Christians; see how
they love one another."

Mrs. Carol ———

EDGAR Z. FRIEDENBERG

knights in chino pants: the vanishing adolescent*

**They behave as if they did not even
know that passion and fidelity are
expensive, but merely assumed that
everyone possessed them.**

Much of the ambivalence of adults toward "teen-agers"
is, I should judge, simply a kind of repressed panic-response to
the liquidation of authority over them. It must be understood,
however, that the loss of authority is real; the adult empire is
tottering. All empires are; this is the era of skepticism about the
relationship between authority and status. It is an error, I believe, to interpret what is happening as a decline in respect for
authority as such. American youngsters today are generous in
according respect to parents, teachers, and other adults who earn
it as individuals; and they are far more perceptive of individual
quality in their elders than they could possibly have been when
all adults were regarded as potentially or actually hostile and
dangerous. But it is true that they are less likely to respect an
adult today simply because he occupies a position of authority.
It is also true that a boy who can be punished for insulting you
is far less frightening—even if he is *very* insulting—than a boy
who offers out of sheer kindness to share his analyst with you because he has noticed, correctly, that you need help worse than
he does.

* Excerpts from a book.

Adults who do not basically like and respect adolescents—and this includes a large proportion of those who make a career of working with them—are badly frightened by the increasingly democratic relationships between adolescents and adults that are coming to prevail in our society. They have become more tense in their attitude toward youngsters, and contribute greatly to the difficulties of young people in our society. Their manipulative and covert hostility demoralizes adolescents and forms the basis of real personal and social problems. . . . Nevertheless, this is probably not too serious a matter, for it is pretty certain to work itself out in the course of time. . . .

What is far more serious is that the emphasis on cooperation and group adjustment characteristic of modern life interferes specifically with the central developmental task of adolescence itself. *This task is self-definition. Adolescence is the period during which a young person learns who he is, and what he really feels. It is the time during which he differentiates himself from his culture, though on the culture's terms. It is the age at which, by becoming a person in his own right, he becomes capable of deeply felt relationships to other individuals perceived clearly as such.* It is precisely this sense of individuality which fails to develop, or develops only feebly, in most primitive cultures or among lower-status social groups. A successful initiation leads to group solidarity and a warm sense of belonging; a successful adolescence adds to these a profound sense of self—of one's own personality.

Personalization is the métier of adolescence. Of all persons, adolescents are the most intensely personal; their intensity is often uncomfortable to adults. As cooperation and group adjustment become pervasive social norms; as tolerance supersedes passion as the basis for social action; as personalization becomes false-personalization, adolescence becomes more and more difficult. Conceivably, it might become again a rather rare event, having no function in the new world of glad-handing primitives happy among their electronic trinkets. But, for the present at least, the old norms of individual character, personal devotion, particular love and hate retain enough authority to make those who remain faithful to them, as adolescents tend to do, extremely troublesome to their contemporaries.

Adolescents often behave much like members of an old-fashioned aristocracy. They maintain private rituals, which they often do not really understand themselves. They are extremely conservative in their dress and tastes, but the conventions to which they adhere are purely those of their own social group; they try to ignore the norms of the larger society if these conflict with their own. They can be extravagantly generous and extravagantly cruel, but rarely petty or conniving. Their virtues are courage and loyalty; while the necessity for even a moderate degree of compromise humiliates them greatly. They tend to be pugnacious and quarrelsome about what they believe to be their rights, but naïve and reckless in defending them. They are shy, but not modest. If they become very anxious they are likely to behave eccentrically, to withdraw, or to attack with some brutality; they are less likely to blend themselves innocuously into the environment with an apologetic smile. They are honest on occasions when even a stupid adult would have better sense.

They are therefore at a considerable disadvantage in many relationships of modern life. Modern life is hostile to the aristocratic social principle. Aristocratic attitudes and modes of action snarl its very mainsprings. They interfere with the conduct of practical affairs and impede administrative action. In busy, anxious, and ambitious people, they arouse anger and resentment; but beneath the anger and resentment there is shame and guilt.

Adolescents insult us by quietly flaunting their authenticity. They behave as if they did not even know that passion and fidelity are expensive, but merely assumed that everyone possessed them. This, certainly, is inexcusably valorous; and it is not excused. But it makes us awkward in their presence, and embarrassed in our approach to them.

Not all adolescents, by any means, retain this quality. There are many who learn to soothe adults ruffled by encounters with their more ardent and challenging peers, and charm them on suitable occasions by an ingratiating youthfulness. When a boy or girl is needed for display, they are available; in the same clothes all the others wear, they look a little—not too much— neater. Having them in charge of the school paper and the student government saves a good deal of wear and tear all around; they are described in their school records as having qualities of leadership.

At certain times and places—perhaps here and now—such boys and girls predominate. Processes comparable to natural selection almost insure that they will. Schools nudge them into the pathways believed to lead to success in adult life and rehearse them for it in carefully designed facsimiles of adult institutions. Student life in the modern high school is now conducted through a veritable rat-maze of committees. The big man on campus is a perfectly executed scale model of a junior executive. It may therefore seem either inconsistent or willfully sentimental that I have described my heuristic model of an adolescent as a knight in shining chino pants.

But I think it is valid to maintain this, not just because I have encountered a goodly few such errant defenders of the faith in the course of half a lifetime, but because I am concerned here with a process of growth rather than with a statistical norm. There is certainly no doubt that modern society has power to corrupt, and that it starts early. But the function of adolescence is growth and individuation, and these can be fruitful only if a reasonable and increasing degree of integrity is maintained.

A youngster who has abandoned the task of defining himself in dialectical combat with society and becomes its captive and its emissary may be no rarity; but he is a casualty. There is not much more to be said about him: one can only write him off and trust that the world will at least feed him well if it cannot keep him warm. The promise of maturity must be fulfilled by those who are strong enough to grow into it at their own rate as full bargaining members.

Must there be conflict between the adolescent and society?

The point is that adolescence *is* conflict—protracted conflict—between the individual and society. There are cultures in which this conflict seems hardly to occur; but where it does not, the characteristic development of personality which we associate with adolescence does not occur either. . . .

But conflict is not war; it need not even involve hostile action. It must, to be sure, produce some hostile feelings, among others. But there need be no intent to wound, castrate, or destroy on either side. Conflict between the adolescent and his world is dialectical, and leads, as a higher synthesis, to the youth's own adulthood and to critical participation in society as an adult. . . . One cannot, therefore, use the inevitability of conflict in adolescence as a justification for actions which hurt adolescents on the pretext of "toughening them up." If "growing pains" are never sickening, heartbreaking, or terrifying, it is equally true that heartbreak, terror, and a sense of insult and violation contribute nothing to growth. They stunt it or twist it, and the grower is more or less deformed. Perhaps the commonest deformation which these cause in persons too young to know how to handle themselves in pain is apathy. . . .

Delinquency, apathy, and seductive fawning are not aspects of the essential conflict between youth and society which constitutes adolescence. They are the consequences of the conflict having gone terribly wrong, and a corresponding wisdom and patience—more than is usually available under actual working conditions—are needed to restore it as a fruitful process. For most young people, of course, things do not go terribly wrong. They go moderately wrong, but we nevertheless grow up, more or less, and conduct ourselves toward the next generation in its need with such humanity as we can muster. . . .

But if the function of adolescence is self-definition, one would expect it to be very difficult in a society which suffers from a dearth of individuality and in which alienation is a crucial problem. And if the instrument of self-definition is the conflict between the adolescent and a basically humane society—which nevertheless has purposes of its own, and more to do than take care of kids—one would expect the self-defining process to break down as that society became less humane and more manipulative. A society which has *no purposes* of its own, other than to insure domestic tranquillity by suitable medication, will have no use for adolescents, and will fear them; for they will be among the first to complain, as they crunch away at their benzedrine, that tranquilizers make you a square. It will set up sedative programs of guidance, which are likely to be described as therapeutic, but whose apparent function will be to keep young minds and hearts in custody till they are without passion. We have by no means gone so far as yet; but the sort of process of which I speak is already discernible. . . .

Adults read their own hopes and fears into the actions of adolescents, and project onto them their own conflicts, values, and anxieties. They take desperate measures to protect the young from imaginary menaces, which are in fact their own fantasies, and to guide them to imagined success, which is in fact surrender. The youngsters, in their turn, respond to this mistrust with even more vigor than could reasonably have been expected, living up to adult expectations with really impressive viciousness.

It is not that adult fears are groundless, or without substantial foundation. The adolescent behavior that disturbs them really occurs, and is really disturbing. However, adult response to the way adolescents act seems often to be influenced more by the adults' own unconscious needs and tensions than by what the adolescents are actually doing. . . .

The most threatening feelings are certain to be deeply repressed into the unconscious; as a result, they are certain to influence action and perception with peculiar potency. . . . First, I believe, is a fear that the adolescent will get out of the adult's control and may also throw out of control situations in which the adult is involved. . . . Adolescents continually disturb the rigid sentinels of the social order. The risks they take also trouble those who love them. . . . The quality of this concern, generated by real affection, is, however, unmistakably different from that of the many adults—be they parents, judges, teachers, or irate citizens—to whom anything unplanned or disorderly is terrible simply because it is uncontrolled.

Second, and less obvious, but equally important among American adults, is a fear of aging. . . . Young people who really do have their lives ahead of them, and who have not yet begun in earnest to make the least of their opportunities, are bound to arouse mixed feelings in their elders. They arouse genuine concern; it is excruciating to watch a youngster, especially one who refuses to listen to you, making what you are quite sure are serious mistakes. But at a deeper level, it may be even more painful when he does not make them, or when they turn out not to be mistakes; when he grasps and holds what eluded you, or what you dared not touch and have dreamed of ever since. Simple envy can be harsh enough. It becomes immeasurably worse if it undermines self-esteem, as it must in individuals who, like many of us, have been taught in childhood that only the successful are lovable. We may hate the young, then, not only for getting what we never had, but for reminding us that since we never succeeded in getting it, we have no right to self-esteem. . . .*

I believe that the growth of hostility toward the adolescent is one more index of the rootlessness and barrenness of modern life; of the intense need for status in a society which provides few stable guarantees of respect on which a sense of personal worth can be based. . . . Integrity—or its lack—must stem from the deepest cultural roots; one is not dealing here with a problem of technique. One may fairly say, however, that whatever is done is more likely to be fruitful if its effect is to improve the conditions of adolescence than if directed toward any other stage of growth. In adolescence, the force of growth itself is most squarely on the side of integrity; it is then that development is most concerned with it.

By helping the adolescent develop good, specific reasons for

---

* (Friedenberg also indicates at some length how and why the adult male's response to adolescent boys—particularly in an open and competitive society—frequently involves "at a much deeper level . . . profoundly irrational and destructive. . . ." the fear of homosexuality, of repressed homosexual feelings.—A.K.)

thinking well of himself, the school can contribute greatly to a stable identity. These reasons *are* competences, and adolescents with the help of good teachers can become very competent in mind, heart, and body. It is essential, however, that the adolescent think of this competence as his own and make it his own. The school must bring itself to recognize and respect a far wider variety of competence than it now does; more particularly, it must learn to accept the student's pride in his own distinction as well as to cultivate his participation in the things it thinks are important.

School ought to be a place where you can not only learn to *be* a scholar, a fighter, a lover, a repairman, a writer, or a scientist, but learn that you are *good* at it, and in which your awareness and pride in being good at it become a part of your sense of being you. More emphasis on the sciences, higher standards, stricter discipline: these, of themselves, will not help at all. They may hinder. A school that, while raising standards in certain academic areas, treats the student more than ever as an object or an instrument, simply becomes a more potent source of alienation.

What is needed is no program of technical training-cum-indoctrination, but the patient development of the kind of character and mind that conceives itself too clearly to consent to its own betrayal. It takes a kind of shabby arrogance to survive in our time, and a fairly romantic nature to want to. These are scarce resources, but more abundant among adolescents than elsewhere, at least to begin with. In the national interest they should be preserved. The greatest safeguard to any democracy is a continuing community of self-respecting young people who understand and accept their relationship to society. The basic unit of such a community is a stable self to respect.

BENJAMIN SPOCK

rebellion in adolescence

**The strongest rebellion may be
expressed in quiet, undramatic behavior.**

Parents and society have always been concerned about
adolescents, and this may be as much a reflection on the worri-
someness of parents as it is on the conduct of youth. . . . There
is lots of misunderstanding, I think, about the meaning of various types of adolescent rebelliousness. Some people assume, for
instance, that draft-card burning is an expression of cowardice
or treachery. Actually, a young person has to have an intense
idealism (whether or not you consider it misplaced) to dare to
do anything so unpopular. And some of the strongest rebellion
may be expressed in quiet, undramatic behavior. . . .

Psychoanalytic experience has taught us that adolescent rebelliousness doesn't consist of just an impatience to be more independent of the parents, in rights and privileges, though it
feels this way to the youths themselves. In the deeper, unconscious layers of the mind it has more of the quality of a resentful
rivalry with the parent of the same sex. This is like the rivalry
of the little boy at four, five and six years of age, when he felt
resentful inside that he couldn't be as big, smart, rich and powerful as he imagined his father to be and that he couldn't compete on an equal basis for the attention of his mother. The little
girl at that same age resented, in her unconscious mind, her
mother's seemingly fabulous privileges and clothes, her possession of a fascinating husband, her ability to grow real live
babies.

The adolescent's rivalry with his parent is much sharper than that of the small child because he now has nearly a full-sized body and aggressive and sexual instincts of high intensity—especially the boy. He realizes that he soon will be a man, with a job, wife and home of his own, and it riles him to have to submit still to the indignities of being his father's child. The girl realizes that it will now be her turn to be the beautiful woman who attracts the men, accepts a husband and has the babies. This gives her the impulse to push her mother aside, though she may be too polite to express this directly unless she is very angry.

Rebelliousness and rivalry in adolescence take many forms, depending on the society to which the individual belongs, his personality, his particular relationship with his parent and whether he is male or female. In the remote mountains of Tennessee and Kentucky, for instance, where life is relatively uncomplicated and where independence is highly valued, a boy of 15 or 16 may graduate to manhood abruptly in one day. When his father angrily orders him to do something that he doesn't want to do he may suddenly, unexpectedly lose his temper, knock his father down and then walk off to the nearest town to find a job. . . .

At the opposite end of the educational scale is the son of an urban professional man. Ever since he was a small child he has accepted the obligation to do well in school as an essential part of the process of becoming a professional man himself, not only in order to meet his family's expectations but also to be able to rival his father's achievements. In this kind of family the father characteristically tries to be a reasonable, generous and encouraging leader to his son. If he feels anger or impatience, he tries to tone it down. These attitudes in the father make it difficult for his son to feel conscious anger toward him or to rebel beyond a little grumbling. To hit his father or even shout at him would be almost inconceivable. Psychiatrists learn that the rebelliousness is there but it finds indirect outlets and quiet forms. Many such boys remain respectful toward their fathers and shift all their irritation toward their mothers. They frequently criticize their mothers' appearance and behavior, blow up noisily when their mothers scold them or remind them of their duties.

A fairly common sign of rivalrousness in the same group, but one that doesn't look anything like rivalry on the surface, is school failure—in high school or college or graduate school—by a boy who has the intelligence and the motivation to do well and who has done well in the past. Sometimes this occurs when the boy first studies a subject that is related directly to his future lifework, especially if he is thinking of following in his father's footsteps. Psychoanalysis may show that in the unconscious mind the academic failure represents in part a fear of competition with the father. Interestingly enough, the hidden fear may be either that he won't be able to do as well as his father or that he may do so much better that his father will be furious. School failure also serves another unconscious purpose. It tortures the ambitious parents; but they can't punish the boy, and he won't feel too guilty, as long as he is consciously trying hard.

This uneasiness about competing with the father may show up in another way. When a boy at 16 or 18 is asked what occupation he's heading for he may answer that he doesn't know yet; the only thing he is sure of is that his father's field doesn't appeal to him at all. Then at about the age of 20 a doctor's son, for instance, may casually drop the remark that he will be taking quite a lot of chemistry this year. "Why?" asks his father. "You have to have it for medical school, of course," the son answers. "But I didn't know you were going into medicine!" exclaims the amazed and delighted father. "Didn't I tell you?" asks the boy in real perplexity. The boy has grown up enough by 20 so that he no longer is afraid of the competition implied in entering his father's field, but there is enough embarrassment left over from the past to make him forget to tell his father about his change of heart.

When a youth from a family with low educational expectations gets into trouble at school (aside from slowness because of mental limitations), it's more likely to be from sassing a teacher or principal because he can't submit any longer to the correcting and nagging, especially when the lessons mean nothing to him anyway; or he defies the authorities by staying away altogether.

When we study the serious delinquencies we see that there is a large element of rebellionsness and rivalry in them. But they also are based on a deprivation of love from early infancy. Before we discuss these, however, it's important to point out that the word "delinquency" is the loosest kind of term. It means different things in different states and municipalities. It is anything for which a youth has been judged guilty in juvenile court. It may include parking a car too long, dumping trash cans on Halloween, running away from home, stealing a few boards from a building site or shooting a filling-station attendant while trying to rob him. The last example is a crime usually commited only by an aggressive, unprincipled character. On the other hand, studies have shown that a great majority of the leading citizens of any town took part in some kind of mischief in youth that would have landed them in court if they had had the bad luck to be caught.

In the serious delinquencies of boys such as vandalism, stealing, armed robbery, sexual assault and brutality, investigation reveals that throughout childhood there was a great lack of parental love and concern, with a lesser or greater degree of cruelty. In adolescence the father (if there is a father still in the home) and the mother are apt to exert little control over such a youth's aggressiveness, and it is then directed mainly against the civil authorities. Serious delinquencies occur much more commonly among poverty-stricken, disorganized families, but they exist also in well-to-do neighborhoods.

The delinquencies of girls usually have much less aggressiveness in them. One of the commonest is running away from home. In doing this a girl will cause great distress to her parents. She also makes the neighbors wonder whether her parents treat her badly. She can indulge her own immature fantasies of finding lovely substitute parents and perhaps also a Prince Charming.

Another fairly common, and more serious, problem with girls is sexual delinquency of a promiscuous or provocative type—they flaunt their misbehavior. Psychiatric investigation shows that though defective parental morals and insufficient affection may be part of the background, the more immediate factor is the girl's impulse to shame and enrage her parents because of an angry rivalry with her mother or a resentment that her father doesn't show her enough attention. . . .

Rebelliousness against parents is a natural, built-in aspect of adolescents. It assists them in giving up the comforts and security of home and achieving real independence. They must also become sufficiently critical of their parents' ideas and ideals to be able to reject those that would be inappropriate for them, or for the times, and to take on others of their own. But all this doesn't mean that parents should take their children's objections and demands at face value—far from it. The successful rearing of children to adulthood and the transmission of family values has always depended on the parents' still acting as parents throughout adolescence, being understanding but watchful, assuming that their own experience and wisdom still have something to offer, making the rules clear even though the rules have to be modified with each successive year of maturation and even though the rules aren't always obeyed, being ready to become firm and occasionally even indignant when gentle persuasion doesn't work.

In America more than in any other country we parents, especially of the college-educated group, have lost a lot of our conviction about how much and what kind of guidance to give our children. The more we have learned about children, the less certain we have become. We have paid much more attention than Europeans have to the new concepts of child development derived from Freud and Dewey, and to the teachings of psychiatrists, educators and pediatricians generally. This is probably because we have come from many countries and backgrounds and have few common traditions; we don't respect our elders;

we move from place to place. We seem to have become particularly fearful that we will make our children resent us or will distort their personalities if we exert too much authority over them. This parental hesitancy has been more marked in relation to adolescent children than to any other age group. Of course, it is the instinct of adolescents to try to emancipate themselves by continually pressing, reproaching and nagging their parents for more freedom and privileges. However, parents should never assume that because youths ask for more freedom they necessarily want it. In fact, half the time when they appear to be demanding it, they are really debating inwardly about whether they are ready for it. But they won't admit this, even to themselves. I've known adolescents to make particularly preposterous requests—to borrow the car to drive to a rather disreputable joint and stay late, for instance—and it became evident that unconsciously they asked for much too much in order to be sure they would be turned down. . . .

I'm not saying that youths wouldn't like to be able to master all worldly challenges at a young age, and I'm not saying that they never want to be given permission to try something more grown up. I'm only saying that they still count on parental guidance, and that often when they demand and complain, they don't really mean it. They certainly resent being talked down to or being bossed arbitrarily. Parents can be reasonable in tone, willing to discuss all the issues, to talk man-to-man. They can show confidence that their children have good morals and good judgment and at the same time act quite sure that the kind of rules and behavior they are specifying are for their children's own protection and good name.

As for those youths—predominantly males—who run into study blocks despite high motivation and intelligence, the first step is to discuss the situation with the school personnel and get their recommendations. This often includes psychiatric consultation. The psychiatrist usually advises psychoanalysis or a less intensive but prolonged course of psychotherapy. (Quick unblocking is uncommon.) The more enlightened universities are now permitting the student who has run into a blank wall or who has lost his sense of motivation to withdraw for a year or two without harm to his academic reputation and then to return when there is evidence that he is back in gear.

HAIM GINOTT

the affluent drop-out[*]

**[My father's] self-esteem has not kept
up with his symbols of success.**

Harris, aged 19, a bright, artistic and rather shy sophomore, dropped out of school. It was an ivy-league college of
his father's choice. The event hit the family like a bomb. His
father tried to bribe him with a sport car and to buy him with
tickets for a round-the-world trip. He was promised paradise
if he only went back to school. The role of education was
stressed to him; money matters were mentioned, and financial
sanctions were implied. Harris withstood both the threats and
the promises. In the following letter he describes the reasons
that led him to his decision.

"My father is a status seeker. His life is a constant search for
emblems of eminence. He uses tokens of power to prove to himself that he has really made it. He rides in a chauffeured limou-
sine. He flies first class. He wears three-hundred-dollar suits and
he lies on the most expensive analyst's couch in America. There
are gold faucets in his bathroom, and Picasso pictures in his office. His mahogany desk compliments the color of his wall-to-
wall carpeting. He has a Finnish sauna and a French bar, but
he does not have a friend in the world. His employees hate him.
He ignores them. He talks only to VIP's. For him people are
business contacts. Old acquaintances are dropped and new ones
cultivated, according to their social standing. With all his
worldly success, Father is insecure and afraid of failure. His
self-esteem has not kept up with his symbols of success.

[*] From *Between Parent and Teenager* by Haim G. Ginott, Ed.D., The Macmillan
Company, New York.

"Now my father wants me to join his middle-class escalator—his security and status get-ahead plan: college, graduate school, family law firm, an executive suite with a deep pile rug and private toilet, a corporate wife and a perfect pension. I don't want any part of my father's ambition, elegant as it may be. My father lives as though there were no other goals: no dreams, no passions.

" 'What are you going to do with your life?' he keeps on asking. He almost dropped dead when I hold him that I had no plans except 'to drift and to paint, to paint and to drift.'

" 'How long will you float like this?' he demanded.

" 'Until enough of my life has flowed onto canvas,' I answered. He looked at me as though I were crazy, and left bewildered and dismayed. And I dropped out of college."

MIDGE DECTER

sex, my daughters, and me

**They must suffer the great hindrance
to growing up of being their mother's friends.**

My adolescent daughters are, as they have been brought
up to be, my "friends." I have two, and they are very different
people indeed; but what I have to say about them here applies
equally to both. We discuss together the day's events in school
and office. We gossip together, within understood limits, about
our respective friends. We share a common pride in the accomplishments, and a common irritation at the naughtinesses, of the
two youngest children in the family. We tell one another jokes—
frequently off-color. We trade cosmetics and minor articles of
clothing. I am as likely to seek out their advice in affairs of
shopping and dress as they are mine.

In our talks, to be sure, we are never exactly equals: I know
a good deal more than they about just those things they are most
eager to know, and have far freer access to that big world they
are so eager to enter, while they on their side hold all the secrets
to that which most disquiets me; still we all manage most of the
time not to be too patronizing. I sometimes think them superior
to me, as they sometimes think me to them. And to some extent
I envy them, as they do me.

Of course, friendship does not truly define the relationship
between us. What defines it—for after all we are mother and
daughters—is a struggle for power. When the friendliness
cracks, as it does with a fair though not permanently disruptive
regularity, it is this struggle which stands nakedly revealed be-

neath. Now, no one of my age and circumstance—a member of what sociologists would call the professional, or educated, middle class in the second half of the twentieth century—can possibly conceal from himself the Freudian implications of this relationship. In fact, no one of my age and circumstance can even mention the subject without being conscious of the idea that a mother and her daughter constitute a primary sexual rivalry. Such indeed, then, must be the case between my daughters and me; how would I, even if I were inclined to, deny it? Nevertheless, that which two of us *experience* as the issue between us in any given hour of battle has far less to do with why we must, at bottom, be contenders than with a whole lot of questions nearer the surface of things. A dispute may arise over something so trivial as the condition of their room, or something so principled as the allocation of their time between work and play, or even something so stark as their choice of friends. These questions, too, boil down to one: the power we struggle for is power over their respective destinies. At least for now, and presumably for the next few years, what is at stake between us is quite simply the fact that they are dependent on me. And I wish them to be and not to be, and they wish to be and not to be.

The struggle is for them an unequal one. For at the moment, anyway, I have the big guns on my side. I have their past record of helplessness and error to use against them and shake their confidence; I have, at least when pushed to an extreme, the unshakable conviction of my right to exercise power; and above all, I have control over money. Their only weapons are to wound with the spectacle of their unhappiness or to hold themselves resisting and out of earshot. These can be very potent weapons—if they were not, all children would be helpless and all parents serene—but they are defensive ones.

Such disadvantages in a relation of power my daughters have in common with every dependent in every age, clime, and culture. They suffer from certain others, however, peculiar to such young girls as have been brought up in their kind of life. For my daughters are supremely children of their time. Whatever their individualities, they are also very much the products of those spiritual pretensions by which their enlightened parents, like all enlightened parents of this generation, chose to bring up their children. In short, they must suffer the great hindrance to growing up of being their mother's friends.

Apart from the emotional burden our casual intimacy places upon them—a burden about which the psychologists have now, too late, a great deal of wisdom to proffer—this intimacy acts as a practical and political handicap of very real dimensions. For it is not merely trite to say the young are trusting. And above all they trust to the appearances of things. Thus in our condition of friendship, an attack of motherhood upon either of them is apt to come quite suddenly and unprepared-for. A casual revelation on one of their parts might become the occasion for a far from casual response on mine. Or I might take them nine-tenths of the way through a discussion or story which is proving to be of the keenest interest and then refuse to go on, overcome by some squeamishness or fastidiousness I had not realized was working inside my nerves; within a single sentence, perhaps, they will have become "too young" to hear what their mother has not heart to utter.

Most of all, they are bereft of the defense of thinking me utterly stupid. They may think so now and then, on this point or that, but they have no really solid base in thought or feeling from which to resist me. Just as they have been brought up from earliest infancy on the assumption that they were being "understood"—this time with sympathy, that time with harshness, but with understanding always—so, too, it has been assumed that they "understand" me. Simple stupidity has never been one of the terms between us. Mothers like me do not believe their children to be incompetent. This may in fact be the prime axiom of our kind of parenthood. We take care to know at every moment of our children's development what the attainments of that moment ought properly to be and make our demands accordingly. (A good deal of fun has been poked at us for this, for we are the comic ladies who sit on park benches poring over our vol-

umes of Spock and Gesell and Bettelheim. But the fun has usually been poked by people who are not entitled to it, by the people who think we ought to respect our children *more;* when what
we are really doing is seeking out the widest range of possibilities to offer our children our respect.) And since we do not treat
them as incompetents, they have no fund of experience from
which in later years to retaliate.

Note, for example, the terms of the current adolescent rebellion against people like us. We are accused of being deficient
in love, not simple enough, too adept at making our way, too
successful. It is not that we know too little of the world—the
major accusation of our own adolescence against our parents—
but too much. They do not strive to alter our definition of reality, for no matter what they say, they acknowledge our competence to do the defining; they simply repudiate "reality" altogether, putting the word into inverted commas with, among
other things, hallucinogens. As it happens, my own daughters'
relation to the current intellectual and social fashions among
their rebelling cohorts is—so far—that of only fairly sympathetic onlookers. So far I have succeeded in spoiling the idea of
direct participation for them. Which is to say, I have managed
to talk them out of it.

And talk is of the essence. We happen to do a great deal of
it in our house; for us as a family it is recreation, too, and
means of survival. But not only by the particular accident of
birth are my daughters surrounded by talk. For all children like
them, words constitute a kind of postnatal amniotic fluid in
which they grow and are both sheltered from and introduced to
their surroundings. On the most primitive level for such children
words have taken the place of physical violence as a means of
instruction and discipline. They have also by and large replaced
that network of instructions and disciplines called "punishment." To be hampered from pursuing a noxious or harmful
activity is to be "told no." Being the denizens of city or suburb,
the children discover the world around them primarily by a
process of giving names to things. Their hours of solitude are

spent alone with the speech of others, in the form of books, television, radio.

The schools in which they spend such a large proportion of the waking hours of their childhood are, of course, veritable waterfalls, floods, volcanos of words, phrases, clauses, sentences, paragraphs. As you might expect, my daughters have gone only to "good" schools—that is to say, the most benign, most attentive, most enriching schools that were available. Thus they have not only been instructed by means of their teachers' use of language, they have also been taught through perfecting their own manipulation of language—in other words, to uncover what might be in their own minds by discussing it aloud. In such schools, the desire to fail can be fulfilled merely by keeping silent. As, indeed, can the desire to fail at home.

The society of the enlightened, then, does not beat or drive its children, does not drill them, but rather nags them, into growing up. And the measure of the children's progress along this path is their capacity to nag in turn. The point about talk is not whether it is a good way or a bad way to bring up the young. As parents have gone—and as societies have gone—the attempt on the part of my contemporaries to give their children certain physical and social freedoms, to confront and harness for good some of their baser impulses, to help them reason their way toward being civilized, to befriend them, seems not so very malign. We are of course doomed by the absurdity of our pretensions—for naturally we are incapable of permitting our children all those things we pretend to permit them. And we are far from being so pure of motive as we imagined—for motives are never pure between adults and the young. Still, we are, I should think, no more pretentious or self-deceived than our own parents, and very likely a good deal less. In any event, my daughters and their friends seem to me far more attractive, more open, and a good deal nicer than I remember myself and my friends in adolescence.

In some ways, however, they seem to me less fortunate than we were. For the point about talk is that it sets up a competition

in which the children, particularly the children of the educated
and enlightened, must lose. Once upon a time, or so I imagine,
children could manage their powerlessness by biding their time.
They could, if they wanted to be comfortable, obey the rules,
and in the face of some unwanted imposition from the authorities or some supposed injustice, take to their closets. Their cor-
poreal selves might be rendered up to Caesar but their thoughts
—undoubtedly of future vengeance—they could keep to themselves.

But my daughters have no means of retreat from the barrages
of those bigger than they: not into the street and not into the
closet. The wider world of school and playmates only confirms
me, for what I have given them of speech is precisely that which
best enables them to get along there. The books they read *I*
have placed into their hands (even the dirty books, with which
they and their friends wile away so many exciting, secretive
hours, they have taken from my shelves, where they stand in full
view). Their imaginative life is one that I as a companionable
mother once encouraged and helped them to invent. Nor are
their hiding places of any use, for I understand and even condone their behavior in taking to them. I am, as it were, huddled
inside with them.

And if either of them stands and fights, she naturally loses.
I know more words than she, and they are bigger words, more
impressive. I can make them do such miraculous and unanswer-
able things as describe an irony, create an analogy, or cite an
apposite witticism. I can dazzle her with words, amuse her
against her will with them, distract her, frighten her, expose her
motives, analyze her character, justify myself with words, and
if need be, simply drown her in them. I can—one of the tricks
of friendship—seduce her into answering and use what she says
as a new supply of grist for my unending mill. Only pure rage
can stop the flow. But my daughters, poor things, are not yet
enough in command of themselves to produce that merciful condition in me without being already in the grit of it themselves.
So they have no recourse but to meet me on my own ground. It

is a predicament from which only the distance and privacy of adulthood can rescue them.

But I, too, am caught in a predicament. Because when I speak to them, I often contradict myself. To the mothers who were trained as I was—by the Freudian precept that children's personalities are shaped not by what used to be called "upbringing" but by the quality of those family relationships into which they enter at birth—our children represent a total responsibility. We do not believe ourselves charged primarily with keeping them healthy and properly sheltered and teaching them the manners of the society into which we will one day send them. We believe ourselves rather to be the very creators of their psyches, their personalities, and above all, their capacities for success and happiness. What such a responsibility demands of us is something more than undying love, more even than wisdom—it demands that we know what is right and what is needed. This is a responsibility I am hardly able to undertake consistently or gracefully for myself, much less for these nearly-grown female creatures who stand opposite me. They naturally do not ask it of me—at least not any longer. But this is the way of our relationship. Without it, I should have to turn away from them. It is too late to go back now.

Thus I contradict myself. I do not always feel what I think; I do not always think what I feel. Or rather, I belie myself— since it is my usual custom to tell them what I think (the words for thought come easier than those for feelings) and only indicate to them, so desperately unfairly, by my sudden passions what I feel.

Nowhere are my contradictions more evident, nor undoubtedly more painful to them, than in dealing with the problem of sex. This problem is about the last genuine one left to the transaction between us. Not that we do not struggle over other things, but we have nothing new to say to one another about these: they have learned what they have learned from me, I have failed them where I have failed them, the rest is for the most part now up to them and fate.

Sex, however, is another matter. As a real issue it is just now coming up in their lives—that is, becoming something they are required to *do* something about. And they are still young enough to ask me, sometimes—usually indirectly—what they should do. And I find myself wishing to the very bottom of my being that they would not.

They ask me, I think, for several reasons. First of all, because they are frightened. Such a to-do is made of sex in these days of the new, supposedly freer attitudes toward it that we are probably succeeding in making it as great a mystery to the young as it was in the era when "leg" was a dirty word: a mystery of a different kind, perhaps, now no longer shrouded in evil but partaking in some of those qualities of quest and conquest of the Holy Grail. In any case, it is partly their timidity that drives my daughters to seek the word of the Authorities, for the comfort, either way, of a denial or of permission.

They also ask me for the simple reason that they believe I know a good deal about the subject. They have not been permitted to assume about me—as the children of my generation, say, permitted ourselves to assume about our parents—that I live in ignorance (in both senses) of sex. I have not permitted it by the conversation, my own and that of my friends, which I have allowed to go on in their presence. I have not permitted it, either, by my style of dress, of behavior, of being. They ask me, too, because to do so is a way, and a very effective way, I might add, of announcing to me that they will one of these days be no longer my satellites but my equals.

But most of all, they ask me because they are too innocent of the danger I represent to them. Like all children raised in the advanced and liberal way, their sophistication and worldliness are streaked with an almost incredible naïveté. This naïveté does not have to do with facts, and certainly not with any of the actual facts of sex, about which they and their friends have a fund of knowledge more complete and accurate than that of many adults I know. Nor have they, since the years of fairly early childhood, acquired any of these facts from me; though once learned, they have often taken pleasure in discussing them with me (out of the desire to show off rather than for information). In fact, had they, as the textbooks recommend, come to me for all this information, they might have found out many of my reluctances in the matter a whole lot sooner. Nor is their naïveté psychological exactly—though its effects on me are clearly psychological—for as I said earlier, they understand me rather well. I suppose their innocence would have to be called spiritual.

Anyway, it has to do with the trust that my seeming openness as a mother has bred in them—so early and so thoroughly that all the disappointments they must have suffered have not served to make them appropriately wary. Our children, so wise to the world in other ways, have very little left of the child's genius for duplicity. They are bad liars and ineffective sneaks. We have deprived them of their natural and indispensable talent for keeping their secrets secret, and with it, of a certain insight into the nature of the dangerous or forbidden.

When I was my daughters' age, I knew exactly how much, for both our sakes, it was necessary for my mother to know about my own personal confrontation with sex: namely, nothing. My daughters have considerably more leeway than that; there, perhaps, is the rub. Sex as a subject is profoundly interesting to people like me. We think about it a great deal, wonder at it a great deal, and discuss it only somewhat less. We are amused by it as a phenomenon, find it comical, take it immensely seriously. We would, if we could, like to know how everyone we see around us conducts himself with respect to sex. And, if it would not entail a psychic monstrosity that no amount of self-deception could keep hidden, we would even like to know precisely how our own daughters and their friends conduct themselves. In short, like the highly emancipated persons we are, our minds are totally the creatures of the most fashionable currents of the culture that surround them.

Yet my daughters, too, are restricted, if not in what they may ask, then in what they may expect to receive an answer to. They are restricted by the intensity with which I wish they wouldn't ask me. All their questions, regardless of how they are put or whether the girls know it or not, can only be directed to one end: ought they, now or in the near future, to engage in sexual relations with one or another young man? And the truth of the matter is, I do not know how to answer.

My uncertainty, to be sure, does not take the form of a simple expression of uncertainty. It takes the form, rather, of a series of confident statements which contradict, supersede, or override one another—or which sometimes simply evade the point. I may, for instance, deride some display of sexual priggishness on the part of a relative, a teacher, or their headmaster—on this occasion planting myself foursquare on the side of the legitimate erotic expression of the children. I may at some other time, and not apparently apropos of them at all, find myself delivering a rather brutal lecture on the horrors of premarital pregnancy— attacking first the criminal immorality of the official posture by which proper contraception and legal abortion are kept out of the reach of young girls, and in the next breath, the criminal irresponsibility of the same young girls in surrendering themselves to something they have not first learned to manage. Or I may, in the name of civilization and decency, take up the cudgels for the boys, attempting to make my daughters aware of the acute suffering inflicted on their male contemporaries by the self-involved experimentation with their powers, *i.e.*, the teasing, of the girls. One of the things I say to them—and naturally it is the one I have the strongest sensation of conviction about— is simply mean: that the adolescent love affairs I have seen do not seem to me to be emotional and sexual adventures at all but, on the contrary, a series of enormous cop-outs. That is, I say, they seem to me to entail nearly all the commitments of marriage, dulling in people so young, and far from providing a wider range of experience, they are actually protecting their participants from having to undergo too much experience. How this must translate to my daughters' discerning and simplifying ears, of course, is: Even if you have sex, it won't be any good.

This particular piece of cruelty to them is not mine alone. In somewhat different (and as I fancy, in far less subtle and clever) form, it represents the defense of an entire generation against the implications underlying its own sexual liberation. If you begin as we all did with the proposition that lust is not only natural but life-giving and good, and if you travel the path from there straight and true, you arrive at complete sexual promiscuity. Lust as an independent value divorces itself from institutions, personal relations, and travels with utter unconcern from creature contact to creature contact. This is, as a matter of fact, exactly how the Puritans understood the matter, and they were right. We understand it, too, in the pits of our stomachs if not in our minds, and scurry about to improvise our excuses. We do not want to be promiscuous, for if lust is simple, the other major human passions—vanity, pride, acquisitiveness—are not. Our marriages barely survive so much of frankness about our desires as we already allow ourselves; and being unmarried is for us an agony of rushing about to stake our claims. And if we do not want promiscuity for ourselves, we will certainly never be able to bear it in our children.

What we want for ourselves and them is to hold on to our imaginings of complete sexual abandon and at the same time maintain the kind of emotional requirements which make such abandon impossible for us. The most notable of our excuses for this is one derived at two removes from a vulgarization of Freud. To wit: a mentally healthy and mature person seeks in sex the deepening and enrichment of an already and otherwise satisfying connection. Sexual conquest as an end in itself is "unhealthy"; in girls it is a mark of self-devaluation, and in boys, of "Don Juanism." On the other hand, an affair with one person undertaken out of curiosity or in a spirit of fun is emotionally irresponsible and therefore "immature." Thus while we promise our children a satisfaction that we had to wrest for ourselves, we nevertheless do our best to block their easy passage to it.

To be sure, we make no point of their having to be married. All of us, I believe, have settled, whether we admit it or not, with the idea that our children will have at least some sex experience before marriage. But we have only retreated to a nearer line of defense. The sex experience they have, in order for them not to earn our opprobrium, must be to some purpose. It must be good in itself, it must improve their lives, it must make them better people. And naturally, it must not end in pregnancy. As for myself, I might wish for the further condition that it take place without either my knowledge or complicity.

I ask too much, I know that. We all do. We always have. But then too much was asked of us, and of our parents, and will be of our grandchildren.

This whole problem is in the end really not my daughters', but mine. They will suffer the cruelties of this alternating titillation and denial that has been their introduction to sex and, like the rest of us, if they are tough enough, or brave enough, or lucky enough, they will prevail. But what will be for them their experience and their life will be for me always the record of my inability as a parent to stand behind that person whose face I had so long ago chosen to show to the world. Not that having such a record is necessarily bad, but the chastening seems to have seeped into every corner of my life. My daughters' education at my hands has turned out to be a far profounder one of me at theirs.

WALTER LIPPMANN

what we offer

**In the face of what has actually
been happening, fathers . . . have all . . .
been unprepared and uneducated men.**

I have at least one qualification for writing about the generation gap. I have lived with two, if not three, of them during my lifetime. To be sure, practice does not make perfect. But it does teach one to realize an important human truth. The movement of events is almost always a great deal faster than the movement of our own minds.

In my youth, for example, the very old politicians who were still around were obsessed with the slogans and battle cries of the Civil War. Nowadays the Administration [has been] trying to convince us that we are fighting the same war in South Vietnam which Churchill and Roosevelt fought a quarter of a century ago against the Nazis and the Japanese. As men grow older and take charge of affairs, they must battle a persistent human tendency to see the world through spectacles that fitted them twenty or thirty years earlier. When they are not successful in distinguishing between what they learned when they were young and what the reality is coming to be now that they are older, generation gap results.

Resisting the tendency to be out of date is especially difficult today, of course, because in our time the rate of change in human affairs has become much faster and much more general and pervasive than ever before in the whole experience of the human race. We may not be better men than our ancestors. But there is a lot more motion in us and around us, and we have, therefore, a better excuse for being puzzled and bewildered. . . .

One great characteristic of the modern scientific and technological revolution is that no one understands all of it, and only the specialists really understand some of the parts. . . . So in the face of what has actually been happening, fathers and grandfathers have, all of them, been unprepared and uneducated men. They do not understand the results of the science and technology about them, and they don't even know how the products which they utilize are made. We cannot expect them to hand down the knowledge one needs in order to live and live well. Young people will have to educate themselves to understand the infinite complexity of the modern age.

What older people may be able to offer is not the translation of modern knowledge, but the transmission of that which is above knowledge, that is to say, human wisdom. The Oxford English Dictionary defines wisdom as "the capacity of judging rightly in matters relative to life and conduct." This is an art which cuts across all specialties. It is possessed by those who have an imaginative feeling for what really matters to human beings, whether they travel in jet planes or walk on foot, whether they are craftsmen in little workshops or hired hands in an automatic factory run by a computer. To be wise is to have a certain familiarity with the deposit of human values that persist in any human environment. On the far side of the generation gap one can find some traces of this wisdom. Those who have good sense, who have an instinct for what will make life interesting, will seize upon this wisdom when it comes their way.

RITA DERSHOWITZ

---

to mr. lippmann

**"[Your] wisdom . . . isn't relevant. . . .
my experiences are qualitatively different. . . .
I am comfortable with interracial social
situations . . . and the mind-expanding drugs."**

The wisdom that may or may not be on the other side of the generation gap simply isn't relevant to my life. . . . An older generation's claim to insight as a result of greater experience is spurious because my experiences are qualitatively different from those of my parents. . . . I am comfortable with interracial social situations, casual use of marijuana and the mind-expanding drugs, and nonrational ways of getting at knowledge, all of which elicit harsh judgments within my parents' value system.

I deeply feel the inadequacy of the values I learned while growing up. Categories of social worth; drive for possession of things and people; the academic definitions of what is worth knowing and doing; the myth of America's good intentions around the world—all of these break down in the search for what is really important, and for a style of life that has dignity. . . .

Television shaped my first impressions of the world beyond the family and affected me in a way it never could my parents. . . . The Negro revolution has significantly touched far more young people than just the activists who made the revolution. The reality changed; Negroes became visible on campuses, and even could be seen holding hands with whites. One could not continue to be shocked by everyday occurrences. The need to respond in a new way changed people's feelings, and in turn led to new ways of thinking about social issues.

Most recently, the easy accessibility and acceptability of drugs has opened a whole new area of possible experiences, of moving inward as well as outward in order to gain self-awareness. In this instance, too, the extensions of the drug culture touch more people than those who actually use drugs. The ethics of the hippie culture—indiscriminate love and openness, the dignity of the individual and the value of human relationships, the destructiveness of rigid external authority—have influenced students who are demanding flexibility and personal relevance of the college curriculum. "Find your own thing, and then do it," is not just new jargon for the same wisdom. It sets up entirely new assumptions about the purposes of any educational institution.

Finally, Vietnam has given the lie to the values we learned at home and in school. The bomb foretold an era of incredible powers for mass destruction, and now this country employs even more terrible refinements on a distant people. I guess I believe that nobility was possible in fighting for this country during World War II, that death was not absurd. But we've left no opening for moral instincts this time, no way to make the destruction finally meaningful. Our statesmen use the rhetoric of other times and other wars, and in so doing they underscore the gap between their reality and mine.

In one sense, the very fact that the old values don't hold true any longer is the great excitement of being young today. . . . The range of possibilities is enormous: with unprecedented economic abundance, one has the real choice of self-imposed poverty; with higher education easily available, one can choose to reject academic learning in favor of other kinds of experiences. These kinds of choices are possible because they don't depend upon our parents' value systems, because they call for new judgments. The younger generation is in the process of synthesizing a new wisdom, and that is the real education.

HARRY GOLDEN

the real iron curtain

When Harvey Haddix of the Pittsburgh Pirates pitched twelve perfect innings against the Milwaukee Braves it was big news not because he lost on a double by Del Crandall in the 13th, but because Harvey was 33 years old.

The real iron curtain is the curtain separating the young from the middle-aged and the middle-aged from the old and the old from the young.

There are cities built specifically for the old, like St. Petersburg, Florida, where there is not a curb. There are developments in California where a playground would look to the residents like some apparatus for the moon. It is no wonder the old are cranky, the young unregenerate and rude, and the middle-aged panicky.

One of the reasons for this division is that we do not believe merit affects the quality of life. Yet Winston Churchill was in his 60s when he became Britain's wartime Prime Minister. When Sophocles was 90 and his sons wanted the courts to declare him non compos mentis, he read his jurors the verses of *Oedipus at Colonus.*

On the Lower East Side, in the crowded tenements, still we had a pretty good idea of what life looked like. We lived with kid brothers, maiden aunts, and grandparents. The result was that we didn't think people belonged in the categories of young, middle-aged, or old—we all of us communicated one way or another. Today, in most suburban complexes, the town at midday is populated only by the women, the kiddies, and the dogs.

We have victimized ourselves by subscribing wholeheartedly to our own myths. We all retire at 65 not because that is when we should retire but because 65 is the most advantageous retirement age for the insurance premiums. We really believe that poets and mathematicians get their gifts early and are washed up at 30. Goethe wrote *Faust* in his 70s. When a 47-year-old bishop becomes a cardinal we say he is young. I submit that our universe is viciously relativistic when it comes to age.

There is little reverence for the old in our society. And because there is none, there is probably less reverence for the young.

MARYA MANNES

---

let's establish
diplomatic relations

**Don't you know that revelation . . . must
be earned. . . ?**

. . . I propose that the satellite nation of Adults—or
Squares, for what else are we now?—appoint a delegation to
draft a note to the nation of Youth, with the purpose of estab-
lishing negotiations, which might, in turn, lead to an honorable
truce. I herewith submit a rough draft of this note. . . :

DEAR YOUNG: If you possibly can, please turn down the volume of your transistors and TV sets, so that you can hear the
quavering voice of your elders. Unaccustomed as you are to sentences more than three words long or, for that matter, to the
English language, try to listen, for this is not a lecture. It's really
a communiqué between states who must—whether you like it or
not—coexist.

First, we would like to dispense with all the unimportant
things about you that seem to alarm a lot of adults and parents,
but shouldn't: One is your looks. When you're clean, they're
great. Hair is both manly and womanly, and the shock of hair
on a boy—when it doesn't dribble below the eyebrows and collar—is far more virile and decorative than the crew cut your
father sported at your age. Sir Lancelot knew it, and so do you.
As for the long, shining hair of girls, it is infinitely more allur-
ing than the teased, spray-glazed bubbleheads of your mothers
and aunts.

If it's sometimes hard to tell you boys and girls apart, in your boots and sweaters and pants and hair, well, to some of us these spell a wonderful freedom and comfort and an honest sense of the body our generation didn't know, and—more important—an end to that arbitrary dividing of the sexes to which we adults were conditioned: the frills and pastels and high heels that were supposed to make little girls (pink) so feminine, as opposed to the little boys (blue) so masculine. The biological differences do not need this kind of artificial typecasting. If anything, true maleness and femaleness are more noticeable the way *you* are dressing, now that you have dispensed with the trimmings of gentility. What we wish you did not dispense with, however, is gentleness: the common courtesy without which even free souls cannot live and work together with any pleasure. You gain nothing from sloppy language except the distaste or hostility of potential allies. The casual exercise of rudeness is not a sign of honesty and independence; it merely shows a calloused heart and a childish mind.

As for the way you dance, we find this diverting if remarkably unsexy in the fundamental sense. It is also profoundly unesthetic. . . . Most of you have beautiful young bodies; but you wouldn't know it the way you use them, either dancing or walking. Your heads hang forward, your shoulders sag, your extremities flip and jerk like clothes on a line, you shuffle and shamble. Man, believe it or not, was supposed to walk erect, and all the finest specimens of the race through the ages have known it. Look at the Spanish men and women who dance: passionate and wild . . . but with enormous dignity of the body. Look at the Greek men dancing, spines erect. And look at yourselves, jerking like demented puppets on a madman's string. Your abstract gyrations may suggest an African fertility rite; but for personal passion, they have nothing on the body-to-body and cheek-to-cheek undulations of your ancestors. . . .

As to this vastly greater sexual freedom you possess, we should count it more a gain than a loss. For you are honest where we lied, and you are open where we were furtive, you are direct where we were hypocritical. Our insistence on romantic love has done us infinitely more harm, some of us believe, than your frank recognition that romance and sexual pleasure do not necessarily go together. You thereby put sex in its place, instead of surrounding it with a sentimental nimbus, and you may . . . be on the way to achieving that true companionship between man and woman which is the only basis for a sound marriage. . . .

What should worry us more about you, perhaps, is a too-early marriage, which leaves you no time to develop by yourself as an individual, to stretch your capacities before you are enveloped in family and domestic patterns. We also hope profoundly that you will exercise more restraint than we did in adding numbers to this desperately crowded world. . . .

Those of you who care enough about the world and humanity to organize and talk and march against a way of life you consider immoral are not the ones that we should worry about. It isn't a matter of whether you are right or wrong, but that you are willing to stand up for what you believe and fight for it, be it civil rights, or peace, or free speech on campus and elsewhere. I wish we could all recognize that it takes as much courage to stand up in public for unpopular causes as it does to fight an unpopular but sanctioned war. The soldier must fight because he is ordered to fight; but nothing except his own conscience forces a boy to expose himself to insult, humiliation . . . and even prison.

No. The protest we adults should be most deeply alarmed about is the one of escape: through drugs, through hallucination, through abdication of self. . . . What we find hard to understand is the extent to which you comfortable young—with money to burn and education to use—would find life so distasteful that you need to buy yourself out of it with kicks and more and more kicks. Hot rods, motorcycles, surfing and sex: these are understandable. But why do you need drugs to give you excitement and revelation when the real world—if you really bothered to examine it—is so full of both? . . .

You want to take a trip . . . to glory without lifting a finger. Swallow something, and you instantly conquer space, time, loneliness, responsibility, consciousness. Have you so little respect for that miracle your conscious mind that you have to submerge and even destroy it to enjoy yourself? Of course, you answer back that this new drug, this frighteningly powerful hallucinogen called LSD, expands and enlarges consciousness. It can, as you also must know by now, permanently shatter it.

But why do you need drugs to expand your senses and gain revelation? Have you ever looked through a microscope at crystal formations? Seen the pattern of earth from an airplane window? Entered the heart of Bach's B Minor Mass? Memorized a Shakespeare sonnet? . . . Watched a woman nursing her child? Skied from the top of a mountain? Have you ever really loved another human being? Don't you know that revelation, like anything wonderful in life, must be earned—by an expenditure of your own will and effort? Do you really think paradise is for free? . . .

You have to give for what you get. And we don't mean this in terms of money. It means giving yourself. . . . giving out of love, whether for others or for a dream of excellence that demands your life. Nothing else will ever really satisfy you. . . . You're right in strongly suspecting words like "success" and "status," because they can be blind alleys, or traps squeezing the life out of your mothers and fathers. And you're right in thinking there must be more to life than earning money or position or membership in the club. That's why some of us wish there were something between college and marriage that would draft you young people—boys and girls alike—*not* for war . . . but for a year of service to society in this great but greatly troubled nation. You are not only desperately needed, but, being needed, would no longer feel the alienation that now drives you to excesses and sometimes despair. You not only would make common cause with all of us, old or young, but would come to grips with reality—of poverty, of disease, of crime, of sacrifice, of courage, of failure, of need—that would give you insight and revelation far beyond anything you find in a powder or pill. You could, indeed, change society along with yourselves. . . .

ARNOLD TOYNBEE

the whole iceberg

I had been living in a fool's paradise. . . .
I grieve for the young.

Inevitably the extremists attract a disproportionate
share of attention, critical and favorable. Both the "flower-chil-
dren" and the deliberate fomenters of violence are minorities.
They are like that one-tenth of an iceberg that is visible because
it protrudes above the surface of the sea. I am therefore mind-
ful of the present-day attitude of boys and girls of the high-
school and university-student age—groups whose behavior is not
flamboyant, but who are no less uneasy and no less alienated
from the ideals and objectives of their parents' generation.

Of course there is always a "generation gap." The rising generation never sees life with the same eyes as its elders—not even
in times and places in which society is relatively static and in
which the younger generation shares with its predecessors a
wish to conserve tradition rather than to make a break with it.
A generation gap of the normal breadth is a symptom of social
and cultural health. If it could be closed completely (but it
never can be), society would stagnate. But in present-day America, and in most of the rest of the World too, the breadth of the
generation gap is abnormally wide.

When students take an active part in politics, this is a sure
sign that the time is out of joint. German students were politically militant at least once before in modern times. I am thinking of the Burschen movement in Germany after the Napoleonic
Wars. This was an expression of disillusionment and embitter-
ment at seeing the spontaneous popular uprising in which the
German people had thrown off Napoleon's yoke being exploited,

for their own selfish interests, by the princes and the aristocrats. In Russia, too, the students were militant politically during the century of growing unrest that culminated in the Revolution of 1917. In these two cases the students' disillusionment with the "Establishment" was certainly justified; and in Russia and Germany then, as in America today, some of the most vehement protesters were boys and girls who had been born with silver spoons in their mouths. Youth is unselfseeking and idealistic by comparison with middle age.

Is the present rising generation's disillusionment equally well justified? This generation is, I think, exasperated with its parents' generation because it feels that this older generation, like the aristocratic *émigrés* who returned to France after Napoleon's fall, "have learnt nothing and forgotten nothing." Though I belong to the super-old generation, I feel this as bitterly as any of my grandchildren, and my feelings, unlike theirs, are born of grievous experience. In the First World War, about half my closest friends were killed fighting in what they believed was "the war to end war." They have been betrayed. War is being used at this moment, in several parts of the world, as "an instrument of national policy," just as if we had not staggered through two world wars into the atomic age. Again, mankind's productivity, and consequent aggregate wealth, has been increased enormously within my lifetime, and in some Western countries this increase has been followed by a mitigation of the age-old inequality of distribution. Yet, in the United States and in Britain today, a sizable minority is still living in poverty and misery in the midst of affluence. There are also many countries in which this shocking contrast is still more extreme and in which the poor are still the majority. Moreover, as between different countries, the gap between the so-called "developed" minority and the "developing" majority is widening.

Thus the young today have good reason for feeling that their seniors have failed to do their duty and, in failing, have handed on to the young a *damnosa hereditas*. Yet, when the young protest, the middle-aged generation is apt to ignore them or to tell them that they are foolish or to prophesy that, when they arrive at sedate middle age, they will become as conservative as their seniors now are. I do not wonder that the young feel outraged. Nor do I wonder that some of them have come to the grim conclusion that resort to violence is the only way in which they will be able to win a hearing and to enforce a change of policy.

Is there any excuse for the myopic self-complacency of which the middle-aged Establishment is, in the mass, undoubtedly guilty? The best that can be said in their defense is that the pace of change has been accelerated to an unprecedented degree by the progress of science and technology, so that it is difficult to make the necessary adaptations within the span of a single lifetime. This perhaps partly explains the middle-aged generation's stick-in-the-mud stance, but it does not excuse it.

> The time is out of joint; O cursed spite,
> That ever I was born to set it right!

I grieve for the young. Whether the older generation is or is not to blame, the time is unquestionably "out of joint." I myself am old enough to have grown up without knowing this cruel truth; by 1914 I was twenty-five, and till then I had been living in a fool's paradise. But, if I were now a child of my grandchildren's generation, I am sure I should make Hamlet's bitter words my own.

IGOR STRAVINSKY

---

the gap is only as
deep as my furrows

QUESTION: *Are you aware of a "gap" between yourself
and the young, Mr. Stravinsky?*

ANSWER: Judging from a news program that I happened to watch for a moment last night and that may have had
the effect of reopening my ulcer, an Arizona-size canyon divides
me from practically *everyone* else. The telecast began with an
announcement about overpopulation that included statistics like
"7.2 people," which are as horrifying to me as Shylock's knife;
by the end of the century the expression "joined the majority"
will mean born rather than died. . . . Then in that alternately
serious and facetious, man-to-man and man-to-woman (and
denture-setting-on-edge) tone, the newscaster read the latest toll
of our "anti-personnel" (*i.e.*, anti-people) bombs. This included
some non-Communists killed by mistake, though happily, in
their case, the next-of-kin will be reimbursed, so the announcer
promised, at the $34 going price *per* non-Communist corpse.
And so far from any trace of doubt underlying this specious re-
cital, the computerized price-fixing of lives and the paying for
them as hunters are paid for pelts was made to sound like a matter for handshakes all around. I switched off at this point for
the sake of my ulcer. . . .

The "gap" between myself and the protesting young, to stop
editorializing and return to your question, is only as deep as my
furrows compared to the chasm separating me from anyone who
can be so mendaciously mouthed to. In fact, as the Sunset Strip,
that dry Ganges for hippie holies (immersions in water not be-

ing in their line) is only a few steps from me, I shall probably apply for membership among the young Hindus myself. As for their elders, it hardly seems to be worth asking whether they know what became of humanity.

*   *   *

QUESTION: What do you expect to be the chief cultural consequences from a society in which more than half of the population is under twenty-five, and to what do you attribute your own rapport with the younger majority?

ANSWER: One consequence will soon be a large crop of sad, the-bloom-is-off, ex-youth, and another, the overthrowing of the biblical tradition of "the wisdom of the elders" by "youth culture." But the mere repudiation of the past in favor of the newest and latest (*cupidus rerum novarum*) is not a new disease in the body politic, and neither is the rejection by young people of an unacceptable reality. I attribute my own rapport with them, a better one than I had with their parents and grandparents at that same age (*everyone* is younger than I am!), to the natural desire to cling to an old man in hopes that he can point the road to the future. What is needed, of course, is simply *any* road that offers enough mileage and a good enough safety record. And my road satisfies these requirements, though the direction in which it extends is not the future but the past. It will soon become a detour, I realize, as newer pavements, newly surfaced and custom-built for new vehicles, are laid down, but I hardly mind that. Detours are often pleasant to travel, far more so than those superturnpikes on which the traffic has yet to discover that the race is not always to the swift.

MALCOLM BOYD

saint or slut?

Saint or slut—it depends on who you're talking to. She is almost oblivious to both judgments made about her. Middle-class in background, educated in the right schools, she is now living among the poor, sharing their life without reservation. Nothing she could have done would have so outraged her former friends and associates.

Because it isn't "charity" but something real. The paternalism is out of it, the risks in. She hasn't time to daydream about the privileges and luxuries she's left behind. She isn't just putting in hours of "doing good" so that she can go back to the party with the proper righteousness. It's not just that she no longer has a hairdresser; she's gone over to the other side.

Some of her former friends accuse her of sleeping around with workingmen in the neighborhood. Others say she's become a fanatic; after all, she looks terrible, and a person has a duty to eat and keep well. They express concern for her future: What will she *do?* What will become of her?

What would make her do it? She doesn't go to church, says she hasn't gone for months, and that it's hopelessly middle-class. Is she just getting back at her father? Wouldn't it have been more sensible to have gotten some government job and done something *effective?* What can she hope to change by doing this?

Perhaps there is something romantic or unhealthy in her decision, but over a bowl of soup at the corner lunch counter she seems quite calm. Tired perhaps, could use some make-up, but she doesn't look unwell. And despite the depressing stories she has of the conditions in which people are living all around her, how is it that she conveys such a sense of hope? Is it something she brought to the neighborhood, or something she found here?

camus in mississippi

A Negro student who has not been able to complete high school but has received an education in participatory democracy and jails is reading Camus in a paperback edition donated by a white liberal in New York.

He is becoming excited by what Camus tells him about the meaning of being a person. He has been struggling with the whole question of motivation. Given his seemingly hopeless future—that is, when he drains off all the sentimental illusions and unlikely possibilities—he has felt alienated from such abstractions as liberty, justice, and the pursuit of happiness. (That last one sounds like a gas.) These have no immediate meaning in his life because he cannot connect them to anything positive in his experience.

Reading Camus, the student perceives something. It's concrete. He still hasn't quite focused on it, but he knows it's there, like a mountain behind some clouds. He's disturbed and strangely exhilarated. Without any false pomposity or preaching, Camus seems to be saying that the struggle matters and has a real point. Not pie in the sky, but now.

The student gets up; he came across a sentence he has to read aloud, if only to himself: "I should like to be able to love my country and still love justice." He's memorized it already.

we want to forget

It's a giant hall in a run-down district of the city. Two thousand teenagers are packed in here—rich kids and poor kids. Someone was singing until a few minutes ago, up there on the stage, but he couldn't be heard over the metallic, harsh beat of instrumental music. The kids weren't listening anyway; they sat in front of him, moving their bodies in time with his. He did grinds and bumps, pulling up his sport shirt over his chest, and they screamed and shouted back to him. Now he's stopped for a short intermission. The juke box is driving, furious noise rocking the room, giving everything a beat, keeping it nervous.

I ask a student—probably seventeen—why there has to be such overpowering and constant noise.

"We want to forget."

"What do you want to forget?"

"Look, some people use alcohol; we use music and noise. It just drowns out everything else. I sit here until I get a headache and then I go home to bed. It relaxes me to come here a couple of times each week. I just want to sit alone and let the music drown out everything I feel."

"But what do you feel?" I asked.

"I feel pressure. We all feel so much pressure. Everybody is at us all the time—do this, do that, don't do this, don't do that. Here we can work out our inhibitions. Our families wouldn't understand if they could see the place or see us here. But it's better for us to be inside this hall listening to music and watching the show than outside on the street fighting. There's so much pent up inside us. Here we can forget it for a little while. So much pressure and tension—we just don't know what's going to happen."

MARSHALL McLUHAN

retribalized makers

**Since TV . . . every American home
has its Berlin wall.**

*When two societies exist side by side, the psychic challenge of
the more complex one acts as an explosive release of energy in
the simpler one. For prolific evidence of this kind of problem it
is not necessary to look beyond the life of the teenager lived
daily in the midst of a complex urban center. As the barbarian
was driven to furious restlessness by the civilized contact, col-
lapsing into mass migration, so the teenager, compelled to
share the life of a city that cannot accept him as an adult, collapses into "rebellion without a cause." Earlier the adolescent
had been provided with a rain check. He was prepared to wait
it out. But since TV, the drive to participation has ended adolescence, and every American home has its Berlin wall.*
                                          —Understanding Media

The cover for *TV Guide* for June 8-14, 1968 consists
of a painting by Salvador Dali. It presents two TV images in
two thumbnails. The thumbs are coarsely textured and carefully
spaced to indicate different worlds. Among other features there
is on the horizon a segment of brain tissue. The new "software"
environment of electric information is literally an extension of
our central nervous system. The interface or touch or "gap"
that constitutes the sense of touch is scarcely acknowledged except among artists. As an artist, Dali understands that the TV
image is profoundly tactile and quite unlike photo or movie.
    Touch is not only the world of musical beat but of the Beats.
It is touch or interval from which stem the multitude of "gaps"

that characterize the TV age: the generation gap, the education
gap, the political gap, the commerce-culture gap, and a great
many more. These gaps require instant and repeated "closure."
It is this closure that is so involving, that requires so much participation from the audience. It is closure that inspires "struggle" and violence.

The new software or electric-information environment is a
world of involvement and tactility that is quite antithetic to the
old visual world of "hardware" services.

Phonetic literacy brought into existence a world of continuous and connected space that is visual in character. This space
creates an environment that has been as imperceptible and unacknowledged through 2500 years of Western history as the new
software, tactile environment is unacknowledged and unper-
cived at present.

The Greek word for environment is *perivallo,* meaning "to
strike from all sides at once." The effect of any environment is,
therefore, numbing, and the larger the environment, whether in
business or in politics, the more numbing it is. That is why perception can be developed only by crossing cultural boundaries,
by getting outside whatever environment we're in.

The Japanese ideogram for nation is a plain rectangle. This
image also means, in Japanese, a prison.

Any culture or system whatever imprisons our perceptions,
turning us into some sort of somnambulists. Professor Brough-
ton of McGill University has recently argued that somnambul-
ism is a motivated state. The prisoners of cultural and technological environments seem to be motivated to ignore them, using
any new environments only as a means of perceiving the previous environment.

In relation to culture as a sort of somnambulistic prison, it
is interesting that the German word, "Volk" or tribal group, is
the same as the word for "cloud." Anthropologists have often
spoken of primitive people as "the people of the dream." The

same anthropologists even today are quite unaware of the fact that preliterate people do not live in the visual space that the anthropologist unconsciously assumes to be a normal or natural space shared by all mankind.

The greatest physicists and biologists have been and still are unaware of the peculiar bias of their perceptual lives, created in them by their acceptance of literacy as normal human equipment.

When people cross boundaries from one culture to another they endanger this sense of identity. People on frontiers, as in the Westerns, are people who have so insecure an identity image that they feel impelled to lead lives of perpetual violence. The most peaceful tribes, when pressed into a condition of interface or friction, become bloody and ruthless. Coexistence threatens their identity image.

Today the TV generation, enveloped in software information, finds it impossible to accept the identity image that was the natural product of the old hardware service environment.

The arts associated with Graeco-Roman literacy, the legal classifications and private patterns of goal-oriented individuals, cannot withstand the pressure of instantaneous and total field information or software. That is why the TV generation, robbed of the old hardware identity, tends to regard the old hardware as the enemy. The effective cause of the "scrubbing" or disappearance of the old identity is actually the invisible electric environment. It is this environment that acts as a mirror in which appears the detested image of the old hardware.

Schools and curricula, objective classified data, represent detachment without involvement and training for goals and jobs that no longer exist.

It cannot be stressed too often that violence does not have a goal. Violence and struggle are themselves the means of creating new identity. It is the irony of a visually oriented society or culture that it has created the conditions by new technology that blind it utterly.

"A burning would is come to dance inane," as Joyce put it.

We ask, "What is the purpose of this violence?" hoping to find out what motive matches it. But violence is not matching but making. It is an attempt to make sense of a world that has destroyed the personal image of the "violent" ones.

The drop-out situation in our schools at present has only begun to develop. The young student today grows up in an electrically configured world. It is a world not of wheels but of circuits, not of fragments but of integral patterns. The student today lives mythically and in depth. At school, however, he encounters a situation organized by means of classified information. The subjects are unrelated. They are visually conceived in terms of a blueprint. The student can find no possible means of involvement for himself, nor can he discover how the educational scene relates to the "mythic" world of electronically processed data and experience that he takes for granted. As one IBM executive puts it, "My children had lived several lifetimes compared to their grandparents when they began grade one."

—Understanding Media

from an interview

QUESTION: The young yearn for the obviously exciting, original thinker, but they couldn't understand you without some basis of comparison. Don't they have to have some sort of formal education?

ANSWER: They can check me out on their own policies. They live in a world in which classified categories are meaningless, and simply dispensing with the accepted methods of looking at things appeals to them. Actually, people in any period and place have always feared their environment; it is the enemy. For the kids, it's the bomb—which eliminates time and space. It's all-at-once. It's total, and it's us. We made it. We put it there. It's our man-made environment.

Q: There is no faith in the control of the bomb?

A: They have a great lack of faith in their parents, as I think they ought to have. . . . It's a great pastime of mankind—opening Pandora's box. But we've never found anything quite that potent before. The kids know we put the bomb there. They can't imagine what sort of people would do that. They have no respect for their parents at all, if only because of the bomb. . . .

Q: One tremendous change is the freedom with which the young live together without the guilt that existed 30 years ago.

A: This is entirely tribal. The younger generation has, in essence, retribalized. In any tribal society, they have complete access to each other until marriage. After marriage, I expect a big tightening up in the future because, in a defragmentized society, commitment, divorce, and infidelity take on much deeper meaning. In an integrated, committed group, any violation isn't a private fault or offense at all; it's an insult, a loss of face for the whole tribe. So they don't hesitate to wipe out offenders. Tribal societies are very rigorous in their morality. Detribalized societies are quite free in their morality, and that's what we've had for 2,000 years.

Q: Will the retribalized young reacquire these values?

A: The austerity, the taboo? It's coming, if they allow the retribalizing to move on. . . .

Q: Are the young of this electronic age lining up against the adult generation?

A: The young insist on much deeper commitments to tasks of all sorts than their parents did. . . . They are not a lighthearted bunch.

Q: Humor has almost vanished from the current scene.

A: Yes, in the private sense. But they have their group of tribal jokes. . . . These jokes without a story line demand much more of the hearer. He really has to work on them. . . .

Q: It is an age of involvement . . .

A: . . . and do-it-yourselfness. You have to provide your own meanings for the jokes, as well as for today's art. This is why people have great difficulty understanding that some of the new poetry began on the assumption that the audience *wants* to provide at least half the poetic process, the creative work. It's the end of consumer-packaged art. Many older people are annoyed that they have to work so hard to enjoy contemporary art. But the kids take for granted that they all get in together and bang around and *make* meanings. . . .

Q: This generation sets enormous store on communicating with each other.

A: In previous generations, people used to imagine that communication occurred more or less inevitably as long as they were within speaking distance; these kids realize communication isn't that easy.

Q: This is a major contribution.

A: However, communication to them is a form of *making*; not just matching this against that, but making something.

In the TV age, Johnny can't read because reading, as customarily taught, is too superficial and consumerlike an activity. Therefore the highbrow paperback, because of its depth character, may appeal to youngsters who spurn ordinary narrative offerings. Teachers today frequently find that students who can't read a page of history are becoming experts in code and linquistic analysis. The problem, therefore, is not that Johnny can't read, but that, in an age of depth involvement, Johnny can't visualize distant goals.

—Understanding Media

R. BUCKMINSTER FULLER

the coming
bloodless revolution

You can't reform a vacuum.

. . . The university student, having attained his first freedom of initiative, his optimum level of metabolic efficiency, bodily coordination, and general outlook, finds that his idealism is concurrently exposed to an awareness of powerful intellectual and technical disciplines. At the same time he is the recipient of frequent science-technology breakthrough news, such as under-the-polar-ice passages of atomic submarines and new achievements in rocketry and electronics. He also receives an overabundance of news concerning world want and political stresses that break into ever more frequent crises.

Logically, the student becomes exasperated and says, "Why can't we make the world work? All the negative nonsense is the consequence of outworn, ignorant biases of the old-timers. Let's join forces and set things to rights." Parading in multitudes, students demand that their political leaders take steps to bring about peace and plenty. The fallacy of this lies in their mistaken, age-old assumption that the problem is one of political reform. The fact is that the politicians are faced with a vacuum, and you can't reform a vacuum. The vacuum is the apparent world condition of not enough to go around—not enough for even a majority of mankind to survive more than half of its potential life span. It is a "you or me to the death" situation that leads from impasse to ultimate showdown by arms. Thus more and more students around the world are learning of the new and surprising alternative to politics—the design science revolution, which alone can solve the problem.

The students are thrilled to realize that it is themselves they must turn to in order to make the world work, through practical use of their university science and technology resources and their laboratory-supported design science capabilities. The students know that they need no more license to invent the tools that will make the world work than the Wright brothers needed a license to invent one of the most needed more-with-less tools— the airplane. The student's task is clear-cut. It is to increase the over-all efficiency of the world's mechanical devices from their present 4 per cent to an over-all efficiency of 12 per cent. This is easy, since over-all efficiences up to 80 per cent are now feasible. The students know that if they invent the right tools, the tools will be used, given the right emergency. And they know that their design science revolution is bound to work because the emergencies to foster its realization are already here. Their revolution is a bloodless revolution that brings peace in the only way it may ever become effective—by elimination of the physical wants that always underlie war.

* * *

Approximately everything man thought he understood will be useless within the next decade. We are going to develop an environment in which the new generation is so protected from the lovingly administered nonsense of grownups that it can develop naturally just in time to save man from self-annihilation. What I call "The Third Parent," TV, brings the babies half-hourly world news as well as much grownup-authored and discrediting nonsense. The students in revolt in California are the first generation of TV-reared babies. They insist on social justice the world around. Imminent change is inexorable.

The most important way in which women are going to accomplish world merging and stability will be through their education *by* their own children rather than vice versa as of yesterday. The Bible was right, "A little child shall lead them."

JACK NEWFIELD

the prophetic minority

We want to create a world in which love is more possible.

Carl Oglesby

Come mothers and fathers throughout the land,
And don't criticize what you can't understand.
Your old road is rapidly aging.
Please get out of the new one if you can't led a hand,
For the times, they are a-changin'.

Bob Dylan

There is a time when the operation of the machine becomes so odious, makes you so sick at heart that you can't take part; you can't even tacitly take part, and you've got to put your bodies upon the levers, upon all the apparatus, and you've got to make it stop. And you've got to indicate to the people who run it, to the people who own it, that unless you're free, the machine will be prevented from working at all.

Mario Savio

A new generation of radicals has been spawned from the chrome womb of affluent America. The last lingering doubts that the Silent Generation had found its voice vanished . . . on April 17, 1965, when more than 20,000 of this new breed converged on the nation's capital to protest against the war in Vietnam. It was the largest anti-war demonstration in the history of Washington, D.C.—and it had been organized and sponsored by a student organization—SDS.

Assembled in the warm afternoon sunshine that Saturday were the boys and girls who had "freedom rode" to Jackson,

Mississippi; who had joined the Peace Corps and returned disillusioned; tutored Negro teen-agers in the slums of the great
cities; vigiled against the Bomb; rioted against the House Un-
American Activities Committee; risked their lives to register
voters in the Black Belt; and sat-in for free speech at the University of California at Berkeley.

They were the new generation of American radicals, nourished not by the alien cobwebbed dogmas of Marx, Lenin, and
Trotsky, but by the existential humanism of Albert Camus, the
Anti-colonialism of Frantz Fanon; the communitarian anarchism of Paul Goodman; the poetic alienation of Bob Dylan; and
the grass-roots radicalism of that "prophetic shock minority"
called SNCC. They were there not to protest anything so simple
as war or capitalism. They came to cry out against the hypocrisy
called Brotherhood Week, assembly lines called colleges, manipulative hierarchies called corporations, conformity called
status, lives of quiet desperation called success. . . .

At its surface, *political* level, the New Radicalism is an anti-
Establishment protest against all the obvious inequities of American life. It says that Negroes should vote, that America should
follow a peaceful, noninterventionist foreign policy, that anti-
Communism at home has become paranoid and destructive, that
the poverty of forty million should be abolished. It is a series of
individual criticisms many liberals can agree with.

At its second, more complex level, this new movement is a
moral revulsion against a society that is becoming increasingly
corrupt. The New Radicals were coming to maturity as [Joe]
McCarthy built a movement based on deceit and bullying, as
Dulles lied about the CIA's role in the 1954 Guatemala *coup,*
as Eisenhower lied to the world about the U-2 flight over the
Soviet Union, as Adlai Stevenson lied to the UN about America's support of the Bay of Pigs invasion. . . . They saw the organs of masscult lie about their movement, the clergy exile
priests for practicing brotherhood, older men red-bait their organizations. Feeling this ethical vacuum in the country, the New
Radicals have made morality and truth the touchstones of their

movement. Like Gandhi, they try to "speak truth to power." Their politics are not particularly concerned with power or success, but rather with absolute moral alternatives like love, justice, equality, and freedom. Practical, programmatic goals are of little interest. They want to pose an alternate vision, not just demand "more" or "better" of what exists. They don't say welfare programs should be better subsidized; they say they should be administered in a wholly different, more dignifying way. . . .

At its third, subterranean level, the New Radicalism is an *existential* revolt against remote, impersonal machines that are not responsive to human needs. The New Radicals feel sharply the growing totalitarianization of life in this technological, urban decade. They feel powerless and unreal beneath the unfeeling instruments that control their lives. . . . And they can only chant "Amen" to Lewis Mumford, who observed, in *The Transformations of Man,* modern man has already depersonalized "himself so effectively that he is no longer man enough to stand up to his machines."

From their fury at arbitrary power wielded by impersonal machines (governments, college administrations, welfare bureaucracies, draft boards, television networks) come some of the New Radicals' most innovative ideas. Participatory democracy —the notion that ordinary people should be able to affect all the decisions that control their lives. The idea that social reformation comes from organizing the dispossessed into their own insurgent movements rather than from forming top-down alliances between liberal bureaucratic organizations. The insistence on fraternity and community inside the movement. The passion against manipulation and centralized decision-making. The reluctance to make the New Left itself a machine tooled and fueled to win political power in the traditional battle pits. The concept of creating new democratic forms like the Mississippi Freedom Democratic Party, the Newark Community Union Project, and the *Southern Courier,* a newspaper designed to represent the Negroes of the Black Belt rather than the white power structure or the civil-rights organizations. It is its brilliant insight into the creeping authoritarianism of modern technology and bureaucracy that gives the New Radicalism its definitive qualities of decentralism, communitarianism, and existential humanism. . . .

Generational conflict is inevitable when a younger, insurgent generation creates its own movement and ethos. . . . The reasons for the discontinuity of radical generations are plentiful and understandable. Some are the irrational psychological consequences of generational loyalties. But enough are political and programmatic so that eighty-one-year-old pacifist A. J. Muste [could] become a patron of the New Left, while twenty-seven-year-old Tom Kahn of the Fabian LID [became] a strident critic.

The New Radicalism is authentically new in its vague weaving together of anarchist, existential, transcendental, Populist, socialist, and bohemian strands of thought. *It is not the logical outgrowth of the older radical traditions in the West.* It is not built upon the same discontents as the Old Left—the depression and the threat of fascism—but upon newer discontents like powerlessness, moral disaffection, the purposelessness of middle-class life—all of which are the special products of an abundant, technocratic urban culture. . . .

In the interest of simplicity I have broken the adult Left down into four broad groupings. One group consists of ex-radicals, now pro-Cold War liberals like Sidney Hook and Lewis Feuer. They see little of value in the New Radicalism and tend to dismiss it in terms of adolescent rebellion against father figures. [They] think America no longer requires major social reforms; only minor technical adjustments that can be made at the top of the society without chaotic upheaval at the bottom. . . .

The second group consists of the Social Democratic Left, represented by Irving Howe and Bayard Rustin. These men . . . share many objectives with the students. But they candidly criticize the New Radicalism for not being sufficiently anti-Communist, for not being reflective enough, for being too romantic, and for its emotional anti-Establishmentarianism. Their sometimes

valid criticisms of the New Left have generated considerable
rancor because . . . the polemical style of their delivery . . . has
exacerbated the political disagreements, which in reality are not
that great.

The third group of over-thirty radicals [typified by Staughton
Lynd] I call the Romantic Left. They have romanticized the
movement's strength and have popularized its most questionable
modes of thinking. . . .

Finally, there is a fourth type of adult leftist, whom I call the
Humanist Liberals. . . . Represented by muckraking journalist
I. F. Stone and writer Arthur Waskow of the influential Institute for Policy Studies, this group has been deeply affected by
the New Radicalism, but has retained enough of its own ration-
alistic identity to see the flaws of the new movements with pierc-
ing clarity.

The Hook-Feuer school of former radicals views reality from
the opposite end of the telescope from the New Left. . . . They
see little pain or suffering, since, as Michael Harrington pointed
out, the Other Americans are invisible men. What they do see,
however, is their own tragic affair with Communism, and they
are determined the new generation should not whore after the
same bitch. On the other hand, the New Radicals have made it
an article of faith to see the world with the eyes of the excluded,
to empathize with them totally, and to speak with them against
leaders and elites. . . .

Lacking the pain and poverty of the excluded, the ex-radicals
would probably agree with Seymour Martin Lipset's opinion that
"Democracy is not only, or even primarily, a means through
which different groups can attain their ends or seek the good society; it is the good society itself in operation." The New Radicals, correctly, I think, would deny that America, because it has
the formal institutions of democracy, is "the good society itself
in operation." Therefore, they call for a "radical reconstruction" of that society. . . .

The ex-radicals have also segregated ethics from politics,
while one of the cardinal tenets of the New Left is that morality

and politics are indivisible. Daniel Bell has written that ethics is concerned with justice, while concrete politics involves "a power struggle between organized groups to determine the allocation of privilege." Or as Lyndon Johnson and others have phrased it, "Politics is the art of the possible." The New Left insists politics become the art of the impossible. It agrees with Max Weber, who wrote, "Certainly all historical experience confirms the truth that man would not have attained the possible unless time and again he had reached out for the impossible.". . .

The FSM at Berkeley crystallized almost all the differences between the 1930's ex-radicals and the New Left. The FSM was anti-status quo, valued ethics above law and order, had its own hip-anarchic style, and included everyone from Maoists to Goldwaterites. So although the Berkeley faculty voted 8 to 1 to support the students against the administration, the most vehement attacks on the FSM came from the typewriters of Dr. Hook and Professors Feuer, Lipset, and Nathan Glazer. . . . Feuer's essay was extraordinary for its emotional content, vituperative style, and generational hostility. He wrote in part:

The conglomeration [the FSM] acts as a magnet for the morally corrupt; intellectual lumpen proletarians, lumpen beatniks, and lumpen agitators wend their ways to the university campus to advocate a mélange of narcotics, sexual perversion, collegiate Castroism and campus Maoism.

First, it should be noted that two in-depth studies of the FSM have been made. One, by Dr. Ralph Heist, a research psychologist, showed the study group of 240 activists was of "above average intelligence" and "much more committed to the process of learning than the majority of students." Another survey, conducted by a group of Berkeley graduate students in political science, revealed:

Most are earnest students of considerably better than average academic standing. . . . Not only are these students among the brightest in the University, but they are also among the most advanced in their academic careers. Nearly two-thirds (64.3%) are upper-division or graduate students.

Second, it seems to me the students were clearly right in their actions and objectives in Berkeley. The controversy began when the administration, without consultation or forewarning, banned political recruiting, fund-raising, and advocacy from a tradition- ally Hyde Parkish twenty-six-feet strip on the campus. Students like Mario Savio, who had jeopardized their lives the summer before in Mississippi, were informed by an unreachable elite that they could no longer collect dimes and quarters for the peo- ple with whom they had worked all summer.

"How many roads must a man walk down/Before you call him a man?" asks Bob Dylan in *Blowin' in the Wind*. The Berke- ley students felt that they were men, entitled to the same civil liberties as off-campus adults. . . . But a faceless administration —with its procedures and committees—told them that they were not men. . . . They all felt like the now immortalized FSM ac- tivist who carried the picket sign that read, "I am a UC student. Please don't bend, fold, spindle or mutilate me." This feeling of *dehumanization by an unfeeling bureaucracy* is something the Hooks and Feuers cannot make a leap of faith to understand, just as Granville Hicks cannot understand the machine-dom- inated nightmares of William Burroughs, and Josh White can- not comprehend the surrealistic images in Bob Dylan's songs. The world has just changed too much. . . .

The New Radicals are speaking harsh truths in a new and irreverent voice. . . . They are saying that the whole society— from the academy to the anti-poverty program—has become too bureaucratized and must be decentralized and humanized. They are saying the draft is undemocratic. They are saying that revo- lutions are tearing the colonial clamps off three continents, and that America must stand with the poor and not the powerful. They are saying that automation is making a guaranteed annual income and a redefinition of work imperative. They are saying that ethics and politics have become divided and must be re- united.

If they are emotional or badly informed about other things, on all these issues the New Radicals are right. The older dissenters should pause and acknowledge these new voices before the Generation Gap becomes a canyon of mistrust.

MICHAEL HARRINGTON

the mystical militants

**A fear of "success," a suspicion
that it would mean the integration of
the oppressed into the corruption of
the oppressors.**

[Today's] young radicals [are] marvelously, and prob-
lematically, American. They are mystical militants, articulating
the authentic miseries of the poor even while maintaining some
of the attitudes of the middle class. They are also one of the
most significant, hopeful developments in recent American life.
. . . I have differences with the young radicals and have on occasion been puzzled, exasperated and even saddened by them.
Yet the happy fact remains that the emergence of a personally
committed generation seeking basic social change is momentous.
They are a minority of their age group, to be sure, but a creative, activist minority who should place their stamp upon the
times. Eventually, and it will probably try the anarchist spirit of
some of them, they are going to lead adult movements and
change this society. Whatever their shortcomings, the New Leftists hold out the hope for a renewal of American social criticism
and action. . . .

When I became a radical in 1948 (the last year of the politics
of the Thirties), it was taken for granted (on the Left) that the
Fourth of July was really a front for the four hundred families.
In part, this was a heritage of European socialist theory, in part
a legacy of the American experience of a Depression which had
demystified so many clichés. One did not get angry that the pow-
ers-that-be lied and cheated and manipulated. That, after all,
was their function in life, just as it was the task of the Left to

create a society which would not need to corrupt its avowed values.

The young radicals of today, it seems to me, did not start with this inherited cynicism. They came to teenage during the American celebration of the Eisenhower years and were, for the most part, not really conscious until after both Korea and McCarthyism. They seemed to have believed what they were told about freedom, equality, justice, world peace and the like. They became activists in order to affirm these traditional values with regard to some ethical cause: defending civil liberties against HUAC, picketing for the life of Caryl Chessman, demanding an end to nuclear testing, fighting for civil rights. The shock generated by the society's duplicity in this or that single issue then opened their eyes to larger, and even more systematic, injustices.

It is, I suspect, this unique Fifties-Sixties experience which gives the New Left its distinctive flavor: a sense of outrage, of having been betrayed by all the father-figures, which derives from an original innocence. And it is also the source of the young radicals' insistence on sincerity and community. They begin, not with an image of the future which was received, in one way or another, from Europe and involves theory and history, but from a sense of the immediate contradiction between democratic posturing and the undemocratic reality. . . .

This intense, even painful, consciousness of American hypocrisy has led the young radicals to people who do not, or cannot, play the national rhetorical game: the left-outs, the outcasts. And it has involved them in a contradiction between mysticism and militancy.

In the iconography of the Thirties, the proletarian was a figure of incipient power and a Puritan sense of duty. The *lumpen* proletarian was despised because he did not belong to a conscious class, because he floated; and he was feared as a potential shock trooper of fascism. By the Fifties, much of the old élan had left the labor movement and, with an overwhelming majority of the people satisfied with Eisenhower, there did not seem to be much of a political perspective for insurgency. At this point a cultural rebellion took place among young people. It was expressed among the Beats who contracted out of the system; it informed Norman Mailer's vision of the white man who aspired to the cool and the hip which white society provoked in the Negro.

As disestablishmentarians, the young radicals continue this tradition of the Fifties. They identify precisely with the *lumpen*, the powerless, the maimed, the poor, the criminal, the junkie. And there is a mystical element in this commitment which has nothing to do with politics. By going into the slum, they are doing penance for the sins of affluence; by sharing the life of those who are so impoverished that they are uncorrupted, values are affirmed. It is honest and moral and anti-hypocritical to be on the margin of society *whether the community organization works or not.* Indeed, there is a fear of "success," a suspicion that it would mean the integration of the oppressed into the corruption of the oppressors.

But, on the other hand, the New Leftists are not Fifties Beats (and, by the way, I do not use the term Beat pejoratively). They are angry militants who see the poor as a new force in America, perhaps even as a substitute for the proletariat that failed. So Stokely Carmichael . . . insists that the Mississippi and Alabama sharecroppers can choose for themselves. He understands that ultimately, to paraphrase an old labor song, no one can abolish poverty for you, you've got to abolish it yourself. And from this point of view, it does make quite a bit of difference whether the community organizing campaign works or not.

An analogy from the Thirties might illuminate the political hope that is here asserted by the young radicals. In 1932 or 1933, many polite Americans believed that if you gave a worker a bathtub, he would put coal in it. And the skilled AFL members thought it preposterous that mass-production machine operators could form *their own* union. On paper, the right to organize was proclaimed by the Wagner Act. In fact, it took at least five tumultuous years of picketing, striking and sitting-in before the CIO turned the brave words into something of a reality. Sim-

ilarly in 1964, America declared war on poverty; and most of
the well-bred citizenry did not intend by that to have field hands
and janitors speaking up for themselves; and the young radicals,
who have this knack of taking America's promises seriously,
sought a surge from below to give meaning to the phrasemaking
on high. But, as I think the New Left realizes, this analogy is
faulty in part. The mass-production workers were, just as radical
theory had said, forced by the conditions of their existence
(thousands of men assembled at one miserable place with common problems and interests) into a solidarity which became the
basis of union organization. The poor, as Tom Hayden noted . . .
are not grouped into incipient communities. A slum street fragments and atomizes people; the two largest groups of the poor,
the young and the old, have little to do with one another; and
even if they could get together, the poor are still a minority of
the society. Therefore it is going to take even more creativity
to help the outcasts into their own than it did to build industrial
unionism.

For a number of reasons the New Leftists shied away [until
recent years] from thinking through the problems posed by their
own militancy. For one thing, they are indeed "American" in
the empirical, activist, anti-theoretical sense of the word. For
another, they rejected the scholasticism of some of the traditional Left formulae (as well as the genuine profundity of the
Left's intellectual heritage), and they were imbued with the
spirit of the civil-rights movement of the early Sixties, where the
willingness to go to jail was more important than political abstractions. . . .

The New Leftists regard the welfare state, rather than the
economic royalists, as the incarnation of the status quo. This is
an almost inevitable result of trying to look at America with the
eyes of the poor. It is very right—and it is a dangerous half-
truth.

The welfare state developed in the Thirties was created by,
and for, the "middle third" of American society: the liberal
middle class and the organized workers. The poor were, and still

are, those who were left behind in the Depression because of bad geographical, occupational or political luck: migrants, farm workers, full-time laborers at poverty jobs, racial and ethnic minorities which came into the economic mainstream at the time of the computer rather than of the assembly line. In addition, the poor include all those who have suffered from a *relative deterioration* in various social-insurance and income-maintenance programs (social security, unemployment compensation, etc.).

The visible enemies of the poor are not the captains of industry but the landlords, shopkeepers and, often enough, the agents of the welfare state. For the welfare state is, of course, ill-financed and bureaucratic, and this distorts the good intentions of many of the fine people who work for it and it reinforces the vices of the bad. So for the poor the welfare state means a humiliating dependence and fear, and requires a constant, cunning battle against authority. The young radicals attempt to articulate these fierce resentments which they discovered in the slums, and the experience does not leave them in a mood for sociological nicety. The welfare state is, they say, a fraud. And the liberals, who actually boast of having created this monster in the name of humane values, are therefore the worst hypocrites.

In formulating this attitude, it is not simply that the New Leftists overlook some history, which youth always does, but that they ignore some *relevant* history. The welfare state did not come out of the Thirties as a result of a liberal plot to manipulate the dispossessed. It was created over the violent resistance of most men of property and wealth, and its creation required a major upheaval on the part of the workers, from the bottom up. Business did not begin its conversion to welfare statism until the World War II discovery that a federal agency staffed by corporation executives was not exactly a class enemy of the rich; and its final conversion to "tax-cut" Keynesianism waited upon the persuasiveness of Lyndon B. Johnson. There was, and is, a very real element of buying off the restless natives in business acceptance of welfarism.

The relevance of this history is that the current welfare-state

consensus is not quite so homogeneous as [some believe]. For
the apparent agreement conceals the latent conflict between the
sophisticated conservatives on the one hand, and the liberal-
labor-civil-rights forces on the other. One can rightly accuse the
liberal welfarists of having been too nostalgically proud of *their*
upheaval to understand the terrible urgency of more change
now as seen from the bottom of society. But it is something else
again to *equate* all present supporters of the welfare state with
one another.

And here I think I come to my most serious criticism of the
New Radicals: that they sometimes expect the poor to act out the
moral values of the middle-class radical who has come to the
slum. I find, for instance, a genuine poignancy in Tom Hayden's
realization that a coalition of the outcasts will not really be able
to change the society and that radicalism can only give itself up
to, and become part of, "the energy kept restless and active under the clamps of paralyzed imperial society. Radicalism then
would go beyond the concepts of optimism and pessimism as
guides to work, finding itself in working despite odds. Its realism
and sanity would be grounded in nothing more than the ability
to face whatever comes."

This attitude is a logical deduction from theory that all the
welfare staters, from Henry Ford to Walter Reuther if you will,
are the same kind of manipulative bureaucrats. For if everybody
but the poor and outcast are "them," then "we" must inevitably
lose, for by definition "we" are not strong enough to transform
a fraud and scandal supported by 60 or 70 percent of the society. . . .

The New Leftists must come up with a strategy which offers
real hope to the other America. And this means making a more
sophisticated analysis of the coalition which supports the welfare state. For the liberal wing of this consensus certainly did
not start with the intention to build a manipulative bureaucracy,
and it maintains values which *could* provide a basis for transforming the present structure. If the social-change movements
of the previous generation must be shaken up by the poor, they

must be shaken up in order to be made allies. To do this requires an intensification of the efforts to organize the slums and ghettos and backwoods as an independent political force. But if there is to be honest hope, that organizaiton must be thought of as the catalyst of a new political majority in the United States. . . . There is reason to hope that these new directions will be taken. . . .

NORMAN MAILER

with souls of interesting dimension

It was the children in whom Mailer had some hope, a gloomy hope. These mad middle-class children with their lobotomies from sin, their nihilistic embezzlement of all middle-class moral funds, their innocence, their lust for apocalypse, their unbelievable indifference to waste: twenty generations of buried hopes perhaps engraved in their chromosomes, and now conceivably burning like faggots in the secret inquisitional fires of LSD. It was a devil's drug—designed by the Devil to consume the love of the best and leave them liver-wasted, weeds of the big city. If there had been a player piano, Mailer might have put in a quarter to hear "In the Heart of the City Which Has No Heart."

* * *

. . . Students began to file up the steps to deposit their solitary or collective draft cards in the bag, and this procession soon became a ceremony. Each man came up, gave his name, and the state or area or college he represented, and then proceeded to name the number of draft cards he had been entrusted to turn in. The numbers were larger than one might have expected. There were almost two hundred from New York, there were much more than two hundred from Boston, and a good number from Yale. As these numbers were announced, the crowd being, when all is said, good Americans, gave murmurs of pleasure, an academic distance from the cry they had given as children to the acrobats of the circus, but not entirely unrelated, for there was something of the flying trapeze in these maneuvers now; by handing in draft cards, these young men were committing their future either to prison, emigration, frustration, or at best, years where everything must be unknown, and that spoke of a readiness to take moral leaps which the acrobat must know when he flies off into space—one has to have faith in one's ability to react with grace en route, one has ultimately, it may be supposed, to believe in some kind of grace.

On the *a fortiori* evidence, then they were young men with souls of interesting dimension, and their faces did nothing to disprove this. None of them looked alike; they had a surprising individuality in their appearance. Some were scholarly and slight, dressed conservatively, and looked like clerks; others were in dungarees, and possessed, like Dickie Harris, the Negro on the grass, that private élan reminiscent of the old cavaliers of SNCC; a few were sports and looked to have eight hobbies, custom cars, pot, draft cards, skiing, guitar, surfboard, chicks, and scuba—not many of these, but Mailer had been expecting none. One tall student from the West, California no doubt, even looked like one's image of the President of the Young Republicans at Stanford, he was handsome enough in conventional measure to have been Number 1 Deke in Delta Kappa Eps. . . .

In a little more than a half hour, the students were done. Now began the faculty. They too came up one by one, but now there was no particular sense offered of an internal organization. Unlike the students, they had not debated these matters in open forum for months, organized, proselyted, or been overcome by argument, no, most of them had served as advisers to the students, had counseled them, and been picked up, many of them, and brought along by the rush of this moral stream much as a small piece of river bank might separate from the shore and go down the line of the flood. It must have been painful for these academics. They were older, certainly less suited for jail, aware more precisely of how and where their careers would be diverted or impeded, they had families many of them, they were liberal academics, technologues, they were being forced to abdicate from the machines they had chosen for their life. Their decision

to turn in draft cards must have come for many in the middle of
the night; for others it must have come even last night, or as they
stood here debating with themselves. Many of them seemed to
stand irresolutely near the steps for long periods, then move up
at last. . . .

*   *   *

A generation of the American young had come along different
from five previous generations of the middle class. The new generation believed in technology more than any before it, but the
generation also believed in LSD, in witches, in tribal knowledge,
in orgy, and revolution. It had no respect whatsoever for the un-
assailable logic of the next step: belief was reserved for the
revelatory mystery of the happening where you did not know
what was going to happen next; that was what was good about it.
Their radicalism was in their hate for the authority—the authority was the manifest of evil to this generation. It was the authority who had covered the land with those suburbs where they
stifled as children while watching the adventures of the West in
the movies, while looking at the guardians of dull genial celebrity on television; they had had their minds jabbed and poked
and twitched and probed and finally galvanized into surrealistic
modes of response by commercials cutting into dramatic narra-
tives, and parents flipping from network to network—they were
forced willy-nilly to build their idea of the space-time con-
tinuum (and therefore their nervous system) on the jumps and
cracks and leaps and breaks which every phenomenon from the
media seemed to contain within it.

The authority had operated on their brain with commercials,
and washed their brain with packeged education, packaged politics. The authority had presented itself as honorable, and it was
corrupt, corrupt as payola on television, and scandals concerning the safety of automobiles, and scandals concerning the leas-
ing of aviation contracts—the real scandals as everyone was beginning to sense were more intimate and could be found in all
the products in all the suburban homes which did not work so

well as they should have worked, and broke down too soon for mysterious reasons. The shoddiness was buried in the package, buried somewhere in the undiscoverable root of all those modern factories with their sanitized aisles and automated machines; perhaps one place the shoddiness was buried was in the hangovers of a working class finally alienated from any remote interest or attention in the process of the work itself. Work was shoddy everywhere. Even in the Warren Commission.

Finally, this new generation of the Left hated the authority, because the authority lied. It lied through the teeth of corporation executives and Cabinet officials and police enforcement officers and newspaper editors and advertising agencies, and in its mass magazines, where the subtlest apologies for the disasters of the authority (and the neatest deformations of the news) were grafted in the best possible style into the ever-open mind of the walking American lobotomy: the corporation office worker and his high-school son. . . .

The aesthetic of the New Left . . . began with the notion that the authority could not comprehend nor contain nor finally manage to control any political action whose end was unknown. They could attack it, beat it, jail it, misrepresent it, and finally abuse it, but they could not feel a sense of victory because they could not understand a movement which inspired thousands and hundreds of thousands to march without a coordinated plan. The bureaucrats of the Old Left had not been alone in their adoration of the solid-as-brickwork-logic-of-the-next-step; no, the bureaucrats of the American Center now liked it as much, and were as aghast at any political activity which ignored it. . . .

* * *

They came walking up in all sizes, a citizens' army not ranked yet by height, an army of both sexes in numbers almost equal, and of all ages, although most were young. Some were well-dressed, some were poor, many were conventional in appearance, as often were not. The hippies were there in great number, perambulating down the hill, many dressed like the legions of

Sgt. Pepper's Band, some were gotten up like Arab sheiks, or
in Park Avenue doormen's greatcoats, others like Rogers and
Clark of the West, Wyatt Earp, Kit Carson, Daniel Boone in
buckskin, some had grown mustaches to look like *Have Gun,
Will Travel*—Paladin's surrogate was here!—and wild Indians
with feathers, a hippie gotten up like Batman, another like
Claude Rains in *The Invisible Man*—his face wrapped in a tur-
ban of bandages and he wore a black satin top hat. A host of
these troops wore capes, beat-up khaki capes, slept on, used as
blankets, towels, improvised duffel bags; or fine capes, orange
linings, or luminous rose linings, the edges ragged, near a tatter,
the threads ready to feather, but a musketeer's hat on their head.
One hippie may have been dressed like Charles Chaplin; Buster
Keaton and W. C. Fields could have come to the ball; there were
Martians and Moon-men and a knight unhorsed who stalked
about in the weight of real armor. There were to be seen a hundred soldiers in Confederate gray, and maybe there were two
or three hundred hippies in officer's coats of Union dark-blue.
They had picked up their costumes where they could, in surplus
stores, and Blow-your-mind shops, Digger free emporiums, and
psychedelic caches of Hindu junk. There were soldiers in Foreign Legion uniforms, and tropical bush jackets, San Quentin
and Chino, California striped shirt and pants, British copies of
Eisenhower jackets, hippies dressed like Turkish shepherds and
Roman senators, gurus, and samurai in dirty smocks. They were
close to being assembled from all the intersections between history and the comic books, between legend and television, the
Biblical archetypes and the movies. . . .

Still, there were nightmares beneath the gaiety of these middle-class runaways, these Crusaders, going out to attack the hard
core of technology land with less training than armies were once
offered by a medieval assembly ground. The nightmare was in
the echo of those trips which had fractured their sense of past
and present. If nature was a veil whose tissue had been ripped
by static, screams of jet motors, the highway grid of the suburbs,
smog, defoliation, pollution of streams, overfertilization of

earth, anti-fertilization of women, and the radiation of two decades of near-blind atom busting, then perhaps the history of the
past was another tissue, spiritual, no doubt, without physical embodiment, unless its embodiment was in the cuneiform hiero-
glyphics of the chromosome (so much like primitive writing!)
but that tissue of past history, whether traceable in the flesh, or
merely palpable in the collective underworld of the dream, was
nonetheless being bombed by the use of LSD as outrageously as
the atoll of Eniwetok, Hiroshima, Nagasaki, and the scorched
foliage of Vietnam. The history of the past was being exploded
right into the present: perhaps there were now lacunae in the
firmament of the past, holes where once had been the psychic
reality of an era which was gone. Mailer was haunted by the
nightmare that the evils of the present not only exploited the
present, but consumed the past, and gave every promise of de-
molishing whole territories of the future. The same villains who,
promiscuously, wantonly, heedlessly, had gorged on LSD and
consumed God knows what essential marrows of history, wearing
indeed the history of all eras on their back as trophies of this
gluttony, were now going forth (conscience-struck?) to make
war on those other villains, corporation-land villains, who were
destroying the promise of the present in their self-righteousness
and greed and secret lust (often unknown to themselves) for
some sexo-technological variety of neo-fascism.

Mailer's final allegiance, however, was with the villains who
were hippies. They would never have looked to blow their minds
and destroy some part of the past if the authority had not brain-
washed the mood of the present until it smelled like deodorant.
(To cover the odor of burning flesh in Vietnam?) . . .

* * *

. . . the demonstrators were not only sons of the middle class,
of course, but sons who had departed the middle class; they
were rebels and radicals and young revolutionaries; yet they
were unbloodied, they felt secretly weak, they did not know if
they were the simple equal, man for man, of these soldiers, and

so when this vanguard confronted soldiers now, and were able
to stare them in the eye, they were, in effect, saying silently, "I
will steal your élan, and your brawn, and the very animal of
your charm because I am morally right and you are wrong and
the balance of existence is such that the meat of your life is now
attached to my spirit, I am stealing your balls." A great exaltation arose among the demonstrators in that first hour. Surrounded
on the plaza and on the stairs, they could have no idea of what
would happen next, they could be beaten, arrested, buried in a
stampede, most of them were on the mouth of their first cannon,
yet for each minute they survived, sixty seconds of existential
gold was theirs. Minutes passed, an hour went by—these troops
were more afraid of them than they were afraid of the troops!
Great glory. They began to cheer. . . .

* * *

. . . one or two principled pacifists practicing total noncooperation were dragged off the 2½-ton trucks, bumped along the
ground, tugged over to the bus, and thrown in by the Marshals.
Bleeding a little, looking dazed, the three or four young men
who arrived by this route were applauded with something not
unlike the enthusiasm a good turn gets in a music hall. Handsome young boys got on the bus, and slovenly oafs, hippies, and
walking wounded. One boy had a pant leg soaked in blood. A fat
sad fellow with a huge black beard now boarded; a trim and
skinny kid who looked like he played minor-league shortstop
took a seat, a Japanese boy, androgynous in appearance, told a
few prisoners around him that none of the Marshals had been
able to decide if he was a boy or a girl, so they had not known—
for he would not tell them—whether a Marshal or a Matron
should search him. This was quickly taken up with pleasure and
repeated down the bus. . . .

* * *

The brutality, by every eyewitness account, was not insignificant, and was made doubly unattractive by its legalistic appa-

ratus. The line of soldiers would stamp forward until they reached the seated demonstrators, then they would kick forward with their toes until the demonstrators were sitting on their feet (or *legally* speaking, now interfering with the soldiers). Then the Marshals would leap between their legs again and pull the demonstrator out of the line; he or she would then be beaten and taken away. . . . yes, the beatings went on, one by one, generally of women, more women than men. . . .

All the while, rumors passed. A demonstrator was already dead they heard—then next that they were all to be taken away and beaten one by one. Now the rumors changed. At X hour, a charge would come down on them. They would be clubbed to death.

It was still possible to leave. It was possible every inch of that slow advance of the Wedge for demonstrators to leave. But they sat there expecting to share the fate of the girls and the boys being beaten now. . . .

So it became a rite of passage for these tender drug-vitiated jargon-mired children, they endured through a night, a black dark night which began in joy, near foundered in terror, and dragged on through empty apathetic hours while glints of light came to each alone. Yet the rite of passage was invoked, the moral ladder was climbed, they were forever different in the morning than they had been before the night, which is the meaning of a rite of passage, one has voyaged through a channel of shipwreck and temptation, and so some of the vices carried from another nether world into life itself (on the day of one's birth) may have departed, or fled, or quit; some part of the man has been born again, and is better, just as some hardly so remarkable area of the soul may have been in some minuscule sweet fashion reborn on the crossing of the marchers over Arlington Memorial Bridge, for the worst of them and the most timid were moving nonetheless to a confrontation they could only fear, they were going to the land of the warmakers. Not so easy for the timid when all is said. . . .

*　　*　　*

A group from the Quaker Farm in Voluntown, Connecticut, practiced noncooperation in prison. . . . Several men at the D.C. jail would not wear prison clothing. Stripped of their own, naked, they were thrown in the Hole. There they lived in cells so small that not all could lie down at once to sleep. . . .

Did they pray, these Quakers, for forgiveness of the nation? Did they pray with tears in their eyes in those blind cells with visions of a long column of Vietnamese dead, Vietnamese walking a column of flame, eyes on fire, nose on fire, mouth speaking flame. . . ? No one will know. . . . But if the end of the March took place in the isolation in which these last pacifists suffered naked in freezing cells, and gave up prayers for penance, then who was to say they were not saints? And who to say that the sins of America were not by their witness a tithe remitted?

KENNETH KENISTON

activists[*]

These young men and women usually had already "proved" they could succeed in the terms that American society uses to define success.

full adolescence and value continuity

I had a good solid family, no parental trouble among themselves or with the kids. My old man is very straight with the kids. That's been very important, because it has kept in the back of my mind all the time concepts like responsibility, seriousness. . . . The values I got from my family, the ones that I've kept, are good. I've pared them and peeled them to fit my own style, but there is a good continuity here. I mean it's a new generation, but there's a lot from my old generation that can't be minimized. Otherwise, I might have flipped out or something like that, or just turned myself off altogether.

This young man, from a relatively apolitical background, links his involvement in the Movement and his escape from "just flipping out and becoming totally alienated" to his continuity with the values of his family. . . .

[Another] young radical's basic perceptions of society . . . are fully in accord with those of his father's. Where father and

---

* These are excerpts from psychologist Keniston's book *Young Radicals: Notes on Committed Youth.* Keniston began his interviews of these members of the "Vietnam Summer" project with certain *un*favorable preconceptions, expecting them to be especially suspicious of his investigations, and "alienated"—although in a different way from "uncommitted" youth.—A.K.

son part company, as the son sees it, is that the father's actions
are not based on his perceptions:

My father, unlike most businessmen—unlike all businessmen I have
met—is probably the most sympathetic toward poor people. I mean he
really understands the injustice. . . . With wealthy liberal people, it is
so difficult for them to feel that. They have a sense that basically what
happens is right. . . . I'm sure my father has a much better understanding of what Stokely Carmichael is about than most people do. But his
point of view would be a very narrow, selfish one. He would say [about
the things that my friends and I are doing now]: "That's great, but let
it happen after I'm dead. You guys can have your way then, but in the
meantime I'm enjoying life."

In most young radicals the positive side of the paternal image
is uppermost, and the negative side emerges only later; sometimes only in apologetic asides. Yet whichever side of the ambivalence is most stressed, there almost always seems to be a
quite conscious split in the image of the father, involving the
picture of him (and by extension his tradition and the older generation) as idealistic, sympathetic, honest, highly principled,
warm, and admirable; but on the other hand, as dominated, hu-
miliated, ineffectual, or unwilling to act on his perceptions of the
world. These two contrasting images help define one of the basic
tensions in these young radicals, the tension between having
principles and acting on them. . . .

. . . The most common adolescent pattern in America involves
what Peter Blos terms "uniformism": a turning away from the
family towards the peer-group culture, acceptance of its norms
as infallible and regulatory, and the use of conformity to peer-
group norms as a means of simultaneously regulating one's own
impulses and attenuating one's family ties. . . . In many instances, involvement with the peer group helps prevent the "normal" turmoil of early adolescence; in some cases, it may also
prevent a real adolescence.

Compared to their more "typical" American contemporaries
. . . these young radicals really *did* have an adolescence, with
all the anguish and the possibilities for growth that this stage

entails. . . . It may be that the very closeness, warmth and encouragement toward independence in some of these families were what made adolescence both possible and necessary. Put differently, many of these families seem to have given their children the strength and the need to challenge, re-examine, and partially reassimilate their parents' values, and eventually to achieve an unusual degree of individuality for themselves. . . .

[But] in these particular young men and women, the move toward radical politics was not a direct outgrowth of what is ordinarily considered "the adolescent crisis." They had long since resolved their first adolescent crisis in a way that almost everyone but themselves would have judged eminently successful. Commitment to the New Left developed out of a later crisis, one that occurred as entry into the Establishment became more imminent. And this second crisis seems less a part of adolescence itself than a crisis at the threshold between adolescence and conventional adulthood. . . .

On the one hand, [their] reluctance to seize the options before them can be interpreted as a reluctance to "grow up": it would probably be so judged by many Americans. . . . Conventional adulthood might mean the loss of that sense of specialness that had been so long with these young men and women; it might mean becoming like the ineffectual side of their fathers, all of whom were in some sense involved in conventional American life. Delaying may therefore represent a childish reluctance to abandon the uncompromising adolescent insistence on purity of principle. But judged from another perspective, their hesitation may reflect strength rather than weakness. These young men and women usually had already "proved" that they could succeed in the terms that American society uses to define success. Most of them had excelled, but had gained scant satisfaction from their own excellence. So judged, their reluctance to take up the jobs, fellowships, offers, and rewards before them might indicate that they were able to demand more, not less, of themselves and of life. . . .

In understanding the continuity of values between these radicals and their backgrounds, it should be recalled that the basic values of the New Left are neither new nor startling. However revolutionary the objectives, however radical the tactics proposed to attain them, the basic values of the young radical are ancient and familiar: the only startling fact is that he takes these values seriously and proposes that American society and the world set about implementing them. Thus, for young men and women like these, who were brought up to believe that prejudice, hatred, and discrimination are wrong, that suffering should be alleviated, that all men should have equal opportunities and an equal say in the decisions affecting their lives, that peace and justice should be sought after, that violence should be minimized, and that men should seek to relate to each other in a human, open, direct, and personal way, the values of the New Left are not at all alien. Also, at the level of even more basic personal values, these young men and women had been brought up to cherish honesty, responsibility, seriousness, and thoughtfulness. Their work in the New Left, far from requiring them to repudiate these values, offered an arena in which they could act on them.

Many commentators have connected radicalism with psychological problems about authority. But among those I interviewed, such problems did not seem especially important. (Doubtless there are other young radicals to whom this explanation applies. In other contexts, I have interviewed young men and women— not radicals—for whom obedience to, or rejection of, authority was in fact a crucial issue.). . . The wariness of these young radicals toward some of their elders seemed less a rebellious projection of hatred of their fathers than a reflection of the very real differences in outlook and style that separate the generations. The early attempts of these young radicals to "work within the System" suggest that their first impulse was to trust authorities and authoritative agencies; it was through experience that they turned away.

It would be wrong, then, simply to call these young men and women rebels against authority. Their early adolescent rebellions were generally brief, and they have been largely resolved into a complex perception of their parents as people. And turning toward the New Left after late adolescence was not so much a rejection of the authority of their parents and society, as a dissatisfaction with themselves—a sense of their *own* inadequacy, of the "wastefulness" of the lives *they* were leading, of the "self-destructiveness" of *their* activities. The principals of their schools, the presidents of their colleges, and some of their potential employers clearly judged their behavior rebellious. But to these young men and women themselves, it felt more like a search. And the resolution of this search was not a simple break with their pasts or with society, but a complex rejoining of both. Part of what they re-established was connection with their own ethical sense, a fusion of action and principle, of will and moral sense, of superego and ego. They thus achieved a sense of being on good terms with their own consciences that is vouchsafed few of their contemporaries. . . .

All of these young men and women agree that the *political* values of their parents are dated—the products of a different generation, irrelevant to the needs of modern America. But their parents' *personal* values—responsibility, seriousness, honesty, concern with people—have been largely accepted, and these personal values now underlie much of the radicals' commitment. Yet at the same time, a powerful motive for radicalism is not only the desire to implement the parents' principles, but is an equally powerful wish to *avoid* the ineffectuality, failure to act, or "compromises" of these same parents. . . .

Out of this complex dialectic of growth has come an unusual degree of psychological integration. Being radicals has enabled them to synthesize previously conflicting needs, to overcome earlier inhibitions, and to resolve many of the "hang-ups" of earlier adolescence. . . .

change and generational
credibility gap

. . . Many middle-class parents moved during their lifetimes from the Victorian ethos in which they had been brought up to the less moralistic, more humanitarian, and more "expressive" values of their own adulthoods. But major changes in values, when they occur in adult life, are likely to be less than complete. To have grown up in a family where unquestioning obedience to parents was expected, but to rear one's own children in an atmosphere of "democratic" permissiveness and self-actualization—and never to revert to the practices of one's own childhood—requires a change of values more comprehensive than most adults can achieve. Furthermore, behavior that springs from values acquired in adulthood often appears somewhat forced, artificial, or insincere to the sensitive observer. . . .

In a time of rapid social change, then, a *credibility gap* is likely to open between the generations. Children are likely to perceive a discrepancy between what the parents avow as their values and the actual assumptions from which parental behavior springs in times of crisis. In the young radicals interviewed, the focal issue of adolescent rebellion against parents seems to have been just this discrepancy: the children argued that their parents' endorsement of independence and self-determination for their children was "hypocritical" because it did not correspond with the parents' actual behavior when their children seized the independence offered them. Similar perceptions of "hypocrisy" occurred for others around racial matters: there were a few parents who supported racial and religious equality in principle, but became upset when their children dated someone of another race or religion. Around political activity similar issues arose, especially during the 1950's. For example, many of the parents of today's youth espoused in principle the cause of political freedom; but most were not involved in politics themselves and some opposed their children's involvement lest they "jeopardize their records."

Of course, in no society do parents (or anyone else) ever fully live up to their own professed ideals. In every society, there is a gap between creedal values and actual practices; and everywhere the recognition of this gap constitutes a powerful motor for social change. But in most societies, especially when social change is slow and social institutions are powerful and unchanged, there occurs what can be called the *institutionalization of hypocrisy*. Children and adolescents routinely learn when it is "reasonable" to expect that the values parents profess will be implemented in their behavior, and when it is not reasonable. There develops an elaborate system of exegesis and commentary upon the society's creedal values, excluding certain people or situations from the full weight of these values or "demonstrating" that apparent inconsistencies are not really inconsistencies at all. Thus, in almost all societies, a "sincere" man who "honestly" believes one set of values is frequently allowed to ignore them completely, for example, in the practice of his business, in his interpersonal relationships, in dealings with foreigners, in relationships of his children, and so on—all because these situations have been defined by social consensus as exempt from the application of his creedal values.

In a time of rapid social change and value change, however, the institutionalization of hypocrisy tends to break down. "New" values have been in existence for so brief a period that the exemptions to them have not yet been defined, the situations to be excluded have not yet been determined. The universal gap between principle and practice appears without disguise. . . . [and] the young see the Emperor in all his nakedness, recognizing the value conflict within their parents and perceiving clearly the "hypocritical" gap between ideal and behavior. . . .

This points to one of the central characteristics of today's youth in general and young radicals in particular: they insist on taking seriously a great variety of political, personal, and social

principles that "no one in his right mind" ever before thought
of attempting to extend to such situations as dealings with strangers, relations between the races, or international politics. . . .

the search for new forms

The post-modern style both mirrors and opposes the contemporary world. It reflects modern history in its fluidity, change,
and openness. It reacts against the impersonality of technological society with personalism, against irrelevant tradition with
generational identification, against technologism, and above all,
against violence. But more than either reflection or reaction, the
style of post-modern youth is a search—a search for new values, for institutional forms, and intellectual formulations that
are adequate to life in the last third of the twentieth century.
And in no group is that search more deliberate and intense than
in the New Left.

It is very easy to find good grounds to criticize the young radicals. Their outlooks are incomplete, changeable, hard to pin
down. They seem "unrealistic" in their firm adherence to principle in the face of social and historical actualities that appear
to demand compromise. They are anti-institutional, even anarchistic, in their fondness for the small-scale, the participatory, and
the face-to-face. They lack any detailed program of specific reforms. They are romantic in their identification with those who
are superficially unlike them, as in their assumption that every
man has a real self waiting to be actualized beneath his social
role. They place great faith in the personal, the at-hand, and the
subjective, yet seek a political effectiveness that requires dealing
in public images and persuasions. They consider themselves involved in politics, yet shy away from the exercise of power.

As obvious and correct as all these criticisms are, they somehow miss the point. To criticize the New Left for not being an
efficient political organization or a complete philosophical sys-

tem is to criticize it for not being what it tries hard not to be. Its political goals are not to win the next election, or the one after, but to increase the social and political consciousness of the American people. And it deliberately avoids a finished philosophy and political program in its conviction that the way the political process operates, the spirit of its participants may be more important than the rhetoric of platforms and promises. The New Left grew out of dissatisfaction with the political forms of the old liberalism and the overly complete formulations of the old radicalism. In the new radical's view, liberal political institutions, however well-organized and efficient, have failed to solve the problems of racism, poverty, and foreign policy. And the older radicalism, despite its coherence as a philosophy, is seen as largely irrelevant to the problems of political action and thought in an affluent, changing, middle-class society. From its first beginnings, the New Left deliberately defined its task as the search for new forms and formulations—a search that few young radicals believe is more than half begun. . . .

These young men and women seek new *forms of adulthood,* in which the principled dedication of youth to the betterment of society can be continued in adult work that does not require blind acceptance of the established System, but permits continuing commitment to social change. . . .

They seek a new *orientation to the future,* one that avoids the fixed tasks and defined lifeworks of the past in favor of an openness and acceptance of flux and uncertainty. In their openness, they stress not ends but means, not goals but style, not program but process, not the attainment of utopia but a *way* of doing things.

They seek new *pathways of personal development* wherein the openness of youth, its fluidity, growth, and change, its responsiveness to inner life and historical need, can be maintained throughout life. Fearful of finished fixity, they look for means of combining social role and personal change so that human development does not slow or cease with entry into society.

They seek new *values for living,* values that will fill the spir-

itual emptiness created by material affluence. The first generation with no need to strive to subsist, to achieve security, or to
augment their status, they turn toward goals of self-expression,
fulfillment, and service, attempting to learn how to live wisely
and well with the unprecedented abundance their generation
takes for granted.

They seek new *styles of human interaction* from which the
participants grow in dignity and strength. Repelled by the impersonality, cruelty, and dehumanization of many modern transactions between man and man, they are looking for ways for
people to remain people and to confront each other in trust and
respect in their daily lives.

They seek new *ways of knowing*, ways that combine intense
personal conviction with relevance and enduring adequacy to the
facts. In a world where the self-evident truths of one generation
become the fallacies of the next, they want an epistemology that
avoids rigidity, dogma, and claims to eternal verity, that permits responsiveness to personal and historical flux, but that
creates the conceptual consistencies by which they can orient
themselves to a world in flux.

They seek new *kinds of learning*, learning that maximizes the
involvement of the intellect in the individual's experience, instead of divorcing the two. The "merely academic" is eschewed
because it gives so little weight to either inner life or personal
experience. What is sought is a means of connecting the knowledge of the past to the experience of the present so that together
they inform life and action.

They seek new *concepts of man in society*, concepts that acknowledge the unique individuality of each human being without denying man's social embeddedness, that stress social involvement without neglecting the special potential that is often
covered by social role. Unwilling to define man as either an
existential isolate or a social cog, they would find a way to recognize both his specialness and his sociability.

They seek new *formulations of the world*, formulations that
give adequate weight to the movement and change that is ubiqui-

tous in their experience. Inheritors of an intellectual tradition that sees stasis as the rule, they search for alternate views that put the flux and process of post-modern life at the center of their views of man, society, and history.

They seek new *types of social organization,* institutional forms that include rather than exclude. Appalled by an immensely affluent society that excludes the black and the poor from its prosperity, angry at self-righteous "help" that devitalizes its recipients, they are trying to create new institutions that will activate, humanize, and strengthen those they touch.

They seek new *tactics of political action* that increase the awareness of those who take part in them and of those whom they affect. Opposing commercialization and manipulation in political life, they propose a politics of dialogue, participation, and confrontation that starts from what is near and immediate, gradually making men more aware of their unavoidable political involvement and responsibility.

They seek new *patterns of international relations,* patterns within which men of diverse nations can respect both their common humanity and their cultural uniqueness. Dismayed by foreign policies that suppress popular demands and oppose the reform of injustice, unafraid of the specter of "Communism," they would allow each people to shape its own destiny free from interference.

Perhaps most important, they seek new *controls on violence,* whether between man and man or between nation and nation. Products of the violence-ridden post-modern world, more aware of man's inner potential for violence than any previous generation, their most constant effort has been to put an end to the violence men do to each other, whether by racist oppression, hidden manipulation, or open war.

No one—and especially not these young radicals themselves —would argue that they have found adequate answers to any of the problems they confront. Most Americans will judge their efforts unrealistic, inconsistent, naïve, misguided, or even dangerous. And many will consider it impertinent of such young men and women to dare to advise their elders so insistently about matters that have puzzled older and perhaps wiser heads for a generation.

However we judge the young radicals, to describe their search is to enumerate the problems of our changing affluent, and violent society, a society that has barely begun to catch up with the dilemmas it has created. The new radicals are right when they argue that our problems lie deeper than a particular election result or a particular war in Southeast Asia. Ours are in fact the problems of a new kind of society trying to find its way in a new kind of world where cataclysm is only a button away. Few of us know how to live wisely and well in such a world: that fact is reflected in the deep malaise, violence, and inner divisions of America and the world. The new radicals are at least confronting the central issues of our time, and confronting them more directly than most of us can afford to. They are asking the basic questions, making the mistakes, and perhaps moving toward some of the answers we all desperately need.

JOHN FISCHER

four choices

> Some of my best friends have been
> revolutionists. . . . the most unfor-
> tunate are those whose revolutions
> succeeded.

. . . The relevant question for the arriving generation
is not whether our society is imperfect (we can take that for
granted), but how to deal with it. For all its harshness and irrationality, it is the only world we've got. Choosing a strategy to
cope with it, then, is the first decision a young adult has to make,
and usually the most important decision of his lifetime. So far as
I have been able to discover, there are only four basic alternatives:

1. DROP OUT. Anyone who takes *Ramparts* seriously
might think that this solution was invented only yesterday by the
Reverend Timothy Leary, and that it can be practiced successfully only in Haight-Ashbury or Greenwich Village, with the
aid of LSD or some other reality-blunting drug. In fact, it is one
of the oldest expedients, and it can be practiced anywhere, at
any age, and with or without the use of hallucinogens. It always
has been the strategy of choice for people who find the world
too brutal and too complex to be endured. Its notable practitioners include many Hindu mystics, certain monastic orders dating
from the early years of Christianity, several Buddhist sects, and
the skid-row bums slumped on the curb with a pint of cheap
wine. The hermit of Mount Athos and the millionaire recluse in
his Caribbean hideaway are both dropouts. So were Diogenes
and Lao-tse. So too is the suburban matron whose life centers
on her daily bridge game and a jug of martinis.

This way of life is, by definition, parasitic. In one way or another, its practitioners batten on the society which they scorn, and in which they refuse to take any responsibility. Some of us (the Squares) find this distasteful—an undignified kind of life, like that of a leech or a kept woman. But for the poor in spirit, with low levels of both energy and pride, it may be the least intolerable choice available.

2. FLEE. This strategy also has ancient antecedents. Ever since civilization began, certain individuals have tried to run away from it, in hopes of finding a simpler, more pastoral, and more peaceful life. Unlike the dropouts, they are not parasites. They are willing to support themselves, and to contribute something to the general community—but they simply don't like the environment of civilization: that is, the city, with all its ugliness and tension.

The joy of simple life among the noble savages has been celebrated by eloquent propagandists, from Vergil to Rousseau. Their precepts have been followed by people as diverse as Daniel Boone and Gauguin. When I was twenty-one, at a time when American society seemed hopelessly bogged down in the miseries of the Depression, I attempted it myself. I applied for a job on an Australian ranch, and if I had been accepted I might be herding sheep today—no doubt a happier and healthier man.

The trouble with this solution is that it no longer is practical on a large scale. Our planet, unfortunately, is running out of noble savages and unsullied landscapes; except for the polar regions, the frontiers are gone. A few gentlemen farmers with plenty of money can still escape to the bucolic life—but in general the stream of migration is flowing the other way. . . .

3. PLOT A REVOLUTION. This strategy always is popular among those who have no patience with the tedious workings of the democratic process, or who believe that basic institutions can be changed only by force. It attracts some of the more active and idealistic young people of every generation. To them it offers a romantic appeal, usually symbolized by some dashing and charismatic figure—a Byron, a Garibaldi, a Trotsky, or a Che Guevara. It has the even greater appeal of simplicity: "Since this society is hopelessly bad, let's smash it and build something better on the ruins." And to anybody with strong Oedipal feelings it provides the special delight of defying the Establishment—that stuffy collection of father-figures whom we all find it so easy to hate.

Some of my best friends have been revolutionists, and a few of them have led reasonably satisfying lives. These are the ones whose revolutions did not come off; they have been able to keep on cheerfully plotting their holocausts right into their senescence. Others died young, in prison or on the barricades. But the most unfortunate are those whose revolutions succeeded—men like Djilas and Trotsky. They lived, in bitter disillusionment, to see the Establishment they had overthrown replaced by a new one, just as hard-faced and stuffy.

I am not, of course, suggesting that revolutions accomplish nothing. Some clearly do change things for the better, as in Mexico and (in spite of Djilas' unhappiness) in Yugoslavia. Elsewhere, as in Algeria and in Ghana during Nkrumah's reign, the change clearly was for the worse. My point is merely that the idealists who make the revolution are bound to be disappointed in either case. For at best their victory never dawns on the shining new world they had dreamed of, cleansed of all human meanness. Instead it dawns on a familiar, workaday place, still in need of groceries and sewage disposal. The revolutionary state, under whatever political label, has to be run—not by violent romantics—but by experts in marketing, sanitary engineering, and the management of bureaucracies. For the Byrons among us, this discovery is a fate worse than death.

Fortunately the young revolutionists in today's America are safe from such a fate. This government simply is not going to be overthrown by violence, within the foreseeable future. Many recruits of the New Left are unwilling to believe this—and since they can't be bothered to study the history of revolutionary movements, they probably are beyond argument. . . .

So long as they limit themselves to demonstrating and wearing buttons, they will be tolerated. But if they should ever become a real nuisance—if they should attempt enough violence to seriously disrupt the life of the country—then the community will suppress them, quickly and harshly. If that happens, a lot of other people will get suppressed at the same time, and many of the most hopeful impulses in American society will be drowned under a new wave of McCarthyism. For the rebels who understand this—the idealists who are determined to remake society, but who seek a more practical method than armed revolution—there remains one more alternative:

4. TRY TO CHANGE THE WORLD GRADUALLY, ONE CLOD AT A TIME. At first glance, this course is far from inviting. It lacks glamour. It promises no quick results. It depends on the exasperating and uncertain instruments of persuasion and democratic decision-making. It demands patience, always in short supply among the young. About all that can be said for it is that it sometimes works—that in this particular time and place it offers a better chance for remedying some of the world's outrages than any other available strategy. . . .

Thirty-five years ago, for example, the generation graduating from college also found the world in a mess. The economic machinery had broken down almost everywhere; in this country nearly a quarter of the population was out of work. Hideous political movements were burgeoning in Europe and Asia. A major war seemed all too likely. As a college newspaper editor at that time, I protested against this just as vehemently as student activists are protesting today. I pointed out to my parents' generation, with what I hoped was burning eloquence, that war was insane and inhuman—and that it was stupid to close down factories when people were starving. The doddering old folks who ran the country obviously were bunglers. If they would just step aside, we youngsters would soon straighten things out.

Oddly enough, something like that actually happened. The generation which came of age in the 'thirties did get the national economy working again—not by revolution, which was widely recommended by the advanced thinkers of the time, but by slow, pragmatic tinkering. As a consequence, though poverty has not yet disappeared, it has been shrinking dramatically for the last three decades. The same generation demonstrated, at considerable cost, that fascism was not the wave of the future. It even created diplomatic machinery for working out peaceful settlements of international disputes. It is true that this machinery has operated only moderately well; but it has forestalled any major war for nearly thirty years—no trivial achievement in the light of earlier history.

At the same time, my generation was discovering that reforming the world is a little like fighting a military campaign in the Apennines: as soon as you capture one mountain range, another one looms just ahead. As the big problems of the 'thirties were brought under some kind of rough control, new problems took their place—the unprecedented problems of an affluent society, of racial justice, of keeping our cities from becoming uninhabitable, of coping with war in unfamiliar guises. Most disturbing of all was our discovery of the population explosion. It dawned on us rather suddenly that the number of passengers on the small space-ship we inhabit is doubling about every forty years —and that already there aren't enough seats to go around. So long as the earth's population keeps growing at this cancerous rate, all of the other problems appear virtually insoluble. Our cities will continue to become more crowded and noisome. The landscape will get more cluttered, the air and water even dirtier. The quality of life is likely to become steadily worse for everybody. And warfare on a rising scale seems inevitable, if too many bodies have to struggle for ever-dwindling shares of food and living space.

So [the young] generation has a formidable job on its hands. But not, I think, an insuperable one. On the evidence of the past, it can be handled in the same way that hard problems have been coped with before—piecemeal, pragmatically, by the dogged efforts of many people. The victories will be unspectacular: perhaps tomorrow the discovery of a cheaper and more reliable method of birth control; next year the development of a high-yield strain of rice. The real heroes will not be revolutionary demagogues, but the obscure teachers who work out better ways to train underprivileged children . . . the businessmen who manage to upgrade unskilled Negro workers . . . the politicians who devise new institutions to govern our metropolitan areas . . . the journalists who persuade a reluctant citizenry that change not only is necessary, but inescapable.

These individual efforts may add up to a surprising sum of accomplishment. For the arriving generation, from what I have seen of it, shows more potential than its predecessors. It is healthier and better educated. It is more idealistic—that is, more willing to work for the common good, rather than for purely selfish ends. If it is (fortunately) pretty skeptical, it certainly is not complacent.

Provided that a reasonable number of this generation choose the fourth strategy, they probably will accomplish more than they now expect. They can't be sure, of course. As they get on with the job, in their step-by-step fashion, they can be sure of only two things. First, that they will get no help from the dropouts, and precious little from the escapees and the professional revolutionists. Second, that about twenty-five years from now they will be upbraided by their children because they have not done enough, and because they will have failed to foresee the arising problems of the next century.

HENRY MILLER
(Interviewed by David Dury)

sex goes public

A new tyranny, a tyranny of the flesh. . . . everyone's having sex . . . but it's [often] so joyless [and] there's no . . . *adoration!*

QUESTION: Are you bored with sex?

ANSWER: One can't get bored with sex. But one is bored with making such a tremendous issue of it. This constant harping on sex all the time is so immature, not just sexually, but socially and politically. It's as though we're a race of adolescents.

Q: But many people would say that you're the one who harps on it in your books.

A: I harped on trying to get at the whole truth of one man: myself. Sex was a big part of that, but no matter how you add it up, in pages or print or words or volumes, it was only a part. It just happened that this was the part that had shock value.

Q: And now you're tired of the shock and the harping?

A: I am absolutely sick of it, and sick of the whole American approach to it, and sick of the way this sexual revolution is going. . . .

Q: Don't you think that all this talk about sex is at least better than the ignorance and secrecy we used to have?

A: Anything's better than that. There's finally been a tremendous change in our attitudes and America is more daring in the matter of sex and expression about it, therefore more honest, which is all to the good and long overdue. But because in the past we have been so goddamned backward about sex, this revo-

lution is causing sex to become a preoccupation. This I find sad,
and even deplorable in many ways. I sometimes wonder if we
can even truthfully call it a revolution.

Q: What would you call it?

A: An adolescent rebellion! And one, if I may say, that is
going the way of most adolescent rebellions—right into a new
status quo, a new tyranny, a tyranny of the flesh.

Q: But isn't the usual way out of suppression to go berserk
at first and then finally balance out?

A: Yes, but we're far from balanced. Because now you've
got the whole *system* getting in on the act. What once was more
or less the opposition is finding ways to exploit the sexual revolution by marketing and advertising. After all, this tyranny of
the flesh reduces the whole thing to purely material terms, which
fits right in with our age-old problem, our exaggerated emphasis
on material things. This may have helped our progress in some
areas, but it's certainly the source of most of our shortcomings,
too, which are unfortunately in crucial areas of the nonmaterial.

Q: So sex becomes a commodity; now that there's more openness.

A: Hell, *people* are becoming commodities, especially
women. Sex is the newest status symbol, another asset you need
to be sophisticated. I can judge only from my own circumscribed
circle, the people I know, what I read, and all the letters and
conversations with readers who tell me their most intimate secrets. But I'm sure that by now Americans are probably having
more sex than anybody. They're certainly devoting more time to
the subject than anywhere I know of. And there's promiscuity
everywhere in this country. But I don't sense the passion and
vitality of sex. It's not in the air here, as it is, say, in France.
Here it's more like everyone's trying to prove a point.

Q: But it's still better than it was in your time, in the Twenties and Thirties, isn't it?

A: There's more quantity, more frequency, sure. . . . During
my time, the girls were so shut in, and you were always being
watched. Now everybody's free about sex, but they're shut in in

other ways. In the old days the great difference was that when we were committing these—What are they calling them? Adulteries? Fornications? Illicit sex? Ridiculous words! When we did it, we did it! We didn't sit around and talk about it first, intellectualize it. There was always pleasure involved. I mean, great fun! For everybody! Joy, do you see? That's the big difference, that element of joy! Joy in sex! You'd have to be a blind man not to see it. In my time, either they weren't having *any* sex because of too much guilt, or they were having wonderfully joyous sex. Now everyone's having sex, the guilty ones probably more than anyone—but it's so joyless, so much of it.

Q: The way you depicted it in your books like *Sexus* and *Capricorn*, was that an accurate picture of the way it was?

A: Sure, but I must say that when I started out and wrote these books which caused such a turmoil about sex, I never thought of myself as an exponent of sex, a sexologist, a professor of that kind of thing, no! With me it was all incidental, like eating and drinking, but an important part of a much bigger thing, a much bigger freedom. I don't think it was ever my aim to make sex itself an important issue. It was always more the *total liberation* of oneself that I was concerned with, not just sexual liberation alone.

Q: Then do you think this sexual revolution is premature?

A: I don't know about premature, but they can never expect to be truly free in sex until they've liberated themselves in the larger perspective. This new standard may be a thrill to some at first, but in the long run it will be just as insufficient and ruinous as the old standard. What we never get at is the most important goal in life. It's what I call spiritual liberation, and that's a religious thing. Which doesn't have anything to do with churches. It's beyond any church! At bottom, it's really like awakening in the true sense, yes, awakening, *spiritual awakening, spiritual liberation!* How can they so consistently, so completely miss that over and over again? It reminds me of the famous saying of the Marquis de Sade just when the Bastille was being torn down and he was being freed at last, a glorious mo-

ment for him, and then he says such a classic thing—he says,
"Français, encore un tout petit effort. . . ." Do you see it? He's
saying, "That's fine, Frenchmen, now just one more little effort!"
And so it is with this business of the sexual revolution, there's
one more little effort needed for Americans to be really free people, and that is *the* effort. Sexual freedom and the effort toward
that should only be one aspect of a movement toward much
larger freedom, to think and act freely and creatively, in every
domain! Just as with all the other freedom movements or revolutions, the civil-rights question, the teen-age thing, the anti-war
protests, the academic-freedom fight—all of it is fine but ultimately pointless if they're not each tied in toward a total spiritual freedom and awakening.

Q: How do you think we can do that?

A: By concentrating only on the big issues and forgetting all
the petty trivia.

Q: Do you consider sex without love to be harmful?

A: There's nothing wrong with sex without love. But much
more is needed. . . . A man has to fall in love. He has to want
something more of the woman and see more in her than an object
to be used. Though I've talked about sex without love, it never
was my thought that this is the supreme goal. In the final analysis, for man or woman, an extended life of loveless sex will be
ruinous, it ruins the psychic health.

Q: What exactly do you think men are missing in the way
they relate to women sexually now?

A: They're missing a lot of things. For one, there's no adoration for women! Now there's another word I would like to emphasize—*adoration!* Where do we have *any* adoration today in
our talk about women and sex? I believe in adoration, not only
in relation to women, but in relation to men as well, where the
man above you is someone you adore and admire and want to
emulate, the adoration for a master. This is completely lost in
our society today. Instead of adoration for women, men now
seem to be just always on the chase. . . .

Q: What about the change in the roles of the sexes that is ac-

companing the changing standards—where the female is gain-
ing more equality and even self-sufficiency? Is this bringing
things more in line with your ideals?

A: It should if the woman doesn't become too aggressive, too
much of the demanding bitch. If she remains the seductress, all
this development could make her that much better *vis-à-vis* the
male. I think the woman derives a lot from her submissiveness,
but only if she has a lot to give and is giving voluntarily, not
because she's dependent or dominated. But the female situation is so complex that she needs to be almost a little bit of each
of these things we talk about. Except for the bitch! I mean, it's
similar to her having to be mistress, lover, wife, mother, all
rolled into one. I can appreciate the woman's role in life and her
whole place in the system of things.

Q: And men?

A: Well, the whole thing about male supremacy has always
been a myth, an illusion from the start. You might say we possessed the strength to put ourselves in seemingly superior positions, as rulers, and we can dominate in that way. Which is sort
of a pseudo-masculinity. But there never were any masters of
their own fates anyway. Where in the hell are they, I'd like to
know. Even the great heroes of history are rather ridiculous in
many ways, aren't they? So this delusion about the almighty
male is being shattered now, with the individual becoming so
much less important in a worldly way. Which should be another
step toward more honesty between the sexes, if the male will
face it and concentrate on mastering himself. Anyone who truly
knows male and female knows that it's the woman who is always
the deciding factor. The man only makes a show. . . .

Q: You never did care much for the idea of the dominant
male, did you?

A: I never cared for any kind of domination. There's no future in it. You can never really dominate another person, another sex, another country. Who's the worse off, the master or
the slave? I say the master. He gets it in the end from the slave,
one way or another. Just as man has gotten it from woman, as

revenge for subjugating her. She has bent his whole psyche, twisted his outlook on life.

Q: That sounds a little like "momism," doesn't it?

A: Maybe so. Except I think men deserve it. I feel sorry only for later generations who pay for the sins of their forefathers. Your generation, you're innocent, but guilty by inheritance. It's up to you to change it. And for your own good—because a woman can't develop as a person if she's being subjugated. It either saps her, or she wastes too much energy in devious retaliation.

Q: The old pretension that a sexual relationship is supposed to lead to marriage has almost vanished. Is this a healthy sign?

A: Why, sure. It always was a very phony terminology anyway. Out of our dictionary of puritanism. I think any of these new tendencies which are leaning toward a more realistic approach to sex or marriage, and to life, are very healthy signs. . . .

Q: Then you approve of the growing trend to living together as husband and wife without going through the legal proceedings, at least not until there are children involved?

A: Oh, yes. . . . Many of our laws long have been obsolete and ridiculous. Intelligent people don't regulate their lives by outmoded laws. After all, if we try to define what a real marriage is, isn't it basically a completely voluntary union? If it's real, there should be no need to enforce it . . . legally. . . . Marriages are made in heaven, and they are unmade in heaven, and then they are over! They last only as long as there is beauty in them, a validity and a reality to them. The important consideration should be to see that the children are taken care of. There's less need now for marriage than ever, and the family itself is so broken, practically disintegrated as an institution. But the adult problems are nothing compared to the damage being done to children. It's sad! So sad that it gets to be laughable when you read all these pompous articles by sociologists and child psychiatrists saying that what children need is love! That's wonderful, but how are they going to get it from these imbeciles who are their parents, who don't even know the meaning of the word love, who don't show any love, even to each other or to mankind in general? Whether the family stays together or not, the children are still suffering. More true attention should be devoted to them. So it's a great big question, but again it brings us back to this problem of spiritual lethargy. . . .

Q: Do you think the erotic content of your books still speaks to young people?

A: I think there will always be a response from young people because the books are new to them; each new crop of youngsters coming up gets the impact fresh. . . .

Q: How do you feel about the way the sexual revolution is being reflected in the arts, in novels, movies, the theatre?

A: My impression is that there's a great deal more pornography today . . . and a great deal less obscenity. Pornography is the roundabout, a leering or lecherous disguise which only adds to the murk; but obscenity—even though it may offend because of its frankness—is forthright, the whole truth, coming out with it cold, shocking if necessary. Obscenity is cleansing, because whenever a taboo is broken, something vitalizing happens, another step toward greater truth and honesty and openness. But pornography exploits the taboo and just serves to reinforce it.

Q: And there's more of the latter?

A: That's the way it looks to me. There also seems to be a lot of cuteness about sex in all the arts too. This might be amusing in a sexually healthy society, but in one that's still basically sick, it's repulsive. The only forthrightness I've seen is devoted to all these perverse and sadistic books and films and plays. They're being fairly straightforward in what they're doing, these more abnormal people. But what are they doing? They're dealing with a very limited area, you know, perversions and dope and all the rest of it. I'm not condemning them. I was just never interested in perversion or sadism of any kind. We're just different types, myself I mean, and someone like Burroughs or Genêt.

Q: Do you see any hope on the literary horizon then, either in sex or the spiritual liberation you speak of?

A: No, I sure don't. Too much is derivative. There's nothing new being said. It's kind of a masturbation: they're not going beyond what has already been done. A few writers broke the ice, giving today's writers the liberty to express themselves. But they're not doing anything new with this liberty. They should be finding new liberations in a thousand different ways, new ways! What's the good of writing more sex novels? They have their place, and always will. But to do it because it's the thing to do, it's the fashion, it's the mode—I deplore that.

More than anything else, I'd like to see someone throw a bomb in the spiritual realm! Open us up that way! Yes! There you are! That's what's needed now, a spiritual explosion! We don't need to read anymore about sex! We're already surfeited with this. The sexual revolution is a *fait accompli,* an accomplished thing. We're not going to retrogress. . . . The point is, there are grandiose problems to be solved, and to be written about, instead of continually writing either about sex or about sadism and masochism and spiritual meanness. Let's tackle the new things! Let's quit telling sad old stories or merely entertaining one another. Let's get going! . . . Everything seems so childish. . . . In magazines, for example, one feels insulted by this "girlie" approach, the nudes they display, children, one-dimensional playthings, mannequins, beautiful and well appointed, but I don't think they're erotic at all, except maybe for teen-agers. And the other crap, the stories, the cartoons, this sex-as-a-commodity idea we talked about . . . it's more for a twelve-year-old. Once in a while there's some worthy editorial writing, but the bulk of even the most sophisticated magazines of this type is pretty shallow. Some say my female characters weren't fully depicted; well, look at *their* depiction of women, purely physical, and they're not supposed to be just picture magazines, so that's no excuse. That's a reverse sort of puritanism, isn't it? Glorifying the female body, but ignoring or denying her as a person. The whole peep-show approach is meant for adolescents from sixteen to sixty, I think. But it's very revelatory. Their attitude is true to the contemporary adolescent reality all around us. Because we aren't mature, the audience isn't mature, so the product is immature. It's too bad publishers can't lead, instead of following like this. But of course when we talk about better approaches, there are always the obstacles that have to be torn down first, the vested interests, the bourgeoisie, the church.

Q: How would you compare the *cool sex* of today's youth with the *metaphysical sex* you talked about so often in your books?

A: I must tell you that the word *cool* is a word I don't like. To play it cool, to be cool, to cool it. The use of that word goes against me. It already has in it the opposite of passion. It means cunning, wise, clever, detached—above all, detached! I'm all for attachment, involvement . . . and the misery resulting from it.

Q: How about all these dance crazes—frug, watusi, jerk?

A: What I call the nonsexual dances, where you stand apart and gyrate, or masturbate. This to me is a passing phenomenon. I only feel sorry that they're dancing apart. Savages can do it wonderfully, but savages make it very sexual. Whereas here it seems just athletic, gymnastics, you don't feel anything erotic. And it seems so narcissistic and egocentric in a bad sort of way. It's like the atom splitting, a break in the polarity; instead of coming together, they're going apart. It's just more evidence of isolation and alienation. In my time, dancing was what you might call a good excuse for sex with your clothes on, that's what dancing was then! The great dance halls on Broadway—O my God!—the lights were dim, the bands were marvelous. And that's all anybody was doing then, this true sex dance, the element of sex was the strongest part of it. Now dancing is almost asexual, it's so palsy-walsy. I've watched my kids doing it. Two men could be dancing these things.

Q: How have you raised your kids? . . . If you forced some moral code on them, they'd just waste a lot of time rebelling against it, is that it?

A: Yes, probably so. I like to keep it as natural as possible in such an unnatural world as this is.

Q: You don't feel as if you've ever given them any guidance about good and bad?

A: Not much. I've never had to. They live their lives and I watch them. Now they're teen-agers, caught up in this sexual revolution themselves. And they're not doing too badly. The only kind of training I ever consciously set out to give them is to awaken them to spiritual values, to think more clearly, to think above all the petty issues of the day—that's what I call most of these problems we're fighting about today, petty problems, ignoble ones! I try to get them to think about life itself.

Q: What about when they come to you with questions?

A: I don't advise, unless I am asked a lot of serious questions or one very blunt direct question. Then I only say, this is what I think, or this is what I would do, this is the way I think it should be done, or how life should be approached. But I'm not necessarily saying that you have to accept what I say as the final answer. I feel that people have to find their own answers anyway.

KATHERINE ANNE PORTER

sex and love: then and now

In *my* time there was . . . a determined effort to identify—or at least confuse—sex with love.

from an interview with roy newquist

The yeh-yeh, the jazz, the hoodlum manners, the tight jeans, all the dreadful little girls who go about looking like Cinderella ten minutes before she was hauled out of the ashes. They were all over France and Italy . . . with boys to match. You want to tell them: "For God's sake, go comb your hair.". . .

I know how bright they are, really, and how good-looking— taller, in better health, in every way better off than we were— and I don't understand how they consent to be so ugly and, worse than that, like tramps. But this is not only of today I am speaking; I'm referring to things I began to notice thirty-five years ago, when I gave up wearing slacks because of the kind of woman I saw wearing them. It isn't any newer than this pornographic-literature thing. And heaven knows pornography isn't new. . . .

Today's youngsters know far too *much* about sex far too early, and it has destroyed something that was rather nice. God knows I'm not for all moonlight and roses—though youngsters naturally have a lot of this in their makeup. But when I was a girl, a girl and a boy together at a party didn't take their minds off each other for one split second, yet all we could do was look at each other. But oh, what a lot we got from those looks. Then, too, the fact that I was instructed to hold off this wild man gave him such importance. He was *dangerous*, don't you see, and it set him up no end.

But they have destroyed something that ought to exist in sex. God knows it's an animal instinct; but we are not four-footed creatures, and when it's debased, we're destroying something profound in human nature. Today's children know so much about sex they can dance without touching each other—narcissistically, by themselves, a ritual that has nothing to do with real dancing. Dancing should provide great pleasure, based on sexual attraction, not on boredom; on attention to one another, not preoccupation with self. . . .

I was brought up in the generation that Miss Stein described as "lost," but I'll be damned if ever I was lost. I always knew where I was. I sometimes wondered how I was going to get out of it, but I knew where I was and how I had got there. I don't think we were lost, straying off somewhere like witless children in the woods; we merely had to work at finding our right way.

Perhaps we represented the real break with the nineteenth century. That century, in very important ways, was an appalling fraud, and we were nurtured on the Victorians, and it took us a while to realize what stuffed shirts they were on the whole—with what strange giant geniuses, like civic monuments!—and to recognize our own world and our own talents.

Look back, now, at the giants of our age, starting with Henry James and Hardy, then Yeats and Joyce and T. S. Eliot, then our whole group of wonderful poets, like Robert Penn Warren and John Crowe Ransom, Wallace Stevens, Allen Tate, Marianne Moore—oh, many! People like that were very grand, and I see some others coming up, now, who are going to last. But we're not the future; we can't judge. We'll have to judge as well as we can, however, to see that the splendid talents of our day aren't neglected or crushed or driven to the wall. . . .

from "letters to my nephew"

Times do change and vocabularies change, too, but in *my* time there was among certain advanced spirits a determined effort to identify—or at least confuse—sex with love; that is, to disprove the old theological doctrine that sex took place entirely below the belt, and love entirely above it. Somewhere in the region of the heart, and if you worked at it, it could sometimes get as high as the brain. Never the twain could meet, of course, unless you were a moral acrobat, which was reprehensible. As I say, the young pioneers set out to disprove this dirty doctrine in two different directions, or schools: First, the most popular, that sex is *all*, just plain sex undiluted by any piffling notions about spiritual overtones, or even just romantic glow—a good hearty low roll in the hay without getting "involved" was the best, perhaps the only, purifying thing in life. The extremists went so far as to say, and claim, they practiced wallows only with total strangers, so that no slag of personal attachment could get into the pure gold of sex. Hence a lot of young women taking up with Italian bootleggers and Brooklyn gangsters, and getting smacked in the eye more than once.

Then of course, not to give only the gloomy side, there were those of this school who picked up with strangers, and wallowed so successfully that in a few days, or weeks, or months, they were setting the alarm clock together to keep an early date at the marriage bureau.

The second school still believed in love: love that began perhaps in the heart, all tender feelings and warm hopes, worked itself up to the head in a community of ideas, and finally got round to exploring the cellar, but only incidentally. That is to say, True Love included Sex, naturally, but it got its innings only after careful preparation in the higher departments of life. Some of these fanatics actually waited until they were married to sleep together, but this was considered very dangerous, because sometimes, when everything else was perfect, sex the louse would be tried and found wanting. It was, therefore, much more sensible to have a few rehearsals beforehand.

But it seemed to me, as time blundered on, that the Foul Sex school was winning because it simply seemed to be more fun. At least in general the male sort preferred it. They seemed to be a touch schizophrenic on that topic, though it is only fair to say the young women had some strange reservations, too. I have heard more than one of that long-vanished generation of liberated young women say she didn't want to marry, but would like to have a baby, just for the experience. A few of them did it, too. A great error, as they realized quickly. The men remained a touch divided between behavior suitable to the vanguard, and certain old-fashioned notions about relations between the sexes. They went on rather furtively dividing girls into the kind they respected, and the other kind. I confess I translated this as meaning the kind they didn't want to sleep with, and the other kind. Also, through some natural perversity of the male, they clung to the notion that they should marry the kind they respect, on the grounds (in other days at least, and I suspect even now) that a woman fit to be a wife and mother should never have any fun thataway. Look at all these horrible little books giving advice on technical procedures and assuring all parties that bed can be wonderful if only the subjects can get rid of their inhibitions and practice a bag of new tricks. I have never read one—the table of contents in the advertisements throw me off, somehow. . . .

There is a third school, to which I long adhered. . . . This is the Stroke of Lightning (*coup de foudre*) or "love at first sight and the hell with theories" school. In this, one beholds (and the circumstances may be of the most ordinary, the time any hour, the place anywhere, the only fixed rule being that it must happen with absolute suddenness, when one is thinking of something, almost anything else) ; an Object irrevocably becomes a Subject— in my case, of course, male—which is instantly transfigured with a light of such blinding brilliance all natural attributes disappear and are replaced by those usually associated with archangels at least. They are beautiful, flawless in temperament, witty, intelligent, charming, of such infinite grace, sympathy, and courage, I always wondered how they could have come from such absurdly inappropriate families. I notice I have fallen into the plural in describing this paragon. It is just as well. The meeting between us is like an exchange of signals with lightning, they also seeing in me whatever improbable qualities they wish me to have. It is a disaster, in fact. We are in love and while it lasts—

It is no good going into details, for while it lasts there simply aren't any. And when it is over, it is over. And when I have recovered from the shock, and sorted out the damage and put my mangled life in order, I can then begin to remember what really happened. It is probably the silliest kind of love there is, but I'm glad I had it. I'm glad there were times when I saw human beings at their best, for I don't think by any means that I lent them all their radiance . . . it was there ready to be brought out by someone who loved them. It is still there, it may have shone out again if they were ever loved like that again. It is just that I knew them better than anyone else for a little while, they showed me a different face because they knew I could really see it—and no matter what came of it, I remember and I never deny what I saw.

ROBERT COLES

---

sex and students

> If I wear a beard and a girl I love stays
> in my room all night . . . I'm a beatnik and in a
> state of moral decline. If I shave and go
> to a whorehouse, buy stocks on the South
> African exchange . . . and sign up for the
> CIA . . . my behavior is unquestioned.

What is happening up there? Are they still debating how long women can stay in the dormitories as though the fate of the world rests on the outcome? Is the college paper filled with the same old words from the same old speeches: morality, integrity, decency, honor? I can hardly believe it sometimes. . . .

I don't know whether I'm ready to face that business again: the pompous, self-righteous officials, noisy with worry about orgasms in young people but discreetly silent when we are sent off to war to kill or be killed; full of reminders about how moral we must be, and responsible to others, not just ourselves, but without a word of concern about the immorality of the slums next door or the dishonest intrigue we've practiced in the Caribbean or elsewhere. They go so very easily from our sexual habits to the broadest conclusions about our honor and our generation's character, but they don't welcome a look at their honor. . . .

If I wear a beard and a girl I love stays in my room all night and I sleep with her, I'm a beatnik and in a state of moral decline. If I shave and go to a whorehouse, buys stocks on the South African exchange that net me a large profit, and sign up for the CIA when I graduate from college, my behavior is unquestioned and my integrity assumed.

Yes, he [was] a civil rights worker in the South, facing continual danger, and thus under a strain. . . . He is against exploitation of any kind—racial, social and economic, or sexual. As he put it: "Segregation and the double standard in sex smack of the same abuse of people. Neither one bothers 'good, decent people' as much as the idea that college students are having sex, or demonstrating, or demanding a revision of courses, or a voice in who teaches them. We're immature and demanding, they say. We'll grow up, they reassure themselves. What they mean by grow up is give up—to sell out, acquiesce and morally die.". . .

One of [his charges] was that in his college, located somewhere between Berkeley and Cambridge, the psychiatrists joined company with the deans to enforce an antique social code by offering two particularly galling contributions of their very own: the ability to obtain information from troubled and trusting students, then offer it shamelessly to administrative officials, and the surprisingly contagious talent of labeling "sick" or "immature" what is new, different or a challenge to the status quo.

A committee of psychiatrists has tried to confront some of the issues brought up, and to some extent caused by, such young men. . . .* What they know best they say most clearly: the college student's sexual life is but another phase in a progressive development of emotional and sexual feelings, the two being rather thoroughly entwined. Consequently, a youth's uncertain sexuality does not struggle for definition without affecting the rest of his life. He is likely to demonstrate highly fluctuating attitudes toward his contemporaries and elders as well as toward sex, so that what is done may not yet be fully enjoyed and what is said or even assertively proclaimed may not necessarily be quite wanted "deep down.". . .

During their study [the authors] found no institution that "published or printed materials that explicitly stated its views toward sexual conduct on the campus." The American student everywhere must deal with lack of candor and evasiveness, with

* *Sex and the College Student,* Group for the Advancement of Psychiatry (Atheneum).

rules all too full of rhetoric, pretentious and fake piety, double talk, innuendo and the kind of picayunish, captious mind that in one college handbook defined a date as "being in the presence of a boy for fifteen minutes." Here is some more from colleges: "coeducation while sunbathing is not permitted"; not only that, but "for every minute that a student is late she will come in five minutes early on the Saturday following her infraction." As the authors explain, with effectively subdued embarrassment, such rules are "almost mandatory in state universities" because parents are voters and have "power to influence the operation of the university."

Under those conditions the sexual issues that commonly face college authorities are hardly likely to receive sensible or fair consideration. . . . The doctors say that a student's privacy should be established, but not overdone. (Some students are not ready for it and would genuinely fear the possibilities it enables or provokes.) As for sex: when "privately practiced with appropriate attention to the sensitivities of other people [it] should not be the direct concern of the administration." (The problem is, however, that there are some "other people" whose sensitivities seem limitless, among them the college administrators themselves.)

Cautiously [the authors] seem to favor making contraceptive information available to students; advising and counseling them on pregnancy and abortion rather than preaching to them or invoking outmoded or inhumane laws upon them; looking at homosexuality as an inevitable, though passing, problem in most youths, and in any event not one solved by anxious or hysterical prurience or vengeance; and, finally, offering sex education because it is useful, but not because it will solve problems that are developmental and emotional, hence resistant to the persuasions of logic and fact. . . .

Since [the authors] are college psychiatrists, it can be assumed that they know their opponents, some probably unappeased even by the following tactful prose: "A certain amount of freedom in the area of student social and sexual interaction with the opposite sex is now taken for granted within limits of personal integrity and public decency." Again, private homosexuality "need not become" the administration's concern. The authors urge "counseling rather than discipline." Freud, who did not deny himself the responsibility of moral indignation, but also failed to achieve any great success in the Viennese academic and medical world, wrote as follows: "It is a great injustice to persecute homosexuality as a crime—and a cruelty, too."

The book gingerly skirts problems very much related to its concern: those of censorship, civil rights and civil liberties, the relationship of class structure to sexual practices and norms, the complicated and at times impossible position of psychiatrists as doctors in danger of becoming negotiators, informers, or practitioners of a kind of military psychiatry. Though the authors have alluded to some of these matters, the unrest in some of our colleges may inevitably require another level of analysis: more sharply critical, more bluntly worded, perhaps less welcome to some people; and for those reasons more decisive.

HARRIET VAN HORNE

the sexual revolution —in living color

Is there any force in the world more fraught with danger?

. . . Television has been as preoccupied with sex as a bridegroom. A thoroughly modern bridegroom, one must add, whose mood is less romantic than clinical. Cool is the word— and faintly obsessive. In the prime evening hours, when entire families are sure to be watching, we have had numberless documentaries focusing on sex. Sex on the campus, sex in the high schools, sex in Sweden, in Las Vegas, in slum areas. Sex by appointment, sex as it is practiced in Protestant, Catholic and Jewish boudoirs. Sex with the pill and sex without it.

The pill, three housewives agreed on a recent TV seminar, has put the magic back into their marriages. They displayed no shyness in answering the question, "Why?" Old-fashioned contraceptives, said one, were a bore and a bother. "By the time I'd made all the preparations," she added, "he'd have fallen asleep." Listening to this trio . . . some viewers may suddenly have longed for the tender grace of a day that is dead. And for the old-fashioned sentiment that held certain matters too sacred for public discussion. . . . The Puritan ethic, writes a sociologist, has become the "hang-loose ethic."

Perhaps because I am closer to television than to other mass media, I have had my eyes opened to some new social patterns that seem to me faintly disturbing. And I am haunted by a particular young girl—a pathetic sort, really—who turns up on my small screen much too often.

She's about nineteen, I'd guess, with slattern hair, lemur eyes, mini-skirt and pale, textured stockings that give her legs the airy grace of tree stumps. Her knees are lumpy, and you feel positive her nails are gnawed to the quick. In the slurred diction that goes with the dress, the times and the hang-loose ethic, this wanton lass, whom I shall refer to hereafter as "the irrelevant virgin," faces the camera and tells us, "I think that for a man the question of a girl's virginity is, well, kinda irrelevant. I mean—well, it's the *totality* of a girl's personality that really hangs him up—y'know?"

. . . Be she an unwed mother in the slums or an accommodating miss from the typing pool, sex is plainly her hang-up. And there's that awful phrase again! "We adults are frightfully hung up on sex," said Dr. Mary Calderone in a TV study called "Sex in the Sixties.". . . Brisk, smiling, handsome, Dr. Calderone . . . is nothing if not candid. "We're seeing an explosion of sexual expression," she said, fairly abeam over the idea. "It's not necessarily the in-bed expression, but in all our communications media—in all our waking thoughts, waking music, waking reading, there's this tremendous explosion, almost an obsession with sex. The *genital* aspects of sex."

On this same program a tweedy, pipe-smoking psychologist remarked, "Kids aren't scared of sex any more." The statement seemed to give him pleasure. He offered it much as an epidemiologist might say, "Yes, thank God, we've finally licked polio.". . .

Not content with merely holding up a mirror to life, television often adjusts the view in the mirror to its own sensational purposes. In "Sex in the Sixties" we had the by-now inevitable views of topless waitresses, nude girlie shows in Las Vegas and the marquees of New York's Forty-Second Street grind houses. Now, do such scenes really contribute to public understanding of the new sexual uproar? We are all aware that these signs of the times exist. To speak bluntly, we are fed up to the eyes with all this pseudoscientific, pseudosociological voyeurism on the part of TV's documentarians.

What we who are a few years removed from campus revelry—
and a few light-years from nude girlie shows—wish TV would
explore is the reason *behind* this sexual revolution. What caused
it? And how much damage has it done youthful, still-plastic
personalities?

It isn't enough to tick off the obvious changes in American
life, as if each one set off shock waves, ending always in the
boudoir. We concede many changes have come about in consequence of: higher education for women, higher incomes, urban-
ization, creeping slums, the poor quality of our public schools,
the birth-control pill, the decline in parental and church authority. But shouldn't we also mention the increasing vulgarization of sex by the mass media and the wanton misreading of
Freud's dicta on the dangers of repression? (The truth is that
Dr. Freud was a conventional, highly moral, happily married
man.)

Unmarried sex, as all those TV programs are at pains to tell
us, is no longer premarital or extramarital sex. It is simply sex
for its own sake. It is sexual pleasure without sexual responsibility. And a school of false prophets and bogus scientists has
hailed these developments as leading the turned-on generation
toward a more meaningful, more rewarding way of life. "There
are no immoral persons or amoral societies," runs a common
argument among the gurus of the new Bohemia. "There are only
differing moral systems.". . . In a breezy but sharply observed
book, *It's Happening*, J. L. Simmons, a sociologist, sum up the
modern sexual ethic this way: "Acquaintances and friends become fleeting lovers, then acquaintances again. Strangers meet
and become momentary bedmates or soul mates, then dance off
to another partner, another scene."

Another partner, another scene. But why? Why, in the space
of a single generation, has so radical a change taken place in our
morality? So far, not one TV documentary has probed beneath
the surface . . . has tried to give the sexual revolution any moral
perspective.

Instead, we hear Dr. Calderone tell us about our hang-up. We hear that complacent pair, Dr. William H. Masters and his aide, Virginia Johnson (authors of *Human Sexual Response*), explain what they're up to out in Saint Louis as they turn their movie cameras (fitted with color films!) on copulating couples. As any Masters-Johnson interview is at pains to tell you, it's all for the greater glory of science. It will enable troubled souls with horrible sex problems to triumph over them. To find a rich, exciting new life in the conjugal—or, more likely, nonconjugal—bed, this time without the whir of movie cameras.

Meantime, only a few critics have bothered to point out that the uninhibited volunteers in this continuing study—sexual exhibitionists ranging in age from eighteen to eighty—can scarcely provide much useful data for average people with normal sex problems; that, in fact, one would have to be markedly abnormal to *volunteer* to make love under hot lights while a doctor and his lady helper operated cameras and took notes.

In his famous essay "Down with Sex!" England's Malcolm Muggeridge says that Americans have made erotica "a mania, a sickness." In America, he points out, dating begins at the age of nine, and "tiny tots who ought to be reading about Peter Rabbit wear padded bras, paint their faces and howl like randy hyenas at the Beatles." He speaks pityingly of "the elderly (dentures gleaming) looking lecherously around" or dozing in their bath chairs over dirty novels and textbooks on the sex customs of the Polynesians.

That society, from the basic unit of the family on through the body politic, is likely to pay a high price for this mania is a matter one wishes TV would explore. But no, we always get the tweedy, pipe-smoking psychologist, nodding benevolently and telling us that "kids just aren't scared of sex any more." The reaction of a parent might well be, "All right, dammit, *why* aren't they? Is there any force in the world more fraught with danger? And never mind the pill. How about the emotional and spiritual dangers?"

The dangers are particularly acute in our society, some observers feel, because we live in an age when people "don't want to get involved." For to become involved with the sorrows, the problems of another human being obliges one to share the burden. Youth today—particularly male youth—seems disinclined to take on any burdens but his own. . . .

"Parents," said one of our young sages recently in a CBS Report called "The Berkeley Rebels," "give you the false idea that a decent man won't marry you if you've had premarital affairs. I refuse to listen to these older people, you know. . . . I look at their marriages. Let's say they don't get a divorce. Let's say they don't even wife-swap. How about all those marriages where these couples stay together and hate each other? They have the gall, the nerve to tell us *we're immoral!* . . . They just floor me.". . .

Interestingly enough, however, this same report did offer a hint of the moral dilemma that seems to be so consistently ignored in most programs of this kind. It came not from the experts but from the irrelevant virgins themselves. "There are lots of people who aren't admitting they're unhappy," one girl confessed. "They appear perfectly free, you know, jumping in and out of bed where there's no love."

And then came one of the most poignant statements heard on a television sex documentary in lo! these many trivial years. "A lot of people are in bed *and* in bed because they need love desperately and sex is not doing anything for them. Sex is destroying them." Precisely what wise men and women have been saying all along. Too much sex, too little love; result: a sad, lost, disturbed human being.

J. L. SIMMONS and BARRY WINOGRAD

happeners

There's little doubt that the capacity to simply *enjoy* sex is greater among youth than among their parents.

the hang-loose ethic

There is an emerging new ethos in America society, which seems most aptly called "the hang-loose ethic.". . . It repudiates, or at least questions, such cornerstones of conventional society as Christianity, "my country right or wrong," the sanctity of marriage and premarital chastity, civil obedience, the accumulation of wealth, the right and even competence of parents, the schools, and the government to head and make decisions for everyone—in sum, the Establishment. . . . When caught by parents or authorities, youths are no longer hanging their heads in shame. Instead, they are asserting the rightness, at least for themselves, of what they're doing. And they are asking what right do their elders have to put them down? . . . An increasing number of "happeners" have reached a level of disrespect so thoroughgoing that they don't even bother to "push their cause." Not only have they dropped their defensive posture, but their own assertiveness has become quiet, even urbane, in its detachment and indifference toward the "other morality." This withdrawal has aroused some of the greatest resentment and opposition, since it is perhaps the gravest affront to an established ethic not to be taken seriously. . . .

Another basic aspect of the hang-loose ethic is a diffuse and pervasive *humanism*. . . . Adherents don't necessarily proclaim the rationality of men or their inherent "goodness," but they do claim that people are precious and that their full development is perhaps the most worthwhile of all things. Killing is a heinous violation of this ethos and so is any action which puts others down, except under extreme circumstances. The most approved method of defense and retaliation is to turn one's oppressors onto the good life they're condemning and to help them resolve hangups which prevent this from happening. If this fails, one may attempt to "blow their minds," to shock their preconceptions and prejudices in some way and hence force them to open their eyes, to re-evaluate, and hopefully to grow. . . .

Another basic aspect of the hang-loose ethic is the pursuit of experience both as thing in itself and as a means of learning and growing. The idea is that a great variety and depth of experience is beneficial . . . as long as you can handle it. This entails a heightened attention to the present ongoing moments and far less concern with the past or future. . . . This courting of raw experience is what gives many people the impression that those participating in the happenings are without any morals whatsoever; that they are selfishly pursuing swift gratification of their impulses. . . . But such judgments are one-sided. Although [these people] see that swingers are breaking standards, they entirely miss the point that swingers are following another, different set of standards; so that arguments between the camps are in reality debates between conflicting ideologies. . . .

Another facet of the hang-loose ethic is an untutored and unpretentious *tolerance*. Do whatever you want to as long as you don't step on other people while doing it. . . . The swingers see most every restriction that modern man has devised as a limitation on directions people can travel [in] and grow. They feel that the irony of contemporary society is that the very restrictions necessary to curb an immature populace prevent that same populace from becoming mature enough to live without restrictions, just as a girdle weakens the muscles it supports. . . .

Without the fuss or the self-righteousness so common among Establishment liberals, the happeners have come closer to integrating the races, religions, and the sexes than any other group. ... A fierce equality is practiced among them, which is appreciative of differences in backgrounds and temperaments. Equality and tolerance aren't abject attempts to make people feel comfortable or wanted; they are dispositions that permit things and relationships to just happen without deliberate forethought and planning. In most happening circles, a Negro is not the recipient of conscious liberal acceptance, but an individual in and of himself who may or may not be a "good" person. Acceptance and participation is based more on how the individual presents himself within the context of the scene, not by preconceived and nurtured stereotypes about the way he is expected to be. ...

This doesn't mean that the swingers will indiscriminately associate with anyone. Like everybody else, they choose their friends, their lovers, their acquaintances and the people they avoid by how well they get along with one another and enjoy doing things together. But they are less down on the people they don't choose to associate with than others generally are, [although] the tolerance stops if somebody is stepping on other people. ...

The ideal person in the hang-loose view embodies traits that are difficult to combine. Being as spontaneous as a child yet being sophisticated and world-wise; being fully self-expressive yet being always in control of oneself. This is the ambiguity of being cool. Being able to dig the ongoing present as it unfolds yet being able to get things done and maintain a competent life of fulfilled commitments and involvements. Being hang-loose from any constraining orthodoxy, yet being courageous enough to follow your own path wherever it may lead and whatever the travails it plunges you into. ...

The happeners . . . take a "liberal" stand on almost every question. . . . They take these stands for granted as the only reasonable and sensible ones, but they usually don't work within organized political parties to bring them about. . . . They see

Communism as at least as odious and repressive as the societies
of the West and probably a good deal more so.

The hang-loose people are not joiners. . . . They tend to shy
away from any kind of conventional ideologies or fanaticisms,
seeing them as . . . compulsions and obsessions rather than noble
dedications. They regard those who are too intensely and dog-
gedly involved in even such highly approved causes as integration and peace a little askance. . . . The villains in the hang-
loose view are people and social forces which put other people
down and hang them up, which teach people to be stolid and
dignified rather than swinging, self-righteous and moralistic
rather than responsible, dutiful rather than devoted. . . .

Along with the repudiation of property as something to work
and live for, the hang-loose people feel less honor bound to fulfill commitments unless they are coupled with personal involvements and attachments. This makes them less dependable workers and spouses, and their lack of steadfastness creates part of
their bad reputation in a society which still harkens to the Calvinist idea of duty. But swingers will not discharge their duties
as students, workers, lovers, or citizens just because someone
else says they *should*. "Should" isn't good enough unless it is
coupled with "want to," stemming either from personal desire
or personal conviction. Concretely, this means that they will
break a law they disagree with, will desert a spouse or friend
they no longer love, will cheat on a test they feel is unjust, will
walk off a job they find odious, and will speak against a war
they feel is dishonorable. . . . Hence, an obvious strategy for
those in the opposition wishing the demise of happening scenes
and their tangential attributes would involve making these people "want to" do something or discharge some particular responsibility. Sadly it is too infrequently recognized that unless
those with the hang-loose philosophy are, at a minimum, tolerated, little progress in the above direction can be made. . . .

Who's going to be left to run the world if everybody turns
on? . . . Who will hold the world together? Maybe nobody will
hold the *present* world together. Who wants to? How much of it

do we really need? How many of our proud items are only consolation prizes? Maybe a newer social order could evolve in
which we would have the real things that we talk about on rainy
nights but never quite seem to achieve? . . .

Many among the older cohort worry whether today's youth
are training and preparing themselves for . . . adult roles. . . .
This worry contains some validity, for many swingers are pretty
unimpressive even judged in terms of their own values and
ideals. . . . But the worry is also ethnocentric and historically
arrogant because the young needn't accept or strive to fill adult
roles as the oldsters choose to define them—and it might even
be best if they didn't. On this issue youth *is* rebellious as it tries
to revamp the more traditional conceptions of a "man," a
"woman," a "career," a "citizen," a "human being." In their
uncertain experimentations some swingers are probably stum-
bling toward what will prove to be more realistic and effective
roles. . . .

Many fear that the accelerating whirl of social change will
prove to be more than human beings can endure. . . . This fear
is based upon some assumptions about human nature which are
unproved and may well be false. A lesson of history seems to be
that human nature is far more flexible than any tribe of historically local judges ever realizes. . . . It may well turn out that the
flux of rapid change is invigorating for the human animal, not
by tying him up in a series of knotty duties, but by letting him
feel free, by letting him walk with bare feet on a dew-drenched
lawn; simply, by letting him hang loose a bit. It may be that
breakdown during change results from a dragging overgrown
rigidity and traditionalism, just as traveling is difficult for a
man in a straightjacket. . . .

sex and love

In a former decade she might have fixed him a cup of tea with
the same grace and for the same reasons. Today she pulls back

the covers and he might be in the kitchen rolling a joint. Maybe this is the beginning of a twosome or maybe [not]. . . . But either way, the experience was . . . meaningful . . . haunted by fewer compulsions from a frustrated or inhibiting past and constrained by fewer promises of the future. And it isn't inevitable; people who happen to be of the opposite sex will often spend great chunks of time together . . . [even] travel across the country together and sleep on one another's shoulder without any sexual . . . byplay whatsoever. Some will go to bed the first night they meet; others spend months in the same company with not a single sexual episode. . . . Those who stay involved with each other over fair durations of time—and this is still the majority —are involved in more ways and share a wider variety of things than unmarried couples did before. . . .

Romantic zeal (and innocence) is still rampant, and of an evening one can find droves of young swains and maidens gazing about with that mixed expression of joy and anguish called Romantic Love. . . . More people are becoming more sexually experienced both in number of partners and in varieties of the act, and sex is losing some of its sacred character along with many of the guilts and fears that previously hounded some who took part in non-marital sexual behavior. . . .

There's little doubt that the capacity to simply *enjoy* sex is greater among youth than among their parents; that they have fewer social and psychological compulsions and are surprisingly competent sexual craftsmen. A brutally simple law of learning is that competence increases with experience, and young people are starting to learn earlier than ever before. Does this mean that they have become self-indulgent libertines? Or, have they recaptured some of the simple human capacity abdicated by overcivilized Westerners? . . .

The sex scene is not an unremited ball. Unrequited love, poor choices, and the disillusionments that troubadours have always sung about are still around. Girls still wait for the guys to move, though their invitations are more direct, less subtly clothed than in the past. And, as with romantic sentiment formerly, companionship and communication are sometimes unconscious or deliberate covers for starkly sexual goals. . . .

Contemporary lovers may move from no contact to complete intimacy with a swiftness which shocks and disconcerts their elders, but these elders are wrong when they judge this to be nothing but widespread promiscuity. Promiscuity does of course exist, but it may be no more common than it has ever been. . . . In fact, for many, the controlling norm has become: sex is fine as long as it is not promiscuous. This vague and general dictum carries with it the obligation to feel that the sexual act possesses, in and of itself, a fine meaning, that it is another form, albeit a higher one, of human relations. . . . It is an easier, fuller, more candid and encompassing style of relating in which the participants do more things together and become involved with each other as companions as well as sex objects to be used or romantic strangers to hang one's illusions and projections on. Partners come to know each other more quickly and more fully as fellow human beings. . . .

tripping—leary and the psychedelic conflict

Even when someone's world view is grim, it is usually stable enough to allow him to move through his days with some coherence; it can be counted upon. But after the trip, the person is faced with what can be a very distressing task—rearranging his patterns and his views and his life. . . .

Dr. Timothy Leary . . . has suggested five dilemmas which psychedelic journeys arouse; a series of fears balanced against a series of yearnings we have paraphrased and expanded as a way of summarizing the psychedelic conflict. The terror of loss of rational control is balanced by the hope of transcending one's hidebound ways of thought and freeing oneself from programmed ruts. The fear of acting shamefully is balanced by the hope of casting off one's social fetters and behaving as one truly wants to. The terror of perhaps really seeing yourself is balanced by the hope of really finding yourself. The fear of disenchantment with one's society and one's position within it is balanced by the hope of insight into the inner workings of one's social environment and of seeing more creative alternatives. And the fear of discovering a "super-normal" realm so pleasant that one will never return is balanced by the hope that one can reach a level of awareness which will transform everything into splendor. . . .

Opponents feel that psychedelic drugs have opened up a Pandora's box of psychotic maladies and damaged lives and societal dropouts. More extreme factions claim that those who trip and those who even want to trip are sick—driven by compulsions which they are too weak to overcome, or else selfishly looking for kicks while decent folks have to work even harder to keep things going. The more moderate opponents simply feel that the drugs are extremely dangerous. . . . [As] one medical man . . . said, "What's the hurry? Let's just take the years we need to thoroughly research these drugs before we allow anyone to use them." But, the proponents argue, do our deadly societal games of atomic cops and robbers, of Black and White, of oneupmanship and onedownmanship, really leave us that much time?

Some of the more contemplative proponents see the opposition as possessing a hysterical fear of what might happen if the masses were liberated [through drugs], like the Church's suppression of the printing press. . . .

HUGH M. HEFNER

some "playboy" views*

**It is our religious tradition that has tended
to look upon woman as a depersonalized object. . . .
Sex is one of the important ways in which . . .
personal identity is established.**

. . . Whatever we call it—sexual revolution or re-examination of our sexual mores—society is in a state of significant sexual transition; but it is less a change in behavior—though there may be a little of that, too—than a change in attitudes toward the behavior. It is, it seems to me, a rejection of our Puritan past . . . a transition from guilt, shame and hypocrisy to a new honesty, a new permissiveness, a new willingness to talk about sex in a frank and open way—a freedom to examine to express, to enjoy.

*   *   *

After 20 years of stultifying conformity, a new generation has awakened America's natural optimism, rebel spirit and belief in the importance of the individual.

*   *   *

The roots of the sexual revolution . . . may go back several decades, but the period of real transition has just begun. For that reason, there is a remarkable difference in the sexual outlook of two generations born little more than 20 years apart. If there is a lack of communication on the subject of sex within the home . . . it is the fault of the parents, [who] still suffer from the sexual suppression of their own childhood. For . . . any real

* From "The Playboy Philosophy."

improvement in the interpersonal relationships between parents and children, we'll have to wait another generation, until the children of today have become the parents.

*   *   *

It is our religious tradition that has tended to look upon woman as a depersonalized object, or possession, by continually associating her with its antagonism toward sex. Sometimes the emphasis has been placed upon the temptation to sin in woman-kind, and sometimes the emphasis has been placed upon feminine purity and chastity; but whether they were considered creatures of the Devil, or placed upon a pedestal, their status in our antisexual society has always been that of an *object*, rather than a *human being*.

*   *   *

There is something sick about a society that accepts detailed descriptions and images of human beings killing and maiming one another, but suppresses any too-precise picture or phrase about the physical act of love. What sort of society is it that tolerates violence, pain and the destruction of life in its books, magazines and movies, but is bothered, embarrassed and even outraged by any too intimate interest in an act of tenderness, pleasure and procreation?!

*   *   *

As society becomes continually more complex, more auto-mated, more impersonal, more conformist, there is increasing reason for concern over the loss of personal identity that people have inevitably suffered. If this trend is to be offset in the fu-ture—and it must be, if we are to survive as a free society—it will require a tremendous emphasis on the importance of the individual and on those things that give a person a sense of iden-tity and individuality. Sex is one of the important ways in which such personal identity is established. . . . It is wrong to suggest that [*Playboy* favors] depersonalized sex. Not unless, by depersonalized sex, we are referring to any and all sexual activity that does not include extensive involvement, commitments and obligations. . . . I certainly think that personal sex is preferable to impersonal sex, because it includes the greatest emotional rewards; but I can see no logical justification for opposing the latter, unless it is irresponsible, exploitive, coercive or in some way hurts one of the individuals involved. [But] I think the best sex, the most meaningful sex, is that which expresses the strong emotional feeling we call love.

* * *

A great many parents tend to manipulate the lives of their children to satisfy their own emotional needs. . . . It is precisely this sort of parental orientation—with the offspring acquiring their fears regarding popularity and social acceptance from their mothers and fathers—that prompts the young to seek the security and status of going steady in high school, becoming engaged in college, and marrying immediately thereafter. . . .

It isn't sexual freedom that Mr. and Mrs. America want for their children—it's the prestige of being well liked, of being pinned, of receiving, or giving, that engagement or wedding ring. It is the kids who, quite naturally, add sex to the relationships. And if they get into trouble . . . dear old Dad is as apt as not to raise the roof, while Mother cries, and both demand to know how their children could have let them down this way—after *all* they've sacrificed in the offsprings' behalf.

Incidentally, I'm not opposed to early dating—it's the "going steady" part of this adolescent social pattern that I question. . . . I just think a young person gets the most out of his or her teens, and is more apt to adjust successfully to the responsibilities of adulthood, if these first years of courtship are spent in the company of a variety of boys and girls. . . .

As far as sex is concerned, I don't favor an entirely free or permissive attitude toward teenagers . . . but I do think we have a tendency in this society to ignore the sexual realities related to adolescence . . . the significant gap between the age a person reaches sexual maturity and the legal age of consent, after which society more or less accepts his or her right to act accordingly. In the years between, a person may be considered a juvenile delinquent for simply doing what adults do and getting caught at it.

* * *

It's easy to understand why a great many people are willing to accept the idea that there is a link between obscenity and delinquency, because it supports the antisexuality that is so much a part of our Puritan culture; and it supplies a simple solution to a complex social dilemma. If the members of society who are sincerely concerned with the problem of delinquency would stop emphasizing these easy answers, which are not really related at all, perhaps they would begin to place greater emphasis where it really belongs. Perhaps they would spend their time, not joining censorship groups, but trying to understand and care for, and about, their own children; and building a better home, school, work and play environment for young people in general.

HARVEY COX

an open letter to allen ginsberg

We drink only because we're thirsty, baby.

Dear Allen: Several weeks ago . . . you asked me a question that has buzzed in my head ever since: "What *is* Christianity going to do about the hippies?". . .

I can imagine one possible scenario of America in 1975 in which not just thousands but millions of youngsters have dropped out of the larger society and tuned in on one of the newly emerging tribes now appearing in the garret sections of our cities. If Haight-Ashbury is any indication of the kind of life they will be leading, it could be a life of quiet, noncompetitive, sensuous communalism. They will chant Hindu mantras, as you and Cary Snyder did at the now-famous "Human Be In" at Golden Gate Park. . . . They will write and read poetry, much of it as erotic as hell. They will share food, clothing, shelter and beds—especially beds—in a way that undercuts the society's preoccupation with property rights. They will experiment with the less addictive hallucinogens, to the dumb horror of their Martini-swilling parents. They will paint their faces in bright turbulent colors, strut through the streets in capes, epaulettes and sashes, and oppose [racism and whatever "war-in-Vietnam" is then ongoing or threatening]. . . . They will be waiting for the collapse of the old order, which they feel sure is imminent, so they can build what you and others of their spokesmen call "a new community of love and full human consciousness." Note to readers: if you think for a moment that your children and mine will be immune to the powerful enticement of such a life you are probably just as "turned off" as Ginsberg says you are. . . .

Remember two things about these youngsters with the weird clothes and inscrutable ways. First, they are the only generation ever born into a world where someone thousands of miles away could incinerate them instantly and without warning in the name of an ideological struggle which means as little to them as the contest between the Guelphs and the Ghibellines. . . . Industrial societies are premised on people's willingness to delay gratification, discipline their emotions, be rewarded later. The Bomb carves a big question mark next to all this. They want it all and they want it *now*. Second, they are the first generation to grow up in an affluent-welfare society. They have none of the unconscious drive, instilled in all of us who weathered the thirties, to be able to *do* something *marketable* so we can eat. . . . The answer to my well-over-thirtyish question about this mundane subject to a lovely young hippie brought a typical answer: "Food?" she asked, as though she had never really considered the question before; then she smiled beatifically and said with consummate serenity, "But food *is*."

At this point, Mr. Ginsberg, the sophisticated Christian theologians must fight down certain intrusive thoughts. One is that disturbing saying of Jesus, "Take no thought for the morrow, what ye shall eat or what ye shall drink or wherewithal ye shall be clothed." This was of course a counsel of perfection, an interim ethic or maybe even a ninth-century scribal insertion. But there are some other intrusive ideas he has to deal with too. The first-century Christian church in Corinth probably looked disturbingly like these ragamuffin misfits and had about the same relevance to its urban power structure. The desert fathers preserved vital elements of human culture during a dark period not by penetrating the imperial power centers but by building a "city in the desert." Some of their experience and visions, if Saint Anthony is any example, allow us to be a little less shocked by the uxorious imagery one finds in the privately printed poetry for sale on Telegraph Street. If the mendicant orders denounced wealth and lived by the begging bowl, the Diggers group in Haight-Ashbury goes them one better: they give away food and clothing and joyously burn ten-dollar bills in little brass urns.

But, like I said, a well-trained theologian has to resist making facile comparisons. . . . The Corinthian Christians had no social action committee because they expected the imminent return of Jesus Christ to judge the kingdoms of this world and establish an era of love and brotherhood. But he didn't come, did he? The desert fathers dropped out because they, poor souls, lived in a period in which the church was hopelessly compromised with the secular world's lust for real estate and earthly power, mistakes we have now firmly left far behind. Haven't we? The mendicant orders gave up their treasures, forsook violence and talked to the birds and the sun because they somehow believed there ought to be a visible difference between the way people turned on by Jesus should live in contrast to those who had not. They had not heard about incognito discipleship. Besides, we've learned as Christians to discount apocalyptic visions. We all know that our civilization—with its universities, student organizations, poverty bureaus and churches—is not really headed for collapse.

I wish I could be more convincing.

But then there's my trump card, albeit a somewhat nontheological one. Your urban descendants of the catacombs, the Calabrian monasteries, and the Oneida community mess it all up, Mr. Ginsberg, with one filthy habit. They smoke pot. Some of them even take LSD. . . . So they are really only adolescent escapists after all, junior junkies. On with the Consultation of Christian Unity!

You say it's funny how adult society can accept the use of some chemicals to induce certain states but recoils in horror at others? Aspirin, tranquilizers, pep pills, Sleepeze, No Doz? That's our trip kit. Then there are Martinis, Rob Roys and double bourbons. Some careless people assert that we over-thirtyers imbibe this stuff to relax, to lower our inhibitions, to help us

enjoy a party, a conversation, even a conference, i.e., to induce
certain states of consciousness. But we don't, of course. We drink
only because we're thirsty, baby, only because we're thirsty.
Anyone who believes that the present laws about marijuana will,
in ten or twenty years, be in the same limbo laws against drinking alcohol now inhabit is just plain wrong. Or he may just be
over thirty.

No, Mr. Ginsberg, I still have no persuasive answer for you.
Oh, I could make a few debater points. . . . There are millions
of people in India and in Brazil today who couldn't care less
about taking an acid trip. They just want something to eat. For
them, despite my lovely hippie informant, food *is not*. Also, the
desert fathers had something going for them you do not. When
the empire fell it didn't poison the desert. But if somebody
pushes the red button we'll all be on the same funeral pyre—
you and me and Billy Graham and Dean Rusk. Haight-Ashbury
will be just as incinerated as Madison Avenue. This is why I
am terribly interested in the effort you're making to relate the
hippies to the new left, to start looking for concrete ways to love
and to change the society we all still live in.

Also, even the hippies' community has its sectarian and internal squabbles, just like the church. And some of the kids I saw
there seemed just a *bit* young to be ingesting Lysergic Acid
Diethylamide. To tell you the truth, some of them looked real
turned *off* to me. Still . . . I realize we Christians have turned
off our share of souls in the millennia we've been in business.
Besides, your question to me was not a defensive one but an inquiry. My answer is you may be right. Chanting *mantras* and
repeating Zen prayers may be as close as you and your unkempt
friends can come to religion, at the moment anyway.

Still, your question makes me wonder whether we theologians
who chant the praises of the new city and hopefully repeat the
promise of technology may need to ask some questions too. Not
to you but to ourselves. Have we looked with real candor at the
price we exact from the young in emotional deprivation and the
erosion of the affective side of life in order to fit them into the

niches of an increasingly rationalized and complex society? Are there some inner values of the garrison-competition-success-performance society about which Christianity should ask some very telling questions? Where in the world of jet schedules, omnipresent deadlines, incessant phone calls and numberless good causes to support do we discover places to meditate, to touch the inner selves of those closest to us, to make love unhurriedly, to walk nowhere in particular, to examine the astonishing form of a child's ear?

Maybe you and your shocking friends are reminding us of something about Christianity we'd almost forgotten, the rhythm of dropping out, listening and then dropping back in. I confess I still perversely hope you and most of the hippies will drop back in someday. Maybe this elemental oscillation between withdrawal and action is something we all need much more than we are willing to admit. Maybe that's just why you bug us. We need places we can go, the secular equivalent of monasteries, to "turn on" again. We even need communities of people who are experimenting with the cultivation of what is essentially human in life, so that when the computers take over the white collar drudgery we are all so caught up in, we won't have to have ourselves committed to the happy farm. And maybe, if we work on all this as hard as we race after the bitch goddess of success and the green stuff the Diggers so ecstatically immolate, we won't even need sugar cubes or fermented grain to help us do it.

Maybe Christianity is finished, Mr. Ginsberg. Maybe it has made its essential contribution and henceforth its impulses will be picked up and carried on by persons and movements it refuses to recognize. But it may also be true that Christianity is only in its infancy, that it will learn to open itself generously to the most threatening and disturbing movements around it, that it can yet provide a revolutionary human vision and a contagious spiritual discipline. And perhaps both of us will live long enough to see which way it turns out.

ALLEN GINSBERG

public solitude

> Control of anger is our problem. . . .
> America's political need is . . . naked
> bacchantes in our national forests.

The present condition of life for American Person is one of deathly public solitude. We've built a technological Tower of Babel around ourselves, and are literally (as in Gemini) reaching into heaven to escape the planet. Now giant overpopulation depends on a vast metallic superstructure to feed and transport all the bodies here together. The stupendous machinery surrounding us conditions our "thoughts, feelings and apparent sensory impressions," and reinforces our mental slavery to the material universe we've invested in. . . .

Abruptly then, I will make a first proposal: on one level symbolic, but to be taken as literally as possible—it may shock some and delight others—that everybody who hears my voice, directly or indirectly, try the chemical LSD at least once; every man, woman and child American in good health over the age of 14— that, if necessary, we have a mass emotional nervous breakdown in these States once and for all; that we see bankers laughing in their revolving doors with strange staring eyes. May everybody in America turn on, whatever the transient law—because individual soul development . . . is our law transcending the illusions of the political state. Soul also transcends LSD, may I add, to reassure those like myself who would fear a chemical dictatorship. I propose, then, that everybody including the President and his and our vast hoards of generals, executives, judges and legislators of these States go to nature, find a kindly teacher or Indian peyote chief or guru guide, and assay their consciousness with LSD. Then, I prophesy, we will all have seen some ray of glory or vastness beyond our conditioned social selves, beyond our government, beyond America even, that will unite us into a peaceable community.

The LSD I am proposing is literal. I hope it will be understood as not *the* solution, but a typical, and spiritually revolutionary, catalyst, where many varieties of spiritual revolution are necessary to transcend specifically the political Cold War we are all involved in.

Anger and control of anger is our problem. Already we have enough insight into politics to be aware of one very simple thing: that we can judge all politics and all public speech and ideology by perceiving the measure of anger manifested therein. All present political parties propose violence to resolve our confusions, as in Vietnam. We might look for a third party, specifically named a Peace Party—referring to individual subjective peaceableness (such as we have not seen in our populace or our leaders) as well as consequent public peaceableness; a party founded on psychology not ideology. We obviously need to feed China and India, not ignore, manipulate, or threaten to destroy them. The earth is yet to be saved from our aggression, and living organic life like unto our own nature be replaced on its surface, which has been overgrown with cancerous inanimate matter, metal and asphalt. And though many mammal species have been made extinct in this century, there are many we can yet save, including ourselves.

Driving out of New York or into Boston at night we see the transparent apparitional glitter of buildings walling the horizon, and we know that these are transient specters. In cold daylight we believe in their finality. But it is that half-dreaming insight of normal consciousness that may provide the direction for our imagination to manifest itself in the material world.

What can the young do with themselves faced with this American version of the planet? The most sensitive and among the "best minds" do drop out. They wander over the body of the nation looking into the faces of their elders, they wear long Adamic

hair and form Keristan communities in the slums, they pilgrim-
age to Big Sur and live naked in forests seeking natural vision
and meditation, they dwell in the Lower East Side as if it were
an hermetic forest. And they assemble thousands together as
they have done . . . in Golden State Park, San Francisco or
Thompkins Park in New York to manifest their peaceableness
in demonstrations of fantasy that transcend protest against—or
for—the hostilities of Vietnam. Young men and women in speck-
led clothes, minstrel's garb, jester's robes, carrying balloons,
signs "President Johnson we are praying for you," gathered
chanting Hindu and Buddhist mantras to calm their fellow citizens who are otherwise entrapped in a planetary barroom brawl.

But there has been no recognition of this insight on the part
of the fathers and teachers (Father Zossima's famous cry!) of
these young. What's lacking in the great institutions of learning?
The specific wisdom discipline that the young propose: search
into inner space.

Children drop out of schools because there are no, or very
few, Gurus. Those elders concerned with this practical problem
might consider that there is an easy practical solution: the establishment within centers of learning of facilities for wisdom
search which the ancients proposed as the true function of education in the first place: academies of self-awareness, classes in
spiritual teaching, darshan with holy men of disciplined mind-
consciousness. One might well, in fact, employ the drop-out
beatniks as instructors in this department, and thereby officially
recognise and proclaim the social validity of exploration of inner
space. Tibetan monks, swamis, yogins and yoginis, psychedelic
guides, Amerindian peyote chiefs, even a few finished Zen
Roshis and many profound poets are already present and available in our cities for such work, though at present they battle
immigration bureaucracies and scholarly heads of departments
of Oriental Religion.

What I am proposing as policy, for us elders, for what community we have, is self-examination as Official Politics; an Official Politics of Control of Anger. With state propaganda re-

versed in that direction, church and university teaching and research in that direction, and requests to the government for vast sums of money equal to the outer-space program; and consequent billboards on the highways, "Control Your Anger—Be Aware of Yourself."

There is a change of consciousness among the younger generations, in a direction always latent to elder America, toward the most complete public frankness possible. As the Gloucester poet Charles Olson formulated it, "Private is public, and public is how we behave." This means revision of standards of public behavior to include indications of private manners heretofore excluded from public consciousness. Thus, new social standards, more equivalent to private desire—as there is increased sexual illumination, new social codes may be found acceptable to rid ourselves of fear of our own nakedness, rejection of our own bodies.

Likely an enlarged family unit will emerge for many citizens; possibly, as the Zen Buddhist anarchist anthropologist Gary Snyder observed, with matrilineal descent as courtesy to those dakinis whose sadhana or holy path is the sexual liberation and teaching of dharma to many frightened males (including myself) at once. Children may be held in common, with the orgy an acceptable community sacrament—one that brings all people closer together. Certainly one might seduce the Birch Society to partake in naked orgy, and the police with their wives, together with LeRoi Jones, the brilliantly angry poet. America's political need is orgies in the parks, on Boston Common and in the Public Gardens, with naked bacchantes in our national forests.

I am not proposing idealistic fancies; I am acknowledging what is already happening among the young in fact and fantasy and proposing official blessing for these breakthroughs of community spirit. Among the young we find a new breed of White Indians in California communing with illuminated desert redskins; we find our teenagers dancing Nigerian Yoruba dances and entering trance states to the electric vibration of the Beatles, who have borrowed shamanism from Afric sources. We find communal religious use of ganja, the hemp sacred to Mahadev (Great Lord) Shiva. There's now heard the spread of mantra chanting in private and such public manifestations as peace marches, and soon we will have Mantra Rock over the airwaves. All the available traditions of U.S. Indian vision-quest, peyote ritual, mask dancing, Oriental pranayama, east Indian ear music are becoming available to the U.S. unconscious through the spiritual search of the young.

Ideas I have dwelled on are mixed: there is some prescription for public utopia through education in inner space. There is more prescription here for the individual: as always, the old command to free ourselves from social conditioning, laws and traditional mores. And discover the Guru in our own hearts. And set forth within the New Wilderness of machine America to explore open spaces of conscionsness in Self and fellow Selves. If there be the necessary revolution in America it will come that way. It's up to us older hairs who still have relation with some of the joy of youth to encourage this revolutionary individual search. . . .

Cutting out, or dropping out, of the culture will not lead to a chaos of individuality: what it will mean, for the young, is training in meditation and art (and perhaps neolitic lore), and responsibility of a new order, to the community of the heart, not to our heart-less society wherein we have read the headline in the *Omaha World-Herald:* "Rusk Says Toughness Essential For Peace."

The "oversoul" to be discovered is a pragmatic reality. We can all tell signs of an illuminated man in business or the church —one who is open-hearted, non-judging, empathetic, compassionate to the rejected and condemned. The tolerant one, the Observer, the Aware. And we see that these souls do influence action. . . .

We have an international youth society of solitary children— stilyagi, provo, beat, mufada, nadaista, energumeno, mod and rocker—all aghast at the space-age horror world they are born to, and not habituated to—and now questioning the nature of the universe itself, as is proper in the space age. . . . What satisfaction is now possible for the young? Only the satisfaction of their desire—love, the body, and orgy; the satisfaction of a peaceful natural community where they can circulate and explore persons, cities, and the nature of the planet; the satisfaction of encouraged self-awareness; and the satiety and cessation of desire, anger, grasping and craving.

Respect for the old? Yea, when the old are tranquil and not nervous, and respect the sport of the young. Holy men do inspire respect. One conservative Vaishnavite Swami Bhaktivedanta moved into the Lower East Side this year and immediately dozens of young LSD freak-outs flocked to sing the Harekrishna Mahamantra with him—chant for the preservation of the planet. But a nation of elders convinced that spiritual search is immaturity, and that national war and metallic communication is maturity, cannot ask for respect from the young. For the present conduct of the elders in America is a reflection of lack of self-respect.

I am in effect setting up moral codes and standards which include drugs, orgy, music and primitive magic as worship rituals —educational tools which are supposedly contrary to our cultural mores; and I am proposing these standards to you respectable ministers, once and for all, that you endorse publicly the private desire and knowledge of mankind in America, so to inspire the young. . . .

LOUIS GINSBERG

allen and i

Satori.

We two—my son and I—differ implicity and explicity on a number of matters and manners. We also have common denominators in which we think we bridge the gap between our two generations.

I charge Allen with conforming to his own conformity, his "caste system." He indiscriminately goes to extremes in denouncing everything in the so-called Establishment or older generation: he throws out the baby with the dirty bath water. He burns down the barn to get rid of the rats. His advocacy of promiscuous sexual indulgence and his use of four-letter words draw frowns. His verse is undisciplined and unselective; often he uses raw material without transmuting it into art or poetry. Further, I look askance at his advocacy of marijuana: I tell him that, since its use is illegal, he should obey the law. Besides, we are not entirely sure that that drug is harmless. I further tell him that his being a guru to the hippies should make him give them better advice than to get hooked on drugs; injustices and social problems and undesirable personality characteristics cannot be remedied by smoking "pot" and other self-indulgence— or by passing out flowers.

On the other hand, I applaud his vitality and energy. He assails corruption and hypocrisy with shock tactics that are salutary. He has magnificent flashes of imagination; his lines lash out, like Whitman's, with sweeping, flagellating power. The visionary side of his poetry expresses his search for the exaltation of the brotherhood of man.

Allen looks askance at my "mechanical" shackles of regular

meter and rhyme. He thinks my lines are too tight and my poetry is old-fashioned. I insist that regular, flexible meter has ineluctable values in being grounded in an elemental instinct for the satisfaction of recognizing underlying patterns. I believe in traditional, though not conventional, rhythm. Together with rhyme, meter roves back to the primitive interweaving of the senses in the tangled roots of elemental time, down to the threshold below consciousness.

Allen and I agree that there are many mansions in the house of poetry. We are not antagonistic but complementary. We believe in poetic co-existence. Moreover, we are held by a filial bond of love. While he is more social and political and I am more philosophical and lyrical, we often have a common denominator in our soaring, at times, on some transcendental plane of a lofty union of brotherhood and/or a revelation of the unity of nature and the world. Often, we two meet in our poetry in a satori.

ROBERT COLES

drugs and dissent*

**Pot and acid challenge our culture. . . .
[challenge] the "ethic" of the "system"
head-on.**

. . . Is there . . . any reason why pot should be outlawed,
why you and I should be denied rightful access to the experiences and sensations hemp and its derivatives have offered millions of people for centuries? Why do even psychiatrists (in
America, that is) find supplies of LSD almost impossible to
obtain, at least legally? . . .

Pot and acid challenge our culture. They are social drugs.
They influence our values and attitudes. Consequently, what
they do to our "nerves" or our moods cannot be described in a
purely psychological or psychiatric way. They are not like seda-
tives or tranquilizers, including alcohol—let alone the thousands
of other drugs that pharmacists dispense—because they arouse,
rather than dampen or ignore, the mind's consciousness, the
mind's awareness of itself, its host the body and its surroundings, that is, the neighbors, the ministers, the police, the mayor
and everyone else who has a say in what is "right" or "wrong."
Minds so aroused may not storm barricades but walk away from
them with pointed indifference or scorn—and perhaps it is more
galling to be snubbed than fought.

Consequently it has to be admitted that the least thoughtful
and most outraged critics are right when they refuse to lump
pot with alcohol, or the side effects of LSD with the by-products
of racism, poverty, bureaucracy or suburbia. There may be six

* Dr. Coles wrote this article early in 1967, so it does not take account of drug-
effects studies made since then. But his basic points seem to me ones we still must
face.—A.K.

million alcoholics in America—their bodies are ravaged to a
degree that pot can never equal, and they kill thousands while
driving to the office or the split-level ranch home, not the pads
of Haight-Ashbury or the East Village—but the martinis those
alcoholics take blot things out rather than highlight them. The
drunk is fed up and tired rather than glowing with vivid, intense
and unusual visions. He wants oblivion. He leaves IBM and the
Pentagon reeling. Inevitably he will blame himself, become his
own critic rather than the college president's, the company president's or Lyndon B. Johnson's. In contrast, the pot-head or acidhead does what the saying urges—he turns on, tunes in and
drops out—but he is drawn *to* something, in fact to himself, for
which he is called a criminal or "sick."

So much of our psychiatric thinking accounts for flights—
from "reality," from fears, from anxieties, from desires that the
person feels to be forbidden, immoral or knows to be illegal or
unconventional—that we think of "sick" people as evasive and
escapist rather than determined and ambitious. We fail to see
what our patients want and do; we only know what is *wrong*
with them. Yet some people say that we the doctors are crazy—
in so far as we are part of this society. They are fleeing *us*, not
their memories or dreams. They openly proclaim their sincere
and convinced despair with what is going on in this country—
and work very hard not only to leave it (through drugs) but to
find a replacement for it among themselves. They are seeking as
well as running, and I do not believe that as a psychiatrist I am
required to call them "abnormal" or such thinly disguised equiv-
alents as "troubled" or "disturbed."

In the conversations I have had with many such youths—they
use pot rather casually, and LSD much more guardedly—I find
them no more in need of psychiatric "help" than many others
who also worry about where in hell we are going, as a nation
and as individual citizens. If anything, drugs make many of
these young men and women more alert, more sensitive to the
feelings they have and to the grim facts of this century. I have
seen some youths overwhelmed by their awakened (drug-

induced, if you will) sensibilities, but at least they are not full of rationalizations and self-deceptions; at least they do not whistle in the dark and become obsessed with the intricacies of the tax form. Anyone who has used pot or acid knows how brutally frank the mind can become with itself when prodded. In that sense hallucinogens do what psychoanalysis does: in each instance the mind's "ordinary" way of dealing with the world is altered, and a greater degree of "awareness" is achieved. Nor is psychoanalysis without dangers somewhat comparable to those experienced by a youth who takes pot, and especially acid. Analysts know that a "transference psychosis" can sometimes occur among even the most normal (apparently) of patients, in treatment with the most skilled of doctors. The patient's defenses are down; he is as it were exposed to his naked self as never before; for a while he feels overwhelmed, indifferent to the "real" world, prey to fantasies, wishes and fears once held firmly under control, and indeed out of sight, out of mind. I am not saying that the various turmoils of psychoanalysis or psychotherapy are the "same" as those brought on by drugs, but I am trying to put the "problem" of drugs in a larger perspective—so that when someone on marihuana or LSD gets in an automobile accident or even tries suicide I am not driven into a state of near hysteria by the eagerly reported and prominently billed news that drugs were "involved."

Every day good law-abiding people who have scarcely heard of iniquitous drugs go wild; they kill themselves or others; sometimes they are even "driven mad" (or so they see it) by their "loved ones," their neighbors, even their doctors. We may "know" that fact, but we seem to forget it, too. We forget that what is "normal" varies; that even madness or cruelty have their styles. One culture does not permit but asks a man to take cocaine; another is shocked at how drugs lead to beards. Some men run amok in the jungles of Asia, with little or nothing but their own inexplicable misery to account for their deeds; and others take a few martinis, complain bitterly about the boss or the way things are going at home, step on the gas of a car whose speedometer goes up to 140 miles per hour—and wrap themselves and any number of other people around a tree, a post, whatever.

I do not see how we can refuse to see the challenge that marihuana and LSD make to our society. They may be called "drugs," and we doctors may want to handle them as a "medical" problem, but much more is at stake. The psychologist William McGlothlin is right when . . . he brings up the social, cultural, religious and economic aspects of drug usage, here and abroad. After all, what Max Weber called the "protestant ethic" was not fashioned to achieve nirvana, or even a resolution of the Oedipus complex. Men were asked to heed their elders, work hard, pray a lot, but think not very much—so that "things would get done." God is transcendent and not (as for so many Asians) immanent, and He is to be reached (by hard work, loyalty, subservience and spurts of initiative) rather than felt. Respites and crutches are allowed (such as alcohol and tobacco) but not the kind of self-regard that challenges the "ethic" of the "system" head-on—and makes the mind's life seem more interesting than the factory's goods. . . .

I have no personal interest in any of the drugs; I do my work and put in my forty-five minutes on the expressway every morning, every night. Yet, it is quite apparent that there are some . . . who not only turn me and my habits down, but do so by "turning off." I fail to see why I should hound them and punish them for the choice they have made, particularly since they may persuade me to have some second thoughts about my own values and actions, about what in my "way of life" I want to defend, or keep at arm's length—or abandon for something better.

JOHN KENNETH GALBRAITH

the hippies*

**For years, I've imagined that
something like this might happen.**

QUESTION: How do you feel about the hippie movement?

ANSWER: Not particularly censorious. For years, I've imagined that something like this might happen—that a growing number of people would not be susceptible to the desire for more wealth and more goods, who would say, "Well, we can get along with very little and have leisure time to cultivate our garden." So the advent of the hippies doesn't surprise me. It seems to be a rather natural concomitant of wealth. But I confess to some considerable misgivings about the association of this movement with drugs. I would be more reassured if I were certain the hippie interests were literary, aesthetic and experimental, rather than involving what seems to me, in my Calvinist way, to be rather contrived and inadequate forms of experience. But this may be a somewhat limited view. I never really get very much pleasure out of alcohol, and I don't smoke, so I undoubtedly speak from a very parochial point of view.

Q: Have you ever smoked marijuana?

A: No, I never have.

Q: Didn't they smoke it in Berkeley when you went to the University of California in the Thirties?

A: We had never heard of marijuana then. Social experiment, sex and alcohol seemed much more plausible forms of excitement in those days, and much more popular. . . .

Q: The hippie love ethic embraces a joyful and unconfined

---

* From a long *Playboy* interview on many subjects.

view of human sexuality. How do you feel about this aspect of what's popularly called the Sexual Revolution?

A: I take a rather relaxed view of these matters. Sex is here to stay. Each generation seems to make up its own rules and abides by its own code of behavior. It's hard to go back to the 19th-century novels, of which I'm extremely fond, without feeling that there was a certain artificiality and stuffiness about the formal relations between the sexes at that time. Certainly, what would look to the Victorians like the enormous revolution that has occurred since has been an improvement. And if further improvement involves further changes, well, I'm still in a highly permissive mood. But you must relate my views to the fact that I've been married only once and happily for 30 years. . . .

ROBERT F. KENNEDY

---

what can the
young believe?

**The young must feel ... like
solitary salmon trying to breast Grand
Coulee Dam.**

More and more of our children are almost unreachable
by the familiar premises and arguments of our adult world. The
first task of concerned people is not to castigate or deplore—it
is to search out the reason for disillusionment and alienation,
the rationale of protest and dissent—perhaps, indeed, to learn
from it. What are they dissenting from—and what do they tell
us about ourselves?

They begin, of course, with the war in Vietnam. We are not
talking about all our young people. . . . The men who fight and
die [in Vietnam], with bravery and endurance equal to any in
our history, are young. There are others . . . on many campuses
who are in favor of escalation—though many who favor escalation also favor continuation of student deferment, their seeming
slogan: "Escalation without Participation." But when a hundred student body presidents and editors of college newspapers;
hundreds of former Peace Corps volunteers; dozens of present
Rhodes scholars question the basic premises of the war, they
should not and cannot be ignored.

These students oppose the war for the brutality and the horror
of all wars, and for the particular terror of this one. But for our
young people, I suspect, Vietnam is a shock as it cannot be to us.
They did not know World War II, or even Korea. And this is a
war surrounded by rhetoric they do not understand or accept;

these are the children not of the cold war, but of the thaw. Their memories of communism are not of Stalin's purges and death camps, not even the terrible revelations of the Twentieth Party Congress. . . . They see the world as one in which communist states can be each others' deadliest enemies or even friends of the West, in which communism is certainly no better, but perhaps no worse, than many other evil and repressive dictatorships all around the world—with which we conclude alliances when that is felt to be in our interest.

Even as the declared foreign policy of our government is to "build bridges" to this new communist world, they see us, in the name of anti-communism, devastating the land of those we call our friends. However the war may seem to us, they see it as one in which the largest and most powerful nation on earth is killing children (they do not care if accidentally) in a remote and insignificant land. We speak of past commitments, of the burden of past mistakes; and they ask why they should now atone for mistakes made before many of them were born, before almost any could vote. They see us spend billions on armaments while poverty and ignorance continue at home; they see us willing to fight a war for freedom in Vietnam, but unwilling to fight with one-hundredth the money or force or effort to secure freedom in Mississippi or Alabama or the ghettos of the North. And they see, perhaps most disturbing of all, that they are remote from the decisions of policy; that they themselves frequently do not, by the nature of our political system, share in the power of choice on great questions shaping their lives.

It would be tempting—but it would be wrong and self-deluding—to trace to the war all the problems of our disaffected youth. Nor can this problem be traced to any individual, or to any Administration, or to a political party; the challenge is deeper and broader. Consider for example our economy: the wondrous production machine which has made us richer, as we count, than any people in history, within which we all find sustenance and support. It is a business economy—which is to say that most Americans are engaged in some form of business. Yet in a survey last year, only 12 percent of all graduating college seniors hoped for a career in business, or thought such a career would be worthwhile and satisfying.

Why? Part of the answer is that the great corporations, which are so large a part of American life, play so small a role in the solution of its vital problems. Civil rights, poverty, unemployment, health, education—these are but a few of the deep crises in which business participation, with a few important exceptions, has been far less than might be expected. . . . We can recignize, and applaud, the work of the NAM in job training, or the work of foundations like Ford and Rockefeller, or the efforts of individuals like Paul Hoffman or Thomas Watson, or corporations like Smith, Kline & French. But certainly business as a whole has not sought out the challenges of the nation's frontier. Of course, it may well be argued that the business of business is to make a profit, that to attempt more is to do less than its stockholders deserve. But does such an argument have relevance, ask the young, when a single company, like General Motors or IT & T, has annual profits greater than the gross national product of any one of 70 nations in the world?

Nor . . . are these young people enchanted with liberal institutions. Labor has been in the forefront of many a great battle. But youth looks with other eyes, and their view is very different: They think of labor as grown sleek and bureaucratic with power, sometimes frankly discriminatory, occasionally even corrupt and exploitative; a force not for change but for the status quo, unwilling or unable to organize new groups of members, indifferent to the men who once worked the coal mines of Appalachia, a late-comer to the struggles of the grape pickers of California or the farm laborers of the Mississippi Delta. This is a one-sided picture, without the dimensions of 50 years' struggle, and the undramatic yet vital work of labor in many parts of the nation today. But there is too much truth in it for us not to understand our children's view—or to ignore the need for change.

We are friends of education, especially of universities; our friends and allies teach there; they are a major force in the liberal community. But listen: "Education [is] by its very nature an individual matter . . . not geared to mass production. It does not produce people who instinctively go the same way. . . . [Yet] our millions learn the same lessons and spend hours before television sets looking at exactly the same thing at exactly the same time. For one reason and another we are more and more ignoring differences, if not trying to obliterate them. We seem headed toward a standardization of the mind, what Goethe called 'The deadly commonplace that fetters us all.'" That might well have been, but it was not, a speaker at a Berkeley rally; it was Edith Hamilton, one of our greatest classicists.

And now listen to a student representative, speaking to a meeting of the Board of Regents of the University of California: "We have asked to be heard. You have refused. We have asked for justice. You have called it anarchy. We have asked for freedom. You have called it license. Rather than face the fear and hopelessness you have created, you have called it communistic. You have accused us of failing to use legitimate channels. But you have closed those channels to us. You, and not us, have built a university based on distrust and dishonesty."

It is impossible to mistake the anguish of that voice. There may be many things in that cry, but one of them is surely a protest of individuality—against the university as corporate bureaucracy, against the dull sameness Miss Hamilton saw also—for in bureaucracy and sameness is the denial of individuality, and the denial that human beings matter; if all are the same, why listen to what anyone says? And if we are not prepared to listen, then men cannot be recognized as more than numbers in statistical collections, a part of the gross national product like so many coffee cups or carpet sweepers.

The nonrecognition of individuality—the sense that no one is listening—is even more pronounced in our politics. Television, newspapers, magazines are a cascade of words, official statements, policies, explanations and declarations; all flow from the height of government down to the passive citizen; the young

must feel, in their efforts to speak back, like solitary salmon trying to breast Grand Coulee Dam. The words which submerge
us, all too often, speak the language of a day irrelevant to our
young. And the language of politics is too often insincerity. . . .

Whatever their differences with us, whatever the depth of
their dissent, it is vital—for us as much as for them—that our
young feel that change is possible; that they will be heard; that
the cruelties and follies and injustices of the world will yield,
however grudgingly, to the sweat and sacrifice they are so ready
to give. If we cannot help open to them this sense of possibility,
we will have only ourselves to blame for the disillusionment that
will surely come. And more than disillusionment, danger; for
we rely on . . . our youth for all our hopes of a better future—
and thus, in a real and direct sense, for the very meaning of our
own lives.

DWIGHT D. EISENHOWER

thoughts for
young americans

The Army isn't what it used to be—and it never was.

. . . Frequently these days I hear your elders say that American youth isn't what it used to be—that young people are short on morals, self-reliance, ambition, energy, idealism and all the other admirable qualities which we older citizens like to ascribe to our own generation. This always reminds me of a wry quip long current in military circles: "The Army isn't what it used to be—and it never was."

Human nature does not change a great deal over the years. The young people of my day did possess many worthy qualities, but we also made our foolish mistakes and we had our share of troublemakers who were a disgrace to society and to their own names. Unfortunately, many people nowadays have become so bemused by the excesses of a small minority of American youth that they forget to note the decency and intelligence of the overwhelming majority. . . . In a good many ways today's young people are *better* than my own generation. Certainly, you are better educated, better informed about the world, have a far broader outlook on life than we did at your age. Moreover, most of you I talk with . . . have fine motives and a sound moral attitude.

Above and beyond these laudable characteristics . . . is the capacity for gallantry and idealism which lies deep within the hearts of American youth. During World War II, I saw millions of young Americans do the tough job that they were called upon to do. They did it courageously and with a simple nobility that both warmed and tore at the hearts of all of us who were there with them. [Recently it has been] happening again in Vietnam. . . . A mother in Iowa . . . wrote Mrs. Eisenhower, enclosing a long and eloquent letter from her [Marine] son. After telling graphically about the horrors of war—the filth, the hardships, his friends who had been killed—and describing with great sympathy and understanding the plight of the Vietnamese peasants, the boy had this to say:

Here we see how badly our military help is needed. For, aside from the Good Lord—no matter what form He is worshiped in—and American assistance, these people have no one left to trust. They are uneducated but not unaware of the terrors of communism.

Those who know me (back home) think of me as a happy-go-lucky person with a light attitude toward life. Well, I have plenty to think about now, and to look forward to—mainly just a quiet and peaceful life in the United States. But to earn that peace and that life, I want to do my part, no matter how minute it may be. I know the price I must pay for freedom.

. . . And this little story could be multiplied by thousands. . . . Morale on the fighting fronts is sky-high; and despite the fact that our young men and women in Vietnam feel a deep revulsion against war, they believe in the fundamental rightness *and the necessity* of mankind's long struggle against despotism and slavery. This, above all the other good reasons, is why I have such abiding respect and affection for the young people of this country. This is why I offer you the following words of advice and encouragement:

INFORM YOURSELVES. These are confusing times. Issues are drowned out by the clash of ideologies, and the protagonists of false doctrines may at times seem as plausible and persuasive as the advocates of the true and the just. In this dilemma, the only sensible approach is to inform yourselves *thoroughly* before drawing conclusions. I suggest not only that you read the newspapers and periodicals but that you also study deeply the history of our country and of all humankind. I particularly recommend to you the basic documents of our American civilization, the Declaration of Independence and the Constitution of the United States. Read them—and then ponder their meaning. . . .

In your study of history, note what despotism, of either the Left or the Right, does to human beings. Note the brutality that is required to establish such a regime. Note how any semblance of self-government always goes down the drain, how people become sheep, puppets for any cause whatsoever, no matter how evil it may be. Note how any who choose to protest are quickly silenced, sometimes permanently. And then ask yourselves whether we Americans, with our shining heritage, should stand aside and let the world fall to the tyrants.

I believe implicitly in freedom of speech. But I also believe that this freedom carries with it basic responsibilities—such as decency, dignity and maturity of thought. If, in the continuing debate over the U.S. presence in Vietnam, after examining both sides, you feel that our country is wrong, you have the right to say so. You do not have the right to do this in a raucous and belligerent way that harms the cause of freedom and in the end will cost additional lives. Freedom of speech is no license for public vulgarity and obscenity. And you do not have the right to violate the law. In my opinion, draft-card burners should be sent to jail —at least for the war's duration.

BE SURE OF YOUR IDEALISM. I am fully aware that many sincere young persons have demonstrated against our activities in Southeast Asia. But it is now a well-documented fact that some of these protests have been organized, led or supported by known communists. Before you jump on that kind of bandwagon, I urge you to find out who your leaders are—and what are their motives. . . .

DEVELOP YOUR MORAL COURAGE. I know that most of our young people do not approve of anarchy on a college campus. Neither do they condone the outbreaks of vandalism, excessive drinking, experimentation with narcotics, licentiousness and outright crime which are indulged in by the heedless few. I suggest, however, that passive disapproval is not enough.

The decent young people of this country could be more active in denouncing, in helping strike down, the evil actions of the irresponsible minority. If the 24,000 students at Berkeley who obviously resented that ridiculous revolt and what it was doing to their school had been as determined and articulate as the 3000 participants, they could have squelched the whole thing in short order.

I know that it isn't easy for a youngster to stand up to a group of companions who are starting out for a night of troublemaking and tell them they are wrong. Nobody likes to be called "chicken." This is a personal problem youth has always faced and always will. But I can say to you from my years of experience that moral courage . . . is essential to self-respect, and its practice brings satisfactions which will continue through all the years that lie ahead of you.

KNOW THE OBLIGATIONS OF YOUR CITIZENSHIP. Democracy's most treasured possession is the vote. It was won for us by those who preceded us, through centuries of bloodshed and travail. To use it is the first obligation of citizenship. Yet only 52.4 percent of those of you between the ages of 21 and 25 voted in our last national election. Moreover, in local elections the record was even worse—often well below 50 percent. Yet good local government is just as important as good government at the national level, in certain fields much more important. For this is where public affairs touch the citizen most directly. . . .

Our two major political parties always need members and workers. Get into the one of your choice, do everything you can to improve it and work at the problems of government. Splinter political groups and factions often attract young persons. I do not criticize such groups, so long as they are clearly dedicated to American principles. Yet I would remind you that the two-party system, ponderous and frustrating though it may be at times, has proved itself the most effective and responsive instrument ever devised for the control of government by the people. When I speak of a two-party system, I mean precisely that—not a one-party system. Any drift toward a monolithic party which always gets its own way negates the very spirit of Americanism. Consequently, the political trends of recent years disturb me and should be a matter for you young people to consider as you begin to participate in public affairs.

GOOD LUCK! I imagine more than one young reader is now saying, "Well, your generation certainly has made a mess of the world. Do you expect us to do better?" I always smile when I hear that cliché. We said it to our parents and teachers when I was young. . . . No, my generation and all the generations of the past have *not* done as well as they should. And, we *do* expect you to do better. Within my lifetime, there has been a fantastic explosion of human knowledge. We have at least placed new tools in your hands. Make use of them, not only for yourselves but for the neglected and impoverished peoples of this earth. . . .

JOHN D. ROCKEFELLER 3RD

the youth revolution: a positive response*

Instead of worrying about how to suppress the youth revolution we of the older generation should be worrying how to sustain it. . . . We badly need their ability and fervor.

For some months past, I have been embarked on the adventure of trying to understand the world of the young, the so-called "youth revolution." In my encounters with student activists, I found that when you are really interested in them, young people will not only talk—they will also listen, even to a considerably over-30 member of the Establishment, whom I'm sure they considered more square than groovy. . . .

Today's youth revolution puzzles many of us. Of course, there is nothing new about youthful idealism and protest. Every generation has had its gap. But we are experiencing something much more than the age-old rebelliousness of youth. Today's ferment is deep and intense. Although the activists are a minority of young people, it is a larger and more vocal minority than ever before. The youth revolt is a worldwide phenomenon, and it displays a tenacity that was lacking in the past. Young people do not seem to be merely getting something out of their systems. Perhaps it is too early to tell, but I do not believe they will slip easily into the comforts of suburbia and the career, leaving behind their idealism and impulse for change. . . .

The young people of today were born after the depression and under a nuclear shadow. In an age of affluence and potential

* From remarks at a Society for the Family of Man Awards Dinner.

Armageddon, they are less concerned about material security and more concerned about basic human values. They feel that time is running out on the great problems—war, racial injustice, poverty. They dislike the impersonalism of large organizations and of rapid technological change. Because of the influence of the mass media and the freedoms of our society, young people today learn faster and mature earlier. They become quickly aware—and deeply resentful—of the differences between what older people say and what they do. In short, the very accomplishments of our generation—in technology, communications, affluence—have served to focus the attention of the young on what we have failed to accomplish.

I want to confess frankly that when I started my inquiry, I was biased. My instincts told me that every much of what young people are doing and saying today basically makes sense and is good. I found this to be even more true than I had thought.

At the same time I do not ignore the disturbing elements of the youth revolution. There are the far-left extremists who say that present society must be destroyed. Their challenge must be met. There are the truly alienated, the loners and drop-outs. They must be helped. There is the use of dangerous drugs. This must be stopped. Too often, while fighting for their beliefs, young people disregard the basic human values and rights which they are espousing. They frequently lack compassion. They are often contemptuous of those who do not fully agree with them. While crying out to be heard, they will shout down a speaker.

Yes, there is much to irritate and disturb the older generation. But we have let ourselves be distracted by the colorful fringes to the point where we miss the central meaning of today's youthful protest. Not only is there tremendous vitality here, but there is also great potential for good if we can only understand and respond positively. This becomes evident if we examine how the youth revolution is manifested in three of the basic institutions of our society.

There is, first of all, the legal framework of society and its attendant issues of violence, social protest, justice, and respect for the law. A major factor distinguishing the current revolt from the past is the skill of young people in the tactics of social protest. They act in ways that would have been hard to imagine for the rebels of my generation. They have learned well from the civil rights movement of the 1950s and the Vietnam protests of the 1960s.

Yet for the most part, young people attempt to work within normal channels to present their grievances and establish a dialogue. They have tried to work through the political system, with their support of Senator McCarthy as the best example. It is they who have made the Peace Corps, VISTA, and the Teachers Corps more than slogans. Many young people are preparing for long-term efforts to change society. For example, law students today are concerned less about trusts and estates and corporate law and more about how just the laws are, how poor people and black people can get a better break before the law.

But even as the majority of young people work constructively for change, severe provocation and even violence have increased as forms of social protest. The protestors are fired by their sense of moral righteousness. They feel they have learned from experience that it is necessary to be loud and demonstrative to get results. It is this behavior that compels attention and strikes fear for the very stability of American society.

The nature of our response is crucial, for it has everything to do with whether there will continue to be violence and whether violence will pay. We must understand that social protest has an honorable history and has a rightful place in any enlightened society. Indeed, it was social protest that brought this nation into being.

At the same time we must recognize that respect for law and the maintenance of order are essential for the protection of everyone in our society. Young people—anyone—who breaks the law as a form of protest must be prepared to pay the penalty and hope for ultimate vindication. But if we stop here we will have failed. The concept of law and order is meaningless without justice. We must be ready to re-examine our assumptions—

and our laws. To do so, we must open channels of communication. We must have dialogue. If we do not—if we think the only answer is to suppress dissent—then the responsibility for violence hangs as heavily on us as it does on those who protest.

Many persons feel today that another of our fundamental institutions—the family—is in trouble. Much has been written and said about the permissive nature of the American family, which allegedly is responsible for many of the ills of today's youth. Yet criticism of American parents' "overpermissiveness" has been part of our society since the 17th-century Puritans. In his penetrating study of our country early in the 19th century, De Tocqueville comments about the domination of youth and their lack of respect for their elders. Even the authoritarian Victorian age was beset with youthful rebellion.

The family provides a framework and a set of guidelines for a child's growth and development toward adulthood. It is the parents' responsibility to give the child love, freely and warmly shared, and discipline, fairly but firmly administered, which in turn means time, attention and interest devoted to the child. In this way, family life plays a major role in determining the stability of the child, and the depth and solidarity of his values.

Children learn much more from what their parents do than from what they say. Many young people state that while their parents talk about love, integrity, freedom, and fair play, their actions are heavily oriented toward materialistic security, comfort and status. They repeatedly point out that they are not rejecting their parents themselves, but rather what they see as the hypocrisy of their parents' double-standard approach to important social values.

Again, the nature of our response is crucial. If I am right that the ferment of youth is potentially of enormous benefit to society, then we might ask: Would we really rather have apathetic and obedient copies of ourselves? More importantly, we might take the criticisms of young people seriously and re-examine some of our basic assumptions. This of course is not easy. We are used to our children listening to us, not our listening to them.

Everyone likes to think that he has done reasonably well in life so that it comes as a shock to find our children believing differently. Change can be very difficult and threatening, especially when the pressure comes from the young. The temptation is to tune them out; it takes much more courage to listen.

When we turn to the third of our basic institutions—the church—we encounter a deep irony. Young people today are committed to values of love, human dignity, individual rights, and trust in one's fellowman. These are precisely the values of our Judeo-Christian heritage. The church has been their proponent for centuries. And yet no institution in our society is today suffering more from the sheer indifference of the young. By and large, they have dismissed the church as archaic, ineffective, and even irrelevant. One young man told me: "There's a genuine religious revival going on, but the church is missing out on it." Another said: "The church could fill a great need in our society, if it would focus less on the divine and more on how to apply Christian teaching to today's world."

The problem again is that the young people perceive hypocrisy. They know the values the church upholds, but they see too little in the way of action and results. Religion to many of them is Sunday-morning tedium instead of a guiding force and an inspiration.

Once again, we must examine our own behavior, we of the older generation. The church is not some impersonal edifice, although all too often it seems that way. The church is what we have made it. Its dilemma is that while its mission should be the righting of wrongs and the active pursuit of the great Judeo-Christian values, we have instead made it for the most part a force for the status quo. By and large, we are much more conservative as elders of the church than we are as parents. The minister who would remain a minister all too often must please a conservative laity, those who support the church financially. The result is that the church loses some of the finest members of the younger generation.

If we have made this situation, we can also change it. Any

dramatic reversal seems improbable. But the young people will come back gradually if the church becomes a place for searching inquiry, for social action, if more of the clergy become involved in today's problems and if the laity support them—and become involved too.

There are common threads that run through all of these basic institutions of our society. The problem is not in our legal system, or the family, or the church. The problem lies in ourselves as people. The crucial issue is not the revolt of youth but the nature of our response to it.

Broadly speaking, it seems to me that there are three possible responses. One is backlash and suppression. We caught frightening glimpses of what this would be like in Chicago and Mexico City. If we choose this route, the only victors will be the small fringe of extremists who want to see our society destroyed. They are playing one of the oldest of political games, that of the *provocateur*. They want a backlash because they know that repression starts a vicious circle that inevitably leads to greater and greater explosions. If we are foolish enough to fall into this trap, then we will deserve what happens to us.

A much more likely response is apathy or muted hostility. We are resentful over the ingratitude and brashness of the young. We think if we cover our eyes and stop our ears their noise and fervor will go away. They don't understand how really complex everything is, we say. Being older, we believe we are wiser. We know that idealism is tempered by time and that realism sets in. Soon the young activists will pass the magic age of 30, and eventually they will be stepping into our vacant shoes. We secretly enjoy thinking about what a tough time they will have explaining to their children why they did not solve all the problems of the world.

This response, or lack of response, basically avoids the issue or yields grudgingly in a kind of tokenism. It is not working very well, and if I am right that the youth revolt of today is something much more than the normal rebelliousness of the young, then it will not work at all in the long run. We will find ourselves constantly pushed toward the brink of backlash.

The greater tragedy will be the opportunity we will have lost. For we know all too well that time is running out on the great problems the world faces. It seems to me that we have a choice. By suppression or apathy, we can make the youth revolution into yet another problem—in which case the burden will become crushing. Or we can respond in positive ways so that the energy and idealism of youth can be a constructive force in helping to solve the world's great problems.

This is the third possible response. It is simply to be responsive—to trust our young people, to listen to them, to understand them, to let them know that we care deeply about them.

Instead of worrying about how to suppress the youth revolution we of the older generation should be worrying about how to sustain it. The student activists are in many ways the elite of our young people. They perform a service in shaking us out of our complacency. We badly need their ability and fervor in these troubled and difficult times.

In my judgment, the key to sustaining the energy and idealism of youth is more direct and effective action on the problems about which young people are concerned—the problems of our cities, of our environment, of racial injustice, of irrelevant and outmoded teachings, of overpopulation, of poverty, of war. To achieve such action we of the older generation must re-examine our attitudes, our assumptions and our goals. We must take as seriously as do the young the great Judeo-Christian values of our heritage. We must be as dedicated as they in fighting injustices and improving our laws. We must have a sense of responsibility individually and collectively for resolving the massive problems of our society.

And secondly, we must revitalize our existing institutions whether they be in education, government, religion, business or politics. They must be made more relevant to today's problems, have a greater sense of mission. At the same time, in support of the initiative of the young, new programs and institutions must be developed which can be effective in areas of pressing social need. Fresh approaches to meeting today's problems are essential.

A unique opportunity is before us to bring together our age and experience and money and organization with the energy and idealism and social consciousness of the young. Working together, almost anything is possible.

If we follow this course each of us will be involved personally and positively in the great drama of our times rather than feeling ourselves to be weary and impotent victims of imponderable forces. The antidote to despair is to be involved, to be imbued with the same spirit that fires the imagination and the efforts of the young. There is a VISTA slogan which captures this spirit: "If you're not part of the solution, you're part of the problem."

JOHN V. LINDSAY

how to change
the world

. . . The future of metropolitan America will be governed largely by our success in strengthening city government, which in turn is dependent on our success in involving more talented, more energetic and more committed people in that government—particularly the young. The members of this generation realize the need for revitalization exists.

A spirit of rebellion exists in the classrooms as well as the streets; the students of America are neither geographically nor psychologically insulated from the slums. The sophomore alienated from his school has much in common with the ghetto youth alienated from his city. Both suffer from an inability as individuals to influence the institutions that can better or worsen their lives.

In the university, the students resent undue regimentation; the immutable dictation of what courses they must take, or what hours they must keep. In the city, the problem is not an excess of attention, but a lack of it; an automatic disavowal of the poor, the black, the unschooled and the jobless. All of it is compounded by the absence of any effective means to compel the establishment to listen, to act, to take down the wall that seals off the Other Generation. The consequent frustration forms the essence of powerlessness in modern society—the loss of will to try for constructive change. It can debilitate—or it can inflame. The absence of hope it engenders was apparent in every one of the American cities where trouble occurred last summer.

The new generation seems more and more to believe in fighting for change in American life. The channeling of that belief to the task of strengthening our governmental institutions is . . . both timely and essential. To those of you who would change the world, [I say] government is the most powerful—often the only —force capable of bringing about that change. . . . You can march and criticize, resist and harangue, and you may affect the course of public opinion and the policies of our institutions. Ultimately, however, you probably will find that the actual decisions are made—for better or for worse—by men in government. Yet, all too often, government has not attracted high-caliber men, and this has been particularly true in the cities. The cities have not been regarded as sources of the prestige, the fame, or the power obtainable in federal or state service. . . .

In New York City we're attacking that snobbery in two major ways: One is by filling top-level positions with established, known men of outstanding credentials. The second is by bringing in young men and women, many of them directly out of college, to serve in staff capacities. (Half of my personal staff is under 30.) Throughout New York City's government, young men and women are working in housing, in public works, in planning, in budgeting, in almost every area of city activity. At the staff level just below the top job, young people are going up against the customary stall of: "We've never done it that way before." They are answering: "Then let's try it this way.". . .

We're not waiting for graduates; we're introducing students into the complexities of New York City government through our widely copied Urban Corps. The project is an application of the Peace Corps concept to the cities. Last summer, we enrolled 2,500 students from 100 colleges and universities. . . . They rode city ambulances to check times, evaluate service and make recommendations on how the emergency system could be improved. They worked with prisoners in rehabilitation projects in city jails. They helped neighborhood residents draw up community-action plans for inclusion in the Model Cities program. . . . They shopped in neighborhood stores to compare prices on the same items. They produced documented evidence that grocery prices often are highest in the most impoverished slums.

The Urban Corps operates throughout the year. We now have five hundred undergraduates and graduate students working fifteen hours a week, for pay, in jobs that are far less academic than they are pragmatic.

I hope it will not be inferred . . . that my administration can be characterized as a children's crusade. . . . [What we have sought is to blend and spark] the judgment and maturity of the veterans [with the vital energy and fresh imagination of the young]. . . .

EUGENE J. McCARTHY

they are protesting <u>for</u>

Bismarck once said that one third of the students in Germany broke down from overwork, another third broke down from dissipation, and the other third ruled Germany. One third of the students in America are not breaking down because of overwork today, although most of them are working very hard. One third are not breaking down from dissipation, although this is a subject that I cannot dismiss lightly. There is evidence of disillusionment and dissipation among the students and young people of America as shown in hippie hairdos, "flower people," love beads, and LSD. Whereas these extremes must be treated as limited and superficial manifestations of rebellion, they must also be accepted as symptomatic of the concern and anxiety that does affect nearly this whole younger generation. . . .

I have been picketed by "hippies" and I have been accused of being part of the Establishment. I have been called a Judas goat for trying to lead young people away from protest and back into the tradition of American political procedures.

It is true that some sensitive young people look upon American society as so big, so impersonal, so chaotic, and so unmanageable that they have chosen to "drop out." On the other hand, I have been reassured by the positive dedication and good will of most of what is called the Next Generation. For despite exotic hairdos and occasional eccentric behavior, this coming generation has demonstrated a deep moral concern about our country's role in making a future of order, of progress, of justice, and of happiness.

This is a generation of protest, of anger, too. Yet most of the anger is not irrational; it is, rather, based on honest inquiry and honest concern. Today's youth are demanding that their questions be heard and that forthright answers be given, if there are such answers. They reject the glib slogans and generalizations that may have served in the past. They are clearly aware of the disparity between the *theories* of democracy, as projected in the language of the Declaration of Independence and the Bill of Rights, and the *realities* of democracy in America today. They are concerned over the processes of politics and government as well as over the substance.

They have no time either for the exclusive caucus and the smoke-filled room or for the customary excuses made for political compromise. They are, instead, protesting against the influences of hidden powers and vested interests. And, particularly to their credit, they have opposed the encroachment of such influences upon the freedom of the academic community in America, whether it be the CIA's financing of and dominance over the NSA, or the improper interference of business and industry on the campus. Their object is to perfect a government that is responsive to the needs of the governed; to improve the processes by which opinions are formed and the will of the people translated into political reality.

Youth today is also characterized by a vibrant desire to find more individual fulfillment than often seems to be "permitted" by the norms of society. They sense that there are unstated but nonetheless stringent limits to the content of the American dream, and they react strongly against those forces—mass production, advertising, and standardized education—that tend to produce homogeneity. . . . This concern, this searching for answers contribute . . . to the health and richness of America. Too often we assume that no one can resist the lure of our packaged society. We glance with suspicion at those who swim against the prevailing tide, but we should look more closely at what is in their hearts and minds.

Many of today's youth respond to selfishness around them with an unprecedented degree of self*less*ness. Good students have left college for a semester or two to work in the civil-rights movement, or to join Head Start or VISTA projects—not because they are rebelling against formal education but because their sense of social commitment and their urge for involvement are more intense than anything we have recently known. . . .

Sometimes youthful protests reflect a degree of childish absurdity. But though some outward forms of protest may not be pretty, the motivation of most young protesters is, I think, something our country need not be ashamed of. Those who march and demonstrate are not so much protesting *against* as they are protesting *for*—*for* an America that is humane and wholesome; *for* an America in which morality replaces expediency, in which the full development of the individual is truly achievable. When people call the youth of today anti-American, I must reply that they are really pro-American in the profoundest sense. They want to bring into being the inalienable rights proclaimed in the early days of the Republic and to develop a structure of new civil rights to be added to the old and traditional freedoms of speech, worship, assembly, trial by jury, and right of privacy.

The new civil rights consist principally of these four: *first*, the right to education, not just at the elementary and secondary levels, but for all persons according to their capabilities—not only those who are most gifted and talented but also those who are handicapped and even retarded. *Second*, the right to a job and to a decent recompense for the work performed. Considering the potential of the American economy, this right takes on a civil character and becomes a responsibility of society and thus a right of our citizens. The *third* right is one of physical health and bodily security. This includes the right to medical attention for those in need and, in a more general way, the right to freedom from poison in one's food, in the atmosphere, in the waters, and to freedom from other forms of physical danger. *Fourth*, the right to decent housing—not just to an isolated existence in a ghetto, but to a home in a neighborhood, in a community—the right to *belong*.

The new generation of Americans is, in a proper and profound sense, a patriotic generation. . . . Albert Camus once defined the true patriot as one who loved his country not for what it was but for what it ought to be. . . . Today's youth strongly affirm that our America need not be an America on the edge of despair; that it can, again, be an America of confidence . . . an America in which trust is the habit of the individual and the spirit of the nation. They believe that America will again be characterized . . . by openness and by hope; that America will sing again. . . .

DAN WAKEFIELD

joan baez:
actually i'm a square*

To many suspicious elders and admiring youngsters
[folk-singer] Joan Baez, with her long black hair and her guitar and her championship of unpopular causes, seems to represent the consummate image of the beatnik-rebel. To this as well
as other sterotype images applied to her, Miss Baez might best
be able to reply in the words of the Bob Dylan song: "It ain't
me, babe." Sitting in an overstuffed chair in [a] modest hotel
in midtown Manhattan . . . Miss Baez casually made what many
fans would consider a terrible confession.

"Actually," she said, "I'm a square. I never was really a
part of the beat scene. I never took drugs or drank or any of
those things. But I try to project—to understand the people who
are involved in that life.". . .

To some she is, as one friend put it, a "celebrity saint," and
she refers somewhat ruefully to those who choose to see her in
a religious context. "I guess," she explains, "that my face is the
kind that people associate with a fairly common religious type,
but actually I'm not anything, as far as formal religious affilia-
tions go." Yet Joan, who was reared in a Quaker home, wrote
for the jacket of one of her record albums: ". . . a friend of mine
told me it would be risky to write about Jesus. I'll risk it. I wonder if Jesus knows what's happening on earth these days? Don't
bother coming around, Jesus."

Her own concern with "what's happening on earth these days"
has led Miss Baez to participate in many controversial causes—

* From a longer article-interview.

the "free-speech movement" of university students at Berkeley; the civil rights march on Washington and the march from Selma to Montgomery, Alabama; the support of pacifist and anti-Vietnam war crusades; and refusal to pay that portion of her income taxes (60 per cent) that is used for military purposes. . . . She has opened an "Institute for Nonviolent Studies" . . . where young people come to read and discuss the works of Gandhi and Thoreau, spend hours in silent meditation and exercise to the rhythm of Beatles records. But despite her concern for a multitude of causes, Joan Baez is not an intellectual or a mystic or one of those single-minded ladies of reform who have no time or inclination for earthly pleasures. Joan owns a sports car, keeps two pet goats named Daisy and Cassandra, enjoys driving to the beach in a jeep and became quite upset when she lost an address book containing the unlisted phone numbers of assorted Hollywood personalities. . . .

When I went to talk with Miss Baez . . . my first reaction was one of relief that she didn't seem at all to fit the image conveyed by some articles I'd read that portrayed her as a "fragile little waif." A solid, self-assured girl, she wore a white blouse, plain brown skirt, stockings, and low-heeled black shoes with gold buckles. Her long dark hair fell straight to her shoulders, and her brown eyes and fine-boned face had an open, reassuringly earthy attractiveness. . . .

When she was graduated from high school in 1953 her father accepted a teaching position at Harvard, and Joan enrolled as a freshman at Boston University. She hadn't wanted to go to college, but entered to please her parents. "Parents," she said, "hang on to their children like grim death, and college is another way for them to keep hanging on. If you have a goal, a profession you want to go into, then I guess you can put up with the extra trivia of college to get the special training that you want. But I just can't see going because your parents or 'society' say you should. I think a kid just out of high school who doesn't really want to go to college might be better off hitchhiking around the country, getting little jobs and learning what life is about. . . ."

Joan didn't stay long at Boston University. "In fact," she confessed, "I only went for about three hours, though officially I stayed for about two months." She left the classroom for the coffeehouses of Boston and Cambridge, where she first played and sang professionally, and began at once to attract a loyal following that has grown to international proportions. [But] she was less interested in commercial success as a singer than in the authenticity of the songs and of her own performance. "When I first started out," she explained, "I had a typical hard-sell manager, and he tried to get me to sign with Columbia Records. I went to their office, but . . . it was very posh, and there were all those gold records of hits on the walls." She signed instead with Vanguard Records, whose offices are a series of loft-like rooms on Manhattan's busy, unfashionable West 14th Street. "As soon as I walked into *their* office, I felt right at home. There wasn't all that bunk and pretension.". . .

Joan's success naturally has made her parents proud, and soothed their original disappointment about her defection from college for the coffeehouse circuit. . . . "My father was very upset when I left college and started singing," Joan said. She smiled and added, "He especially didn't like the idea of my being in coffeehouses, with all those 'hairy' people hanging around. But it's understandable. He spent his whole life trying to give his children an education and send the three of us to college. My younger sister didn't even start—she was more of a rebel than I was."

But Joan was not the same kind of rebel as were many of her young admirers. . . . "I used to sit up all night long and cry a lot, sometimes," she recalled, "but I never went all the way, like a lot of the kids in Cambridge and Greenwich Village who end up getting their days and nights mixed up and smoking pot and all that. I feel sorry for the ones who do. It only *seems* like those 'free' kids are 'free.' All I have to do is look at their faces, and after that nobody could convince me that they're having a good time.". . .

I asked Joan if she had never been tempted by the promises of "consciousness-expending drugs" or "instant insight," as advertised by the self-appointed priests of the LSD cult. She explained why she hadn't. "I get a big bang out of life as it is," she said. "Living so fully, I can't imagine what any drug could do for me. Also, from seeing the people who take it I feel that it must be worthless and frightening.". . .

Although Joan has often been linked with Dylan as a kind of double idol of the youthful protest movement, has sung duets with him, and has admired a number of his songs and recorded them in her album "Farewell, Angelina," she feels that he has become too cynical and bitter. "The kids idealize Dylan more than me," she said. "For that reason I think he should help them more, not play up to their negative feelings. What they *think* they want to hear is that 'nothing matters,' and in a way, that's what his newer songs tell them. I say just the opposite; I believe everything matters, and you have to take a stand."

If Joan can no longer find herself in harmony with Dylan, neither is she in tune with any contemporary cult or group, be it middle-class suburban or campus Marxist. When she talks about love, as she often does, her conception of the word, it seems to her, is not that of either group, or perhaps of any group at all. . . . She is appalled by the "lack of love in our whole society.

"I wonder," she said, "if love is such a scary thing everywhere. To love means you also trust; you open up. But people are petrified of doing that because they're afraid of getting hurt." Certainly she doesn't see contemporary marriage as an answer to the search for love. "From what I've seen of it, marriage today is mostly a farce. . . ."

One of the basic problems, Joan continued, is that "kids feel they have to marry—otherwise they'll be social outcasts. So they take the first person who comes along. Or they fall in love, and with the first little problem they get scared. Sometimes they

just get married as a way of trying to hold a relationship together. I think they ought to live together first, to try it. I don't
see how two people can get married before they've tried it out."

Nor does Joan feel that love is necessarily found in a radical
political commitment. "I once got hooked into a meeting at
Berkeley," she told me, "where everybody turned out to be a
Marxist. In the course of the discussion I made the mistake of
saying something about 'love.' Everyone got very uncomfortable
and started talking about dialectics. . . ."

Joan's own politics are more emotional than intellectual—
the response of one who has a natural sympathy for the under-
dog. Her response is also that of one who loves life and so is
repelled by destructiveness and violence, regardless of motives.
Her approach to all of life probably can be summed up best
with a single line from a poem by W. H. Auden: "We must love
one another or die.". . .

"I must have been eight years old when I started carrying the
world around on my shoulders. I remember one time when I
walked into the kitchen, my mother and some neighbors were
talking. Suddenly I was worried about all the people in the
room. How were they? What would happen to them? And I remember that my mother came over and 'wiped' a frown off my
face and told me to smile.

"Then once when I was fifteen, I was riding in a car on a road
that went alongside a railroad track. As a train went by I caught
a glimpse of a girl about my own age. I had the most peculiar
feeling that we were really the same person; I felt if she was
hurt, *I* would be able to feel the pain; I felt that I was a part of
all children; that I was everybody.". . .

THE BEATLES:
JOHN LENNON and
PAUL McCARTNEY
(Interviewed by
Mitchell Krauss)

turn on, stay in and change it!

**What's it got to do with some man
with one eye?**

KRAUSS: Do you think that, seven, eight, nine, ten years ago, young people were less awake to the realities of . . . .

LENNON: I think they're becoming more aware each generation, you know. . . .

McCARTNEY: More aware, but no one's quite sure what it is they're aware of. . . .

Q: Young people [are] always rebelling against the older generation. But this rebellion has gone so much further. . . .

L: Yes. What will the next one be like, you know?

Q: They'll rebel against you. . . .

L: Yeah, depending on what we turn into.

McC: You know, you've got your life and you're faced with choices in it. . . . And for us, you know, suddenly being rich and famous, and in a position to do something, we've got a choice of doing either what most people do, which is just making more money, and getting . . . more and more things, or trying to do something which'll help. . . .

Q: But what do you think about the young people?

L: Well, I think they're young, and trying to find out.

McC: They seem to be trying to—to stop wars. . . . It may be just . . . silly to try, but it may be good.

Q: . . . But the word anarchy has been used to describe some of the youth.

L: . . . There always will be that element. . . . It's—"Well, what can we do about all that?" I mean, what can you do really but wear a badge, or stand up and shout? . . . The choices are now shouting or let it roll. . . .

McC: Everyone needs someone to say, "This is how you do it." You know—"Now this is what we want you to do.". . . We make guesses; they're not always right. . . . It'd be great if we knew what it is you [should] do, because we're in a good position . . . just to [tell] all the people who want to know how you do it. . . . Because there are so many phony institutions saying, "This is how you do it"—and . . . you know, nobody can believe them any more.

Q: The whole idea of whether you get involved, or whether you stay out of it; whether you're turned on, or whether you're turned off—how do you feel about it?

L: Well, we believe you should turn on and stay in, and change it.

McC: Drop in, sometime.

Q: . . . Do you mean getting involved in the establishment, in institutions?

L: No, to change it, because unless you change it it's going to be there forever. So the only thing to do is to try and change it, not replace it with another set of Harris tweed suits. But just change it completely. But how you do it we don't know.

Q: Now you went to India and spent time with the Maharishi. . . .

L: Well, we sort of feel that Maharishi for us was a mistake, really. Meditation we don't think was a mistake. But I think we had a false impression of Maharishi, like people do of us, you know. . . .

McC: . . . He had great answers. Because he said you can

sort yourself out . . . that you can calm yourself down, just by doing this very simple thing, you know. And it works, that bit of it. . . .

L: He's giving out sort of recipes for something that—[but] he's still creating the same kind of situations which he's giving out recipes to cure. . . .

McC: He's okay, you know, he's okay; but the system's more important.

L: Something seems to have gone out of it.

McC: It always goes by the board, that bit. You know, people watch Maharishi, or watch us, you know, and just don't think about the system, don't think about what it's about. . . .

Q: He got you to stop taking drugs, you've been quoted as saying.

L: No he didn't; we'd stopped taking drugs a couple of months before we met him. . . .

Q: You feel that drugs are not necessary any more for what you want to achieve?

L: I don't know. . . . I'm not making any statements about what I'm going to do for the next sixty, or whatever it is, because I have no idea any more. . . . I just have a vague goal.

Q: . . . Do you think that [other] young people . . . ought to try the same path that you do?

L: No, we don't—we don't give instructions on how to live your life. . . . They can judge for themselves what happens to us, with Maharishi, with drugs, and with whatever we do. . . .

Q: Some people probably say to you, "Why don't you cut your hair shorter? Are you just wearing it that way to be different?

L: . . . We please ourselves. What's it got to do with some man with one eye?

Q: . . . This business of color prejudice . . . this doesn't have any significance in the mind of many of your young people?

McC: . . . It seems to be older people, really, that've got that hangup. . . .

L: Yes, and musicians . . . their vibrations don't usually have this . . . they get that scene sorted out as soon as they meet other musicians. Because it's the music that counts. . . .

McC: Someone can play a guitar, it doesn't matter what color hands he uses.

L: But it also doesn't matter for the carpenter, and the bricklayer, and all that. . . . Well, those people are sick, you know. And we might all be sick, but their manifestations of sickness are pretty . . . horrible really, frightening. . . .

Q: What are your views about the Vietnam war?

L: . . . It's all part of the same insane scene. . . . It's just insane. . . .

McC: You know, whoever's right and whoever's wrong. . . . there's only that much world. . . . It's just insane. . . .

Q: Well . . . what do you do, when you talk about the establishment, and you try to put something in its place? . . .

L: We are all part of it as well. . . . So it's just to change it any way you can; if you think you can, you know, that's all you can do. . . .

BRUCE JAY FRIEDMAN

the new sound*

**An insistent, deep-probing, suffocatingly
sexual beat that laces through your middle
to pull at stale, long-unplucked cords
of youth. . . . you simply fall before the
Olympian onslaught of all that raunchiness.**

It has been called bad, dirty, offensive, loud, obscene,
and it may be that much of this labeling is deserved. Yet it seems
to me that much of rock-and-roll music is also sweet and innocent, tender and vital, and that a visit to this world is a chance to
roll back the membrane of youth's dreams. You peer inside and
then you put one foot in and before you know it, you are strolling
around and have decided to buy some property so that you can
always return. You may notice that, in a curious way, you have
always lived there.

The first visit is a dizzying, zigzag ride through a Coney Island jungle. The music and lyrics flail out at you, choked with
alien sounds, some of them expectedly raucous, hyena-like, others gentle, soft as tongues. There is advice you don't need, suf-
focating chichés, but then flashes of skin-pinching wisdom,
sounds and talk so current they make your teeth chatter.

It is a tangled world, where often simplistic, brain-dulling
lyrics are blended with spiraling, vine-entangled, suddenly
thrilling, cathedral-like backgrounds. Boys sound like girls, girls
like boys, authentic Negro rhythm and blues singers turn out to
be deep-banged David Copperfield types from the slums of
Liverpool. Children slip into manhood almost in mid-record,
and for a while the whole world seems to be named Bobby. A

---

* From a longer article written several years ago but continuingly valid and
illuminating.—A.K.

thigh-slapping country boy makes himself heard, a crowd of harmonizing nuns, chanting hipster rabbis, strange, sexless creatures from Australia, surfers from L.A. Latins swing into view *(Hey, baby, you want to dance with me?)* trailing groups of spindly, gospel-cloaked Negro girls who sing with a new pride snatched from Civil Rights marches. . . .

There are the voices of winners *(I'm in love with her and I feel fine)* and, more often, the sound of losers *(Mr. Lonely)*. Riding through so much of it is the sound of youth—jukebox tinkling, defiant brattiness, skirts swishing, grown-up putdowns, kisses refused, engines grunting, swirling rumps, guitars, loneliness, backs suddenly turned, movie-house wrestling and death on the highway. . . .

There is a musical explanation for it: the big bands became outmoded, uneconomical. A small group of kids could do the same job, cost less. But you feel there is more. It is as though the kids are huddling together, fearful of standing alone, afraid to hear the sounds of their single voices.

Some of the groups are chaotic, cannibal-like, unruly gangs, just moving and shouting, really, as if to drown out the massive Jack Ruby chord of absurdity that has been struck in the land. If they move enough, moan enough, cry and entreat enough, it will all go away. Others do a numb, glazed-eyed, much-sought-after "dumb sound." You know about this one if you have ever gone all the way down the line in argument with an adolescent, watched him retreat behind a final, immovable, no-grown-ups-allowed barrier. The "dumb sound" exists behind this last sullen barricade. . . .

And then there are the groups that send out a sound tying rock and roll of all shades together, an insistent, deep-probing, suffocatingly sexual beat that laces through your middle to pull at stale, long-unplucked cords of youth. The music is innocently sexual in the style of a young, pretty girl who crosses and rocks her legs while knitting argyles. If you give it a chance, the best of the music . . . will steal into your blood, and whether you are

Albert Schweitzer, U Thant or Ladybird Johnson, don't bet that your feet won't begin to move.

It cannot, of course, be explained, any more than you can explain why a boy is in love with monster movies one day, leopard frogs the next, *Playboy* bunnies the day after that. Trying to sort out rock-and-roll tastes is like making sense out of the contents of an enormous shoulder bag belonging to every American teen-age cheerleader. . . .

The music may be untamed, chaotic, but it is this very quality that has rendered the r-and-r radio-station managers, the people who decide what to play and not to play, modest and humble. No man among them feels confident that he can pick hits, can say for sure what the kids will like or reject. They are not only modest but awestruck, flabbergasted by the many tails of this rock-and-roll dragon. A record company man talking: "The standard procedure is for a group of these kids to make a hit, sell a million records and then, two months later, be right back in the butcher shop in Topeka wondering what in hell happened to them."

"Sound" is the word that reels triumphantly through all echelons of the r-and-r industry; you'd better have a distinctive one if you are going to be around longer than four and a half minutes. A deejay invites his audience to listen not to a record but to a sound, the way a fashion house shows off a look. The records that succeed wear their sounds like identifying badges; you can tell them miles away, in the dark or with one ear tied behind your back. Lesley Gore—spunky, ripe-apple fresh, no nonsense, and if you're a boy she'll knock sense into your head *(I don't wanna be a loser)*; the Zombies—tense, thin-chested, sex-frightened *(If she tempts you with her charms, tell her no, no, no, nononononono)*; the Righteous Brothers—unshaven, dressed up for the first time, like Mafia men suddenly thrust into Sicilian choirs; Dobie Gray—pimpled, falsely cocky, scared out of his wits though in with the In crowd; the Beachboys—lonely, rudderless, moaning, riding twenty-foot waves to an uncertain fu-

ture; Petula Clark—platonically intimate, the girl who feeds
you broth, tides you over a bad affair. . . .

The search for new sounds goes on with the same assiduity
the Pentagon uses in rooting out new weapons. Sound is the passport, the currency of acceptance, just as the new kid on the block
had better have a gimmick, a scar, a great-one-handed set shot,
an uncle on the cops. You forget how important sounds are to the
young. When I was sixteen, a fellow stole my girl by imitating
a police whistle each time I spoke, tugging down twice on an
imaginary toilet chain and holding his nose. Youth seems to go
after new sounds just as it might new experiences. . . .

It was WMCA [a key r-and-r station in New York] that converted me to rock and roll. Before that, my safe, protected radio
musical world was bounded on the left by Perry Como, on the
right by Hugo Winterhalter. In a daring mood, I might surrender to Frankie Laine. One day, I drove to a car wash, the
radio tuned in to a "good music" station, guaranteed to keep me
corruption-free with plenty of Sinatra and Mantovani. Driving
off later, I noticed that the dial had been turned, and I was listening to a sinful group called the Beatles singing *I Want to
Hold Your Hand*. It wasn't sinful. It was sweet, young, something pure about it. I drove on. The Dixiecups sang about going
to the chapel. No sin-pit swallowed me. A girl named Dion War-
wick very quietly broke my heart with *Walk On By*, and that did
it. I stayed in the car and listened for hours. A new kind of
salted peanuts. It got so I could hardly wait to get into the car
each morning to drive to the office. And I wasn't alone. There
had always been a kind of consanguinity between my book editor and me, something that ranged beyond literature. I had never
been able to dope it out. One day, jokingly, I mentioned a song
I had heard by the Velvelettes. He came back with the Miracles,
the Flames, fed me snatches of songs that went back eight years.
A savage rock-and-roll fan. Explained everything.

In some fields, a pro is a man who plays hard, picks up his
check, then couldn't care less about the sport until game time the
next day. Not so in rock and roll. Among the deejays, you sense

a fevered, day-and-night commitment to the music. "This isn't background music, ever," Joe O'Brien of WMCA told me. "It's there in the foreground. You don't put it on and have yourself a pleasant chitchat. You listen, participate. It's arrogant, aggressive, positive, slaps you right in the face. You listen or turn it off." Nor could he deny the sexuality. "But it's primitive, honest, flesh-and-blood, the way an authentic belly-dancer stacks up against some of the losers you see in the night clubs. . . ."

There is plenty of opposition to rock and roll, but to O'Brien, the hysterical pitch of the dissidents was due to a lack of effectiveness in their own lives. "But let's face it, you get 2,000 kids screaming, rotating their bottoms, half of the boys with hair down to their armpits, and they're a pain. So the adults forget about the music. It can be four kids singing an innocuous lyric about folks not understanding them, but it's the spectacle that's hard to take. The adult reaction becomes violent, irrational."

O'Brien thinks of rock and roll as the first music ever addressed directly to the vast teen-age world. The music of the 1940's? Unaware, really, of anyone under twenty-five. Yet Steve Lubunski, WMCA's general manager, knows that his station has an 80 percent adult audience, "if you define adult as eighteen and over. The same mother who bawls out her daughter for listening to us will send her off to school and then steal a little listening of her own. Plenty of hip-swaying in there, too. Why? It's a nondemonstrative society. The executive feels silly admitting he has the time of his life with the Beverly Hillbillies. You have a lot of adult r-and-r enthusiasm, but much of it on the sly."

Lubunski agreed the music had a directness, jumped out at you, tended to make you feel young, that the rthythm was sexual and that it all represented forbidden fruit to the kids, a language of rebellion. Some of the songs were written by old Tin Pan Alley types, but the slightest touch of cynicism, of pandering, would be smelled out. Kids and puppy dogs could always tell.

Some rock-and-roll music is plain, all-out funky; and some of it is tender and powerful, elaborately threaded, obviously rooted in the classics. And there is yet another sound—a distillate of the very worst (or best) in soap opera, fake novels about youth, every wrong notion Hollywood ever had about young people, the very worst in clichéd soda-fountain philosophy. Yet the lyrics are lousy on such an exquisite, classic level, and are backed up by music that is so thunderously positive and sexual, that you simply fall before the Olympian onslaught of all that raunchiness. Good God, you groan to yourself the first time you hear *Dawn (Dawn, go away I'm no good for you . . . hang on to him . . . think what a big man he'll be . . . the places you'll see . . . Now think what the future will be with a poor boy like me).* But the music has already ensnared some dark, second-rate, insufferable chamber of your psyche. . . .

You are never quite sure whether to invade certain worlds. The drug-and-dream world is one; and scuba divers very often have this feeling of uncertainty when they probe some new underwater palace and are observed coolly by strange, aristocratic creatures of the deep.

Perhaps rock and roll is such a world. There is the early-kiss taste of young mouths in this music, the fragrance of a starch-covered young girl's skin and the time when holding hands meant more than strategic hamlets in Vietnam. Who knows how threatening this is to middle-aged arteries? But why be upset about it? Why want to wipe it out? To be impatient with the music is to be impatient with things just budding. In seconds, a young boy climbs to the top of a tree, panther-like stands on the top branch. Triumphant. Later, at the dinner table, blue jeans slick, peas in his lap, he slides off his chair, disappears beneath the table. Teen-age music climbs to the top branch, also takes the table falls. But they are dazzling climbs, fascinating falls.

RALPH J. GLEASON

like a rolling stone*

I was a prisoner of logic.

Hail hail rock 'n roll,
Deliver me from the days of old!

Forms and rhythms in music are never changed without produc-
ing changes in the most important political forms and ways.

Plato said that.

There's something happenin' here. What it is ain't exactly clear.
There's a man with a gun over there tellin' me I've got to be-
ware. I think it's time we STOP, children, what's that sound?
Everybody look what's goin' down.

The Buffalo Springfield said that.

For the reality of politics, we must go to the poets, not the poli-
ticians.

Norman O. Brown said that.

For the reality of what's happening today in America, we must
go to rock 'n roll, to popular music.

I said that.

For almost forty years in this country, which has prided itself
on individualism, freedom and nonconformity, all popular songs
were written alike. They had an eight-bar opening statement, an
eight-bar repeat, an eight-bar middle section or bridge, and an
eight-bar reprise. Anything that did not fit into that framework
was, appropriately enough, called a novelty.

* From a longer essay.

Clothes were basically the same whether a suit was double-breasted or single-breasted, and the only people who wore beards were absentminded professors and Bolshevik bomb throwers. Long hair, which was equated with lack of masculinity —in some sort of subconscious reference to Samson, I suspect— was restricted to painters and poets and classical musicians, hence the term "longhair music" to mean classical. . . .

And the Beatles appeared ("a great figure rose up from the sea and pointed at me and said 'you're a Beatle with an "a" ' "— Genesis, according to John Lennon). They came at the proper moment of a spiritual cusp—as the martian in Robert Heinlein's *Stranger in a Strange Land* calls a crisis. Instantly, on those small and sometimes doll-like figures was focused all the rebellion against hypocrisy, all the impudence and irreverence that the youth of that moment was feeling vis-à-vis his elders. Automation, affluence, the totality of instant communication, the technology of the phonograph record, the transistor radio, had revolutionized life for youth in this society. The population age was lowering. Popular music, the jukebox and the radio were becoming the means of communication. Huntley and Brinkley were for mom and dad. People now sang songs they wrote themselves, not songs written *for* them by hacks in grimy Tin Pan Alley offices.

The folk-music boom paved the way. Bob Dylan's poetic polemics, "Blowin' in the Wind" and "The Times They Are A-Changin'," had helped the breakthrough. "Top-40" radio made Negro music available everywhere to a greater degree than ever before in our history. This was, truly, a new generation—the first in America raised with music constantly in its ear, weaned on a transistor radio, involved with songs from its earliest moment of memory. . . .

The dance of the swing era, of the big bands, was the fox-trot. It was really a formal dance extended in variation only by experts. The swing era's parents had danced the waltz. The fox-trot was a ritual with only a little more room for self-expression. Rock 'n roll brought with it not only the voices of youth singing their protests, their hopes and their expectations (along with their pathos and their sentimentality and their personal affairs from drag racing to romance), it brought their dances.

"Every period which abounded in folk songs has, by the same token, been deeply stirred by Dionysiac currents," Nietzsche points out in *The Birth of Tragedy*. And Dionysiac is the word to describe the dances of the past ten years, call them by whatever name from Bop to the Twist to the Frug, from the Hully Gully to the Philly Dog. . . .

In a short few years [the] companies that dominated the recording market, the huge publishing houses that copyrighted the music and collected the royalties, discovered that they no longer were "kings of the hill." Instead, a lot of small companies, like Atlantic and Chess and Imperial and others, had hits by people the major record companies didn't even know, singing songs written in Nashville and Detroit and Los Angeles and Chicago and sometimes, but no longer almost always, New York. It's taken the big ones a few years to recoup from that. First they called the music trash and the lyrics dirty. When that didn't work, as the attempt more recently to inhibit songs with supposed psychedelic or marijuana references has failed, they capitulated. They joined up. . . .

So the stage was set for the Beatles to take over—"with this ring I can—dare I say it?—rule the world!" And they did take over so thoroughly that they have become the biggest success in the history of show business. . . . With the Beatles and Dylan running tandem, two things . . . have been happening. The early Beatles were at one and the same time a declaration in favor of love and of life, an exuberant paean to the sheer joy of living, and a validation of the importance of American Negro music.

Dylan, by his political, issue-oriented broadsides first and then by his Rimbaudish nightmare visions of the real state of the nation, his bittersweet love songs and his pure imagery, did what the jazz and poetry people of the fifties had wanted to do—he took poetry out of the classroom and out of the hands of the professors and put it right out there in the streets for everyone.

I dare say that with the inspiration of the Beatles and Dylan we have more poetry being produced and more poets being made than ever before in the history of the world. . . .

Speaking of the importance of new styles of music, Plato said, "The new style quietly insinuates itself into manners and customs and from there it issues a greater force . . . goes on to attack laws and constitutions, displaying the utmost impudence, until it ends by overthrowing everything, both in public and in private." That seems to me to be a pretty good summation of the answer to the British rock singer Donovan's question, "What goes on? I really want to know."

The most immediate apparent change instituted by the new music is a new way of looking at things. . . . The old ways are going, and a new set of assumptions is beginning to be worked out. I cannot even begin to codify them. . . . But I think there are some clues—the sacred importance of love and truth and beauty and interpersonal relationships. . . .

Among the effects of "what's goin' on" is the relinquishing of the belief in the sacredness of logic. "I was a prisoner of logic and I still am," admits Malvina Reynolds, the composer of "Little Boxes," but then goes on to praise the new music. And the prisoners of logic are the ones who are really suffering the most —unless they have Mrs. Reynolds' glorious gift of youthful vision.

The first manifestation of the importance of this outside the music—I think—came in the works of Ken Kesey and Joseph Heller. *One Flew Over the Cuckoo's Nest*, with its dramatic view of the interchangeability of reality and illusion, and *Catch-22*, with its delightful utilization of crackpot realism (to use C. Wright Mills's phrase) as an explanation of how things are, were works of seminal importance. No one any longer really believes that the processes of international relations and world economics are rationally explicable. Absolutely the very best and clearest discussion of the entire thing is wrapped up in Milo Minderbinder's explanation, in *Catch-22*, of how you can buy eggs for seven cents apiece in Malta and sell them for five cents in Pianosa and make a profit. Youth understands the truth of this immediately, and no economics textbook is going to change it. Just as—implying the importance of interpersonal relations and the beauty of being true to oneself—the under-thirty youth immediately understands the creed patiently explained by Yossarian in *Catch-22* that everybody's your enemy who's trying to get you killed, even if he's your own commanding officer. . . .

At this point in history, most of the organs of opinion . . . are in the control of the prisoners of logic. They take a flick like *Morgan* and grapple with it. They take *Help* and *A Hard Day's Night* and grapple with those two beautiful creations, and they fail utterly to understand what is going on because they try to deal with them logically. They complain because art doesn't make sense! Life on this planet in this time of history doesn't make sense either—as an end result of immutable laws of economics and logic and philosophy.

Dylan sang, "You raise up your head and you ask 'is this where it is?' And somebody points to you and says 'it's his' and you say 'what's mine' and somebody else says 'well, what is' and you say 'oh my god am i here all alone?' " Dylan wasn't the first. Orwell saw some of it, Heller saw more, and in a different way so did I. F. Stone, that remarkable journalist, who is really a poet, when he described a *Herald Tribune* reporter extracting from the Pentagon the admission that, once the first steps for the Santo Domingo episode were mounted, it was impossible to stop the machine. . . .

Kesey and Heller and Terry Southern, to a lesser degree in his novels but certainly in *Dr. Strangelove*, have hold of it. I suspect that they are not really a New Wave of writers but only a *last* wave of the past. . . . In almost every aspect of what is happening today, [the] turning away from the old patterns is making itself manifest. . . . The Negro performers, from James Brown to Aaron Neville to the Supremes and the Four Tops, are on an Ed Sullivan trip, striving as hard as they can to get on that stage and become part of the American success story, while the white rock performers are motivated to escape from that stereotype. Whereas in years past the Negro performer offered style in performance and content in song—the messages from Leadbelly to Percy Mayfield to Ray Charles were important messages—today he is almost totally style with very little content. And when James Brown sings, "It's a Man's World," or Aaron Neville sings, "Tell It Like It is," he takes a phrase and only a phrase with which to work, and the Supremes and the Tops are choreographed more and more like the Four Lads and the Ames Brothers and the McGuire Sisters.

I suggest that this bears a strong relationship to the condition of the civil rights movement today, in which the only truly black position is that of Stokely Carmichael, and in which the N.A.A.C.P. and most of the other formal groups are, like the Four Tops and the Supremes, on an Ed Sullivan-TV trip to middle-class America. And the only true American Negro music is that which abandons the concepts of European musical thought, abandons the systems of scales and keys and notes, for a music whose roots are in the culture of the colored peoples of the world.

The drive behind all American popular music performers, to a greater or lesser extent, from Sophie Tucker and Al Jolson, on down through Pat Boone and as recently as Roy Head and Charlie Rich, has been to sound like a Negro. The white jazz musician was the epitome of this. . . . Today's new youth, beginning with the rock band musician but spreading out into the entire movement, into the Haight-Ashbury hippies, is not ashamed of being white. He is remarkably free from prejudice, but he is not attempting to join the Negro culture or to become part of it, like his musical predecessor, the jazzman, or like his social predecessor, the beatnik. . . . For the very first time in decades . . . something important and new is happening artistically and musically in this society that is distinct from the Negro and to which the Negro will have to come, if he is interested in it at all, as in the past the white youth went uptown to Harlem or downtown or crosstown or to wherever the Negro community was centered because there was the locus of artistic creativity. . . .

The basic creed of the American Federation of Musicians is that musicians must not play unless paid. The new generation wants money, of course, but its basic motivation is to play any time, anywhere, anyhow. Art is first, then finance, most of the time. . . . This [extends] the attitude that gave Pete Seeger, Joan Baez and Bob Dylan such status. They . . . never have been for sale in the sense that you can hire Sammy Davis to appear, as you can hire Dean Martin to appear, any time he's free, as long as you pay his price. You have not been able to do this with Seeger, Baez and Dylan any more than Allen Ginsberg has been for sale either to *Ramparts* or the C.I.A. Naturally, this revolt against the assumptions of the adult world runs smack dab into the sanctimonious puritan morality of America, the schizophrenia that insists that money is serious business and the acquisition of wealth is a blessing in the eyes of the Lord, that what we do in private we must preach against in public. Don't do what I do, do what I say.

Implicit in the very names of the . . . organizations that these youths form is an attack on the traditional, serious attitude toward money . . . not only [in the names of] the groups themselves . . . with [their beautifully irreverent] imagery: the Grateful Dead, the Loading Zone, Blue Cheer or the Jefferson Airplane—all dating back to the Beatles with an "a"—[but also in] the names of their business companies: Frontage Road Productions (the music company of the Grateful Dead), Faithful Virtue Music (the Lovin' Spoonful's publishing company), Ashes and Sand (Bob Dylan's production firm—his music publishing company is Dwarf Music). A group that gives light shows is known as the Love Conspiracy Commune, and there was a dance recently in Marin County, California, sponsored by the Northern California Psychedelic Cattlemen's Association, Ltd. . . .

Attacking the conventional attitude toward money is considered immoral in the society of our fathers, because money is sacred. The reality of what Bob Dylan says—"Money doesn't talk, it swears"—has yet to seep through.

A corollary of the money attack is the whole thing about long hair, bare feet and beards. . . . Recently I spent an evening with a lawyer, a brilliant man who is engaged in a lifelong crusade to educate and reform lawyers. He is interested in the civil liberties issue of police harassment of hippies. But, he said, they wear those uniforms of buckskin and fringe and beads. Why don't they dress naturally? So I asked him if he was born in his three-button dacron suit. . . .

To the eyes of many of the elder generation, all visible aspects of the new generation, its music, its lights, its clothes, are immoral. The City of San Francisco Commission on Juvenile Delinquency reported adversely on the sound level and the lights at the Fillmore Auditorium, as if those things of and by themselves were threats (they may be, but not in the way the Commission saw them). A young girl might have trouble maintaining her judgment in that environment, the Commission chairman said.

Now this all implies that dancing is the road to moral ruin. . . . During the twenties and the thirties and the forties—in other words, during the prime years of the Old Ones of today—dancing, in the immoral words of Bob Scobey, the Dixieland trumpet player, "was an excuse to get next to a broad." The very least effect of the pill on American youth is that this is no longer true.

The assault on hypocrisy works on many levels. The adult society attempted to chastise Bob Dylan by economic sanction, calling the line in "Rainy Day Woman," "Everybody must get stoned" (although there is a purely religious, even biblical, meaning to it, if you wish), an enticement to teen-agers to smoke marijuana. But no one has objected to Ray Charles's "Let's Go Get Stoned," which is about gin, or to any number of other songs, from the Kingston Trio's "Scotch and Soda" on through "One for My Baby and One More [*One More!*] for the Road." Those are about alcohol and alcohol is socially acceptable, as well as big business, even though I believe that everyone under thirty now knows that alcohol is worse for you than marijuana, that, in fact, the only thing wrong about marijuana is that it is illegal. . . .

[And marijuana smokers] do not think they are doing anything wrong, any more than their grandparents were when they broke the prohibition laws. They do not want to go to jail, but a jail sentence or a bust no longer carries the social stigma it once did. The civil rights movement has made a jailing a badge of honor, if you go there for principle, and to a great many people today, the right to smoke marijuana is a principle worth risking jail for.

"Make Love, Not War" is one of the most important slogans of modern times, a statement of life against death, as the Beatles have said over and over—"Say the word and be like me, say the word and you'll be free.". . .

There's another side to it, of course, or at least another aspect of it. The Rolling Stones, who came into existence really to fight jazz in the clubs of London, were against the jazz of the integrated world, the integrated world arrived at by rational processes. Their sons, from "Satisfaction" and "19th Nervous Breakdown" to "Get Off of My Cloud" and "Mother's Little Helper," were antiestablishment songs in a nonpolitical sort of way, just as Dylan's first period was antiestablishment in a political way. The Stones [moved], with "Ruby Tuesday" and "Let's Spend the Night Together," into a social radicalism of sorts; but in the beginning, and for their basic first-thrust appeal, they hit out in rage, almost in blind anger and certainly with overtones of destructiveness, against the adult world. It's no wonder the novel they were attracted to was David Wallis's *Only Lovers Left Alive*, that Hell's Angels story of a teen-age, future jungle. . . . Nor is it any wonder that this attitude appealed to that section of the youth whose basic position was still in politics and economics (remember that the Rolling Stone Mick Jagger was a London School of Economics student, whereas Lennon and McCartney were artists and writers). When the Stones first came to the West Coast, a group of young radicals issued [a] proclamation of welcome [which read in part]:

Greetings and welcome Rolling Stones, our comrades in the desperate battle against the maniacs who hold power. The revolutionary youth of the world hears your music and is inspired to even more deadly acts. We fight in guerrilla bands against the invading imperialists in Asia and South America, we riot at rock 'n roll concerts everywhere. . . .

We will play your music in rock 'n roll marching bands as we tear down the jails and free the prisoners, as we tear down the State schools and free the students, as we tear down the military bases and arm the poor, as we tatoo BURN BABY BURN! on the bellies of the wardens and generals and create a new society from the ashes of our fires. . . .

But rhetoric like that did not bring out [one January day] to a Human Be-In on the polo grounds of San Francisco's Golden Gate Park twenty thousand people who were there, fundamentally, just to see the other members of the tribe, not to hear speeches . . . but just to *BE*.

In the Haight-Ashbury district the Love Generation organizes itself into Job Co-ops and committees to clean the streets, and the monks of the neighborhood, the Diggers, talk about free dances in the park to put the Avalon Ballroom and the Fillmore out of business and about communizing the incomes of Bob Dylan and the Beatles. The Diggers trace back spiritually to those British millenarians who took over land in 1649, just before Cromwell, and after the Civil War freed it, under the assumption that the land was for the people. They tilled it and gave the food away. The Diggers give food away. Everything is Free. So is it with the Berkeley Provos and the new group in Cleveland—the Prunes— and the Provos in Los Angeles. More, if an extreme, assault against the money culture. Are they driving the money changers out of the temple? Perhaps. The Diggers say they believe it is just as futile to fight the system as to join it, and they are dropping out in a way that differs from Leary's. . . .

[But] even *Ramparts*, which is the white hope of the Square Left, if you follow me, misunderstands. They think . . . that political activity is the only hope, and Bob Dylan says, "There's no left wing and no right wing, only upwing and down wing," and also, "I tell you there are no politics."

But the banding together to form Job Co-ops, to publish newspapers, to talk to the police (even to bring them flowers), aren't these political acts? I suppose so, but I think they are political acts of a different kind, a kind that results in the Hell's Angels being the guardians of the lost children at the Be-In and the guarantors of peace at dances.

The New Youth is finding its prophets in strange places—in dance halls and on the jukebox. It is on, perhaps, a frontier buckskin trip after a decade of Matt Dillon and Bonanza and the other TV folk myths, in which the values are clear (as opposed to those in the world around us), and right is right and wrong is wrong. The Negro singers have brought the style and the manner of the Negro gospel preacher to popular music, just as they brought the rhythms and the feeling of the gospel music, and now the radio is the church and Everyman carries his own walkie-talkie to God in his transistor. . . .

"Nobody ever taught you how to live out in the streets," Bob Dylan sings in "Like a Rolling Stone." You may consider that directed at a specific person, or you may, as I do, consider it poetically aimed at plastic uptight America, to use a phrase from one of the Family Dog founders.

"Nowhere to run, nowhere to hide," Martha and the Vandellas sing, and Simon and Garfunkel say, "The words of the prophets are written on the subway walls, in tenement halls." And the Byrds sing, "A time for peace, I swear it's not too late," just as the Beatles sing, "Say the word." What has formal religion done in this century to get the youth of the world so well acquainted with a verse from the Bible? . . .

These songs speak to us in our condition, just as Dylan did with "Lookout kid, it's somethin' you did, god knows what, but you're doin' it again." And Dylan sings again a concept that finds immediate response in the tolerance and the antijudgment stance of the new generation, when he says, "There are no trials inside the Gates of Eden."

Youth is wise today. Lenny Bruce claimed that TV made even eight-year-old girls sophisticated. When Bob Dylan in "Desolation Row" sings, "At midnight all the agents and the superhuman crew come out and round up everyone that knows more than they do," he speaks true, as he did with "Don't follow leaders." But sometimes it is, as John Sebastian of the Lovin' Spoonful says, "like trying to tell a stranger 'bout a rock 'n roll."

Let's go back again to Nietzsche.

Orgiastic movements of a society leave their traces in music [he wrote]. Dionysiac stirrings arise either through the influence of those narcotic potions of which all primitive races speak in their hymns [—dig that!—] or through the powerful approach of spring, which penetrates with joy the whole frame of nature. So stirred, the individual forgets himself completely. It is the same Dionysiac power which in medieval Germany drove ever increasing crowds of people singing and dancing from place to place; we recognize in these St. John's and St. Vitus' dancers the bacchic choruses of the Greeks, who had their precursors in Asia Minor and as far back as Babylon and the orgiastic Sacea. There are people who, either from lack of experience or out of sheer stupidity, turn away from such phenomena, and strong in the sense of their own sanity, label them either mockingly or pityingly "endemic diseases." These benighted souls have no idea how cadaverous and ghostly their "sanity" appears as the intense throng of Dionysiac revelers sweeps past them.

. . . "Believe in the magic, it will set you free," the Lovin' Spoonful sing. "This is an invitation across the nation," sing Martha and the Vandellas, and the Mamas and the Papas, "a chance for folks to meet, there'll be laughin', singin' and music swingin', and dancin' in the street!"

Do I project too much? Again, to Nietzsche. "Man now expresses himself through song and dance as the member of a higher community; he has forgotten how to walk, how to speak and is on the brink of taking wing as he dances . . . no longer the *artist*, he has himself become *a work of art*."

"Hail hail rock 'n roll," as Chuck Berry sings. "Deliver me from the days of old!"

I think he's about to be granted his wish.

STANLEY KRAMER

---

scrambled put-ons, or who's copping out and how?

I think there will be a massive return to utter simplicity.

When I attended college in the 1930's, it seemed that almost all the art majors wanted to write the great American novel or the great American play. Today, the young creative talent wants to make the great American film. Or, to be more truthful, the great film. I'm not sure he cares about its being American, or even thinks it can be. Godard doesn't make American films. And the student of cinema wants to be Godard—not William Wyler or George Stevens or John Ford.

The reason has to do with the purposeful widening of the Generation Gap—the desire of the young to move as far as possible from the common denominators they and we have known. In more practical terms, the motivated story form—with its emphasis on a beginning, a middle and an end—is not the approach of the new film creator. He takes the viewpoint that Godard has said a story might have a beginning, middle and end—but not necessarily in that order. And sometimes, it seems, not necessarily with all three, either. The new art issues the challenge to the "once upon a time" hacks that "film can be art for art's sake. You conventional filmmakers seek content and form. We seek effect, fragmentation, improvisation, technique. If you can't feel the emotional essence of it, you can't understand it. If you have to *ask* what it means, man, you'll *never know*."

This leads to something called the "put-on." It happens on film all the time now—but is in no way limited to film in the "new art" approach. Now the put-on leads to the adoration of technique. The "nouvelle vague," the "neo-realists" and the "angry young men" have opened the gates to interrupted dialogue, mismatching, jump cuts, super-imposures, split screens and the camera as primary weapon in the director's bag. Technique covers a multitude of sins. It relieves the need for a motivated development, lightens the burden on the story-teller by its stress on the strictly visual. It is a mistake to refer to this kind of filming as a "director's medium." The privilege of being a director in a director's medium involves the responsibility of long arduous collaboration with the writer, nothing less. That part of the director's function in picture-making can be compared to an iceberg—three-quarters of it is unseen beneath the surface. This is where concept is forged and where there is improvisation more unbridled and imaginative than any 60-day "free association" schedule can manage. This is where there is collaboration in what is a collaborative medium. . . .

The primary objection to "Guess Who's Coming to Dinner" was the fact that . . . I made a film about a problem miscegenation—which the university student maintains does not exist. . . . A surprising number of them said bluntly, "That's no problem for us. We accepted this a long time ago.". . .

Maybe it is no problem for *them* to fall in love with a girl of a different race, or vice versa. But they take no cognizance of the fact that they live in a world in which their own fathers and mothers and relatives and friends and neighborhoods do constitute for them a problem. They are so right—and the sunset side of the gap is so wrong—but that's part of the very real problem.

Another objection was Sidney Poitier's characterization. "It's pretty old-fashioned to make the character of the Negro so pure and simple," they declared. "You made him such an ideal fellow, we knew from the beginning that she would marry him."

The big point, of course, is that everybody in the film was de-

liberately made ideal. The film is an adventure into the ludicrous
—the characters so perfect that the only conceivable objection to
this marriage could be . . . the pigmentation of the man's skin.

I heard most often that the film was a "cop-out" because, to
be real, Sidney Poitier would have had to [be] a postman—
like his father. That's really some other story—on some other
economic level. Actually, the white family in this story might not
have been attracted to a *white* postman.

They didn't want more love scenes between Sidney Poitier and
Katharine Houghton—they wanted them in bed, period. I
pointed out that whether or not they agree with the premise of
the picture, I was dealing with an eight-hour time span in the
girl's home with her family there—and if they were a *white*
couple I'd still have a very difficult time getting them into bed.
[But] the students tend to react to a subject and make generalizations without the training to demand: *which* story, at *which*
time, in *which* place.

Nine out of ten of the most informed collegiate youth in history took the position the film could not make its way south of
the Mason-Dixon line. This despite their earlier accusations that
it was too mild, too benign. [Actually] the film has been doing
smashing business everywhere, including Atlanta, New Orleans,
Houston and all points south.

Vietnam and the draft will have to take the blame for thrust-
ing upon [students] a decision which we're unable to make for
them in a war which isn't an official war and which divides us.
That's enough for bitterness and for the desire of youth to divorce itself as far as it can from everything we know or promise.
We find young filmmakers no less desirous of departing from all
our norms and most of our heroes.

But the seeds of the next revolution are planted during this
one. I think there will be a massive return to utter simplicity.
It remains the purest form, the most difficult to attain. When a
woman buys an exclusively designed gown, it is the design with
the simplest lines which is the more expensive and the more brilliantly engineered and cut. Not the brocades and beads and

bangles. These are the manifestations of the more obvious techniques—the overloading of the design—perhaps even to obscure the basic flaws.

And sentiment—oh, sentiment, the whipping boy of [today's] film buff. How many creative cowards have refused to play *the* scene at the risk of seeming overly sentimental and loosening an onslaught from the bogus intellectual critics. Underplay it, symbol it, technique it—but don't shoot it straight. Or if you must shoot it, don't commit yourself to it by making it simple enough to be reacted to for what it is.

This new unsmiling generation may occupy itself with the dire foreboding of its music, with the serious faces and apartness of its dance. But I wish for its vast multitude of filmmakers a little more humor, about themselves and about us. Even if they blame us for the whole damn mess, let it not be because we've been evil—but rather because we were somewhat ridiculous.

WILLIAM KLOMAN

the groove of the future

**The truth of a thing is the feel of it,
not the think of it.—Stanley Kubrick**

From the look of things, there are some difficult days ahead for middle-aged theater and film audiences. But if they are willing to make the effort, they just might find out what their kids are all about. The new direction being taken by film and drama strongly reflects what might be called a sensory reorganization among the younger generation. This new wave makes not only greater demands on its adult audience, but it makes qualitatively different ones from those that have been made in the past. The difference is the difference between understanding and groovin'.

The media explosion has, in effect, rearranged the kids' minds and put them way ahead of their parents in their openness to the best of the new art. The way most adult Americans respond to drama stems in part from the way people used to be taught to interpret literature—especially poetry—in high school. The assumption was that any work of art, or any part thereof, could be reduced to a declarative sentence. Teachers used to tingle with pleasure when a student showed he could change a lush image of daffodils into something like "It says the poet's girl friend has yellow hair." The result was a strong preference for writers who just *told* you she had yellow hair and cut out all the nonsense in between. People grew up with their artistic receptors atrophied beyond repair.

Ballet and symphonic forms suffered too. Whole generations

of children were driven away from such music by being told that every measure "meant" something, as if the composer were keeping a secret. "It's for me to know and you to find out," composers and choreographers were supposed to be saying, with the result that nobody gave a damn because it was too hard to "find out."

Thanks largely to innovators in popular music—by which I mean the Beatles and Bob Dylan—all that is over now. Children, and more slowly, adults, are discovering that music is for listening. The yellow submarine might be a Nembutal pill, but it doesn't really matter much. The song is its own message, and won't sit still for footnoting. Academic types still dissect Dylan lyrics for obscure references, because that's their thing. The rest of us know by now that that's not the way to hear a song. Gertrude Stein's epigram about roses has come of age.

The "American Tribal Love-Rock Musical," *Hair*, [will probably] be the *West Side Story* of the sixties. The difference between the two shows illustrates how far we've come in a decade. *West Side Story* had vigorous music, but a smarmy social conscience. It now seems awfully dated. In good liberal fashion, it romanticized the lower classes to within an inch of their downtrodden lives. Events have outrun its message, and the vision of slum gangs dancing into battle would probably strike today's young audience as odd, if not funny. . . .

Hair's godparents are Marshall McLuhan, Herbert Marcuse, and Norman O. Brown, the prophet of polymorphous perversity. Not only do white girls in *Hair* dig black boys (and black girls dig white boys, in a number that may set the Supremes back five shades of pancake), but boys, black and white, dig each other. Love, in *Hair*, comes interracial, intrasexual, and in multiples of three. As well as the regular way.

RCA Victor, which will publish the Broadway-cast album, threw a little press conference after one of the previews, and a few of the participants complained that they couldn't follow the show's story line. Before Tom O'Horgan, *Hair*'s director, could rise to the defense of the book, a girl in the company responded,

"Man, we're not asking you to follow anything. Just to dig what's going on. That's what it's all about—opening up your mind."

Marat / Sade was in the same bag. It was tolerated as an amiable freak. People admitted that it was excitingly staged, but found it hard to "understand." No one seems to have suspected that it represented the theater of the future, but now that *Hair* has arrived, *Marat / Sade* comes neatly into perspective, and its point is belatedly clear. It was never meant to be understood, in any traditional sense. It was meant to be "dug." And "digging" a work of art requires, for most of us, a radical alteration of our habits of perception. *Marat / Sade* and now *Hair* bear the same relationship to an Ibsen play that a collage does to a realistic landscape. The new theater insists that its audience relinquish their demand for traditional structure. "A play is not a novel," it says. "A play is a collage of dramatic effects which calls for groovin', not understanding."

To groove means to yield yourself to the flow of activity around you. To be "with it," as a phonograph needle is "with" the record groove, responding to its microscopic impressions. Swinging with the sound. Groovin' requires a lot of personal freedom, and a lot of self-assurance. It is the antithesis of uptight perception, in which one accepts only what he can comfortably categorize. Groovin' consists of opening your senses to what is happening, without anticipation or imposition of logical structures. The new art is often devoid of traditional dramatic tension, which depends upon sequential progression for its effect. Chevrolet was on the same track when it tried to convince people that the fun was in the going, not in the getting there.

Groovin' also includes the ability to receive several clashing stimuli simultaneously. Singers in the aisles compete with dialogue on stage, and both are enveloped in lighting effects which theatergoers struggling to "understand" will find distracting. The effect—like that of montage in films—is one of sensory bombardment. It is intentional, not undisciplined.

Hair is a celebration, not a story. It celebrates the human body, marijuana, love and sex. For the first time on a Broadway stage, the human body is shown completely naked. That, too, is part of the collage we are asked to dig. The gesture is graceful and affecting. To ask what the scene "means" is to miss the point and to force drama back into the tired categories our best playwrights would like to overcome. There it is, people—the human body. Dig it.

In 1957, the tag-line of the "Officer Krupke" number in *West Side Story* was thought daring. The songs in *Hair* include a catalogue of forbidden drugs, sexual practices, and words. Reciting them on a Broadway stage in 1968 is not shocking. It seems more like an overdue exorcism of fear. We are in a much healthier state when nice people in evening clothes can admit that such things exist in the world. And most of the nice people in evening clothes will go home happier.

Hair's presence helps restore relevance to the theater itself. For too long, drama has failed to affect, to touch or involve audiences. Beside a play like *Hair*, the plays of Tennessee Williams, for example, seem like exercises in voyeurism. Williams showed us life through a plate-glass window. Today's theater is designed for audiences who prefer boutiques to show windows. They want to be surrounded by the merchandise. They want to touch it.

Watching *Hair*, I recalled a talk I had with Leonard Cohen, a Canadian poet who . . . along with nearly every articulate young person . . . today, believes himself to be a revolutionary. "My feeling is," Cohen told me, "that as our revolution gets more and more powerful, it will become invisible. You won't know where the hell anybody is." At the *Hair* press conference, a reporter asked, in effect, which members of the company were real hippies, and which ones were actors. It was a lovely moment of truth, because the entire cast just smiled.

If Cohen is right, *Hair* is a transitional piece of drama. Perhaps the final glorification of the visible revolution. Stanley Kubrick's *2001: A Space Odyssey*, however, is a film that has made the jump Cohen spoke about. Masked as a science-fiction thriller (reviewers who took it at face value found it boring),

Space Odyssey is, in fact, a deeply subversive film. What the film subverts are all the familiar categories of time and space, our habit of linear-sequential perception, and our painfully cramped concept of the erotic. In this respect, the story line is incidental. It could as easily have been about racing drivers or the Trojan War.

What matters is the obsessive attention Kubrick paid to shapes in motion, and his disregard for traditional dramatic continuity. Like *Hair*, *Space Odyssey* has broken loose from the novel and is exploring the possibilities of its own medium. It is the sort of thing Andy Warhol has been doing badly for years, but Kubrick makes it work.

People attuned to cookbooks are sometimes blind to poetry. *Space Odyssey* is poetry. It asks for groovin', not understanding. It says, "Observe the spaceship moving toward its goal." Some time later, after we have been shown every possible angle of the ship, it may reach its goal. People restless to "get on with the action" miss what the real action is. Natural groovers—children especially—surrender themselves to the form and are able to experience the contours of the ship in motion. Natural groovers supply their own message. Concentration on a single object reveals many layers of possibility in the object: Machine is beauty, Machine is sex. The audience comes away enriched only if they open their heads and experience what is put before them. They have to know how to groove. I suspect that much of the critical hostility to *Space Odyssey* originated in the theater lobby during intermission. Critics (some of whom seem to dislike movies and wish they were more like books) met their friends and found that nobody was able to verbalize what the film, so far, had "meant.". . .

When authors and directors begin playing in a new key—begin, in fact, to reach out and play on the human sensorium with their gloves off—traditional forms of criticism become inadequate. As they attempt increasingly to generate feelings rather than "messages," criteria will have to be established to evaluate their success. The first requirement of a new criticism is to recognize the breakdown of traditional sensory divisions. Groovin' requires the unification of the five senses into one receptor. Today's children do this naturally, and their parents, if they respond to the Beatles, already know how to do it with music.

In music, film, and drama, we are entering the age of the feelie. Rational methods of perceiving the truth about man and his world seem to have failed us, and are being abandoned. "The truth of a thing," Stanley Kubrick says, "is in the feel of it, not the think of it." Kubrick's dictate is the motto of the younger generation of film makers and dramatists. . . .

ROLLO MAY
(Interviewed by Alexander Klein)

we must create myths
and goals together

**When the old myths disappear, youth
has to look within.**

MAY: The permissive parents in my generation have done their children a disservice in agreeing with everything and removing the controls. That gives youth more anxiety, takes away their chance to struggle with the older generation, their chance to assert themselves, to test their strength and establish their freedom in a successful struggle against the parent generation. Now if parents have capitulated to start with, and the parent generation is a frightened generation, it shrinks up, becomes more like a neurotic, more rigid.

In turn, the young people have no myths. The myths and symbols have disintegrated. By myth I mean that view of myself which gives me identity, a sense of being, a style of life. It used to be that a set of ceremonies helped you get born, educated, confirmed, married, told you how to bring up your children, even helped you die. Now none of those have the same cogency. So, in addition to the problems caused by parents' overpermissiveness, youth has been struggling to come of age in a society in which there have been no basic, viable, fully-accepted myths and symbols available to be incorporated into the self.

KLEIN: Even the myth of material success has evaporated for many middle-class youth. Partly because they've been brought up in affluence and take it for granted; partly because they believe they see this affluence as ashes in their parents' mouths.

A: The point is, when the old myths disappear, youth has to look within, to undertake the lonely, confusing task of finding new myths on which to base identity. Hence the mood of apathy in the early 1950's. Temporarily there just were no clear, acceptable goals. So we come to the beatniks, and then the hippies, in a sense the most extreme movement in modern youth against the values of society. They deny nine-to-five work, and they may be a bit premature, but in a few years none of us is likely to work nine-to-five unless we want to. They are against the old ideas that there can only be sex when there is love and marriage and that marriage is "forever." What they are after is *authenticity* of relationship *in the moment*. They ask, "Is this relationship authentic now, is the affection real, is the understanding real?" It's a cogent critique of the artificiality of society.

I've been out to California and spent some time with the hippies. And I find them a very sound corrective to my own Protestant work ethic. But the problem for the hippie is fidelity, the lasting quality of love, of relationship. They seem to believe that emotion is only existential and momentary. Fundamentally, I'm afraid, the hippies don't have a system of goals and values that has staying quality, that can offer a lasting, positive, viable way of life to the future.

Q: But suppose the hippies' acceptance of affections which are temporary but "honest, authentic" were spread out in breadth and time, with hundreds of thousands, perhaps many millions, living a hippie life-style their entire lives. They enjoy fleeting "loves," but in a sense pervasive ones because they know that they can always feel love and consummate their feelings with partners reciprocating the feeling, without necessarily focusing on one person for very long, and—significantly—without being badly hurt by a partner's shifting affections (or guilty about themselves turning to a new love) because the new myth says this is fine and good. And new, authentic, non-ulterior-motivated relationships are always available. And both sexes will have economic security, with the children brought up communally, tribally and/or by professional, paid but loving "parents." Might such a life-style be preferable to the pattern many now have of serial polygamy and of guilty, hurting "unfaithfulness" (with each relationship-end a painful loss and failure for at least one partner) and with no social form for bringing up the children?

A: I think there's a possibility that some people would have greater fulfillment that way. Whether it could be made workable and lasting is hard to say. The strange thing, for example, is that there are very few beatniks and hippies who remain that way for long. I think it's essentially a youth movement and a corrective movement. It is saving a lot of young people from going to mental hospitals. It's a positive form of protest, as neurosis and psychosis are negative forms. The hippie movement serves as a kind of support, a kind of constructive group therapy, if you will.

Q: Are you suggesting that a larger proportion of hippies are disturbed than, say, youth who opt for conformism such as getting a job in a corporation and "fitting in?" Perhaps just as high a percentage of the conformists are just as sick and are saving themselves by a sort of "conformist group therapy"?

A: Oh, yes. In fact, I think there may be more latent mental illness among the conformists who fit in neatly with society. I'd say the conformist is more likely to end up a patient in my office than the hippy. Many hippies achieve personality integration by this kind of natural therapy and then function better in general society.

Q: Are parents jealous of what they conceive, consciously or not, as the younger generation's hedonistic life?

A: Yes, the older generation envies the new values of youth.

Q: . . . Which they claim to decry.

A: Yes, the older generation certainly is hypocritical and confused. We are at a point of transition in history. I believe that just as the classical period in Greece went into the Hellenistic period and then collapsed, so the period that began at the

Renaissance started to collapse in the Victorian period, became more rigid (like a neurotic before he collapses) and did collapse in 1914. And ever since we've been in a transitional period, without myths and symbols, without mooring posts. This is the transitional period that precedes the birth of a new age which we don't yet have. And this, essentially, is the reason for the extreme conflict between youth and age at this time. We are going to live in the new world whether we like it or not, but we don't yet know what the new world's going to be. . . .

Now let me go to the revolt at Columbia. The real reasons for that revolt were complex, including the lack of communication, the lack of students' adequate role in the running of the university. Columbia had become a stultified, rigid place, administratively. For the first couple of days I was all for the students. But then a change occurred. They didn't have long-term values worked out. They didn't really have an understanding of the concept of freedom. The philosophers they follow are Rousseau-esque—like Paul Goodman and Erich Fromm—who seem to believe chiefly in what to be against, and that if you act against those things everything is going to work out beautifully. Well, it doesn't work out beautifully.

One has to be able to plan, control and aim for things. Soon the power that was in the student revolt became its own end, and they may have become somewhat drunk on power. The vacuum of goals was filled by the joy-in-power of actually paralyzing the university. Paralysis seemed to be the goal. Now this I cannot but be very much against.

Q: But isn't rebellion generally a reaction *against* things? Particularly youthful rebellion. So I ask rather why are the *adults* failing to respond with meaningful reforms and programs? Why do the adults act as if youth were their irreconcilable enemies? So the young say to the older generation: You keep messing things up and you have no answers for anything; and even when we yell all you can say is you hate the *way* we yell.

A: What you're really saying is that both young and old are

bankrupt with respect to goals. That is true. In this transitional period we have to work goals out together, and they've got to be worked out in the deeper aspects, the irrational aspects of life, as well as in rationally explicated aims.

PHYLLIS McGINLEY

the new breed of parents

**If domestic virtue is decaying, the real
cause is found in the rapid disappearance
of the family horse and buggy.**

There is nothing pundits love like a crisis. Give them
something to deplore and they are happy as a child with a
Popsicle. They can view with genuine alarm, cry authentic woe
and ruin. And of all the topics for lamentation, the collapse
of the American family is the most reliable. It is as handy now as
it was, no doubt, when some early colonist set up the first gazette
and needed a paragraph of prophecy to titillate readers. We
know the problem bothered Cotton Mather. Jonathan Edwards
thundered from various pulpits that God had His eye on household rebels. Even in what seems to us the safe, patriarchal era of
the late Victorians, oracles were warning of catastrophe.

"Ever and anon," wrote a doomsayer . . . at the beginning of
the century, "rises a cry that the home is perishing from our
midst and civilization must perish with it."

Then he went on to explain what he believed was at the root
of that doom. He had to reach farther than his hand-wringing
brother today. There was no Dr. Spock to blame, no space program; the country was threatened by no unpopular wars, few
divorces, fewer precooked dinners. The Bomb was not so much
as a gleam in a scientist's eye, and the word "alienation" had
not entered the mass vocabulary. . . .

"If domestic virtue is decaying," he continued, "the real
cause is found in the rapid disappearance of the family horse

and buggy. That conveyance preserved a sweet and delicate atmosphere of family ties. The citizen, shaken loose from his safe domestic base by much streetcar straphanging, takes to socialism and drinking. The matron, without the steadying discipline of *having to get home in time to feed the horse* [the italics are mine] gads and grows extravagant.". . . .

There is consolation in knowing that our ancestors faced dilemmas which, quaint as they sound now, must have seemed in their era as disturbing as ours. It is soothing to read that more than 100 years ago moralists were concerned over the downfall of parental authority. Children were called "selfish and willful," and communities bewailed the "decay of discipline and the alarming development of juvenile depravity."

The consistent message seems to be that the American family has *always* been in crisis, yet has always muddled through. And I, by nature an optimist, cannot entirely despair. From my suburban terrace I survey the betrayals, the accidents, the triumphs of middle-class American life (which is the life of an enormous majority of citizens and the only one I can write about with conviction) and feel a kind of hope. Certainly this amiable village is as thorned with problems as any other community of its type. Generation misunderstands generation. Ideas and ideals of sex, politics, religion, the arts, have been radically altered in so brief a time that all heads swim. Here, too, we come across drugs circulating in schools and youth in flight from authority. But for one thing, these are the noisy singular, not the ordinary quiet, examples of family life in our region. (Most of us are on good terms with our children and grandchildren; we are trusted and loved by our descendants.) And for another, parents here have never before worked so hard at understanding the forces of chaos that imperil their young. There is little abdication, simply concern. We have begun to realize that parental failures have not necessarily caused these rifts and tensions; only the world around us all.

At base the American family, I rosily believe, is in pretty good condition, considering the brutal buffeting it has taken during the 20th century. Scarred but intact, it survives. It has not abandoned its aspirations; merely changed society's shape and its own.

For there has been a revolution. It was apparent as long ago as the First World War, quickened in the next few decades and has come, during the present years, to high climax. Yet it *is* a revolution rather than a mere rebellion. The wheel of time has turned full circle, wholly revolved. We are back where we began, on a frontier. That large, warm, papa-dominated Victorian family group is what we look back to wistfully, thinking it the norm. Actually it existed for less than half a century and then chiefly in fiction. That it is envisioned today as an image of lost contentment only demonstrates the persistence of legend. Families now resemble that vanished concept far less than they do the pioneer clusters at the start of our country's history. Like the pioneer families, they face a wilderness where few trails have been blazed, few signposts erected. Though the wilderness is moral and psychological rather than geographic, its dangers are real. . . .

New England's Pilgrims came here in bands large enough to ensure some clinging to the old behavior. But even they, fanning out from Plymouth to wider territories, lost touch with inherited customs. Later travelers into strangeness forgot them altogether. They were forced by circumstance to adopt new creeds, new standards of domestic life. Authority fell away, children grew mutinous, and sexual morals relaxed, as they tend to do in any time of change. We think of our ancestors as prim and stern. Except in the heart of New England, they were nothing of the sort. They were earthy. Separated from what [Oscar] Handlin calls "monuments of his past," the man of the frontier shrugged off moral taboos. Courtship became casual, marriage often undertaken without benefit of clergy. Even in Massachusetts, stronghold of European tradition, sexual conduct was haphazard. If the young of today seem bent on inventing temptations for themselves, they have early precedents to follow. We smile tolerantly at the picturesque custom of "bundling." Yet going

to bed together, even with a presumed pine board between them
to hamper embraces, must have appeared to young couples then
as inciting as today's unchaperoned meetings in college dormitories. Many a pioneer bride went to her marriage wearing, in
the ballad phrase, "her apron high." And the farther west the
settlers pushed, the weaker became antique notions of decorum,
harmony, order.

Living conditions did not permit such luxuries. Each family
had to fend for itself. And that family consisted usually of a
solitary unit—parents and children only, no older folks. Whatever shelter they inhabited had to be built by their own hands.
So houses were small and cramped, and elegance impossible
where help was scanty, children always underfoot, and wives as
necessary in the fields as their husbands. There was "alienation"
among those forest families, and loneliness on the prairies.

In this decade, I repeat, the frontier returns. Under the impact
of sociological pressures, pillars topple, established mores crum-
ble. Religion, custom, common opinion—none is strong enough
to regulate the new liberty. Ours is a bracing but a foreign climate. And people of my age can learn to breathe its air but cannot shelter our young from the winds that blow upon them.

My generation was spared the worst of the storm. We had our
Depression and our War. But we were able to earn our livings
and bring up our children during a time when standards, however frayed and fraying, were still familiar. On our side we had
the weight of solid social approval (or disapproval) to guide
us. Extramarital experiment, however widespread, was not publicly condoned. If we had heard of marijuana it was distantly—
as a mysterious dissipation prevalent only among jazz musicians. *Lady Chatterley's Lover* and *Ulysses* were still the most
scandalous reading we had undertaken. A "blue" joke in the
theater set the town rocking. Nor had we spent our entire lives
in the knowledge that annihilation of the planet was not only
possible but perhaps imminent. Dachau was unknown to us; and
the plight of the Negro had not been made vivid. Safe, a little
smug, we lived by old dogmas and inherited creeds.

We were not people of the forest. It is our descendants, now in their 20's and 30's and forming family units of their own, who must nearly unassisted mark the roads, forge new cultural values, invent a different civilization. . . .

Early marriage is this generation's reality. So is the necessity for do-it-yourself-manship. So is the blurring of distinctions between those tasks that belong to women and those to men. All were phenomena of frontier existence and have revived today. So also have certain deprivations that still harass Americans—a lack of permanence, services and ordinary housing space. Most immediate is lack of space. Where now are the houses that can mingle children, grandparents, servants and dependents in comfortable juxtaposition? Certainly not in cities, seldom even in the suburbs where novice families can afford to live. Moreover, necessity has bred desire. No longer do the generations *wish* to live together. Privacy has become their passion as it was often the passion of the frontiersman. The newly married consider it an inordinate hardship to live with parents. They will rent a loft, pitch a tent, inhabit a trailer, go to any lengths to escape the company of in-laws.

And parents, in turn, feel no inclination to spend even old age with their offspring. Today, over and over, one hears a slogan repeated by every aging couple, "All we hope is we'll never have to stay with our children." Pensions and savings and Social Security have made the hope attainable in most cases, and one supposes it works for the best. Still, from a romantic point of view, it seems a ruthless and lonely concept. Grandfather is no longer in a niche by the fire but in an expensive nursing home. Grandmother is dispensable. Generations no longer have the power to pass along their wisdom, if any, to blossoming families. And those families lose not only unpaid help and entertainment but the capacity for generosity.

. . . There is recently another tendency in middle-class life that elaborately frustrates the closeness of generations. This is the policy developed by large corporations of sending their junior executives shuttling about the nation. From city to city they are shifted like puppets, from job to job, and from one suburb to another. Each move confronts the family with an alien society, a varying culture. Kansas City is not Los Angeles. New York's customs differ from Houston's, and Montana's from Connecticut's. Yet over 10 or 20 years young parents and their children often have to adjust to such a variety of places. It makes for flexibility. It also makes for disruption of fixed values. Not only are the parents cast adrift by each move, but the children are disoriented. Continuity is sweet to the juvenile mind, one of the prime stabilizers of adolescence. Sensing their children's confusion, parents attempt to make home itself a bulwark. Families draw ever more tightly together into a cellular group, as covered wagons used to form a fort-like circle against marauding Indians. Each transportation is a new wilderness. And to guide them the travelers have only one compass, one North star —their personal beliefs and ideals. Unsupported by the wisdom of any stable community, they must work out a bond strong enough to bind them through the years.

As they must do it without ethical guideposts, they must also frequently depend on no actual labor except their own. . . . In few other epochs have parents been forced so single-handedly to cope with houses, jobs, children. Before, there was always a neighbor, an aunt or a grandparent to see the family through childbirth or an illness. Now the recently married, even the well-to-do, have no such solace. They go it alone.

As a consequence they have developed a remarkable self-sufficiency. Union-wage artisans are either unavailable or beyond their economic reach. So fledgling professors learn to be carpenters and refinish their own attics. Salesman lay bathroom tiles. Ingenious accountants paper their walls, repair plumbing, build garages. There seems little feeling of resentment about such an atavistic pattern of hardship; only a continual drawing together. Youthful fathers know about changing diapers as their wives understand electric cables. Indeed, the young appear to court difficulties. . . .

The kind of fastidiousness that yesterday's middle classes

strove for disappears along with vanished cooks and nursemaids. Still, there are more important gains. It speaks well for the health of an economy that domestic service is no longer the sole opportunity open to the unskilled. And that the under-served refuse to complain is also good. I believe with all my heart that children forced early to accept household responsibility will grow up more adaptable and stronger of character than the generation before them. I even predict that among them will be fewer adolescent rebels. For from the time they are born, the children of today fit totally into parental arms. No intrusive presence comes between mother, father, offspring. Where parents go, there goes baby—to the store, the party, the skiing weekend. The cabin in the clearing fostered no stricter bond.

So far, my metaphor has been elastic enough to explain most new vagaries. I have yet to mention one significant [element] which, at first, may seem to throw the analogy out of joint. That is the matter of wholesale prosperity.

Those who hacked from virgin territory a new civilization were largely the less privileged of the population. They owned little except a set of tools, a team of horses or oxen and whatever dowry of household goods the wife had brought to marriage. They expected nothing much except hardship. Theirs, they knew, would probably be a marginal living and a spare old age.

Today we drown in affluence. Youthful families cannot even remember hard times. They have romped through a world where, no matter how rigorously their parents had fought for an economic foothold, they themselves have been conditioned by security. Few of them have gone short of food, clothing, education. (I speak again, of course, about the middle classes. Slums and ghettos are aberrations spotlighted ever more fiercely as society in general continues to flourish.) All have grown sleek as race horses in body and mind. They have been fed fluoride and vitamins; they have been immunized and vaccinated and orthodontured within an inch of their lives. Specialists have removed their tonsils, and psychologists their inhibitions. Many have made it to college. Medicare and old-age subsidies will insure their futures. And for them, everywhere is [lucrative] employment. . . .

But to inhabit such an extraordinary economy is itself a form of pioneering. So vast a prosperity becomes a frontier hardly yet explored. The habits and casts of mind it engenders are quite different from those of any people before their time. Not too many years ago, for example, debt was a disgrace. A mortgage was something to be wiped out with all possible speed, burned in a ritual ceremony. Nowadays mortgages are considered assets, [to] be paid off in a future where sums now owed will presumably have dwindled in purchasing power. . . . The national theory of deficit spending has become a personal one. Young families buy houses on time, furnish them on credit, vacation by flying-now-paying-later, entertain on expense accounts. Thrift as a virtue has lost its appeal.

Those of my era, for whom balancing a budget was considered crucial (for the country as for households) turn apprehensive eyes on the progress of our cavalier descendants. We cannot always understand their goals and grails.

"Here is my youngest son, John, graduating from Harvard with honors," complained a distracted father to me the other day, "and all he plans to be is a teacher in Harlem. He doesn't seem to care about getting ahead." What this parent cannot appreciate is that the very glut of opportunities proffered our children has made them contemptuous of the material values that guided us. John, his father thinks, ought to study medicine or law or business, ought to be embarking on some financial course earmarked "security." But John has known nothing *but* security. Now he wants adventure. He also longs to spend himself for the good of society.

The new generations have tender consciences. They can afford them better than could we who were so engrossed in trying to ward off from our front porches the wolves of the Depression. . . . We in youth wished to make our fortunes. Many now yearn to make a world. I call that very hopeful indeed. If the American family seems threatened—by the impact of violence and war, by frequent divorce, changing sexual attitudes and a general atmosphere of wariness toward established religion—it is also protected by this fresh concern for the rights of human beings.

Advancing this cause becomes the cement of family relationships. Boys and girls meet in picket lines, marry for love of justice, together rear children imbued from the cradle with the conviction that they must give service to humanity. Something larger than financial gain freshens their days. They are never bored (and boredom can hugely endanger felicity) since they own a hundred outlets for their surplus energies. They enlist for duties among the poor. They work on ecumenical committees, pressure their congressmen, sustain the arts. Fathers who might otherwise pass their evenings watching television now nightly knock on neighborhood doors, petitions in hand. Mothers with children packed off to school give importance to their mornings by attending lectures on sociology or instructing the retarded or working for the League of Women Voters.

They may live strenuously. But they are a free people. Medicine has enabled them to bring children into the world when they are most wanted. The economy has allowed them—women as well as men—to follow careers or not, as they choose. And prosperity permits them to expend both their lives and leisure on projects that enrapture them.

I like what I see. I admire the new generation. And I believe the American family has never before had a better chance for a rewarding life, for enlightened liberty, and for the pursuit of its own and everybody else's happiness.

ERIK H. ERIKSON

youth today and the year 2000

"Hedonistic" perversity will soon
lose much of its attractiveness. . . . but
there may . . . be no predictable society to
"come back to."

i

IN RESPONDING to the inquiry of the Commission on the Year
2000, I will take the liberty of quoting the statements put to me
in order to reflect on some of the stereotyped thinking about
youth that has become representative of us, the older generation.
This . . . is prognostically as important as the behavior of the
young people themselves; for youth is, after all, a *generational
phenomenon,* even though its problems are now treated as those
of an outlandish tribe descended on us from Mars. The actions
of young people are always in part and by necessity reactions
to the stereotypes held up to them by their elders. To understand
this becomes especially important in our time when the so-called
communications media, far from merely mediating, interpose
themselves between the generations as manufacturers of stereotypes, often forcing youth to live out the caricatures of the
images that at first they had only "projected" in experimental
fashion. Much will depend on what we do about this. In spite
of our pretensions of being able to study the youth of today with
the eyes of detached naturalists, we are helping to make youth

in the year 2000 what it will be by the kinds of questions we now ask. So I will point out the ideological beams in our eyes as I attempt to put into words what I see ahead. . . .

I would assume that adolescents today and tomorrow are struggling to define new modes of conduct which are relevant to their lives.

Young people of a questioning bent have always done this. But more than any young generation before and with less reliance on a meaningful choice of traditional world images, the youth of today is forced to ask what is *universally relevant* in human life in this technological age at this junction of history. Even some of the most faddish, neurotic, delinquent preoccupation with "their" lives is a symptom of this fact.

Yet, this is within the context of two culture factors which seem to be extraordinary in the history of moral temper. One is the scepticism of all authority, the refusal to define natural authority (perhaps even that of paternal authority) and a cast of mind which is essentially anti-institutional and even antinomian.

I do not believe that even in the minority of youths to whom this statement is at all applicable there is a scepticism of *all* authority. There is an abiding mistrust of people who act authoritatively without authentic authority or refuse to assume the authority that is theirs by right and necessity. Paternal authority? Oh, yes—pompous fathers have been exposed everywhere by the world wars and the revolutions. It is interesting, though, that the word *paternal* is used rather than *parental*, for authority, while less paternal, may not slip altogether from the parent generation, insofar as a better balance of maternal and paternal authority may evolve from a changing position of women.

As a teacher, I am more impressed with our varying incapacity to own up to the almost oppressive authority we really do have in the minds of the young than in the alleged scepticism of *all* authority in the young. Their scepticism, even in its most cynical and violent forms, often seems to express a good sense for what true authority is, or should be, or yet could be. If they refuse "to define natural authority," are they not right if they indicate by all the overt, mocking, and challenging kinds of "alienation" that it is up to *us* to help them define it, or rather redefine it, since we have undermined it—and feel mighty guilty?

As to the essentially anti-institutional cast of mind, one must ask what alternative is here rejected. It appears that the majority of young people are, in fact, all too needy for, trusting in, and conforming to present institutions, organizations, parties, industrial complexes, super-machineries—and this because true personal authority is waning. Even the anti-institutional minority (whom we know better and who are apt to know our writings) seem to me to plead with existing institutions for permission to rebel—just as in private they often seem to plead with their parents to love them doubly for [being rejected by] them. And are they not remarkably eager for old and new uniforms (a kind of uniformity of nonconformity), for public rituals, and for a collective style of individual isolation? Within this minority, however, as well as in the majority, there are great numbers who are deeply interested in and responsive to a more concerted critique of institutions from a newer and more adequate ethical point of view than we can offer them.

The second factor is an extraordinary hedonism—using the word in the broadest sense—in that there is a desacralization of life and an attitude that all experience is permissible and even desirable.

Again, the word *hedonism* illustrates the way in which we use outdated terms for entirely new phenomena. Although many young people entertain a greater variety of sensual and sexual experiences than their parents did, I see in their pleasure seeking relatively little relaxed joy and often compulsive and addictive search for *relevant* experience. And here we should admit that our generation and our heritage made "all" experience relative by opening it to ruthless inquiry and by assuming that one could pursue radical enlightenment without changing radically or, indeed, changing the coming generations radically. The young have no choice but to experiment with what is left of the "enlightened," "analyzed," and standardized world that we have bequeathed to them.

Yet their search is not for all-permissibility, but for new logical and ethical boundaries. Now only direct experience can offer correctives that our traditional mixture of radical enlightenment and middle-class moralism has failed to provide. I suspect that "hedonistic" perversity will soon lose much of its attractiveness in deed and in print when the available inventory has been experimented with and found only moderately satisfying, once it is permitted. New boundaries will then emerge from new ways of finding out what really counts, for there is much latent affirmation and much overt solidarity in all this search. All you have to do is to see some of these nihilists with babies, and you are less sure of what one of the statements as yet to be quoted terms the "Hegelian" certainty that the next generation will be even more alienated.

As for the desacralization of life by the young, it must be obvious that our generation desacralized their lives by (to mention only the intellectual side) naïve scientism, thoughtless scepticism, dilettante political opposition, and irresponsible technical expansion. I find, in fact, more of a search for resacralization in the younger than in the older generation.

At the same time society imposes new forms of specialization, of extended training, of new hierarchies and organizations. Thus, one finds an unprecedented divorce between the culture and the society. And, from all indications, such a separation will increase.

Here, much depends on what one means by the word *imposes*. As I have already indicated, in much of youth new hierarchies and organizations are accepted and welcome. We are apt to forget that young people (if not burdened with their parents' conflicts) have no reason to feel that radical change as such is an imposition. The unprecedented divorce we perceive is between *our* traditional culture . . . and the tasks of *their* society. A new generation growing up with technological and scientific progress may well experience technology and its new modes of thought as the link between a new culture and new forms of society.

In this respect, assuming this hypothesis is true, the greatest strains will be on the youth. This particular generation, like its predecessors, may come back to some form of accommodation with the society as it grows older and accepts positions within the society. But the experiences also leave a "cultural deposit" which is cumulative consciousness and—to this extent I am a Hegelian—is irreversible, and the next generation therefore starts from a more advanced position of alienation and detachment.

Does it make sense that a generation involved in such unprecedented change should "come back to some form of accommodation with the society"? This was the fate of certain rebels and romantics in the past; but there may soon be no predictable society to "come back to," even if coming back were a viable term or image in the minds of youth. Rather, I would expect the majority to be only too willing to overaccommodate to the exploiters of change, and the minority we speak of to feel cast off until their function becomes clearer—with whatever help we can give.

---

ii

Having somewhat summarily disavowed the statements formulated by others, I would now like to ask a question more in line with my own thinking, and thereby not necessarily more free from sterotypy: Where *are* some of the principal contemporary sources of identity strength? This question leads us from diagnosis to prognosis, for to me a sense of identity (and here the widest connotation of the term will do) includes a sense of anticipated future. The traditional sources of identity strength—economic, racial, national, religious, occupational—are all in the process of allying themselves with a new world-image in which the vision of an anticipated future and, in fact, of a future in a permanent state of planning will take over much of the power of tradition. If I call such sources of identity strength *ideological*, I am using the word again most generally to denote a system of ideas providing a convincing world-image. Such a system each new generation needs—so much so that it cannot wait for it to be tested in advance. I will call the two principal ideological orientations basic to future identities the *technological* and the *humanist* orientations, and I will assume that even the great politico-economic alternatives will be subordinated to them.

I will assume, then, that especially in this country, but increasingly also abroad, masses of young people feel attuned, both by giftedness and by opportunity, to the technological and scientific promises of indefinite progress; and that these promises, if sustained by schooling, imply a new ideological world-image and a new kind of identity for many. As in every past technology and each historical period, there are vast numbers of individuals who can combine the dominant techniques of mastery and domination with their identity development, and *become* what they *do*. They can settle on that *cultural consolidation* that follows shifts in technology and secures what mutual verification and what transitory familiarity lie in doing things together and in doing them right—a rightness proved by the bountiful response of "nature," whether in the form of the prey bagged, the food harvested, the goods produced, the money made, the ideas substantiated, or the technological problems solved.

Each such consolidation, of course, also makes for new kinds of entrenched privileges, enforced sacrifices, institutionalized inequalities, and built-in contradictions that become glaringly obvious to outsiders—those who lack the appropriate gifts and opportunities or have a surplus of not quite appropriate talents.

Yet it would be intellectual vindictiveness to overlook the sense of embeddedness and natural flux that each age provides in the midst of the artifacts of organization; how it helps to bring to ascendance some particular type of man and style of perfection; how it permits those thus consolidated to limit their horizon effectively so as *not* to see what might destroy their newly won unity with time and space or expose them to the fear of death— and of killing. Such a consolidation along technological and scientific lines is . . . now taking place. Those young people who feel at home in it can, in fact, go along with their parents and teachers—not too respectfully, to be sure—in a kind of *fraternal identification,* because parents and children can jointly leave it to technology and science to provide a self-perpetuating and self-accelerating way of life. No need is felt to limit expansionist ideals so long as certain old-fashioned rationalizations continue to provide the hope (a hope that has long been an intrinsic part of an American ideology) that in regard to any possible built-in evil in the very nature of super-organizations, appropriate brakes, corrections, and amendments will be invented in the nick of time and without any undue investment of strenuously new principles. While they "work," these super-machineries, organizations, and associations provide a sufficiently adjustable identity for all those who feel actively engaged in and by them.

All of us sense the danger of overaccommodation in this, as in any other consolidation of a new world-image, and maybe the danger *is* greater today. It is the danger that a willful and playful testing of the now limitless range of the technically possible will replace the search for the criteria for the optimal and the ethically permissible, which includes what can be given on from generation to generation. This can only cause subliminal panic, especially where the old decencies will prove glaringly inadequate, and where the threat or the mere possibility of overkill can be denied only with increasing mental strain—a strain, incidentally, which will match the sexual repression of the passing era in unconscious pathogenic power.

It is against this danger, I think, that the nonaccommodators

put their very existence "on the line," often in a thoroughly con-
founding way because the manifestations of alienation and commitment are sometimes indistinguishable. The insistence on the
question "to be or not to be" always looks gratuitously strange
to the consolidated. If the question of being oneself and of dying
one's own death in a world of overkill seems to appear in a more
confused and confusing form, it is the ruthless heritage of radical enlightenment that forces some intelligent young people into
a seemingly cynical pride, demanding that they be human without illusion, naked without narcissism, loving without idealization, ethical without moral passion, restless without being classi-
fiably neurotic, and political without lying: truly a utopia to end
all utopias. What should we call this youth? *Humanist* would
seem right if by this we mean a recovery, with new implications,
of man as the measure, a man far grimmer and with much less
temptation to congratulate himself on his exalted position in the
universe, a self-congratulation that has in the past always encouraged more cruel and more thoughtless consolidations. The
new humanism ranges from an *existential* insistence that every
man *is* an island unto himself to a new kind of humaneness that
is more than compassion for stray animals and savages, and a
decidedly *humanitarian* activism ready to meet concrete dangers and hardships in the service of assisting the underprivileged
anywhere. Maybe *universalist* would cover all this better, if we
mean by it an insistence on the widest range of human possibilities—beyond the technological.

But whatever you call it, the universalist orientation, no less
than the technological one, is a *cluster* of ideas, images, and aspirations, of hopes, fears, and hates; otherwise, neither could
lay claim to the identity development of the young. *Somewhat*
like the "hawks" and the "doves," the technologists and the universalists seem almost to belong to different species, living in
separate ecologies. "Technological" youth, for example, expects
the dominant forces in foreign as well as in domestic matters to
work themselves out into some new form of balance of power
(or is it an old-fashioned balance of entirely new powers?). It

is willing, for the sake of such an expectation, to do a reasonable amount of killing—and of dying. "Humanist" youth, on the other hand, not only opposes unlimited mechanization and regimentation, but also cultivates a sensitive awareness of the humanness of any individual in gunsight range. The two orientations must obviously oppose and repel each other totally; the acceptance of even a part of one could cause an ideological slide in the whole configuration of images and, it follows, in the kind of courage to be—and to die. These two views, therefore, face each other as if the other were *the* enemy, although he may be brother or friend—and, indeed, oneself at a different stage of one's own life, or even in a different mood of the same stage.

Each side, of course, is overly aware of the dangers inherent in the other. In fact, it makes out of the other, in my jargon, a negative identity. I have sketched the danger felt to exist in the technological orientation. On the "humanist" side, there is the danger of a starry-eyed faith in the certainty that if you "mean it," you can move quite monolithic mountains, and of a subsequent total inertia when the mountain moves only a bit at a time or slides right back. This segment of youth lacks as yet the leadership that would replace the loss of revolutionary tradition, or any other tradition of discipline. Then there is the danger of a retreat into all kinds of Beat snobbishness or into parallel private worlds, each with its own artifically expanded consciousness.

---

iii

As one is apt to do in arguing over diagnosis, I have now overdrawn two "ideal" syndromes so as to consider the prognosis suggested in a further question presented to me:

Is it possible that the fabric of traditional authority has been torn so severely in the last decades that the re-establishment of certain earlier forms of convention is all but unlikely?

. . . I would not expect a future accommodation to be characterized by a "coming back" either to conventions or to old-fashioned movements. Has not every major era in history been characterized by a division into a new class of *power-specialists* (who "know what they are doing") and an intense new group of *universalists* (who "mean what they are saying")? And do not these two poles determine an era's character? The specialists ruthlessly test the limits of power, while the universalists always in remembering man's soul also remember the "poor"—those cut off from the resources of power. What is as yet dormant in that third group, the truly under-privileged, is hard to say, especially if an all-colored anticolonial solidarity that would include our Negro youth should emerge. But it would seem probable that all new revolutionary identities will be drawn into the struggle of the two ideological orientations sketched here, and that nothing could preclude a fruitful [polarization] between these two orientations—provided we survive.

But is not the fact that we are still here already a result of [this] polarization. . . ? If our super-technicians had not been able to put warning signals and brakes into the very machinery of armament, certainly our universalists would not have known how to save or how to govern the world. It also seems reasonable to assume that without the apocalyptic warnings of the universalists, the new technocrats might not have been shocked into restraining the power they wield.

What speaks for a fruitful polarization is the probability that a new generation growing up with and in technological and scientific progress as a matter of course will be forced by the daily confrontation with unheard-of practical and theoretical possibilities to entertain radically new modes of thought that may suggest daring innovations in both culture and society. "Humanist" youth, in turn, will find some accommodation with the machine age in which they, of course, already participate in their daily needs and habits. Thus, each group may reach in the other what imagination, sensitivity, or commitment may be ready for activation. I do not mean, however, even to wish that the clarity of opposition of the technological and the humanist identity be blurred, for dynamic interplay needs clear poles.

What, finally, is apt to bring youth of different persuasions together is a change in the generational process itself—an awareness that they share a common fate. Already today the mere division into an older—parent—generation and a younger—adolescing—one is becoming superannuated. Technological change makes it impossible for any traditional way of being older (an age difference suggested by the questions quoted) ever to become again so institutionalized that the younger generation could "accommodate" to it or, indeed, resist it in good old revolutionary fashion. Aging, it is already widely noted, will be (or already is) a quite different experience for those who find themselves rather early occupationally outdated and for those who may have something more lasting to offer. By the same token, young adulthood will be divided into older and younger young adults. The not-too-young and not-too-old specialist will probably move into the position of principal arbiter, that is, for the limited period of the ascendance of his specialty. His power, in many ways, will replace the sanction of tradition or, indeed, of parents.

But the "younger generation," too, will be (or already is) divided more clearly into the older- and the younger-young generation, where the older young will have to take over (and are eager to take over) much of the direction of the conduct of the younger young. Thus, the relative waning of the parents and the emergence of the young adult specialist as the permanent and permanently changing authority are bringing about a shift by which older youth will have to take increasing responsibility for the conduct of younger youth—and older people for the orientation of the specialists and of older youth. By the same token, future religious ethics would be grounded less in the emotions and the imagery of infantile guilt, than in that of mutual responsibility in the fleeting present.

In such change we on our part can orient ourselves and offer orientation only by recognizing and cultivating an age-specific *ethical* capacity in *older* youth, for there are age-specific factors that speak for a differentiation between morality and ethics. The child's conscience tends to be impressed with a moralism which says "no" without giving reasons; in this sense, the infantile super-ego has become a danger to human survival, for suppression in childhood leads to the exploitation of others in adulthood, and moralistic self-denial ends up in the wish to annihilate others. There is also an age-specific ethical capacity in older youth that we should learn to foster. That we, instead, consistently neglect this ethical potential and, in fact, deny it with the moralistic reaction that we traditionally employ toward and against youth *(anti-institutional, hedonistic, desacralizing)* is probably resented much more by young people than our dutiful attempts to keep them in order by prohibition.

At any rate, the ethical questions of the future will be less determined by the influence of the older generation on the younger one than by the interplay of subdivisions in a life scheme in which the whole life span is extended; in which the life stages will be further subdivided; in which new roles for both sexes will emerge in all life stages; and in which a certain margin of free choice and individualized identity will come to be considered the reward for technical inventiveness. In the next decade, youth will force us to help them to develop ethical, affirmative, resacralizing rules of conduct that remain flexibly adjustable to the promises and the dangers of world-wide technology and communication. These developments, of course, include two "things"—one gigantic, one tiny—the irreversible presence of which will have to find acknowledgment in daily life: the Bomb and the Loop. They together will call for everyday decisions involving the sanctity of life and death. Once man has decided not to kill needlessly and not to give birth carelessly, he must try to establish what capacity for living, and for letting live, each generation owes to every child planned to be born— anywhere. . . .